CULTURES AND SOCIETIES IN TRANSITION

CULTURES AND SOCIETIES IN TRANSITION

India, Russia and Other CIS Countries

Edited by
Manu Mittal

SHIPRA

ISBN: 978-81-7541-417-4

First Published in India in 2008

Cultures and Societies in Transition: India, Russia and Other CIS Countries

Published by :
SHIPRA PUBLICATIONS
115-A, Vikas Marg, Shakarpur, Delhi-110092 (India)
Tel. : 91-11-65277210, 22500954, Fax : 91-11-22458662
Email : info@shiprapublications.com
www.shiprapublications.com

Foreword

Socio-cultural transition in any society, in any country is a natural and inevitable process. It has been observed that when a particular socio-cultural system outlives its utility and value, it is replaced by a new system. The nature of transition may be sudden and drastic or may be gradual over a long period. Russia is one of the striking examples of two drastic all encompassing transitions which took place in a period of a single century. October Revolution of 1917 has been an epoch making event in world history. With the establishment of the first socialist state many socio-cultural experiments were made for the first time. A new political, economic, social and cultural set up emerged in difficult and struggling conditions in Russia. Seventy years of Soviet rule has been described by social scientists in various ways, as a new path breaking experiment with varied degree of success to total disaster of Soviet experiment, depending on the ideological disposition of the analyst.

The disintegration of the Soviet Union in the last decade of the XX century was one of the most striking events of the last century. The change was so sudden and total that it took sometime to access the full implications of changes. Russia and CIS countries had gone for total political and economic transformation resulting in drastic transformation in socio-cultural life of these countries. The ongoing transition has become the focus of studies of various scholars. The scholars presenting papers in the International Seminar on "Culture of Societies in Transition" organized by the Centre of Russian Studies, JNU made an attempt to understand, analyse, comprehend and evaluate the process of recent transition in Russia and CIS countries. While analysing culture and society in transition in Russia, Indian scholars made an attempt to compare the process with socio-cultural transition in India in the last century which were substantive but much more gradual, less volatile and painstaking.

The papers presented in the Seminar "Culture and Societies in Transition" held in JNU would stimulate discussion on the subject which has created a lot of interest among scholars. The papers published under the editorship of Dr Manu Mittal will enable the scholars to get a deeper insight in the recent changes and transformation in Russian society and culture.

The process of transformation in CIS countries has been comparatively less focused. Some of the papers of the seminar which have been published in this book take up the nature of socio-cultural transformation in Central Asian countries, which were formally part of the Soviet Union. Scholars from Central Asia who presented papers in the seminar have given a thorough analysis of heir view point regarding these changes.

In the papers presented, the concept of socio-cultural transition has been analysed from sociological, psychological, historical, economic and philological angles. Scholars have tried to evaluate how globalization of culture had its effect in the process of transition. Resultant changes at times have taken place quietly, at times in a volatile manner. The process of globalisation, which is related to the all encompassing changes connected with info-tech revolution have given a new dimension to culture and society. The emerging society is trying to find ways to balance their traditional and modern cultural identities.

Thus a very topical subject involving Russia, Central Asia and India has been discussed from a broad prospective, as well from certain specific angles. Scholars from Russia, Central Asia and India contributed papers which will give better insight about the forces which are going to shape the future developments of these countries. Thus a clearer picture of the process of transition taking place in these countries will help to promote better understanding and relationship between India, Russia and other Central Asian countries.

Prof. Sankar Basu
Professor
Centre of Russian Studies
Jawaharlal Nehru University
New Delhi

Preface

The last two decades have seen a tremendous change in the world order. As political, economic and social changes sweep across the globe and geographical boundaries get redrawn, so are the economic, social and cultural boundaries, constantly changing. The term 'globalization' acquires a meaning much beyond economies to represent the globalization of culture and the search for and advent of a 'new' culture or a change in the established, that many traditional societies, as well as those in a state of dynamic flux, are sometimes silently and often turbulently witnessing.

While societies undergo such transition, so does culture – both in its popular form and in its deepest fabric. As the rapid change of the post-technological, post-modern society on the info-tech highway spawns new thought, language and literature, there are societies that are groping to find and reconcile their ancient as well as new cultural identities.

As independent India went on to make rapid strides in all spheres, the decades of the 50s, 60s and 70s – of socialistic-mixed economy gave way to reforms and the current state of liberalization and privatization. Whereas on one hand modern resurgent India is emerging as a regional and technological power, it still remains rooted in tradition and the ancient. Consequently there are ever changing social scenarios with a multitude of cultures – both Indian and foreign – often blending, sometimes co-existing, at others clashing and at times fusing to give new meaning to or finding new forms, identities and expression in arts, language and literature.

The metamorphosis of USSR into independent countries that now form the CIS is not geopolitical alone. Ironically, literature and language that once strove to unite the Soviet Union now appear to have become instruments of division. While the new independent States in their assertion of national identities want to distance themselves from Russian Language, Literature, art forms as well as literary and cultural traditions and heroes, they are often struggling to find their own cultural voice. And yet, new writers and artists are being born and new cultural tradition being created.

These developments, transformations, and the cultural-history that is in the making, as well as the similarities and the differences in processes that are silently taking place in India as well as in Russia and other CIS counties need a close study and understanding. More so, since India, Russia and some other CIS countries have ethnic, cultural, trade, strategic and political links that extend back centuries.

In order to provide a platform for scholars and experts from various regions to meet, interact, share, exchange and deliberate, an International Seminar on *Cultures and Societies in Tradition: India, Russia and other CIS Countries*, was held at the Centre of Russian Studies, School of Languages, Literature and Culture Studies, Jawaharlal Nehru University, India from 8-10 February 2006. Sponsored by the Indian Council for Cultural Relations, the Seminar was attended by more than 150 international experts, views and scholarships of some of whom are presented in this book. This volume, I am sure will provide glimpses and insights that resonate of similarities and yet are as diverse as the fields of work and regions that these experts come from.

Manu Mittal
Centre of Russian Studies
Jawaharlal Nehru University
New Delhi

Acknowledgements

The journey that began as an inner quest for understanding from diverse yet convergent dimensions, the impact of globalisation, new technologies as well as the rapidly changing world order on human life, culture and society, has found form in this book. I am indebted to all whose support has made this possible.

The first landmark on this journey was my being able to organise the International Seminar on *Cultures and Societies in Transition: India, Russia and other CIS Countries* in February 2006. I am grateful to the Jawaharlal Nehru University for giving me the opportunity to do so as well as for providing a publication grant which made the second landmark – this book - possible. I express my thanks to Prof. B.B. Bhattacharya, Vice Chancellor, JNU, for his support. A nebular idea crystallised and took shape only due to the unstinting support of the Indian Council for Cultural Relations. I am thankful to the ICCR as well as its former Director General Shri Rakesh Kumar, and its current Director General Shri Pavan K. Varma for the interest and encouragement I received from them. I am grateful to all the experts who have contributed their views, insights and experiences weaving richness into this book.

I express my gratitude to all my colleagues and the staff at the Centre of Russian Studies, School of Language Literature and Culture Studies, JNU, especially Professors Varyam Singh, Sankar Basu, R. Kumar, R.N. Menon, as well as Kiran Singh Verma, Meeta Narain, Nasar Shakeel Roomi, and Ajoy Karnati for their suggestions and help.

I am indebted to Prof. S.A. Khavronina, who thirty years ago as my *guru* at the People's Friendship University, Moscow, initiated me into the world of Russian language, literature and culture. Responding to my request she came and contributed in her grand inimitable way. My special thanks to my friends Professors V.M. Shaklein, Vera Stepanenko, Fedor I. Pankov, Irina Polyakova from Russia and Azad

N. Shamatov from Uzbekistan for their presence and academic contributions, and cine′-stars Ajay Devgan and Kajol for having urged celebrated film-maker Prakash Jha to participate and share his views on cinema and socio-cultural transition as well as to screen and discuss his film *Apaharan,* for which I am obliged to him.

Pranav Mittal deserves special thanks for his able assistance and working even at odd hours in coordinating the Seminar and in editing and designing this book. I also thank Dr. N.K. Sharma and Shri Dharamvir for their valuable contributions, Indira Musaeva and Kaizurina Mittal for reading and correcting the manuscripts, my students and Shobhana for their help and running errands, and Susan Thomas, Manoj Chandran and Sangeeta Kashyap for their untiring secretarial and organisational assistance. My husband Sunil, who has always stood by me in all my ventures provided ideas and help in many different ways.

As in all journeys, keep moving we must. Between the Seminar and the publication of this book one of our illustrious contributors Dr. Neelmani Upadhyay passed away, moving beyond to eternity.

Meanwhile for all of us the passage continues, with unceasing transition in our personal as well as socio-cultural lives.

Contents

1

The Voyage of Socio-Cultural Evolution in India and the CIS

Manu Mittal

Moving - as we always do - from one socio-cultural era to the next, transition is perhaps what we perpetually live in! One may wonder: Is it a continuum one is traversing or is one moving from one discreet socio-cultural time and space to the next?

Yet, perhaps, no one particular time in human history may have seen such rapid and global socio-cultural transition as we are all witnessing today. All in about the last one hundred years, with most of it having occurred in the last few decades. Indeed we are living in exciting and turbulent times!

Fast and far-reaching changes that have, and are, greatly influencing the history of our times are taking place in Asia, Latin America, and Europe and in some way or the other in every country of the world. These processes of transition and transformation have their effect much beyond their epicenters of occurrence. They may be understood as part of the modernization drive and the global movement towards a one-world system based on the western model of democracy and economy and are so, understandably fraught with the import and influence of the culture where they come from, especially as ever-increasing global exchange and communication take place.

Transition and transformation differ in meaning. While transition is supposed to be a type of change that takes a society from a defined social and economic structure, through a planned structural change, to another defined structure, transformation implies a less defined and possibly more chaotic change. Very often today, societies undergoing change witness both transition and transformation in their form, structure, and dynamics. And the rate of change is often so rapid, that before individual, system and social adaptation to a set of changes takes place, the next set of changes is already occurring. If fragile, the individual or the system may be stressed to the point of collapse or undergo only superficial change while deeper changes take more time to set in, and may never actually do so. Societies and communities with old cultures rooted in strong traditions may survive this transition and transformation better by drawing on their cultural strength and engage in cultural dialogue or experience a confluence and amalgamation of cultures, yet, may also experience polarization of the forces of change and those resistant to change and so be ground for cultural conflict and confusion.

With the movement from 'walled culture' to 'world culture', the term 'globalization' acquires a meaning much beyond economics to represent the globalization of culture and the search for and advent of a 'new' culture or a change in the established, that many traditional societies, as well as those in a state of dynamic flux, are sometimes silently and often turbulently witnessing.

As independent India went on to make rapid strides in all spheres, socialistic-mixed economy gave way to reforms and the current state of liberalization and privatization. Whereas on one hand modern resurgent India is emerging as a regional and technological power, it still remains rooted in tradition and the ancient. Consequently there are ever changing social scenarios with a multitude of cultures – both Indian and foreign–often blending, sometimes co-existing, at others clashing and at times fusing to give new meanings to or finding new forms, identities and expression in arts, language and literature.

The transformation of the USSR into independent states that now form the CIS is not geopolitical alone. Ironically, literature and language that once strove to unite the Soviet Union now appear to have become instruments of division. While the new independent states in their assertion of national identities want to distance themselves from Russian Language, Literature, art forms as well as literary and cultural traditions and heroes they are often struggling to find their own cultural voice. While there is cultural revivalism yet, new writers and artists are being born and new cultural traditions being created.

India has always been a pluralistic society, generally tolerant to diversity, with many cultures and sub-cultures co-existing. In India, many cultures and faiths, ways of life, dress and food habits, traditions and rituals, are united. Different Indian religions such as Hinduism, Buddhism, Jainism, Sikhism, Islam, Christianity, a variety of sects, and varying tribal religious beliefs co-exist. And this diversity exists in Indian languages as well.

Socio-linguist Jennifer Bayer has aptly summed up the India scenario by saying:

"The Indian political, economic and socio-cultural contexts occur under conditions of a multi-structural whole. Its economy centers around agriculture (now technological prowess as well) wherein feudal, pre-capitalist and capitalist structures co-exist. Its political system is the manifestation of the local *panchayat* system with a combination of international political systems. Its socio-cultural make-up is the combination of Great Traditions with Little Traditions. Its Industry is a spectrum, ranging from Information Technology to small-scale industries. Its legal system ranges from the local *panchayat* system and tribal customary laws to the district, state, high and supreme courts. Its people are composite groups, a combination of caste and class, of *'jatis'* and *'non-jatis'*.

In such a setting where collective sharing of cultures contradicts collective rights and group identities, a discussion on cultures in transition is bound to encounter complexities." Yet, India sails on, historically adopting and taking into its fold cultural traditions that arrived and continue to do so from far and near.

Let us look at the scenario in the CIS. As Biserka Cvjeticanin has observed that the cultural diversity and pluralism in the countries that were part of the USSR and the East European Block became very visible after the breakdown of socialism. These countries have long histories, strong cultural traditions and rich cultural heritage that they preserved. The processes of transformation that began with the collapse of socialism have brought into a sharper focus the question of cultural identity of these countries. The new countries that emerged in Central Asia and Eastern Europe now seek to assert their nationalistic, ethnic, and cultural identities, and are re-examining their history in search for new values, historo-cultural heroes, literature, mythology and new modes of linkage and cooperation on the global level (as can be seen in Europe). Due to the lack of democratic traditions and other historic reasons, the centralized vesting of authority still continues in some of the Central Asian States.

The initial hope and hype of the historic changes in the CIS began to be questioned when serious doubts arose whether the path of change spelt evolution and authentic development or one of strife, unemployment, social, ethnic and religious conflicts, increased crime in the wake of poor social security and the breakdown of socially cherished value systems. In this process of transition and adoption of market economy brought the whole social structure into a state of uncertainty and tension for what was taking place was 'social transformation' and not just 'transition'. It also became evident that the process simply required that they should adjust and adapt to Western models.

State funding of Cultural activities in these CIS and East European countries, which used to be high in the socialistic era has dropped to a meager low. As the role and function of the State in culture and its development and sustenance dissipated there have been attempts to privatize and commercialize cultural infrastructure and institutions: whether these be museums, films, theatre, art, dance and music; activities like the printing and publishing of books. Due to lack of support and training high caliber artists have left in exodus for the greener pastures of the West. The mass media and new communication technologies have been importing content or modeling it along the lines of the West and so there is hardly any development at local levels. While local talent starves, cultural conflicts raise their head.

Since the State which was supposed to be the 'hand' that 'controlled' culture vanished and private support is missing the current situation is best summed up by the Polish historian Bronislaw Geremik who has remarked: "Today the State no longer has a bad conscience, and sponsors and patrons do not have it yet. Neither the one nor the other support culture."

Here one may also pause and ask what is culture? What is society? And what transition are we talking about?

We all know that culture encompasses the values, traditions, norms, customs, arts, history, folklore, and institutions that a group of people, who are unified by race, ethnicity, language, nationality, or religion, share. It comprises of the common beliefs and practices of a group of people. Culture is the integrated pattern of human knowledge, belief, and behavior that depends upon man's capacity for learning and transmitting knowledge to succeeding generations. It is indeed the integration pattern of human behavior that includes thoughts, communications, actions, customs, beliefs, values and institutions of a race, ethnic, religious or social group. Culture is the way of life of a group of people. This includes what they wear, how they govern themselves, their religious rites, other rituals, learned behavior of people, which includes their belief systems and languages, their social relationships, their institutions and organizations, and their material goods - food, clothing, buildings, tools, and machines.

On the other hand, 'society' is a close knitted framework composed of a group of interacting people who share a geographical region, a sense of common identity, and a common culture. It is an extended social group having a distinctive cultural and economic organization. While culture and society are anthropological entities, Transition here is just a passage: the act of passing from one state or stage to the next that results in a transmutation. It is the movement across a threshold into another phase as the result of the interaction of relevant factors during the previous phase.

"Culture", "Society" and "Transition" might be different words, with different independent meanings and connotations but when they come together, they represent a powerful dynamic phenomenon of everlasting ongoing transformation.

Culture has eternally been in the process of rapid metamorphosis, and one effect of this was the catalyzing of a desire for personal metamorphosis. A tendency emerged for individuals unconsciously to seek experiences of transformation in order to fit into a culture in transformation, hence giving birth to universal cataclysm and metamorphosis!

It is not difficult to see a similarity between the pre-historic migration of man from one place to the other and the movement of tribes and ethnic groups from one geographical region to the other creating 'shared common culture zones' without clear national or geopolitical boundaries, and the unifying conquests of Ashoka the Great or of Alexander of Macedonia; or the spread of thought and belief-systems through religions such as Buddhism, Christianity, Islam, Hinduism and others which spread far and wide; and the appearance in the modern world of cyberspace as a force leading to a radical increase in cultural interconnection and related shifts in patterns of personal identity.

So goes on this voyage of cultural evolution. A never-ending voyage!

2

The Process of Cultural Transition in Russia

Sankar Basu

The process of transformation of the socio-cultural life of Russia in the last two decades has coincided with the political and economic upheavals in the country. Russia was under going drastic changes in its political and economic systems which was clearly reflected in the cultural life of the country. Along with the political stagnation during the eighties in Russia, there was a feeling of stagnation in the field of Russian culture dominated by the stereotype concept of "Socialist realism". A basic contradiction in the Soviet cultural life was evident. The "official culture" was not capable of any further development and the emerging dissident (unofficial) one did not have a proper base to create a significant impact on social consciousness.

Though the official culture conformed to the ideological dictate, there was an urge for cultural dissent, a longing for getting out of rigid ideological controls. Ordinary men as seen in every day life did not conform to the ideal image of "builders of communism". However, the dissident literature did not try to politically destroy the Soviet system (although it was often accused of it). In the best works of this group the main characters had the strength to provide intellectual, spiritual and moral resistance to totalitarianism. The dissident writers were able to provide invaluable spiritual examples of tenacity and independence of thought. This was the main reason for the cruel persecution of dissidents. Differences in the cultural sphere were transmitted to the political as well. By the seventies, seven thousands persons were condemned for dissidence. A.J Solzhenitsyn, V.P. Nekrasov had to immigrate, the violinist Rostropovich, the famous film director Tarakovsky, director of theatre Leubimov and many others had to leave the country. They were representatives of the cultural elite, whose works and stand on public issues seemed to the authorities endangering of the Soviet state. The dissident culture was an amalgam of the style of life and thought of literary personalities, who created conditions for self expression. This kind of culture united varied personalities who did not want that the conditions for their creative work should be predetermined or monitored.

Political, social and later on the economic process which had been unfolding since 1985 has changed external cultural conditions. The process of liberation of consciousness from enslavement was unstoppable. People understood that rulers are not capable of conducting open or truthful communication with the society, on whose behalf they conduct their policy. Among the members of the Party there was no common position with regard to the aim, problems and limits to "openness". Words and emotions, which were too long under control, just burst onto the pages of newspaper and journals. It seemed that the key to the destiny of Russia would be found soon in the merciless and truthful knowledge of the past. That is why there was such a passion for polemics on controversial historical questions. In fact, it was not a search for scientific truth, but new historical consciousness of the nation was being developed in the hope of finding the real road to Russia's destiny. After getting out of the clutches of Party dictates and the Government, the Press fell into an even crueler trap set by moneyed people.

To run a well known publication it was necessary to cater to popular tastes by providing information about social scandals, or be dependent on the advertisements of big business and MNCs. Slowly the character of the press changed, many newspapers and journals appeared full of gossip. Its aim was not to provide information and education but to entertain the readers. Used to constant supervision, ordinary Russians were not ready for independent choice of economic, political, social and cultural behavior. The reforms were from the top, the people were offered freedom of action. Many thought that once more some experiments were being conducted on them it could lead to some catastrophe.

Collapse of a familiar set-up, loss of social status always result in crisis, that is why any reform is accompanied by a socio-cultural crisis of a more or less intensity or period. At an individual level such crisis is expressed in the 'loss of meaning of life', as man cannot with authenticity judge what tomorrow may bring to him and to his family. On the level of the society this crisis manifests itself in destroying the demarcations of different social strata; submerging moral norms.

After the disintegration of the Soviet Union in 1991 such a socio-cultural crisis started developing with unusual intensity. The deep crisis of the social consciousness was the result of loss of former worldly certainties, norms and stereotypical behavior. But the most difficult suffering of the people was the loss of habitual hierarchy of values.

Soviet men lived at two levels: real and mythological. Earlier motivation of life came from a myth that the Soviet citizen belongs to a wonderful and progressive country, which was moving towards a "bright future". Later it turned out that the wonderful future was simply not there and the state which in the past seemed so powerful was in no mood to protect its own citizens. The prestige of different professions underwent a change. Professions which could quickly earn money became prestigious. Culture reached a stage of chaos and confusion. Parody crept in all the spheres of culture, abolishing stereotypes and clichés but unable to suggest any thing new to replace it.

Russia started feeling an intense crisis of cultural identity at all levels. A period came when irony became the medium of expression indicating instability and vacillation of the cultural process. The subject of parody became the literary and artistic heritage, values and norms of Soviet culture. A specific feature of Soviet culture was that it was regulated not by the market, but by the Government. Ideology was its integral part and commercial considerations were secondary. Now the situation has drastically changed, the mass culture has an audience, which is ready to use its produce. This explains the great success of the first Russian 'soap operas'.

The process of making culture relevant to the contemporary world led to the imitation of the West, mainly following the American example. American film studios started determining the youth's tastes and trends. Imitation is useful for culture, only if it does not stagnate after a point.

Demolition of the values of Soviet culture was not accompanied by constructive activities directed towards acquring a new image. It seems destruction was taking place much faster than accumulation of new creative power for producing new literary works.

An important feature of the culture of post Soviet period had been to place literature at the periphery. The writer is no more an "engineer of the human soul". Now he has to get into a dialogue with the new market forces. Literary art has started acquiring unusual variety of genres and styles. As a result readers get the opportunity to over- come the limitations of a one sided approach, and learn to formulate an objective picture of the world. Literature of the period of openness allowed to form an understanding that in the world (besides class priorities), there are other values in the world. Return to those was an important achievement of literature.

Literature of the period of reconstruction could still preserve its leading position. In a confident manner it was opening up new themes, by focusing on the most critical stages of social reality. The journal "New World" published Aitmatov's "Plakha" which for the first time dealt with the problem of drug addiction. Later on Dudintsev's "White robes" was published, which deals with obscurantism in the field of science during the forties. Published during this period Rybakov's "Children of Arbat" depicts the devilish picture of Stalin's time. The social novels of Dudintsev, Rybakov and others were created on the same principles, as works of critical realism of the 19th century.

Along with traditional literature, post modern literary works made their appearance. It did not place before it any social problems. It was found that for the first time after many years of a monolithic character, Russian literature has formulated in principle a very different artistic trend. This trend is often called "the other prose", by referring to its proximity to post modernist trends in world literature. "The other prose" tried to forget the past, did not try to forecast the future and got engaged in the psychological sphere of "contemporary man in the modern world". The characteristic feature of this trend was a refusal to have any social responsibilities or morality. It puts forward in the forefront the aesthetic purpose of literature and at the same time the writers have a skeptical attitude towards attaining higher social ideals. Some of the characteristic features of this literature are: insignificance of place of action, social back- ground of the characters, introduction of the author in the story as its main character, aphoristic character of the work, back of definite ideas and above all an ironic attitude and approach.

The new literature broke up the usual framework of permissible limits, criticizing not only the hierarchy of values, but also the language of literature. They did not want to spare anything that they received as heritage, and insisted on the right of the author and the hero to willfully arrange textual timings. The other prose or poetry aptly expressed the scattered attitude of modern man in the world. The prose of Petsukh, Popov, Petrushevskaya, Murzakov and other authors of the New Wave became a reflex response of the author to his immediate environment. The new literature determines the characteristic features of contemporary socio-cultural situation, the loss of identity of man, his perplexity, one who has lost a familiar cultural reference point. The feeling of uncertainty gave rise to an ironic attitude to the present reality. Prose and poetry of post modernism tries to determine the relationship between author and text, between text and reader. Such type of prose and poetry one could find in the literature of the beginning of XX century, when man felt unstable and uncertain in everything that took place around him. At the time the writer tried to play with literary language, attempting to find new ways to describe the world. May be after finally desacralizing words and images a new beginning will be made; and a constructive not destructive time for culture, will set in.

The Modern Russian cultural process is characterized by a remarkable mosaic of character along with contradictions in style and world views. It is continuing to develop because of the widening field of cultural activities. At this point the problems of cultural inheritance have to be solved. Historical link of culture with the past assumes continuity of moral, intellectual and spiritual life of man. From the second half of the nineties interest in the classical heritage of Russian culture can be noted. An important sign of interest in classical works has been expressed in its rediscovery, in the effort to give it a new contemporary interpretation.

In the nineties, considerable attention was paid to the spiritual heritage of Russian thinkers of the 19th and 20th centuries. The works of Berdyaev, Fedotov, Rozanov, Bulgakov and others were published. As a result the condition for a dialogue with the culture of the Silver Age and the Russian immigrant literature of the 20s to the 40s opened up (which in fact was kind of continuation of the literature of the Silver Age). When a major culture of a major country is undergoing a feeling of loss of values, the search for spiritual self identification becomes a very important factor. The formation of cultural values of this "New Russia" is becoming possible due to the inclusion of the mechanism conducive to the activation of a higher culture which will create new values and meanings. However, for the present one can find only certain trends and tendencies of cultural creation, which does not allow us to speak about the active vertical line of Russian culture above its horizontal existence.

The solution to these problems requires time and new cultural priorities, which the society itself must become aware of.

REFERENCES

1. Blum, D.W. ed. *Russia's Future: Consolidation of Disintegration Boulder*, Co., 1994.
2. Boym, S.Common Places. *Mythologies of Every Day Life in Russia.* Cambridge M.A. 1994.
3. Bremmer, T and R.Taras, eds. *New States, New Politics: Building of Post-Soviet Nations*: Cambridge, 1996.
4. Dunlop, J.B. *The Rise of Russia and the Fall of Soviet Empire*, Princeton, 1993, 1995.
5. Lapidus, G.ed. *The New Russia: Troubled Transformation.* Boulder, Co.1995.
6. Moore, J.L.ed. *Legacies of the Collapse of Marxism.* Fair Fox, V.A. 1994.
7. Saikla, A and W.Maley eds. *Russia in Search of its future.* Cambridge, 1995.
8. White, S. et al., eds. *The Politics of Transition: Shaping a post-Soviet Future*, Cambridge, 1993.
9. Алексеев Л.М. История инакомыслия в СССР. М. 1992.
10. Громов Е.С. Сталин: власть и исскуство. М. 1998.
11. Жолковский А.Н. Блуждающие сны. Из истрoии русского модернизма.М. 1992.
12. Кричевская Ю.Р. Модернизм в русской литературе; Эпоха Серебряного века. М. 1994.
13. Плимам Е. Г., Пантин И.К. Драма российских реформ и революции. М.2000.

3

"New Currents in Russian Poetry" Mikhail Epstein's *After the Future*

Abhai Maurya

After decoding the term post-modernism as "after-time" (in parenthesis) M. Epstein in the context of post-Soviet literature backed it up with the statement "Actually, we are experiencing a kind of post-futurism."[1] He reinforced this notion with the formulations of authoritative Russian philosophers with a view to establish that "after-time" or "post-futurism" or still better, "after-futurism" relate to the Shakespearean "seven ages" of man. A smattering of such axiomatic utterances garnish even the preface of the book "*After Future. The Paradox of Post-modernism and Contemporary Russian Culture*". Picking up Diderot's words from his letters to Catherine II to the effect that Russia was "a fruit that rots before it ripens"[2] Epstein sought to prove the point that "the future of fruit turned out to be in the past."[3] By citing the pronouncements of Russian thinkers: "Russia's fate is one of needless ventures based on being born soon and soon collapsing" (Prince M. Shcherbakov); "We grow but don't ripen" (Petr Chaadaev); "We were born well, but grew up very little" (Vasily Rozanov)[4] Epstein would have liked us to compare all these statements with F Dostoevsky's words "the premature exhaustion of the mind and imagination of our society as yet so young but grown so untimely decrepit."[5]

Thus while analysing the recent literary processes in Russia M. Epstein applied the term post-modernism rather sensationally. After all it sells well when you are being 'different', a bit of 'oddball'. But Epstein is not so original. The term post-modernism was extensively employed by Leslie Fiedler and lhab Hassan in 1960s with "premature approbation and even with a touch of bravado".[6] Ihab Hassan saw the "prelude" to post-modernism in what he had termed as "the literature of silence" or "anti-literature" which was a product of "outrage and apocalypse" that had been raging in the world in the face of which "human tongue is speechless in fright and ecstasy".[7] Leslie Fiedler was quick to discern the "complex alliances" of literary imagination "with silence, with obscenity, with madness, and even with those postsexual states akin to mystical trance"[8]

How could Mikhail Epstein lag behind? He in his monograph *After the Future* displays similar touch of bravado in dismissing the very thing that had existed in Russian literary and cultural scholarship hitherto and propounding a host of most bizarre hypotheses.

Writing on "New Currents in Russian Poetry..." he states that "the poetic currents" that had appeared in the beginning of 20th century, i.e. symbolism, acmeism and futurism had towards the end of the century got metamorphosed into "a new poetic triad: metarealism, presentism, conceptualism"[9]. He further elaborates that while metarealism and conceptualism are the new incarnations of symbolism and futurism respectively, presentism is a kind of arithmetical mean between the two, "Presentism, like acmeism before, strives to sail between Scylla Charybdis."[10]

To begin with Epstein in his book briefly discusses the most general features of post-Soviet Russia literature (up to 1995). He is right to suggest that the paradigms have been shifting gradually in the Russian literature over a few decades: in 1950's and 1960's there was a preponderance of words like "sincerity", "openness", "the confessional", "boldness", "freedom from inhibition" and so on. Subsequent to this the poetry, for example, was taken to "nature", "origin", "memory", "warmth", "kinship", nativity" . These, according to Epstein, were only "half-concepts", "half-images". In post-Soviet times there, inevitably, had to be preponderance of terms like "culture", "meaning", "myth", "custom", mediation", "reflexivity", "polysemy" and so on[11] At this stage major part of poetry, according to Epstein, became "a form of self-consciousness for culture, reflecting the relativity and diversity of sign systems."[12] He cited the sonnet by Alexander Eremenko to prove his point:

> ... in the dense metallurgical forests,
> where chlorophyll production was in progress,
> a leaf fell. Autumn had already arrived
> in the dense metallurgical forests.
> And stalled up in the skies forever

are a tank truck and drosophila fly.
Pressed down by the resultant force,
they're stranded in a flattened clock.
The last hawk-owl is broken and sawed up.
And with an office push-pin he's been tacked
to an autumnal bough, head-down,

he hangs and ponders in his head:
why, with such an awful force,
have binoculars been mounted into him!

Thus the life in modern day Russian poetry, according to Epstein, is "not equal to itself; it grows insofar as it is transformed and made more complex by culture." Modern poetry is "cultural to the utmost, not in the sense of culturedness as evident knowledge, but in the sense of culture as the accumulated memory or spiritual continuity that broadens the content capacity of each image."[13]

As stated above, in subsequent sections of the chapter on 'New Currents in Russian Poetry' Epstein has dwelt at length on the triad of metarealism, conceptualism and presentism.

The works of metarealism, according to Epstein, display the tendency towards greater complexity of poetic language in contrast to the simplification and primitivisation discernible in conceptualism. Metarealism does not mean the negation of realism. It, according to Epstein, is an expansion of realism "into the realm of things unseen, a complication of the very notion of realism, revealing its multidimensionality, irreducible to the level of physical and psychological verisimilitude and including a higher, metaphysical reality."[14] In other words metarealism is a realism of multilayered and multistrand realty which could be connected to each other by a myriad of intertwining "passages and interchangeabilities"[15] Epstein affirms that the stylistic current of metarealism is discernible in the works of Olga Sedakova, Elena Shvarts, Ivan Zhdanov, Victor Krivulin, Dmitry Shchedrovitsky, Vladimir Aristov, Arkady Dragomoshchenko and others. In metarealism, according to Epstein, the image is raised to the level of supra-artistic generalisation, converting it almost into a myth. Epstein cites a few stanzas from the poetry of Orga Sedakova, wherein one finds that standardised norms of contemporary literary language stand pulverised and the meaning plays a hide and seek game, slipping and sliding at will, making her poems extremely complex:

> Can it be, Maria
> that frames alone do creak,
> that panes of glass alone do ache and tremble?
> if this is not the garden–
> then let me turn back,
> to the quiet, where things are thought out,
> it this isn't the garden, if the frames are creaking
> because it can't get any darker,
> if this isn't The garden,
> where hungry children sit by apple trees
> forgetting the fruit that they've tasted,
>
> where no light can be seen,
> but breath is more dark
> and the healing of night is more trusty …
> I know not, Maria, this sickness of mine.
> It is my garden that rises above me.

According to Epstein, in metarealist works it is not possible to separate the direct meaning from the figurative ones or to break the metaphoric similarity from symbolic correspondence. Indeed, in materialist poetry "metaphor is again revealed as metamorphosis, as an authentic intercommonality, rather than the symbolic similarity of two phenomena."[16]

Thus metarealism has also been termed as "metaphorical realism" by Epstein because it is the "poetry of that reality which is hidden within the metaphor, uniting its divergent meanings, the literal and figurative."[17] Thus Epstein has termed Sedakova's poetry as "poetry of transfiguration"[18]

It is in this context that Epstein dwelt at length on the penchant of poets like Zhdanov and Eremenko for metaphor which is why they have been called "mataphorists" by Epstein. In fact Epstein has coined a new term called metabole with a view to encompass the totality of the content of metaphoric poetry. The metabole, according the Epstein, is "an image that cannot be divided into the two halves of literal and figurative meaning, of an object described and the similarity ascribed to it; it is the image for a doubled and yet unitary reality."[19] In the poetry of metaphorists the metaphor is sought to be overcome from within and attempt is to move away from dichotomy to an intrinsic unity wherein movement is, in the words of Epstein, "from the external similarity of distant objects to their necessary copresence in one expanded reality."[20] Through metabole the metarealists poetry undertakes a kind of quest for some sort of "wholeness that is not reducible to the simple identity of all phenomena as in the case of metamorphosis; nor does it separate them through the contingency of similarity, as in the metaphor".[21] Epstein compares the metaphor and the metabole in the following words: "If metaphor is a shard of myth, then metabole is an attempt to restore wholeness of an individual image appointed to draw near to myth, to the interpenetration of idea and realia, insofar as this is possible in contemporary poetry."[22]

Epstein after declaring the metarealism as the new incarnation of Russian symbolism missed the point that the latter was not a monolithic phenomenon. Nor did he discuss the philosophico-aesthetic positions of metarealists without which the analogy between the two remains unsubstantiated.

Firstly, the Russian symbolism had been divided into three generations. V.M. Zhirmunsky has identified "Three Waves" among the Russian symbolists. These waves are concretely associated with the three generations of Russian symbolists: the first represented by Konstantin Bal'mont and Valery Brusov, second by V. Ivanov, A. Belyi and A. Blok and, finally, third by M. Kuzmin.[23] Secondly, rather more importantly, Russian symbolism philosophically had been an extremely motley phenomenon: one wing, i.e. the one spearheaded by Dmitry Merezhkovsky and Valery Bal'mont were drowned in retrograde mysticism through and through (no wonder the were called "chyornye magi", i.e. the poets of black magic). Dmitry Merezhkovsky, for instance, being an extreme case among them, thought that "Mythology was a religion."[24]

Moreover, D. Merezhkovsky through his brochure "On the Reasons of Decay and About the New Trends in Modern Russian Literature" written in 1893 had put the entire blame for the downslide of Russian literature around that time at the doorsteps of the theories espousing social commitment of literature, which, according to him, had led the literature into a blind alley. Blaming squarely the aesthetic theories of Chernyshevsky, Dobrolyubov, Pisarev the author went as far as to say that their theories had created a sort of literary materialism and they were responsible for the vulgarisation of the literary taste, which is "the taste of crowds."[25]

Konstantin Bal'mont continued to sing this very refrain. In his article "Elementary Words about Symbolists Poetry" Bal'mont devotes a significant part to contrasting of symbolism and realism: "Realists are always simple observers, whereas symbolists are always thinkers. … While the poets-realists look upon the world naively, like simple observers, submitting to its material base, the poets-symbolists … penetrate deep into its mysteries."[26]

Writing under the spell of Nietzsche early symbolists were subsumed by the cults of 'devil', 'people as herds', motifs of escapism, loneliness, death and so on as if to say that "evil disappears under the breath of death"[27] like smoke.

At the very outset of his literary life Brusov came under the spell of the philosophy of Kant and aesthetic ideas of Schopenhauer. However, Brusov did not limit the content of art to mysticism alone. In other words Brusov discarded the scientific method of cognition in favour of the intuitive one: "These are the gaps, those moments of ecstasy, of super-sensual intuition, which offer alternative conception of universal phenomena, which penetrate deeper than their external layer into their very crux."[28]

However, Brusov did not share Merezhkovsk'y view that mysticism should be the sole source of content of art. After the revolution of 1905 Brusov is clearly having a fresh look on his aesthetic positions.

The second wave of Russian symbolism is represented by younger symbolist poets like Vyacheslav Ivanov, A. Belyi and A. Blok, S. Slov'yov and others. The 'younger symbolists', as they came to be known as, strove to overcome the individualistic reticence of the 'elder' brothers, position of extreme subjective aesthetism and the abyss of abstractness. Moreover, the acuteness and intensity of the social situation obtaining in Russia at that time soon compelled the symbolists to climb down from the soaring heights to the ground reality. They were forced to pay attention to the question about Russia's fate, life of people, about revolution. Moods of depression and extreme pessimism of 'elder' symbolists yielded place to the expectations of imminent storms with which the air in the Russian sky of the first decade of 20th century was laden very heavily.

A. Blok became the biggest star among the generation of 'younger symbolists'. Blok, for Instance, wrote around this time: "Poets cannot be "aesthetic individualists", or "pure symbolists" or "mystical realists", or "mystical anarchists", or "cathedral individualists. ..."[29]

The symbolists like Valery Brusov and other young symbolists had reviewed their philosophic-aesthetic positions in favour of revolution, particularly after the revolution of 1905.

Brusov's collection of poems *Urbi et orbi* (*To the Whole World*) had a stunning effect on Blok. The poet as if had suddenly woke up to the themes of contemporary life. He was compelled to feel the acuteness of the problems and contradictions of the contemporary life. No wonder in 1903 he wrote the poem *Factory* which is replete with the realistic episodes from the lives of "the beggarly" workers who were being "tormented" to death.

Thus the theme of human suffering gradually began to permeate Blok's poetry, even thought he had abstractly romantic ideas about the incipient changes, about the imminent revolution. The world of *Wonder Lady* turned out to be illusory and ephemeral, "a temple washed in azure reflection of the skies". The mysticism, as he wrote in his diary, turned out to be an exercise in emptiness, in vacuity. Blok gradually drifted towards the civic poetry, "Like the decadents, the younger symbolists accepted the revolution of 1905-1907 without the slightest hesitation."[30]

Conceptualism, according to Epstein, is a stylistic current which embodies within itself "a certain conception, or some conceptions, which the critics or interpreters draw out." [31]

In other words in place of "a work with a conception" we have to deal with "a conception as the work". The conceptualists create a rupture between "the idea and the theme, the sign and reality", which becomes a sort of stylistic principle with the conceptualists. In conceptualist poetry we discern "the petrifaction" of language making conceptualism, thus, "a workshop for producing scarecrows, ideologically figurative formula, that are hastily covered with a slovenly sackcloth of linguistic fabric"[32]. Epstein sites following poetic lines by Dmitry Prigov to prove his point:

The outstanding hero –
He goes forward without fear
But our ordinary hero–
He's also almost without fear
But first he waits to see:
Maybe it'll all blow over
And if not – then on he goes
And the people get it all.

Since conceptualists intend to demonstrate the self-sufficiency of a formula or conception they try to make the language as "arbitrary, inorganic, unsanitary" as would be possible. Conceptualist works, thus, are a sort of "criticism of artistic reason" leading to the unmasking of "lyrical soulfulness" which produces "a skeleton of an idea-engendering construct."[33] In other words, conceptualism creates a sort of primer of stereotypes by removing from them "the aura of creative mist and lofty animation" so that their "vulgar nature as signs called forth to stimulate the most elementary reaction to love and hate, 'for' and 'against'"[34] could be subverted conclusively. The use of minimal !inguistic means leads to "the depletion and deadening of language itself. … Conceptualism unequivocally reflects the reality of that milieu from which it arose and spread, or more precisely, its apparent, empty "idealness"[35]

While drawing the analogy between Russian futurism and conceptualism Epstein forgets that the former was an ultra-revolutionary literary current. The only plausible similarity between conceptualism and futurism seems to be the attempt at demolishing the language or attempt at stripping the language of its multifarious paraphernalia that had been made both by Futurists and conceptualists. Futurists had thundered: "We have turned the syntax topsy-turvy."[36]

Probably another feature that could be seen as common to both the stylistic currents is the rejection of the things and the ideas of past. Russian futurists clamoured for "throwing away of Pushkin, Dostoevsky, Tolstoy … etc. from the steamer of modernity[37], whereas the conceptualists had been pulverizing the conceptions of recent socialist past, more often than not. But here the analogy ends. Russian futurists were revolutionaries fiercely agitating against bourgeois individualism and calling for the promotion of the spirit of "we", i.e., prevalence of the spirit of collectiveness as opposed to the egocentrism inherent in the "I" of a person obtaining in the poetry of conceptualists. More importantly, for the futurists the quintessence of the aesthetics lay in the 'Word' with capital letter, whereas for the conceptualists, as defined by Epstein, the greatest virtue resided in the conception that they chose to subvert, more often than not. Indeed, contrary to Epstein's assertion, there seem to be more points of divergence between Russian futurism and modern day conceptualism, a fact that has been totally obscured by Epstein.

The third stylistic current, i.e. presentism encompasses the poetry of presence. In Epstein's words, "Presentism affirms the presence of an object, its visibility and tangibility, as the necessary and sufficient conditions of its meaningfulness. Between the extremes of poetic monism (the merging of object and sense) and dualism (their separateness) a medial approach to reality is sketched out, close to a phenomenological description."[38] In other words, according to Epstein, a poetic work of this current consists of diverse views obtaining about one and same object. The views may spread out in succession of each other or they could form a conglomerate of different perceptions forming a totality of "the manifestations of its actual essence"[39]. Epstein considers poets like Aleksei Parshchikov, Ilya Kutik, Alexander Eremenko as the poets of presentism. He has cited following stanzas from Parshchikov's poem as an example of sum total of ways in which the "catfish" is perceived in different situations, i.e. in water, on land, while waking and sleeping:

> It seems as if he's dug out in the water, like a trench.
> Surfacing, he thrusts out a wave above his head.
> Consciousness and flesh compress themselves more tightly.
> He's altogether like a backway from the bedroom to the moon.
>
> And if you dip your hand into the underwater byways
> they'll turn and speak to you, telling fortunes by your palm.
> A kingfish on the sand flounders ringingly
> and goes could, like a key in its thickening lock.

In the poetry of Alexander Eremenko, Mikhail Aizenberg, Tatiana Shcherbina, and Nina Iskrenko, Epstein finds that the movement is from the "archetype, through kenotype, to stereotype"[40] Presentism thus occupies the intermediary zone, i.e. the diapason between the two opposite poles of metarealism and conceptualism the way acmeism had been situated between symbolism and futurism.

In our opinion presentism is hardly comparable with Russian acmeism, wherein one discerned an attempt at creating a kind of balance between the high-flying mysticism on the one hand and *mundaneness* or earthliness of life as obtaining Russian poetry, on the other. Unlike symbolism the poetry of acmeism was against the phenomenon of escapism from life and its concomitant manifestations. The credo of acmeists lay in the simplicity of vision and its expression in literature. In their attempt to avoid extremely apparent and extremely mystical in their poetry acmeists had sought that the poetic word "carried out the function of calling out the things and phenomena by their apparent names, while at the same time it accomplished the function of metaphorical values."[41]

It is quite obvious that there is nothing common between acmeism and presentism and Epstein had undertaken a vacuous exercise to artificially establish the analogy between the literary triads of early 20th century Russian literature and its counterpart obtaining around the threshold of 21st century.

Epstein has also discussed the avant-garde literature that he discerns in the latest Russian literary processes. He is of the view that "the avant-garde continues and develops the ancient principle of nonrepresentationalism."[42] In Epstein's opinion "the avant-garde is intimately linked to the apocalyptic worldview that achieved its zenith in early Christian times, but thereafter was pushed aside for many centuries by the traditions of secularized religiosity."[43] Epstein goes on to say that "the avant-garde is the art of building an image to frame this world in the process of its passing away, as it sheds its apparent, worldly surface. This is the realism of an apocalyptic age that has realised the unstable and spectral nature of all worldly arrangements. This is apocalyptic realism."[44]

Here again it has to be pointed out that the avant-garde was the most revolutionary and radical strand among a host of protest movements that had obtained in art and literature in the beginning of 20th century. It is, however; quite significant to note that that both modernism and avant-garde had their origin in protest against the existing order of things. Yet, differences between the two were equally important.

Indeed, the difference between modernism and avant-garde largely lay in the extent and the intensity of protest against the values of their culture and against their fear of being subsumed in that culture. In modernism the attempt was to reflect on contemporary society and changing social and aesthetic vision and to ponder on their modernity in an innovative manner but within the limits and restrictions that are self-imposed largely due to the reactive and defensive postures of modernist writing.[45]

In avant-garde writings modernism's social antagonism was stretched to a tenuous extreme. It almost approached nihilism, and its formal innovation, i.e., attempts at finding an aesthetic language of newness and future, became strident experimentalism.[46] Moreover, avant-garde adopted decisively militant postures and it directed all its aesthetic activism at pulverizing the institution of art and the social conditions that were responsible for the quagmire of stagnation in which art and literature were trapped around that time.

Thus, we can see that there is not an iota of similarity between the avant-garde of early 20th century literature and the "apocalyptic avant-garde" as discovered by Epstein in modern Russian poetry or prose. Why Epstein's American translator Anesa Miller-Pogacar has rushed to support the his view in this regard is not at all difficult to understand.[47]

M. Epstein has also generously used the terms like the "last literature", "tired literature" in his work under reference. Picking up the threads from 19th century Russian literature Epstein discerns that the "superfluousness" of 19th century Russian literature had got metamorphosed into the "somnambulism" in the "last literature", i.e. the literature of Soviet era. Quoting Valeria Narbikova's novella *The Appearance of Us* Epstein wholeheartedly supports Narbikova's assertion to the effect that "somnambulists are predominant in a last literature: characters who have not managed to accomplish anything or think anything through, who immediately drown in apocalyptic fog."[48] Epstein also cites the examples of Tatiana Tolstaya's stories like "Peters", "The Circle", "The Okkerville River", "Sleepwalker in the Fog" and Shukshin's story "Oddballs" (*Chudiki)* to substantiate his point. Whether or not these somnambulist characters are comparable with the 'superfluous people' of the yore is yet to be substantiated. Nevertheless, Epstein by resorting to such a comparison has undoubtedly unleashed a discussion that literature like history repeats itself in its "cyclical development"[49]. But whether this "development" is "cyclical" or spiral is a moot point. Further, if it is the latter, i.e. the spiral, the question still arises as to whether or not the spiral is moving downward or upward.

It would be saying the obvious that Mikhail Epstein has used the method of comparative study of literature with a view to create a dazzling effect much against the letter and spirit of the comparative method as the comparison would be a barren exercise if it is not undertaken with a view to establish the laws or objective factors that give rise to the similarities or correspondences under discussion. However, the inter-literary or intra-literary mutuality can hardly be ignored. Even though Epstein has undertaken a strenuous exercise, the results would have been far more convincing had the comparison been backed up by a discussion on the factors generating the resemblances. However, in that case Epstein's whole enterprise would have come crumbling down like nine pins as there seems to be no basis for such correspondences to obtain.

REFERENCES

1. Epstein M., After the Future, *The Paradoxes of Postmodernism and Contemporary Russian Culture* (translated into Eng. by Anesa Miller-Pogacar), 1995, p. XI
2. Epstein, p. XII
3. ibid.
4. ibid.
5. Cited by Epstein from *The Brothers Karamazov*, trans. David McDuff, London, Penguin Books, 1993 p.800
6. Hassan Ihab, *The Post modern Turn: Essay in Post modern Theory and Culture*, Ohio University Press, 1987, p. 86.
7. ibid., p. 204.
8. ibid. p. 12
9. Epstein, p. 19
10. Epstein, p. 20
11. Epstein, p. 22
12. Epstein, p. 24
13. Epstein, p. 29
14. Epstein, p. 37
15. Epstein, p. 38
16. Epstein, p. 40
17. ibid.
18. ibid.
19. Epstein, p. 44

20. Epstein, p. 46
21. ibid.
22. Epstein, p. 47
23. Zhirmunsky V.M., *Teoriya literaturyi, poetika, stilistika* (*Theory of Literature, Poetics, Stylistics*), Leningrad, 1977, p. 106
24. Merezhkovsky D S., *Taina tryokh* (*Secret of the Three*), Moscow, 2003, p. 80.
25. *Russkaya literature XX veka, Khrestomatiya (Russian Literature of 20th Century, a Reader*), Leningrad, 1991, p. 464
26. Ibid., p. 465
27. Bryusov V., in the poem "Умереть, умереть, умереть! (Die, Die, Die!):
    "И я понял, что зло род дыханием твоим (смерти – A.M)
    .... исчезает как дым."
28. A.G. Sokolov, *Istoriya russkoi literaturyi kontsa XIX nachala XX (History of Russian Literature of the End of the 19th and Beginning of the 20th Century)*, Moscow, 1979, p. 157
29. Emanuel Swedenborg, *Heaven and Hell* (New York: E.P. Dutton), p. 473
30. Лотман М.Ю. "Символизм", *Русская литература XX века* ("Symbolism", Russian literature of 20th Century) , p.28
31. Epstein, p. 31
32. ibid.
33. Epstein, p. 32
34. ibid.
35. ibid.
36. *Русский футуризм* (Russian Futurism), compiled by Teryokhina V.N. and Zimenkov A.P., Moscow, p. 42
37. *Литературные манифесты* (*Literary Manifestoes*), compiled by Brodsky N.L. and Sidorov N.P., Moscow, Agraf, 2001, p. 129
38. Epstein, p. 48
39. ibid.
40. Epstein, p. 49
41. Panov M.V. *Стилистика* (*Stylistics*), quoted from Русская литература, op. cit., p. 45
42. Epstein, p. 56
43. Epstein, p.57
44. ibid.
45. See Russel Charles, *Poets, Prophets and Revolutionaries*, Oxford University Press, New York, Oxford, 1987, p. 5-14.
46. Eagleton Terry, *Literary Theory: an Introduction*, Oxford, p. 41
47. See Miller-Pogacar Anesa, *Introduction*, Epstein, pp 1-16
48. Epstein, p.74
49. See the table: Epstein, p. 79

4

Impact of Social Transition on Russian National Identity

A.V. Yegorova

According to a Russian saying, each generation has to endure some hardships. For the generation of my grandparents it was the Great Patriotic or the Second World War. For my parents it was the complicated time of postwar reconstructions. When applying the saying to my generation, I would certainly state it is true for perestroika and following it, the reform times of the nineties. As the audience is probably aware, a method of "shock therapy" was applied to cure the economic disease. Although such an approach was extremely painful to millions of Russians, only a few arguments opposing this political and economic course could be heard publicly which were mainly raised by western analysts and journalists. This was the starting point for the present crisis of national identity.

The period since then to now is sufficient enough for making conclusions on crucial nation-size changes. The transition has impacted the society such that contemporary Russian society is extremely heterogeneous. The economic gap between the elite and the indigent has led to polarization of subcultures. At the same time the concern is that there are not enough evidences of research in cultural values shifts. Research projects in general are expensive, and this might be a possible reason for a lack of such projects dealing with modern Russian subcultures in the field of social psychology. However, there are public opinion surveys which are published regularly on various issues. According to a recent survey by Pew Global Attitudes (*Inostranets,* #41, 2005) only 23% of respondents were satisfied with the general situation in the country, while 31% considered themselves to be at the bottom of the society. The gap between the highest and lowest levels continues to widen.

This striking difference between the two sections of the society can be observed even on the national television programs. Quite recently, a journalist succeeded in showing the tremendous gap between the two subcultures on a prime time channel. While on the first day social meetings of the "golden youth" revealed those things which are highly valued by the off springs of the business and political elite: dress code – pretentious dresses and luxurious accessories, behavioral code: artificial joviality and smiles, on the following day the audience sympathized with marginalized homeless children, who are called "бомжи" in Russian. The event covered by the television was a birthday celebrated in a basement, thereby showing the difference in the manner of celebrations. My proposition is that now the values of these anti-pole subcultures are so different, that their native Russian language is the single uniting element for the elite and the marginalized Russians. Certainly, not the whole bulk of the language, but its most general part, most commonly used vocabulary. The divergence starts at an early age, in places of socialization for children (nurseries, day-cares, schools). Because of the different settings, qualifications of the teaching staff and the environment, students acquire different education, which includes attitudes and morals. They have an unequal access to further education. At present there are no strong evidences of efforts towards reducing these inequalities.

A lack of respect towards the authority of the people of "high" culture – i.e. writers, film-producers, actors and others, who used to be called "интеллигенция" since they were engaged in intellectual work and were considered to share high values and ethics, can also be seen as a sign of cultural crisis today. The hunt for financial prosperity and political profits has brought a change in the people's outlook. According to surveys, they no longer serve as the role models for the youth, but instead criminals and business people (or in some cases both) often do. The latter as role models are to a certain extent imposed by the mass culture.

Changes in gender relationships followed social shifts. The business lady, a new type of a Russian woman emerged and brought about a phenomenon which was previously uncommon – the gigolo phenomenon. It should be noted that this phenomenon has not been rejected by the society. The reason for this, in my opinion, lies in the fact that labor by itself has ceased to be a value. Instead personal success, no matter by what means, is highly valued. 'The end justifies the means' seems to serve as the new motto for a considerably large portion of the society.

When virtues are vague, attempts are made to find those things which can unite – ethnic roots or religious beliefs. Unfortunately, quite often such attempts manifest themselves in disrespect and humiliation towards strangers. Crucial social changes have influenced intercultural relationships. One of today's acute social problems is intolerance towards other cultures and subcultures, an extreme form of which are crimes for racial and religious reasons. While intolerance has never been a state policy, quite unexpectedly the slogan "Russia for Russians" is heard frequently in everyday life. A recent evidence of religious intolerance was the reaction of the orthodox masses to the words of the Russian Minister of Education that in the near future a text book for secondary school students will be published which shall be titled "Survey of World religions". A negative reaction was soundly expressed by means of noise and objection and the argument raised was that – "We are an orthodox nation". The question that arises is – what is meant by the 'Russian nation'? Does this refer to only a certain part within the Russian Federation?

The lack of a national idea is obvious. It has become a routine to forward one social project or another as an attempt of declaring it as a possible national idea which could unite the citizens and strengthen their feelings of national identity.

When thinking of such a national idea, some propose a project aimed at improving living conditions or the conditions of the highroads, others – on savings people's lives and preserving their health, developing sports facilities. In general they might be classified as social projects. Yet such objectives, despite their importance, could not serve as a national idea, since they lack ideology. Ideology helps to realize and estimate relationships in the society. None of these projects have such an aim. We are still in search for one.

5

Mass Media and National Identity in Multi-Cultural Society of Russia

In Search of a Balance between Toleration and Freedom of Expression

Veronica V. Usacheva

Characterizing mass media, we recognize that one of its main functions is defining (in the broad sense of the word) social reality and the place a person occupies in it. Most of modern social scientists could agree with Peter Kareithi, who believes that "we make sense of our world from the stories we are told. From these stories we construct the sense of who we are and, more importantly, who we are not. The construction of that difference - of the 'other' - is crucial to the discourse of race". Besides, an important characteristic of modern mass media is the fact that they take an active part in the formation of the system of personal and social values. They are able to integrate a society, and to promote decrease of social tension in it. But also they can provoke the crisis in society, play a destroying role.

Nowadays the Russian mass media pays much attention to the correct imaging of different nations and races. This situation has many reasons. Among them – the search for national identity, the desire to solve the problem of migration, and repeated actions of skinheads. The pattern of national identity creation seems rather simple if believe that it provides the society with major orienting factors: indicating who belongs to the society and who is alien to it, what is considered to be a norm of behaviour and what differs from it. However, in modern times this simplification could not satisfy new goals and approaches oriented on cooperation of different nations, co-existence of different religions and traditions.

Mass media coverage of this important subject inevitably causes various reactions in the society. Unfortunately, accusation against mass media for its prejudice to the people of other race and nationality, cultures and even other appearance is a common thing in modern Russia.

The period after disintegration of the Soviet Union is characterized in the majority of studies as a complex social and cultural crisis. At once, spiritual values as well as standards of behaviour, which formed the basis of self-identification of a personality, lost their significance. Purposes generally accepted in society lost their meaning. This brought about destabilization in society and affected common national identity "Soviet people". As a result, many issues of ethnicity, nationality and race – earlier kept in silence and considered a taboo – have rapidly acquired an unusual salience and topicality.

In such a situation the image of an "alien" in Russia has gained in importance. The crisis of national identity was projected not only on foreigners, but also on ethnic groups inside the country. Moreover, sometimes inter-religious relations and contradictions between regions and between particular regions and the central government aggravated the situation. Social and economic problems, even a competition for labour places could be explained as an ethno-confrontation and furthermore like an antagonism.

The mass media had their role in spreading the image of an "alien" all over the country. Thus, we approach the problem of responsibility of mass media to the society. Nowadays we can hardly speak about responsibility of mass media in Russia. That is why we frequently meet with images of an "alien", i.e. enemy in mass media. This situation hampers the progress of creating the identity of "Rossians".

"Blacks" inside Russia (the popular term for people of Caucasian origin)

The crisis of national identity in the Nineties had a negative effect on the economic, social and international position of Russia. The present political elite look toward stabilization of the status of Russia in international relations and creation of identity of the "*Rossians*" (citizens of Russia) as a common Russian national identity. The main potential danger for it is a possibility of stirring up a feeling of dissatisfaction and enmity towards the "aliens". As history has it, an "enemy" can be easily found both inside as well outside the country, and this can lead to more dangerous situations, namely repressions of nations and war conflicts. But without the notion of national identification, that requires prudence and caution from the political leaders, there is no way out of the crisis, i.e. creation of a uniform national civic identity is imperative for the country.

The analysis the image of an "alien" in Russia on the materials of the mass media makes it possible to conclude that the problems which were raised in Russian mass media demonstrate strong concern of the public opinion about manifestations of xenophobia, nationalism and racism in Russian society. The components of the image of an "alien" in these materials are as follows.

First, the concept of the "blacks" is popularly understood as "aliens" with a negative accent. This concept in Russia is partly connected with Africans, but mostly with Caucasian peoples as well as peoples from the former Soviet Union Asian republics. To ameliorate the situation mass media replace the "blacks" for "person of Caucasian nationality". This term is supposed to legitimate the notion of "alien", so that it loses its negative emotional colouring of the "blacks". Moreover it gives it a certain official colouring. Despite all this, the term has a strong negative tinge in public consciousness, as it denotes persons, perception of whom is connected with potential danger. This feeling is aggravated by the critical atmosphere prevailing in particular parts of the Caucasian region and by streams of refugees with whom a common people connects his troubles. The term has an offensive character, but its pseudo-official form plays the role of a "fig leaf".

Next, in electronic mass media there is no visual (at least) presence of ethnic minorities, whose appearance alone could give an impression that alongside with the "white" majority there live "coloured" minorities in the country. This was typical for the Ninetieth years. The situation changed in the end of the decade and new faces have appeared on telescreens.

Lastly, a considerable proportion of materials about the "blacks" concentrate on the negative aspects of social life. They are criminality, violations of administrative regulations, corruption, drugs, diseases etc. All of these are considered to be ethnic characteristics of suspected. This suggests the existence of "ethnic criminality". Hence, this develops an ideal situation for sparkling off hatred towards a particular ethnic group and for the local population develops an idea of a "black threat". Quite often such materials contain examples of hate speech.

It is important to underline, that the notion of "black threat" has nothing to do with official policy or ideology. Moreover, the official authorities oppose it in every possible way. Nevertheless, it could be termed a socially conditioned mood or perception. "Black threat" can change from ethnic chauvinism at worst to eurocentrism at best.

The content analysis of the news programs on TV let us make a conclusion that the diversified phobias, both ethnic and social in character, had influence upon the Russian society. It seems, the main source of a danger in mass opinion is migration, and, as result, the dominant phobia is "migrant phobia". Not always this phobia has a trace of ethnicity. But, it is easier to identify it as ethnophobia.

The main ethnophobia's object is people of Caucasian origin (particularly, North Caucasia and Transcaucasia). "Caucasian Phobia" is a new term, appeared recently with increase of Caucasian Diaspora in other regions of Russia. Some researchers reckon it is the most commonly used sort of the ethnophobia in modern Russia. Besides, image of "profiteer-Caucasian" has roots in mass perception as far back as Soviet Union period. This image provoked (and still provokes) negative emotions among people.

In mass media materials depersonalization of representatives of minorities promotes intolerance. But individualization /personification – specifying of names, professions, gender characteristics, mention of family, children etc – contributes to their "humanizing" and gains the sympathy to them.

According to the prevailing view among researchers, in the last decade (from 1995) two social groups express their enmity against 'other' ethnos more intensively - young people and "bureaucracy". It is generally accepted that youth are particularly sensitive to the changes in the national consciousness. It is not only Russian specificity, this is a widespread phenomenon. Youth aggression against aliens, others ethnic or race could be marked almost in all countries of Europe, in Australia and so on.

Social responsibility of the journalists, editors, and mass media at whole, takes on special significance. In fact, they give names or create names for social phenomena, moreover point out and establish the reasons.

It is easier to tell the stories, which based on stereotypes and prejudices, rather than to investigate the phenomena, to explain complex historical and social context. In addition the fright is a great tool for manipulation and national issue is a simple instrument for determination of political issues, for political goals on Post-Soviet space.

The migration is considered the main source for increase of population in Russia. Therefore a fear of migrants will be present in Russian society and its realization will depend on mass media

The "Blacks" outside Russia

What is the image of Africa and Africans are using in Russian mass media? And what is the role of mass media in creation of an image of representatives of other races.

Here are the results of the monitoring of the news from Africa in news blocks of the NTV channel. The sampling includes the foreign news of the NTV Channel's[1] program "Segodnya" ("Today") of the eight-month period from September 1, 2000 till May 1, 2001.

We have found out that during the period under study in the news program of NTV-Channel there were fifty-two stories, in which only twenty-two African countries had been mentioned. Almost the half of these stories (twenty three) told about Africa indirectly. As regards emotional influence, out of 52 stories six were positive, twenty – neutral and twenty-six – negative.

Mass media very often uses Africa and countries of the continent as "terrible matching": for example, in the story about grave condition of Yugoslavian economy, this country has been compared to such countries of Africa as Zambia or Sudan. The countries of the continent are usually represented as a standard of poverty.

Stories about leaders, political and public persons are very rare. We can tell that there is No Africa in persons (in faces). The continent is faceless and impersonal. The image of Africa at telecast is also amusing and terrible, generally corresponding to children's poem "Children do not go to Africa for a walk", with a detailed set of trapping threats and dangers.

---

1. NTV was the leading Russian commercial TV-channel, famous for democratic views at that period

To sum up it is necessary to tell, that in general the Russian mass media followed common for the Western world tendencies in coverage of Africa. Moreover, the countries of the West are represented as a certain idea and pattern of development, and only South Africa – as a "gleam of hope" for the continent of incipient savagery and chaos.

The image of Africa, as to my mind, is not the main image of "alien" for Russia. However, it is undoubtedly important and necessary for Russian mass media. When the public opinion in Russia, proceeding from the political idea about multipolarity of the world, identified the position of Russia as the "other" culture in relation to Western culture, Africa in the Russian mass media received the role of the "other" culture in relation to the Russian one. The image of Russia became a connecting link in the chain "Western World – Africa" allowing to emphasize the "civilised character" and "developed nature" of Russian society. As a result, the following argumentation has appeared: "while Russia barters raw materials for hi-technologies at the West, to Africa Russia sells its own technologies, which are competitive but cheaper than Western. While Russians go West to study, Africans look for cheaper but qualitative education in Russia". And image of Africa in Russian mass media helps to realize this purpose.

As noted earlier, Russian mass media, as a rule, present material in light of Western values and corresponding advantages as compared to other cultures. Such an attitude denies originality and values of other peoples, predominantly those of Asia and Africa. As a result, the image of Africa is treated as a manifestation of an "alien culture", inferior to the Russian culture. By this contrast between "wild Africa" and "civilized countries of the West", Russia is *a priori* associated with the latter.

The image of Africa in the Russian mass media, as a whole, discredits the idea of balanced informing. Frequently journalists use narrow-minded stereotypes, which have been formed in the previous epoch. The situation is aggravated by the fact that there are not enough news and publications of the authors, who visited Africa or had deep comprehension of its problems.

On the way to solve the problem

The image of the "blacks" is perceived as a certain chaos, destroying or capable to destroy the stability of Russian society and culture. This stereotype must be broken. The peoples of Russia have been living together many generations and other perspectives for the future would not be foreseen. In these conditions the creation of "civil national identity" – the *Rossians* – is one of the vital purposes for Russia. The basic provisions which prohibit the spread of inter-ethnic dissension and discrimination on the basis of racial identity were written in the Civil Code of the Russian Federation, in Mass Media Act of 1991, in the currently in force Constitution of the Russian Federation of 1993 and other legal acts. Despite the declaration of these norms, the mechanisms of their implementation are badly developed. In this connection we pin hopes on judiciary reform being nowadays carried out. The active role of public organizations and commissions should be also essential. They could perform the monitoring of materials of mass media for racism and chauvinism and prepare recommendations for the authorities including licence commissions. The propagation of political correctness, causing jeers among the majority of journalists, is obviously necessary condition for operation of mass media.

Nowadays the appeals to be politically correct are audible more often from the part of the State officials, and not from mass media community. So, after terrorist acts, the authorities and officials declared in reply to the questions of mass media about the "Chechen track" in the terrorist acts: "... it is a mistake to look for any national track ... Terrorists, first of all, have neither nationality, nor religion". At the same time on the pages of the respectable newspapers it is possible to find, for example, a such sort of allegations: «The main distributors of drugs in Russia are the representatives of the criminal ethnic groups, among them the main places were occupied by Tajiks, Azerbaijanis and Nigerians" or "more and more pronounced ethnic character of criminal groups are to be observed».

During the last years in Russia the "Concept of State National Policy of the Russian Federation" and also "5-years Federal Programme of Forming Tolerant Attitude and Prophylaxis of an Extremism in the Russian Society" for mass media and the education have been approved. These and other acts of the authorities testify their concern about the problem of creation of national identity and give hope, that the solution of the problem will be found out and applied in life.

REFERENCES

1. Kareithi P. *Global Narratives of Race in Rhodes Journalism Review*, N20. *(www.rjr.ru.ac.za)*
2. Malahov V. *"Skromnoe obajanie rassizma" i drugie ctatii ("Discreet Charm of Racism" and Other Articles). Moscow, 2001*
3. *Neterpimost' v Rossii: starye I novye fobii (Intolerance in Russia: Old and New Phobias). Moscow, 1999*
4. Usacheva V. *Obraz Afriki v rossiiskih mass media (Africa's Image in Russian Mass Media) in Asia and Africa Today, №11, 2003*
5. Usacheva V. *"Svoi" i "Chuzhie" v zerkale sredstv massovoi informatcii ("Our" and "Others" in the Mirror of Mass-Media: Coverage of the Pogrom in Tsaritsino-market, October 30, 2001) in "Chuzhie" zdes' nr hodjat. Radikalnaja ksenophobia I politicheski extremism v socio-culturnom prostranstve sovremennoi Rossii ("Others" not allowed here. Radical Xenophobia and Political extremism v social and cultural space of modern Russia). Moscow, 2004*

6

Three Centuries in Cultural Transition of the Kazak Society

Güljanat Kurmangaliyeva Ercilasun

The basic criteria in studying the cultural transition would be music, theatre and cinema; games, dress, food consumption, café and restaurant culture, guest reception, shopping, and mass media as main determining and indicating topics. What kinds of changes have occurred in each of these fields in the Kazak society? Indeed, these topics need to be compared during three centuries: 19th century, as a traditional period, 20th century as a socialist period, and 21st century (i.e. last decade) as a capitalist period. Furthermore, the impacts of globalization on the cultural values in Kazakstan also need to be explored.

Music of the Kazaks in the 19th century is now called folk music, and composers are called folk composers. 19th century-Kazak music was mostly performed by *dombyra*, Kazak national music instrument. Furthermore, the main themes of the 19th century-Kazak music were nature, wild animals and birds, philosophy of life, ethics and values, beauty, and lyric themes.[1] Additionally, cattle breeding reflected on the music as a natural part of the life. Indeed, horse takes an important place in music genre, since horse was accepted as a loyal friend of a *jigit*, Kazak young man.[2]

1. *Jiyrma bes, Shapibay-au, Top shengel, Qaratorgay, Ayqyzyl Gul* and many other songs serve as examples for this genre.
2. *There are plenty of songs, devoted to the horses or at least they were mentioned, in the 19th century-Kazak life; for instance,* Akbaqay, Eki jiren, Alqonyr, Boz jorgha, Uzengi bau taralgy al, Kulager, Manmanger *and so on.*

Music of the 20th century was affected by the Socialist ideology. A specific genre, glorifying Socialist leaders, has appeared in this century. Collective work, transition to the agricultural life, for example, cotton rising, crop and rice cultivation, began to take place in the Kazak music. World War II showed also its impact on the music themes.[3] Nomadic life of style was no more praised. New kinds of musical instruments, especially Western, such as violin or contrabass and new terms as orchestras, bands and ensembles entered to the Kazak life in the 20th century.

Music in the 21st century has all genres and all musical instruments. However, the beauty of voice does not have much importance any more. With the assistance of developed technical systems, computers, it is possible to correct all defects. Having financial sources and physique have become enough to become an artist, even a star. Importance is given neither to the voice qualities, nor to the meaning of the songs. As for the genres, the youth admire rap and hip hop. It even affected their style of wearing. Surely, this does not mean that traditional music is lost; however, traditional style of music and *dombyra* is mostly liked by old people and only small part of the young generation.

As for the theatre and cinema, in the 19th century, *aytis* can be estimated as an ancestor of theatre and cinema among the Kazaks. *Aytis* is a competition among two or four people; there would be two sides competing and producing straight away. *Dombyra* was also used in *aytis* in most times. Actual problems and important questions were also expressed and discussed in the *aytis*. The sides could also joke or criticise each other friendly. Producing straight away with rhymes and playing an instrument at the same time required high poetic, artistic and creative skills. Different ceremonies could take place of the modern cinema and theatre in the 19th century.

In the 20th century, the Kazaks were introduced with modern theatre and cinema. Many Kazak film directors, actors, artists and scene writers became famous in the 20th century. Theatre developed and took a significant place in the social life. Importance given to the theatres can be observed in the theatre buildings; all theatres were

---

3. *Aq maqta, Terbeledi tyn dala, Aq biday, Jas Qazaq, Kyzyl Sunkarlar, Beybitshilik saqtalady, Aq kogershin and etc.* are examples of the 20th century-genre.

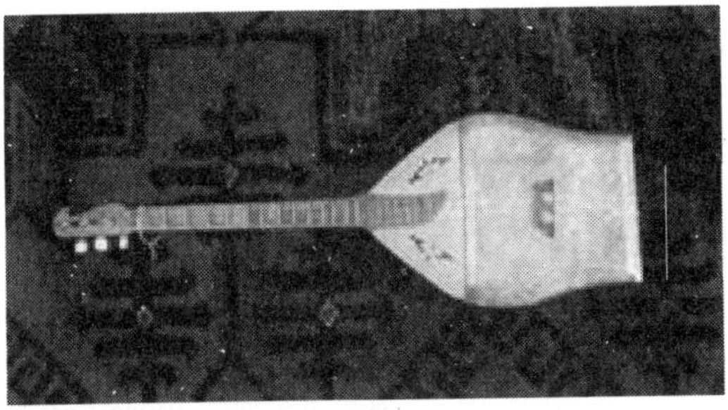

Dombyra, Kazak national musical instrument[4]

grand and splendid buildings throughout the Soviet Union. People were wearing chic dressings to go the theatre. As for the cinema in the 20th century-Kazakstan, similar to the other republics of the Soviet Union, mostly Soviet films were in the vision. Imported films were mostly limited to such countries as Poland, Romania, China, etc. Besides, there was another country which took a significant role, it was India. Indian films created a different and special sector in the 20th century-Kazakstan. Some people made their preparations before going to an Indian film, by taking the handkerchiefs for crying. Kazak people know very well some Indian actors. For example, Raj Kapoor, Amitabh Bachchan, Hema Malini, Anil Kapoor, Mithun Chakroborty, Rekha, Govinda, Sri Devi and many other Indian actors and actresses are well-known and popular in Kazakstan.

Theatre and cinema in the 21st century changed slightly its shape. Theatre had some financial problems in the first years following the dissolution of the USSR, but the Kazak government pays attention also to the cultural development. Besides, intelligentsia continues to attend theatres. Cinema is full with Western films, it would be an incredible situation during the Soviet period; new films come to vision almost at the same time with the USA, and new cinema saloons are equipped with all modern techniques. Moreover, home cinema systems are quite developed at present. VCD and DVD consumption become higher and cable TV and satellites provide people with many films on different channels.

Games were actually played collectively in the 19th century Kazak traditional society. National games, such as *kökpar*, men on

4. Source: http://www.president.kz/articles/culture/culture_container. asp? lng=ru&art=musik

horse play as two commands and compete for a mutton or goat, *kyz kuu*, competition of a man and woman on horse, *bayge*, competition of horses, etc. were played collectively, and these games were mostly played in ceremonies. Among everyday games there were *asyk*, to play knucklebones and *altybakan*, a big swing, where several people could stay at once. "In the nights, the Kazaks come together and enjoy; they narrate tales and listen to the musicians playing musical instruments…" (Levshin, 1996: 297).

As for the games in the 20th century, chess and draughts were most popular. National games became less and less known. Especially chess contests were held, even in the classes and schools.

As there is an observable return to traditional life, national games became popular again in the 21st century. In ceremonies, many contests of the national games are held. Besides, the globalizing age show its impacts, too. Since computer using becomes more popular, the computer games, such as "Counter strike" and "Age of Empires", can be played everywhere. Furthermore, in many corners, there are game machines and clubs, where it is possible to play different games and lose money. Latter subject gradually becomes to form harm to the society. Machine game hazard make pupil and students fail to attend the courses and bring harm to the relations with family.

Dress in the 19th century was as how we now call it national dress. Women wore long dress, ornamented waistcoat, boots, and hat or scarf. Dresses also changed according to age, social and marital statuses. Men wore broad trousers, shirt, waistcoat, hat and silver belt. Ornaments were embellished by hand work. Materials were brought by merchants, but leather clothes were prepared by the Kazaks themselves.[5] Leather, cotton, felt and fur were the most utilised materials in the Kazak dresses (Zeland, 1885: 20).

In the Soviet times, scarf of the women was prohibited and young women almost did not use it as a whole. Long dresses and other elements of traditional clothes were preserved among the aged women and on a less scale among the aged men. Younger generation started to follow the fashion. Standardisation throughout the Soviet Union reflected also on the dresses of the Kazak people.

When we came to the 21st century, it is possible to see Christian

---

5. For more information about the leather producing and commercial activities, see *Kazakstan Tarihı*, 1994: 198-199.

Dior, DKNY, Yves Saint Laurent, Mango and other famous marks. There are grand shops of worldwide famous marks in Kazakstan. While it was a deficit to find imported goods during the Soviet period, now it is difficult to find clothes of local production. As a striking example, jeans was a very fashionable and deficit cloth in the 20th century, whereas now even children in cradle wear it.

Food consumption in the 19th century was in a traditional style. The Kazak traditional foods consist of meat in the first place (especially horse meat is valuable), milk and pastry. *Beshparmak* (dish made up mainly of boiled meat and paste, and this dish is counted as a national dish number one) and *palau* (dish made up mainly of meat, rice and carrots) are the most popular plats among the Kazaks. *Sorpa*, *manty*, *bauirsak*, *chakchak*, *kospa*, *kurt* and *irimshik* are some other dishes of traditional cuisine. The Kazaks drank *kymyz*[6] and tea[7]; *kymyz* was made at home; whereas, tea was mostly imported from China in the 19th century (Valikhanov, 1985: 259, 261).

Kazak National Cuisine[8]

6. *Kymyz* is fermented mare milk. *Kymyz* is a very old beverage among the nomadic people; for instance, monk Rubruck noted *kymyz* with the word cosmos, as early as in the 13th century (Ospanuly, 2005: 94).
7. The Kazaks mostly drink black tea with milk. Furthermore, according to N. Zeland, who spent some time among the Kazaks, The Kazaks liked tea very much, but it was not always possible to get it (Zeland, 1885: 19).
8. Source: http://www.president.kz/articles/culture/culture_container.asp?lng=ru&art=cooker

During the Soviet period, national cuisine preserved its place, but some new dishes entered to the life of the Kazaks. Especially potatoes obtained an important place in the cuisine. Making and drinking *kymyz* became rare, but tea consumption became higher[9]. Moreover, in the 21st century, it is possible to see that cuisines became richer. National foods still preserve main place, but at present one can easily find European, Chinese, Turkish, Korean, Indian, Japanese, and Arabic cuisines in Kazakstan. It is possible to claim that impacts of globalization can be observed in the cuisine, too. Besides, *kymyz*, as a national beverage, still preserves an important place in the Kazak culture; however, rate of its consumption cannot be compared with the traditional period. Tea is still important drink in life of the Kazaks; they can drink it 4-5 times a day.[10] Nonetheless, coffee starts to compete with it in the last decade.

It is not possible to say anything about the café and restaurant culture for the 19th century, since there were not cafés and restaurants at that period. Surely, there were *caravansarays*, offering meal and accommodation; however, it was a different practice. Therefore, we will compare 20th and 21st centuries in this category. In the Soviet period, there were dining rooms and few restaurants in a city. Dining rooms and dining halls were mostly situated in institutes and institutions. The prices were not high. Besides, they worked in a Soviet mentality; that is, the clients were not important for them. The clients waited in the orders, took, ate and brought the dishes back. There were working hours, and if clients come and it is a time to close, they surely close the dining halls. Earning money or satisfying the clients did not mean anything. They were not earning from there,

---

9. Since the 20th century, tea has being imported mostly from India.
10. In the 21st century, tea is still being imported from India. However, export of Indian tea has fallen significantly fallen in the last few years. For example, in 2002, India exported 52.24 million kilograms of tea to the CIS as against 76.22 million kilograms in 2001. (http://www.telegraphindia.com/1030421/asp/business/story_1893225.as). This fall was probably caused by the reason, which was also expressed earlier by an Indian delegation, visiting Moscow, that there was wrong labelling of packets in Russia. There have been found to contain blends of teas from other countries, but labelled as Indian tea (http://www.hinduonnet.com/businessline/2001/01/03/stories/140365y4.htm).

it was a state institution; therefore, it was not important, it was much important to close and rest. As for the restaurants, the prices were high there. Clients surely were people who had higher incomes than usual people. Service was relatively better, but still not comparable with present, capitalist period. In the capitalist period, as it was already mentioned above, there are many kinds of cuisine from many parts of the world, and surely there are plenty of café and restaurants.

Normally, a coffeehouse or café "shares some of the characteristics of a bar, and some of the characteristics of a restaurant. As the name suggests, coffeehouses focus on providing coffee and tea as well as light snacks. Other food may range from baked goods to soups and sandwiches, other casual meals, and light desserts. In some countries, cafes may more closely resemble restaurants, offering a range of hot meals, and possibly being licensed to serve alcohol"[11]. In Kazakstan, cafés are also close to restaurants; they offer hot meals, alcohols; but restaurants are more expensive and have better qualities than cafés.

The Kazak hospitality is evaluated as a practice of totally different mentality from the Western viewpoint. Guest reception was a usual activity for them in the 19th century. There was a concept "Guest of God"; that is, guest is sent by God, and host must accept this guest whom he sees for the first time[12]. Host must feed the guest and even feed his horse, and to find him a place to sleep. The Kazaks had such a mentality that they were saving meals, good foods for the guests but did not eat themselves. They were hosting the guests cordially.

Guest reception slightly changed in the 20th century. It is still one of the very important and most preserved traditions among the Kazaks. They still give to the guests everything they can. Change happened with the practice "Guest of God", people started to inform the hosts and in most cases people whom you do not know do not come as guests.

In the 21st century, guests are still important in the society. Still people invite, prepare, serve and do their best. Nevertheless, there is a new practice, which came by globalization. This is an invitation of a guest to a café or a restaurant. People start to choose easier practices. That's how guest reception traditions are subjected to the changes.

---

11. http://en.wikipedia.org/wiki/Cafe
12. For more information, see *Kazaktın Köne Tarihı*, 1993: 385-386.

Shopping is another subject which had transitions throughout three centuries. Earlier, in the traditional periods, there were not fixed shops, there were mobile ones; merchants came to the Kazak steppes.[13] The Kazaks also went to the grand bazaars of the sedentary regions. Shopping was realized in such a way.

In the Soviet period, there were big supermarkets called *TsUMs* (Central Universal Stores) or *GUMs* (State Universal Stores) throughout the USSR. There was one such a big store in every city. In the standardised country, there were also shops called *Detskiy mir* (Kid World) in every city. There were grocer's shops, all similar everywhere. In provinces, there were two-three stores that sell everything similar, not with many alternatives. Houses, furniture, accessories, dress; even water glasses were almost the same everywhere in the USSR.

It would be incredible that one day, actually in the 21st century, there would be plenty of shops and shopping centres. As it was already mentioned above when we dealt with the dresses, it is impossible to count how many shops there are now. At present, in Kazakstan, one can find everything he / she looks for.

As for the mass media, it is impossible to talk about the TV and radio in the 19th century; there were newspapers and magazines in the Kazak steppes. Nonetheless, the literacy degree was lower; and transportation and communication was a problem in the vast Kazak steppes. The impacts of the newspapers and magazines were significant, because they were the tools used by the Kazak intellectuals to enlighten and educate the society, and they played important role in socio-cultural transformation of the Kazak society. Nonetheless, newspapers and magazines were not mass-circulation media tools in the 19th century.

During the Soviet period, the mass media was harmed by ideology. Literacy degree become very high, many newspapers and magazines started to come out, radio and TV played a significant role in the society. There were also regional and professional newspapers and magazines. Radio and TV had limited channels and had uninteresting broadcast programmes. Speech and thought freedom

---

13. Travelers, who visited the Kazak steppes in the 19th century, describe trade activities in details. Such records can be found in the notes of travelers like Levshin, Radloff, Valikhanov, and Zeland.

was obviously lacking in mass media. For instance, even in a recipe book authors had to firstly praise the socialism and the establishment of the Soviet Union, before they could publish it. Generally, there were about three-four TV channels totally in Almaty, the capital of the KazSSR even in the last years of the USSR.

In the 21st century, now there are plenty of newspapers, magazines, radio and TV channels. Capitalism and globalization brought their rules. Cable TVs offer about 60-70 channels, satellite TVs offer more than 350 channels. If to have money, it is possible both utilise as a consumer and even become a producer.

In sum, after having compared cultural changes in three centuries, it is possible to evaluate that the Kazak society is enjoying the market economy and freedoms at present. The most important question might be the preservation of cultural values and traditions, where I believe that they still do preserve important and positive sides of the traditions. Three centuries brought different political, economic, social and cultural environment and different transitions for the Kazak society. I do not assess it as a progress or regress, but rather evaluate it as a socio-cultural change. Three centuries include different pictures in the Kazak society.

REFERENCES

Kazakstan Tarihı Kone Zamannan Buginge Deyin (Ocherkter), Kazakstan Respublikasinin Ulttik Gilim Akademiyası, Sh. Ualihanov ątındagi Tarih jane Etnologiya Instituti, A.H. Margulan atındagi Arheologiya Instituti, "Kazakstan" damu kori, Almaty, Dauir, 1994.

Kazaktın Köne Tarihi, Almaty, Jalin, 1993.

Levshin, A.I., *Opisaniye kirgiz-kazachiih, ili kirgiz-kaysatskih, ord i stepey*, Almaty, Sanat, 1996.

Radloff, Wilhelm, "Kazaklar ve Kyrgyzlar", *Türkler*, 2.cilt, s. 368-376.

Ospanuly, Eraly. "Cosmos, otkrytyi monahom Gil'omom de Rubrukom", World Discovery Kazakhstan, 2005/04 (5), pp. 94-98.

Valikhanov, Chokan, *Sobranie Sochineniy*, vol. IV, Almaty, 1985.

Zeland, N., *Kirgizy (Etnologicheskii Ocherk)*, St. Petersburg, 1885.

7

Indo-Persian Literary Culture and Central Asia

Through Iranian Perspective

S.A. Hasan

In a similar fashion as the West has tried to rename the Persian Gulf and derive strength from new order in West Asia, the Russians and their allies are now bent upon creating certain disputes among the Central Asian countries in terms of their socio-cultural identity. In order to remain independent and stable, the Muslim countries of Central Asia need commitment from within for giving more teeth to their age- old common culture and tradition. The very purpose of coming out of the unified Russian umbrella does not mean to invite another threat from the market oriented mind of the Western colonialists. In spite of the fact that without Russia there can be no military balance in the region since Central Asia lacks resources, military facilities, professional and technical skills, yet it must be mentioned here that this is the same Russia that for many years has exploited these countries, bringing them on the verge of bankruptcy and poverty. On the other hand, Russia being a super power has always deprived these Muslim republics of their technical and technological resources and skills, and is now attempting to convince the Central Asian countries to seek help from her in order to face the current challenges.

The most difficult situation today is the crisis of identity of the Central Asian countries. We have witnessed over a period of time that the Central Asian Studies throughout the globe have been placed under the Russian Studies' circle whereas, frankly speaking, neither as a part of spirit nor the affiliation of language, literature and culture they show their similarities with any aspect of Russian identity.

The centuries old language and literature of Central Asia has been over shadowed by sixty four years of Slavic domination.

When talking of Persian literature the mind invariably turns to the glory and richness of its past. The pomp and grandeur of Persian culture has often been portrayed in the writings of Central Asian intelligentsia; and so, it remains a subject of interesting discussion among the social scientists and men of letters, within and outside this region. Today, even the biggest enemy of Central Asia too admits to the fact that the jewels of Persian culture has enriched not only its next door neighbours but has also thrown its rays on the people living even in the remotest parts of the world. The sweetness of Persian language and its vast literature has contributed a lot to this campaign over the course of history.

The Central Asians have always been very proud of their language, literature, ideology and culture. In spite of heavy odds and many socio-economic upsurges, they have tried to protect their dignity and preserve their identity. One must give credit to them that even after accepting Islam and considering Arabic language as the medium of their religious discourses and decrees, they have kept no stone unturned in order to resist against Arab culture and therefore, have not made any compromise vis-à-vis their national language.

Ferdowsi's great epic "Shahnameh"(The Book of Kings and Heroes), is an important landmark, not only in the renaissance of the Persian language and literature that has remained practically unchanged for thousand years, but also in its expression of national identity. Having undergone for more than three centuries and having assimilated the Muslim faith to make a new culture out of it, the Central Asians saw themselves described in Shahnameh as a people possessed on ancient traditions and yet imbued with fresh vitality and aspirations. Ferdowsi is one of the rare poets who managed to depict vividly the inner soul of the people. His heroes and their struggles for justice stem from the most ancient popular traditions and from all the legends of Central Asian mythology in which any Central Asian can recognise himself.

All through the Muslim history, the Central Asians maintained their own identity. In the realm of mind and intellectual research, they acted in accordance with the standards common to the whole of Muslim community, whereas in their personal, emotional and aesthetic lives, they lived in a different world. Avicenna, who was to remain for centuries the unique master of medicine of unprecedented philosophical-psychological dimensions, and who produced outstanding works (Al-Shifa, & Al-Qanun) in philosophy and medicine in Arab tongue, was highly proud of being an Iranian speaker.

The feeling of dissatisfaction with oneself and confession of man's inability to explain the mysteries of life are the main features in the works of Omar Khayyam, who's Rubaiyyat (quatrains), express it with deep anguish and sorrows. In order to ease his anguish, this mathematician and astronomer sought in the wisdom of nations and explanations that he found to escape the vanity of philosophers and theologians, he took refuge in epic narration. The toleration that emerges from Omar Khayyam's thoughts is characteristic of Central Asian culture and literature and is to be found at all times in the Persian books.

It was only the middle of the 19th century when deep rooted Central Asian culture got diluted by so called protectors as to adopt a new colour and to co-ordinate with the new-born nationalistic feelings.

The concept of 'Nation', from which the term Nationalism has been derived, appears for the first time during 14th – 15th centuries in Europe. During this time people belonging to the same linguistic groups, living in the same territory and practising almost the same types of traditions, began to think of themselves as one. This gave encouragement to the monarchs, whose powers were curtailed to a large extent by the feudal lords. Consequent upon the emergence of this national identity, the people lent support to the monarchs who were able to establish nation-states in England, Spain, France, Prussia, Russia and other countries. Thus nationalism in its historical concept implies such a belief of oneness among the people on the basis of language, territory, customs, traditions and others such outward manifestations which can be easily discerned. In the post-feudal age, the concept of nationalism has come to stay and in all the later political developments, this concept has played a very important role.

In the Iranian context, the people of pre-constitutional movement (1905-6) in Iran have often been accused of not having this concept. True, this concept of nationalism was absent in the 18th or early 19th century Iranian psyche, but as the national movement started taking roots in the country; one finds a rapid development of this idea.

The economic expansion of European nations reached its climax during the nineteenth century, and it is from this date that the process of modernisation in the Iranian society may be said to have begun... Slowly and gradually Iran came under the influence of rival interests. As a result of these developments Iran was placed deep down to its misfortunes. J.B.Fraser describes the tragic state of Persia in these words... "... all orders seem on the point of suspension, and a disposition to anarchy obtains, which certainly would end in some revolution, were it not for some counterpoises connected with religion and peculiar political situation prevailing in the country, that tend to preserve things as they are, and to resist every cultural efforts at improvement. The insecurity on life, limb, or property even for the passing day, produces a corresponding mistrust among the individuals; the servant distrusts his master, the master his servant.... The worst is that there is no rational prospect of amelioration, no point from which to look forward to a happier state of society, for there is not hope of any change in the system of government."[1]

In the beginning of 20th century Iran was occupied by the Russians in the north and the British in the South. During this period, Iran experienced intense foreign subversions whose manifestations were the domestic political turmoil and the disorders at that time. A number of eminent scholars of Iran have expressed their deep sorrows against such torturous developments in Iran. Md. Hejazi's famous novel 'Homa' and his well-known short story, 'Shirin Kela' could be the best example of their disagreement. Sa'eed Nafeesi too, has registered his protest in the form of a story titled 'Khanah-i-pedari'.

The twenty years of Reza Shah Pahlavi's dictatorial regime, a short period as it was, were crucial in the history of Iran... During this period various changes took place in the Iranian society. These changes led to an enormous development of intellectual creative thought. Changes not only in behaviour, but in dress too became an outward symbol of the new way of perceptions. Reforms in the field of education, according to the European pattern, were the basis of essential cultural changes. In 1934, a university after the name of Reza Shah Pahlavi was founded in Tehran covering all basic branches of contemporary learning, such as medicine, technical sciences, natural philosophy, veterinary sciences, agriculture and fine arts etc. fell in the same line.

The development of press and book publishing (both by state and private publishing houses) greatly added to the popularisation of educational progress. Some purist tendencies that manifested authority at that time led to the enhancement of freshly born nationalistic feelings in Iran. The purists aimed at removing foreign influences from the language, especially Arabic ones and replacing them by neologisms or archaisms, brought into life again. Sa'eed Nafeesi, Bahar Mashhadi, Mohammad Hejazi, Poor-I-Dawood, Sadegh Hedayat and Jamalzadeh played a leading role in this regard. Jamalzadeh's "Farsi Shekar Ast"[2] initiated this discussion.

New Persian literature writing was also progressing. Some text-books dealing both with works of Persian writers and translations from foreign literature appeared. It is worth mentioning that the translations from European languages into Persian have given a new direction to the modern literature of Iran. It was mainly through translated documents that the Iranians came across Western culture, art, tradition, idea, style etc. This time Iran had moved into a modern era and assumed a central place in the world affairs with extra-ordinary speed. The rapidity of these events caused great concern to the intellectuals and guardians of traditional Iran. Fearing the consequences, many of them could not dare to promote their opinions, and many of them utilised this opportunity to come out openly declaring themselves as rebels. A group from within these protectors of traditional Iran deliberately avoided confrontations with the government and through suggestions and advises registered their reactions and discharged themselves from responsibilities.

Mohd. Ali Eslami Nadushan, who was born in 1925,is known, as his cultural, political articles written for the leading magazines of the country and published in 1962, under the heading of "Iran ra az yad Nabarim"(Let us not forget Iran) earned him reputation and lent his ideas some weight. The centre of his interest is a confrontation with European civilisation so for as it fosters or retards the developments of Iran in its traditional perspective. His ideas can be briefly condensed as follows:

"The East has woken up and no longer wants the Westerners to decide its fate. As long as the Western countries hesitate to accept this reality, tension and friction can not be eliminated."[3]

"Our culture is deep and daily reality for the great mass of Iranian people. Classical poetry, popular poetry and songs, tales, proverbs and ancestral wisdom express a deep-seated humanism that guides men and women in their daily lives."[4]

"…. Another development that has begun to be noticed in Iran is in the popularisation of arts. A dreadful kind of popular music, a cheap pulp literature, and a generally dread cinematic output are among the most striding out puts of this popularising trend. In Iran it is increasing fast as a result of blind imitation of what is happening in the west."[5]

"Referring back to the strength and identity that lie within traditions, I propose that in Iran the ancient code of 'good thought, good words and good deeds' are revived. Its full implications and applications should be taught and made into a national discipline."[6]

'Gharbzadegi' by Jalal Ale-Ahmad is considered to be a numerous work in the same spirit which could best be translated as 'Obsession with Westernisation' which is highly topical and acute in the context of Iran. The author aims to fight the ever- increasing foreign influences affecting Iranian culture and social life in its own way corresponding to the political conditions of the country. Here I would like to mention a few examples of the same author:

"The process of modernisation as interpreted or encouraged by the West, contained many erroneous elements and much veiled domination. The value of freedom, democracy and justice has often become a mere means of exploitation."[7]

"The demands of rationality and objectivity constitute the very foundation of western outlook. If such an outlook has resulted in great achievements where machinery and the physical world are concerned, we must admit that it has been much less successful in dealing with the human conditions. Human sciences founded on rational objectivity are today suffering setbacks and defeats."[8]

"As for administration and industry, they have to appeal to an increasing number of Sociologists and Psychologists so as to lessen the evils of dehumanising bureaucracy. Why should we follow the same road? Do we have to assess our degree of civilisation by referring to the ills of western civilisation? We can certainly adapt the techniques and methods of industrial and administrative organisation to the demands of our social and cultural life, as long as we do not forget the value that our traditions attach to man and to human relationships."[9]

"In the West, since the last war, the Social Scientists have had much to say on the subject of resistance to change. They have claimed that the cultural traditions and beliefs in non-western societies are a barrier to progress. Such an allegation reflects two attitudes. The first is, consciously or unconsciously dominating and establishing a western hegemony over the whole world; the second is to model the world according to a western model. All the achievements of the west in technology serve as an argument to justify such an attempt at uniformity. As a result of such campaigns, many Asian countries paid attention to such temptations."[10]

Mohd. Ali Eslami and Jalal Ale Ahmad, both the scholars have discussed at length the evils of Western Culture in Iran. In this small article, I have documented only a few quotations; yet there are many more things to be acknowledged. Whatever may be the contention of their feelings, but their sentimental attitudes, towards their national identity and grace, can easily be discerned in the writing of these scholars who have sharpened their instruments to kill the western model of culture as to preserve the true picture of Iran on a spotless canvas.

At the beginning of the 20th century, there was a great enthusiasm for the adoption of the Western Model. Taqi Zadeh, one of the most respected representatives of elite had openly declared, "We must westernise ourselves, body and soul"[11]. Fifty years afterwards, in the 1960s, he repented and admitted the importance of a cultural identity. Today, among the new generation of poets, writers and artists, belonging to the different schools of thoughts, there is not one who wishes to become westernised in body and soul.

The dominance of Persian continued in this region to a considerable degree until the beginning of the 20th.Century in spite of new political, economic and cultural conditions, not least under influence from Europe, sponsored gradual simplifications of style. Thus there emerged contemporary standard Persian. At the same time, Tajikistan under Russian and Soviet rule developed its own literary language which is -based on local dialects and written in the Russian alphabet. Iranian Persian ceased to be the accepted standard form of vehicle of expression. It is still in vogue in Afghanistan, but decreasingly so as it is the official language beside East Iranian Pashto.

Persian was cultivated at the courts of the Ottoman rules, several of whom are known for composing Persian poetry. Literary Ottoman Turkish is a virtual substance of Turkish and Persian (with all of the latter Arabic loan elements). Similarly, Urdu, the language of the military camp, developed under heavy Persian influence. Persian first entered India with the conquest of north-west India by Ghaznivid armies in the eleventh century. Four centuries later, Persian in its classical form was chosen as the court language of the Mughal kings (1530-1857), who were major patrons of Persian literature and poets from Iran, unlike the contemporary Safavids in Iran. It was at the courts of India and Turkey where many of the major traditional dictionaries of Persian were compiled from the fifteenth to the eighteenth centuries, many with grammatical treatises. Simultaneously, there developed in India a Persian vernacular, and it was from the Indian scribes and secretaries that the English officers of the East India Company, many of whom wrote grammars of Persian, with all its local idiosyncrasies. Persian was abolished in its last official bastion-the courts of law-in 1837 by the authorities of the East India Company.

In the 10th.century AD Seljuk and his generation fought in wars which broke out between the Samanids and Sultan Mahmud of Ghazna. The Saljukes were nomadic Turkoman who at first disliked city- life, civilisation and religion and, after taking to Islam they became begotten due to their simple nature. But in the same era of Saljuk dynasty the language and literature advanced and poets like Khayyam, Nasser Khosrow and Anwari; and scientists such as Ghazali and Sanai emerged. Malikshah and Sultan Sanjar patronised such poets and scientists. The Saljukes brought Islamic Asia which extended from the farthest part of West Afghanistan to the coasts of Mediterranean Sea under one rule. By encouraging the Muslims, the Saljukes repelled the crusaders of the Byzantine army.

The literary interactions between India and Central Asia continued until the establishment of USSR. Amir Khusrow, Mirza Abdul Qadir Bedil, Mirza Ghalib and finally Allama Iqbal earned great popularity throughout Central Asia. Needless to mention that Iran, due to certain reasons ignored the valuable services made by the Persian scholars of India until the Islamic Revolution but, on the other hand, Central Asians loved and admired them from the bottom of their heart.

There have been five eminent poets of Indo- Persian traditions in the Indian subcontinent of which Khosrow, Bedil and Mirza Ghalib are of Central Asian origin. Khosrow the poet of India extolled his forefathers and made bridge between the people of India and Central

Asia. Similarly, Bedil forged unbreakable link between the two regions of Asia. It has been rightly commented that Bedil is the gift of India to Central Asia. After the Russian integration of Central Asia, the people of the Central Asian republics namely Tajikistan and Uzbekistan began to discover their traits and culture in the works of Bedil alone. They took strong fancy to him and worshipped him as their Muse and Oracle. Every Central Asian house hold has the Divan of Bedil besides the holy Quran. The people of the region adore Bedil as their national poet who represents all their ethos and aspirations and every word of the poet is considered by them as divine voice. The poetry of Bedil fits into their cultural fabric and infuses a lively spirit in their music and dance. The language of Bedil is a natural blend of Farsi which is widely spoken and understood by the majority of the people of Central Asia. In nut shell, Bedil is a house hold name in Central Asia and represents the highest intellectual standard of the region. Intellectuals of the region Sadruddin Aini and others held Bedil in their highest estimation and placed him on the pantheon of worship.

Mirza Ghalib, the leading poet of India boasted himself of his ancestral heritage from Samarqand.

One of the leading short story writers has beautifully criticised the Russian invasion in his story entitled "Friendship of the Aunt Bear". The title subtly points to a famous fable regarding friendship of a man and a bear where bear sits awake by the side of his sleeping friend to guard him. When it sees a fly sitting on the nose of his friend, it tries to get rid of the fly, but irritated by the fly's obstinacy of coming and sitting again and again on his friend's nose, the bear picks up a big stone and aims it at the fly. The fly flies away but the man is killed.

This story clearly points out that the left wing of the Muslim countries, which solely depended on their Russian friends, and follow them blindly were heading towards the same fate as that of the man who befriended the bear. According to the author, Russians are not very sharp, at the same time; he found them quite aggressive like bears.

With the advent of Russian colonialism in Trans- Caucasian region and the British hegemony in the sub-continent, these relations became gradually weak because the two colonialist powers, with different cultures and aims, got control over this region. Though Iran was not colonised but had to undergo many hardships because of the rivalry of these two powers in the north and the south. Till before the victory of communism in Russia, contacts did exist at individual levels between the people of India and Central Asia and those of Iran and Turkistan, even though these relations had no definite aim or direction. But with the establishment of the Soviet Socialist Republic of Russia, even these contacts came to an end. Under the new Socialist rule, Turkistan was divided into five republics, all formal relations with whom were possible only through the USSR. More than eighty years passed by and with the disintegration of the Soviet Union, it came to be known that the people of this region have still preserved their identity in the same way as India and Iran. It was due to the common socio- cultural linkages between Iran, India and Central Asia that the colonialists could not resist against the traditional foundations as the Iranians too during their struggle against the Western cultural onslaught brought down the Pahlavi regime.

Though the colonialists try to equate the local traditions with fanaticism and condemn them, the realities of the societies of Iran, India and Central Asia are something else. The people love their traditions and consider them as invaluable heritage.

Today the civilised Eastern and Asian societies are under the threat of Western cultural attack which has launched a full scale war against local traditions by using technology and immense material resources at its disposal. The West wants to bring the Eastern people under its control by alienating them. It wants to create markets for its consumer goods and get hold over vast resources of raw material and cheap labour.

The nations, which are blessed with distinct identity and ancient civilisation, should struggle against this conspiracy by exchanging among themselves their experiences and capabilities. Some narrow minded people raise issues like that of fundamentalism and claim that the culture of the time of Babur was the annihilator of the Indian culture or that the Iranian or Islamic culture is against the Turkish culture.

Political leaders of these countries have to show their will to confront this conspiracy. Taking into consideration the vast potential of Iran, India and Central Asia, the signing of a the memorandum of understanding between the Islamic Republic of Iran and India for cooperation in progress and development of the Central Asian Republics by using the transit facilities and availing of scientific and industrial capabilities, are all the initial steps for future wide ranging co-operation and which are the reminder of the glorious history of the region. The enemies of revival of the previous glory of these nations claim that to acquire technology and achieve economic development, there is no way except following the West. This claim must be treated bogus and redundant.

REFERENCES

1. Narrative Journey Into Khorasan.pp.175-76
2. The first short story written in Persian language.
3. Iran ra az Yad Nabareem, M A Eslami Nadushan, Yaghma, Tehran pp.27
4. Ibid.pp.29
5. Ibid.pp.36
6. Ibid.pp.41
7. Gharb Zadegi, Ferdows, Tehran, 1373 pp.172
8. Ibid. pp.197
9. Khedmat va khyanat-i- Raushanfikran, pp. 87
10. Ibid. pp. 132
11. Roohani Nezhad, Nehzathai-Melli, Rvesh, Tehran, pp. 29

8

Society and Culture in the Twenty-First Century

Role of Science and Religion in Development

Mahnaz Merchant

A very striking feature of our times is the accelerating rate at which change occurs. The magnitude and speed of the changes that humankind has undergone in the past century and a half have been unparalleled in our history. In every area of human endeavour a great deal of new knowledge is being generated, and old practices are being rejected one after another. At this point in history, no one can possibly deny that society, in all its aspects -- social, economic, political, religious and cultural -- is going through a process of fundamental transformation.

"In this past century and a half, every country and region of the world has seen old structures swept away through radical reform or revolution. There is no doubt that ideals motivating these deliberate, sometimes violent, attempts to change society have often been extremely noble and laudable. Yet, it is now an historical fact that these attempts have, by and large, failed to generate this sense of purpose, the values and the standards of behaviour that are essential for the creation of a new society. The unavoidable conclusion we reach when we examine the present times is that old moral codes and belief systems have proven entirely inadequate when faced with the challenges of an age of transformation." [1]

During the cycle of human life, an individual passes through the stages of infancy, childhood and adolescence, before undergoing the transition to adulthood. We achieve great clarity about the meaning of our times if we accept that humanity, in its collective life, also goes through similar stages, and that we live at a time when mankind has emerged from its childhood and stands at the threshold of maturity.

The turbulence and upheavals that prevail in society today can then be seen as characteristic of adolescence, which is the period of transition. The onset of maturity, of course, brings new capacities and presents new demand for which the attitudes, thoughts and habits of childhood are inadequate. The challenge now facing humanity is to leave behind the ways of youth and to develop those qualities and capabilities that will allow it to respond to the requirements of a new age.

We often hear however, the voices of traditionalists, of those who romanticize the past urging us to go back to old ways. The fact is, however, that return to the standards of the past is not possible, for the forces released during this period have set in motion a process of transformation that is clearly irreversible.

The pressing needs of the current age call for a reassessment of the underlying assumptions of the political, social and economic arrangements that prevail from the local to the global level. If we are to give impetus to constructive social processes that advance the prospects of peace and enhance human well-being, all the world's inhabitants must become directly engaged in a search for appropriate values, ideas, and practical measures that address the challenges of the present hour.

As humanity emerges from a century of upheaval and startling change, its need for moral and spiritual renewal becomes ever more apparent. That the twentieth century was a century of both darkness and light-revealing the capacity for human depravity as well as human achievement-underlies the confusion that pervades our times. A deepening moral disorientation threatens social institutions and the fundamental bonds that define human relations.

It is essential, then that we should develop a profound awareness of the reciprocal relationship between personal growth and organic change in social structures. We cannot develop virtues and talents in isolation, but only through effort and activity for the benefit of others. (Idle worship and prolonged withdrawal from society, advocated by some philosophies of the past, neither promote individual development nor aid the progress of mankind.) People whose sense of purpose focuses only on the development of their own potential soon lose objectivity and perspective. With no outside interactions and social goals, how does one judge one's own progress and measure one's development? Morality centred on the self only leads to subtle forms of ego -- combinations of guilt, self-righteousness and self-satisfaction.

"Social advancement we know arises from the ideals and shared beliefs that held society together. Meaningful social change results as much from the development of qualities and attitudes that foster constructive patterns of human interaction as from the acquisition of technical capacities. True prosperity- a well being founded on peace, cooperation, altruism, dignity, rectitude of conduct and justice-flows from the light of spiritual awareness and virtue as well as from material discovery and progress." [2]

What uniquely defines the human experience is the transcendent component of life. It is this dimension of existence that enriches, ennobles and provides direction to human beings. It unlocks the creative capacities within human consciousness and safeguards human dignity.

A strict materialistic worldview reflects a profound error of conception about human nature itself. Unless the development of society finds a purpose beyond the mere amelioration of material conditions, it will fail to attain even modest goals of political and social stability. A purpose must be sought in the spiritual dimensions of life that are so central to human identity and human dignity. It is the spiritual aspects of existence that enriches, ennobles and provides direction to human beings and ensures its prosperity.

Thus we must strive to develop a concept of prosperity whose goal is not just efficiency but the promotion of equity, social well-being, service to others, justice, social harmony and cohesion, and the creation and preservation of beauty-whether man-made or of the natural world. It must be a prosperity that promotes respect for human rights and awareness of our responsibilities to the common weal, recognizes that the interests of the individual and of society are inseparable, and fosters equality and partnership of women and men. Protects and nurtures families, shares and harnesses the fruits of science and technology for the whole of the human race and follows a path of social advancement that safeguards the world ecosystem.

"Throughout history, civilization had depended upon science and religion as the two principal systems of knowledge that have guided its development and channeled its intellectual and moral powers and contributed to the advancement of civilization. The methods of science have allowed humanity to construct a coherent understanding of the laws and processes governing physical reality and to a certain degree the working of society itself. The insights of religion have provided understanding on the deepest questions of human purpose and initiative."[3] This does not refer to sectarian movements or distortions of religion, but a system of knowledge, which explores the deepest motivations of human behavior and provides the spiritual principles to guide action.

The knowledge system of religion is concerned with the nature of the social order, societal structure, processes and the moral fabric of collective life. It leads to the stirring of the human spirit that provides energy, motivation and insight for individual and societal transformation. It is the knowledge system of religion that engenders community learning and empowerment.

We have to go to the level of systems of knowledge because development of society and cultures rest on the foundations of the various disciplines of modern science in which we have all been educated, irrespective of where we are from. Most of us have been influenced by the Western tradition, which has defined the disciplines and the professions that we bring to the field of development. Whether we are anthropologists, sociologists, economists, agronomists, doctors, social workers, or educators, the knowledge system that underlies our thinking and according to which policies are formed, plans made, and programmes created comes essentially from that tradition. At some point in the evolution of Western thought, which is so strongly rooted in the period of the Enlightenment, it was decided by the academia—by the intellectual powers of Europe and North America—that science and religion were in conflict with each other. As a result the knowledge system of the West became extremely secular. The question of religion and spirituality was either rejected entirely or, at best, left to the realm of individual personal concern, far from the public domain where important decisions about the structures and processes of society are made.

Religion should be just as scientific in its method as science. It helps us understand spiritual principles and translate them into concrete action. Can humanity develop without both knowledge system of science and religion? We need both of them in our efforts towards social advancement. We need to have a systematic exploration of the complementary roles of science and religion in the development of society and culture. How they can work together in a synergistic manner to erect harmonious and equitable social systems. We have extremes in religious fundamentalism and we have extremes in scientific fundamentalism, both of which have proved disastrous. What is being suggested here is a look at the relationship and complementary roles of science and religion?

Observations of the conditions of the world around us can leave no doubt that the way we look at and understand this essential relationship must change profoundly. It is clear that the old conceptions of these relationships have not been able to withstand the pressures of the age of transition; the forces that have shaken the very foundations of human society have corrupted some of these relationships, have shattered some, and have rendered others meaningless. Ironically, many of these distortions seem to be the results of material progress, which in itself is desirable. One way of looking at the present dilemma is to regard it as the failure of materialism. When in the early part of the twentieth century, and perhaps in the closing years of the nineteenth century, it became possible for humanity to come together as one for the first time because of scientific, technological, and cultural advances, the leaders of humanity, especially those in the West who held large shares of power, made some gross miscalculations. They made terrible mistakes. One mistake was to assume that material considerations and material development were the only things worth pursuing—that material considerations were the main determents of human existence. They basically forgot, or ignored, the spiritual nature of humankind. They made a fundamental mistake about the nature of the human being. They read human nature wrong. In all the theories they advanced, in the literature they wrote, in the educational programmes they spread around the world, and in the economic systems they took to every part of the globe, whether falling into the Marxist or the Capitalist camp, they misjudged human nature—this, despite the brilliance of their thinkers and having the entire power of science behind them. They somehow reached the conclusion that what mattered most was to improve material conditions, initially naïvely through economic growth, but later through a host of complementary factors. They failed to realize that unless two civilizations—material civilization and spiritual civilization—advance hand in hand, humanity cannot prosper.

"There is a wide difference between material and divine civilization. With force and punishment material civilization seeks to restrain society from mischief, from inflicting harm on societies and committing crime. But in divine civilization, the individual is so conditioned that with no fear of punishment, he shuns the perpetration of crime, sees the crime itself as the severest of torments, and with alacrity and joy sets himself to acquiring the virtues of human kind and spreading light across the world. "[4]

Taken together science and religion provide the fundamental organizing principles by which individuals, communities and institutions function and evolve. Utilizing the methods of science allows people to become more objective and systematic in their approach to problem solving and in their understanding of social processes, while drawing on the spiritual inclinations of individuals provides the motivational impetus that begets and sustains positive action.

The emergence of a just social order calls for a pattern of social interaction that cultivates the moral and creative capacities latent in human nature; it embraces a concept of prosperity in which material advancement makes possible new avenues of intellectual, cultural and spiritual expression rather than being an end in itself; it anticipates the emergence of a world community, the consciousness of world citizenship, the founding of a world civilization and culture.

Our present civilization rests on an economic structure that is fundamentally unsound. "There is more food, money, and goods today than there has ever been in history, yet poverty is far from being eliminated. Although the world population is large, it is not so large that the people need to go hungry or forgo basic health care, basic education etc. Today we have a strange education that a tiny fraction of world population owns and controls almost everything material while the majority of the people have to struggle and split, the small remainders that is left". "Something is fundamentally wrong with our economic model. Even though machines and computers save a huge amount of time and money, people today are working longer hours per day as an average than before the industrial revolution-before the invention of machines. It is truly ironic we have machines that can do the work of the thousand individuals yet people are working more today than when machines were invented. In the 'developed' world millions of people are unemployed while at the same time those in paid work are working longer hours! How can this be? The industrial system appears to have failed in the task of sharing the available work-and leisure time for family life and community service equitably. Currently our values glorify material pursuits above all else. Money prevails over principles. Fortunately this sad state of affairs is gradually changing partially because the economy today is generating sorrow and discontent on a massive "planetary" scale. Since happiness and contentment are not material objects, therefore they have not associated material price."[5] Essentially we need spiritual solutions for economic problems. Most people work to make money, so that they can spend it. Is this concept of work adequate for a society that is striving towards a non-violent civilization founded on spiritual principles? Is money really the best way to motivate work? How do patterns of social cooperation, collective learning and community empowerment develop? Where does a dynamic, self-sustaining vision of social progress come from?

"The significant problems we face cannot be solved at the same level of thinking we were at when we created them." (Albert Einstein)

We have to go deeper and redefine the very premises and assumptions on which development rests. And it is in this task that I am suggesting we cannot rely solely on science. It is true that we have to turn to science as that knowledge system which studies the material universe and teaches us how to generate material means for the advancement of humanity. But we must also turn to religion, by which I do not mean a specific religion or a specific sect, but religion as the spiritual heritage of humankind, as the knowledge system that studies the powers of the human spirit and which concerns itself with the demands and the desires of the higher nature of the human being, the society it lives in and its culture.

Science has to accept that it does not have the answer to every question about human existence. For while science can figure out the "how" of the universe, it cannot bring meaning to existence. Insights into profound questions of meaning are to come not from science, but from its co-partner religion.

The questions that have been raised in this paper are some very fundamental questions regarding our very approach to development. What do we define development as? Should we redefine development? Should we look at something new? Is it possible that the answer lies in a new discourse, a discourse that looks at other systems of knowledge that contribute to the advancement of humanity and not just science?

Having spoken at some length about the complementary role of science and religion let me introduce the work that we do for promoting the Discourse on development from the above perspective. The initiative began in India in November 2000 when the National Spiritual Assembly of the Bahá'ís of India in collaboration with the Institute for Studies in Global Prosperity (a research based institute fostering research and dialogue on new development concepts and strategies) hosted an international colloquium on the theme of "Science, Religion and Development" in India. The project engaged over 100 influential development organizations in the country, NGOs, UN agencies, civil society and inspired national media coverage. Other cosponsors of the program were UNICEF, IDRC-Canada, WHO, Department of Secondary and Higher Education of Human Resource Development Ministry of the government of India.

Marking out a distinctive contribution to the promotion of the social advancement, the event set the stage for symposia of the same kind in Africa, Latin America and Malaysia. The goal of the Colloquium was to foster a discourse that explores how a substantive interaction between scientific methods and religious resources can promote the building of human capacity.

One observation that the discourse has made is that decision-making has been made on a fundamentally materialistic outlook of development. We have looked at the human beings and their nature as only material and we have totally ignored their spiritual nature. Some of the example of wrong assumption is that 'everything can be understood and dealt with in material terms.'

The discourse on Science, Religion and Development is proposes as a new paradigm. It opens up new avenues of inquiry and activity that can expand understanding. An important goal is to use this understanding to engage and influence decision-makers at all levels of society. The decision-makers include people right from the family to the civil society, industry, educational institution, the government, the policy makers etc. It is an attempt to analyze and learn to correct such fundamental errors in conception of the decision makers of humanity. Its mandate is to further expand the growing network of organisations/individuals interested in the discourse on Science, Religion and Development and its promotion.

I take this opportunity to invite you to study the documents of the discourse and welcome your valuable comments about its conceptual elements.

REFERENCES

1. Dr. Farzam Arbab-Living in a Rapidly Changing Society: Transition to Maturity.
2. The Universal House of Justice-Century of Light.
3. Concept Paper of the Colloquium on Science, Religion and Development, (November 2000, New Delhi).
4. Abdul-Bahá. Secret of Divine Civilization (Wilmette, Illinois, USA: Bahá'í Publishing Trust, 1971).
5. Mahatma Gandhi and The Bahá'ís-Striving towards a Non-violent Civilization (New Delhi, India, Bahá'í Publishing Trust, 2000).

9

Impact of Globalization on Culture

One World Culture

Neelmani Upadhyay

The world has become a global village, so goes the euphemism. Science, technology, the way of living and thinking are not limited to a particular country but have become transnational with satellites in the orbit for purposes of information and imagery. The world has become closer. We today have the view of the earth, its geography, people and resources from the sky above and it presents a marvelous sight of harmony and unity in a miniscule manner. The telecommunication and electronic media with high speed and transport make it possible to reach out to any person anywhere in the world to alleviate his distress or to rejoice in his victories. The world has become so close but the question arises whether it is well knit. Have our hearts united and have we become emotionally integrated? Herein comes the concept and need for one world culture.

Cultural Osmosis

'East is East and West is West and the twains shall never meet' so wrote the poet. Today there is no cultural separation between the East and the West and instead they are coming closer and closer towards understanding each other. There is a cultural osmosis and we are witnessing the intermixture of different cultures. Any idea, invention or innovation anywhere gets across the other part of the world with the help of print and electronic media. We are no more like islands sundered from the rest. In the last few decades, especially the eighties, we witnessed the breaking down of the two opposing blocs — the communist and the capitalist represented respectively by U.S.S.R. and U.S.A. and there was talk of the uni-world. The nineties were different and the 21st. century has made a lot of difference and the ideas of one or the other blocs are percolating and intermixing. There is neither a pure capitalist economy nor an unpolluted socialist economic order and there is an imperative synthesis. These are happy signs and augur well for realization of long- cherished ideal and dream of one world culture.

The cultural osmosis can be actualized in systematic manner and organized way. We have to move in the right direction and give the necessary momentum and magnitude to it. We can specify the different stages as follows;

1. There should be cultural exchange between different countries and the Departments of Culture and allied councils should take positive steps. The writers, thinkers and artists from performing arts should go to study the cultural patterns of different countries.
2. In publicizing our wares we should not overstress the separate and divergent aspects of our culture. We should underline the similarities and common features of the cultures.
3. We have to clear our minds of narrow loyalties, bigotry, rituals and dogmas and stress the essential core underpinning the humane aspects. We have to set our minds free from blinkers and ensure right response and receptivity.
4. We have to maintain our cultural identity but at the same time we should emphasize the universal aspects of the culture. This dynamic equilibrium between the racial and universal aspects of culture has to be maintained. Mahatma Gandhi, the Father of the Nation, was right when he said that ,we should keep our windows open so that the winds of change visit us from outside but we should refuse to be swept off our feet
5. The affinities and common features of the different cultures have to be diligently worked out and there should be meetings and conferences, free interplay and mutual exchange of our cultural aspects and achievements. We should be tolerant enough in understanding the viewpoints and cultural milieu of different countries. The understanding is the key to this one world culture. Rabindranath Tagore

was very right when he said, "When we do not understand we cannot be just".

Need for One World Culture

The need for one would culture is strongly felt by all understanding intelligentsia of the world, the world is sitting on the volcano and the nuclear holocaust and total annihilation are staring at us. There is the talk of star wars and lethal nuclear war heads can reduce the entire world to rubble. Science with its analytical mind and amoral attitude has equipped the leaders with weapons of devastation. There will remain no victims and vanquished. We have, therefore, our hopes in United Nations and its different agencies. The establishment of W.T.O. (World Trade Organization) has been a step in the right direction. We have to curb our chauvinism regarding our cultural values and institutions. Science has brought the world close but it is the philosophy, values and culture which will cement world peace and understanding and will pave the way for one world culture.

We should adopt positive and affirmative approach to unity and peace. Our efforts should not just be confined to the removal of conflicts and controversies but one should rather take concrete steps for emotional integration and unity of the world. We generally work on the level of importing technology. Science, technology and inventions all are part of civilization. Culture is inward looking whereas civilization is outward looking. The superstructures of civilization are imposing but the fabric of culture is subtle and the warp and weft of culture are thoughts, attitudes, values and ideals. A country can lack in civilization but may be rich in culture. We have to reach to the inner being of the people in different countries and should try to enrich their inner world with glowing ideas and noble thoughts. The great American seer and essayist Emerson was right when he said that the greatest things are fashioned in the silence of our minds. We have to establish bulwarks against unabashed consumerism, lewd obscenity, and vulgar display of wealth, titillating but ultimately degrading distractions and unbridled pursuit of power paying no heed to the purity of the means.

Attributes of One World Culture

It is easy to talk vaguely about one world culture but to define its parameters is not an easy task. We witness the emergent trends of one world culture and these can be broadly summed up in these seven attributes:

1. **Tolerance**: We have to encourage tolerance at various levels. The greatest enemies of one world culture are fundamentalism, bigotry, obscurantism, superstition and dogmatic approach to the problems of life. We have now to lay more emphasis on co-existence, partnership, goodwill and interdependence, Tolerance is the key to all these virtues and is the core of one world culture. Tolerance is not weakness rather is thrives on broadmindedness and benevolence.
2. **'Vishvaneedam':** One Creator, one Home. Our Indian seers have included in golden letters the ideal of 'Vishvaneedam' i.e. one Creator, one Home. The oft-repeated Sanskrit Shloka clarifies this succinctly:

   अयं निजः परो वेति गणना लघुचेतसाम्।
   उदारचरितान्तु वसुधैव कुटुम्बकम्।।

   This is mine and this is others as the concept of small minds. For the large-hearted ones, the whole world is one family. Yajurveda emphatically declares it:

   वेनस्तत् पश्यन् निहितं गुहासद्
   यत्र विश्वं भवत्येकनीड़म्।
   तस्मिन्निदं संचविचैति सर्वं
   स अतः प्रोतश्च विभुः प्रजासु।।
   य (वा.) 32/8

   The loving sage beheld that
   being hidden in mystery
   where in the universe comes
   to have one home:
   Therein unites and there from
   emanates all

The Omnipresent One is warp
and woof in the created things.

Needless to add, the United Nations and such organizations are concrete steps in this direction.

3. **Sarva-Dharam-Sambhav** (Secularism): The third cardinal attribute of one world culture is secularism which is unfortunately portrayed as one opposed to religion. We should remember that one can be religious without adhering to any religion. The right word is Sarva-Dharam-Sambhav. The bane of Indian politics today is that in early years of electioneering it was communalization of politics and it was then followed by politicization of crimes and now it is communalization of politics. It is eating at the vital roots of our polity. We have to check this malady otherwise it will assume monstrous proportions. The truly religious person has respect for all religions and it is the small minds that create dissensions, strifes and violence.

4. **Faith in Ourselves and the Destiny of the Universe:** An adherent of one world culture believes in the destiny of the universe and firmly believes in himself. To him life is not meaningless and purposeless 'a tale told by an idiot signifying nothing'. Faith and self-confidence are keys to the well-being and happiness of the world. Kalidasa rightly says:

   जगतः पितरौ बन्दे श्रद्धाविश्वासरूपिणौ।
   याभ्यां बिना नपश्यन्ति सिद्धाः स्वान्तस्थमीश्वरम्!

   I bow to the universe parents — Shiva and Parvati who symbolize faith and self- confidence. The seer even cannot have the vision of the ultimate Reality seated deeper in our hearts. Will Durant so pithily underscores this faith and self-confidence and gives the clarion call to 'speak out'. He says, "We have been silent too long and part of our tardy righteousness may well be due to the loose ends flow of sap in our flesh. No matter, let us speak out. Let us say humbly but publicly that we resent corruption in politics, dishonesty in business, faithlessness in marriage, pornography in literature and the theatre, coarseness in language, chaos in music and meaninglessness in art. It is time for all good men to come to the aid of their party, whose name is civilization".

5. **Self-Esteem and Sanctity of Life:** The man or for that matter woman of one world culture has respect for all forms of life, 'givas'. Here comes into play the concept of eco-culture. There should be proper synthesis between Nature, animals and man respecting and supporting one another. We today talk about environmental degradation, problems of development and depletion of natural resources. We must have respect for ourselves and should take any life of animal, bird or any creature as sacred. Self-esteem and sanctity of life signify and strengthen one world culture.
6. **Humility and Learning Attitude:** The hauteur of know-all person and superiority of the race hinder fostering one world culture. A truly cultured man is not rude, arrogant and haughty but is rather humble, genial and good tempered man. He tries to learn the good things about other cultures and is ever eager to learn. It is rightly said that the really educated man is he who is always ready to learn and I would add that he is truly cultivated person.
7. **Divine Consciousness and Unity In Diversity:** The diversity of the world is for its color and glory. It should not create any mental block and artificial barriers. The universe is essentially one and there is 'Sat-Chit-Anand'- Truth-Consciousness and Bliss pervading the entire universe, It is this divine feeling that leads to the realization of unity in diversity.

'एकं सद्विप्रा बहुधा वदन्ति'

He is one and wise men talk in numerous ways about Him.

Cultural Linkages

We need to develop appropriate strategies and programs to visualize and actualize one world culture. We have to propagate it at the right forum. This will create the awareness and would pinpoint the need to establish one world culture. The collective effort of the individual seekers of Truth will crystallize the contents, methods and techniques of one world culture.

There are different organizations like universities and institutions engaged in spreading the cause of world peace, progress and enlightenment. There is need to coordinate the efforts of all these universities and institutions of higher learning so that there are no duplication and overlapping leading to squandering of scarce resources. It may be Yoga including Kundalini Yoga, ancient insights of learning, cultural ambience, etc. we have to establish different cultural linkages for optimal results and efficacy.

The one world culture is for 'Sarvajanhitay, Sarvajan-sukhay' — the welfare of all and the happiness of all. This task is stupendous and difficult but we have to take the first step. We have to invoke the Divine Powers for making one world culture a reality and pray with the Vedic seer

'आ नो भद्राः क्रतवो यन्तु विश्वतः'

(Rig-Veda 1-89-1 let noble thoughts come to us from every side.

REFERENCES

1. Hindu – Sanskriti – Ank (Kalyan) Special Number – 24th year. Samvat 2050, pp. 904.
2. Language, Education and Culture by D.P. Pattanayak, Central Institute of Languages, Mysore Ed./991 p. 289.
3. Bhavan's Journal, Mumbai, September 24, 1978, p. 13.
4. Bhavan's Journal, April 8, 1978, Vol. XXIV- No. 18, p. 72.

10

Psychological Aspects of Cultures and Societies in Transition

N.K. Sharma

Change is the eternal law of nature. The transition that the societies and cultures have undergone in the past say 40 years is phenomenal; be it scientific, social, fiscal or Psychological. As a Psychiatrist I view these changes in my own way, which may not be the same way as viewed by many in this august gathering and at the outset I would like to submit my apologies for any expressed views which may not fit in the frame of orientation of the members of the house, though I would be happy to discuss the same, if required and permitted by the chair.

Let us start by viewing the psychological aspects/effects of transition from the beginning of the human life – birth, and for that we look at the institution of marriage. In the earlier times, marriage was considered to be a divine phenomenon. Today it has transitioned into an affair of mutual convenience, resulting in the high index of separation/divorce. Biological urges result in the birth of a child. The prevailing practices of female feticides and the consequent reversed gender ratio are a cause of great concern. The transition has also brought with it the choice of choosing the timing of the birth of your baby, under the specialized guidance of the acclaimed fortune tellers and the fortune makers and that too without having to undergo the tedious process of delivery and saving upon the precious time to be devoted for other better activities (kudos to Obstetricians). Now that the child is born, it is a fulltime job rearing it up and for the working couple. Maids and crèches have provided a viable alternative, though the psychological aspects of this trend, both upon the parents and the infant are pretty adverse, irreversible and lifelong. The lack of adequate breast feeding notably has its hazards upon the physical and psychological health of both the mother and the child. In fact the seeds of personality disorders are sown primarily here at this stage.

Childhood: The Childhood period is badly marred by lack of parenting skills, premature schooling, absence of peer group learning and lack of modeling. Child battering, sexual abuse of children and even child labor are known phenomena. The prevalence of childhood psychological disorders being enormous has necessitated the formation of a separate branch of Psychiatry.

Adolescence: This child, often inadequately and dispassionately reared up, enters into the arena of adolescence wherein he has to establish his identity. Under pressure from ambitious and image-seeking—from the society, parents and the over demanding academic needs from the schools, the bearer only has to satisfy his all instinctual needs in the bedroom watching TV and playing videogames, that too if he /she has a good rapport with the surrogate mother, who alone can allow him/her till the arrival of fatigued parent/s and then starts the nagging. The root of drug abuse, delinquency, psychopathy, violence and all other deviances can be traced to adolescence.

Adulthood: Today's adult faces serious challenges in the college or in the university. You all know of the sexual offences, the menace of ragging, drugs and substance abuse, violence, pornography, cyber-crimes, misuse of communication devices, availability of 24hr entertainment channels (I do not know to which segment of our population it caters to), owing to vast improvements in the respective fields. Further, the educational system, the malpractices in the selection systems, gross politicization of all institutions of learning coupled with rampant corruption, has made sailing difficult for the saner segment of our youth, which statistically is in majority and hold the command of the future of this country. With the process of globalization much in vogue, the resultant brain drain is a matter of serious concern. Our top young technocrats are whisked away through what is proudly called "in campus selection" and their services are effectively utilized overseas, but in turn push them towards unsettlement in life. The large-scale migration within the country itself has its share of miseries to both sides. The scenario in metros of the country is dismal.

The concept of single hood, single parenting, unwed mothers, pre and extramarital sexuality with its ill effects including the HIV AIDS epidemic, do need mention here. The changing/weakening value systems in the society is leading to enormous stress, evident from the rising indices of suicides, litigations, murders, crimes, terrorism and alcohol and drug abuse. Religious confusions, political extremism, lack of discipline, loss of character, inadequacy of role models in the present society are some of the areas of concern and need to be addressed.

Old-age: Someone very aptly said – "Old age is the most unexpected event in a human being's life". We have transitioned to a time where the well-being of this section of the society lies in a state of neglect. Yesteryears' Joint Family system, unique to India, is now on the verge of extinction. *Saas bhi kabhi bahu thi*, we are left with a definitive impression that there is no scope for a caring son to look after his aged parents without sacrificing his peace within his nuclear family. This gives a push towards the concept of old-age homes, the scenario wherein is far from satisfactory.

It causes me great pain to look at the rising prevalence of psychological disorders in our country, and the insufficient availability of mental health professionals. In a country of over a billion, mental health professionals constitute a shrinking group of a merely 3500 trained professionals, of which a sizeable number is eagerly awaits migration to countries like the United Kingdom, New Zealand, Canada, United States of America and others who invite them with equally welcome open arms. This is where our journey of continuous social and cultural transition has brought us. Where do we go from here and what do we do to modify the process?

11

Globalization and National Culture Development

Zarrin Abdukhalik-Zade

It is well known that globalization is a typical peculiarity of the contemporary world, which is why scholars from around the world pay special attention to this phenomenon. It was not by chance that this very issue was discussed in Istanbul (Turkey), at the 21st World Philosophy Congress. The event was devoted to the topic "*Philosophy Confronted with World Problems*".

Globalization and the challenges that it brings to the society, culture, and to human beings, induces the international society to examine the essence, causes, factors and consequences as well as further prospects of this process. The study and analysis of national culture transformation in the modern globalization conditions is particularly topical. It touches upon all spheres of society: economic, political, socio-cultural, etc. What will be the response of national culture as unique phenomena of social life to these processes? What can be the consequences of total globalization, which does not take into consideration the peculiarities of national cultures?

The scholarships mark the ambiguity and irregularity of globalization. At the same time there exist different opinions about genesis, nature, factors and consequences of the above-mentioned process.

In general, globalization is considered as an expansion and intensification of social relations and institutions within space and time; so that the events, taking place in other parts of the world, greatly influence the everyday life of people. On the other hand, the activities of the local communities may have significant global consequences. Globalization suggests that the majority of social, economic, political, cultural and other connections and relations acquire the worldwide character. At the same time it demonstrates the growth of the interaction level both within some definite states and between the states.

However, what is new for globalization is its penetration and diffusion into such spheres of activity as technology, administration, law and others, and also constant intensification of collaboration through modern communities and new information technologies.

Through the understanding of the sense and contents of the phenomenon, a definite attitude towards this process is being formed. We distinguish between adherents of globalization – globalists and their opponents – anti-globalists. The latter (anti-globalists) think that the process can weaken the state sovereignty, be detrimental to national identity and inequality between the rich North and poor South and lead to conflicts between states and civilizations. It goes without saying that under globalization, along with positive and progressive phenomena, such as trade and communications development, increase of interstate contacts, military and political collaboration, economic and ecologic security, new technologies, some negative processes are also increasing. They are: the increase of worldwide criminality, international terrorism, drug-dealing, expansion of radical ideas, etc. As a result of intensive distribution of information, aggression has become accessible and available. Such information has anti-social character and stimulates demoralization of the youth. Another example is a growth in the number of people with untraditional sexual orientations. It should be noted that while such relations are considered a feature of freedom in the Western society, the same are impermissible and prohibited by religion. Some lines of the Koran state: "If one of you commits such adultery, both of you will be sentenced to punishment." (The Holy Koran, Sura 4, Ayat 16, translated by Kulieva E., Saudi Arabia, Medina.)

In the history of Oriental philosophy there are many utterances and statements concerning destructions of society, which begin with moral and spiritual corruption of the society members. In Central Asian culture the moral dogmas of Zoroastrianism – the unity of good intensions, good word and good deed prevailed. After Central Asia was conquered by Arabian Khalifat, Islam was transformed into the ruling ideology. On the whole, as the spiritual values of Islam did not contradict the existing moral priorities, the process of Islamisation progressed quickly and without serious controversy.

An important role in the spiritual culture of Central Asian nations belongs to Sufism – religious philosophic doctrine based on the rules of behavior and obedience of pilgrims striving at comprehension of a divine truth. The primary condition for comprehension of truth is the obligatory fulfillment of all Shariat laws and formation of such moral values as industry, decency, modesty, love to knowledge, homeland, avoidance of mercenary-activities, selfish demands to material benefits, violence, etc. This doctrine greatly influenced the creative work of the outstanding poets and thinkers such as Saadi Sherazi, Alisher Navoi, great astronomer Mirzo Ulughbek, great physician Abu Ali Ibn Sina and other historical figures.

It seems to us that in order to avoid spiritual degradation of a person and society as a whole in the globalization conditions, we must observe human values through the development of national cultures and the dialogue of various civilizations. However, such dialogue must be based on the mutual respect and understanding of different cultures, which is not possible without drawing into each other the cultural values of one another.

During the era of globalization, the moral problems that the society faces makes it search for solutions not merely within their own culture but outside as well. Philosophy from time immemorial has remained pivotal for human society. Many scholars are eager to study Oriental philosophy today, where the problem of moral perfection of a person occupies an important place.

After Uzbekistan proclaimed its independence, a new perspective starting from around the 90s has emerged. In 2001, the department of Modern Oriental Philosophy and Culture was opened at the Tashkent State University of Oriental Studies. In 2005, the major 'Modern Oriental Philosophy and History' was introduced. Over a hundred 100 students study the philosophy of Near and Middle East, as Indian, Japanese, Chinese and Korean philosophy and great scientific research work is also held.

I would like to mention that we are deeply interested in the extension of collaboration with Oriental philosophy as it may demonstrate mutual scientific interest.

12

The Origin of the Cult of Fertility

Central Asian and Indian Rock Art

Debal Dasgupta & Vishwas H. Sonawane

The Upper Paleolithic Period

The Upper Paleolithic period (40,000 -10,000 BP), also known as the Flowering Paleolithic, saw an astonishing number of human cultures, marking a great sense of aesthetics in the artistic reflections of various kinds. Tools made were of a great variety, including different types of semi precious stones and bones. They also used bone, horn, ostrich egg-shells, ivory and made necklaces and other personal ornaments. They carved the so-called Venus figures, ritual statuettes and made drawings on rock shelters and cave walls.

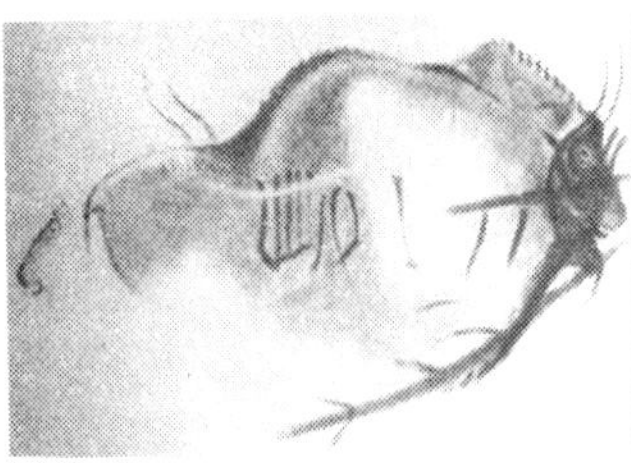

The first forms of symbolic communication are believed to have originated during the Upper Palaeolithic Period, during which the ice ages continued and anatomically the modern Homo Sapiens Sapiens evolved. Evidence of symbolic communications, like gestural and / or graphic, is noticed and the earliest human-mediated symbols are found. Some of these take the form of carvings and others are found on rocks along with beautifully painted images, curious markings / symbols etched onto the walls.

"Symbolism" is a term closely intertwined with communication. Human beings think and communicate by using symbols. Words are symbols for material items and concepts and written expressions are graphic symbolic representations of those words and ideas. All writing is symbolic in nature. Therefore, proceeding with this hypothesis, one can say that all rock art embodiments of semiotic expressions bear a great meaning for their authors as they attempt to communicate a meaningful entity or idea. In a society, devoid of phonetic writings, all forms of graphic representations are very meaningful for the preservation and communication of thoughts and ideas. Rock art is also viewed as a means of a communication system and any symbolism, depicted thereupon, is understood to be conveying something. They certainly reflect on the aesthetic taste, developed by the prehistoric community. Though many of these art objects are highly abstract in their nature, some of them can be regarded as symbolic, while the others are rich in their descriptive details. Symbols are often considered as material representations of abstract concepts. There are often no visually obvious associations between the symbol and the entity, which it represents. Typical non-iconic art is far more likely to be symbolic than their iconic counterparts. The latter is only symbolic when a depiction of the object refers to an abstract concept.

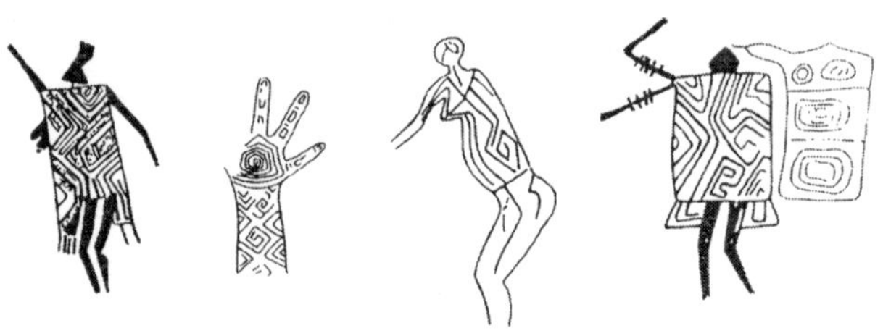

Such an understanding is based on archaeological finds, as reported from Chandravati (India), Mezin (Ukraine) and some other archaeological sites, dating back to the Upper Paleolithic Period. In this regard evidences obtained from Bhagor I (Son Valley, Madhya Pradesh, India) offer an important clue, quite convincing of the triangular shaped natural sandstone with concentric triangles, found placed on a raised, circular platform of rubbles, and based on ethnographic parallels obtained from the same region. It is identified as the earliest shrine of the Mother Goddess (*богоматери-таі*). Many specialists, who studied the Paleolithic statuettes and other artefacts depicting Mother Goddess or the Symbol of Fertility, differ in details and interpret them as cultic subjects, amulets, idols etc, reflecting the idea of maternity and fertility.

We refer to designs, engraved on a bracelet, carved from a single piece of mammoth ivory found at Mezin, Ukraine, which is identical with the engravings resembling spiral rhomboids on the fluted core of chert from Chandravati (Sonawane, V.H., 1997, Upper Paleolithic Art of India: A Fresh Look, Purakala, 8/1-2). They consist of a pair of parallel lines moving clockwise from the centre, forming two intertwining spiraling arms. The present paper deals in the fact that this in all probability had a deeper significance than pure decoration.

The Engraved core along with blades, burins and cores, showing close affinity towards Upper Paleolithic Lithic Industry, were found near Chandravati, the capital of the Parmaras of the Arbuda Mandal near Mount Abu. One of the two spiraling arms of the design engraved on this core bears a series of short diagonal lines whereas the other arm is significantly left plain to render a foreground and background effect of the sign. The incompleteness of the design, damaged as a result of later flaking, indicates that the engraving preceded its use as a core. The engraving also indicates the artistic abilities of its creator who could produce this sharp and accurate geometric motif, and is one of the finest works of its contemporary.

In drawing parallels with rock art of the Indian sub-continent one notices a strict codified repertoire in their respective styles and use of space as if they were the parts of a widely understood communication system, that much later may have also transformed into **tantric yantras**, and that they are distinguished by a very high degree of craftsmanship and characteristic uniformity of intricate designs.

Bhimbetka	Cheel Daant	Cheel Daant

Mahadeo Hills	Kathotiya

Shri Yantra

Yoni Yantra

Kali Yantra

Devi Yantra

The earliest drawings were clearly pictorial representations. These were adequate to describe concrete objects but were not capable of portraying abstract ones. A rebus of sorts began to develop so that the pictograms that represented an object such as a deer or an ox would also represent that sound. An example may be by drawing

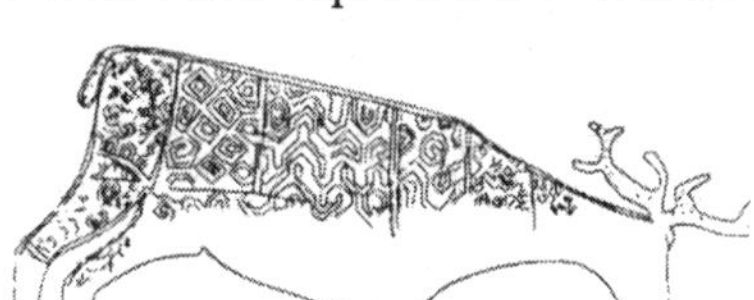

the picture of a bee to represent the sound 'bee'. This led to a huge proliferation of meanings and uses for signs / sounds. Over a period of time, the graphic representations of signs became more and more abstract. The above paintings, comprising of intricate geometric patterns, are most conspicuous stylistic features of the earliest style (Neumayer, Erwin, 1993, Lines on stone: The Prehistoric Rock Art of India, New Delhi).

These designs are often indicated as Labyrinthine and are composed of rhombic meanders and honeycomb patterns along with their multiple derivatives. They, most often, cover large parts of the virgin surfaces of rock shelters. In several other rock paintings they are found as designs or ornamentations of the body, both for animals and human beings. Such animal figures are identified as deified animals (Misra, V.N., et. al. 1985, Recent Advances in Indo-Pacific Prehistory,), whereas, the rectangular shaped torso of female figurines are also adorned with such intricate geometric patters. All these seem identical with the engraved design on the Chandravati core.

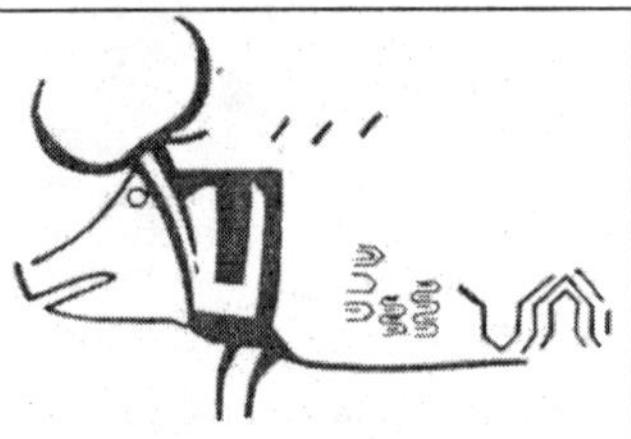

Bhimbetka

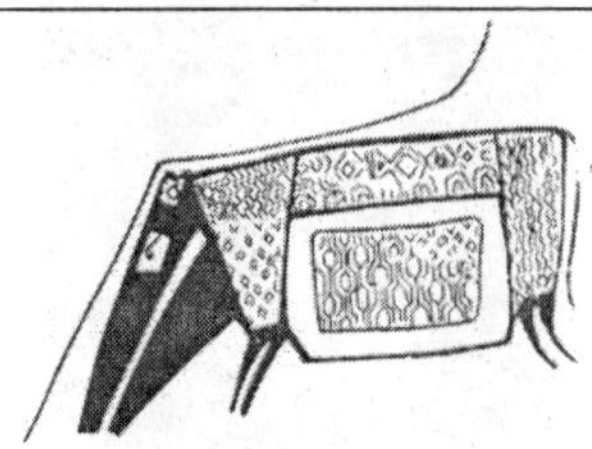

Bhimbetka

Firangi

Urden

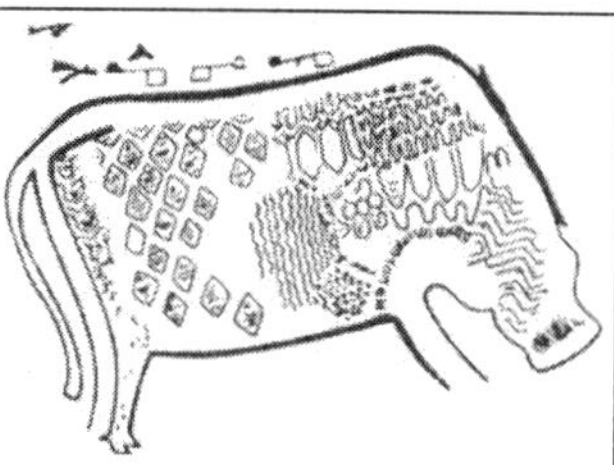	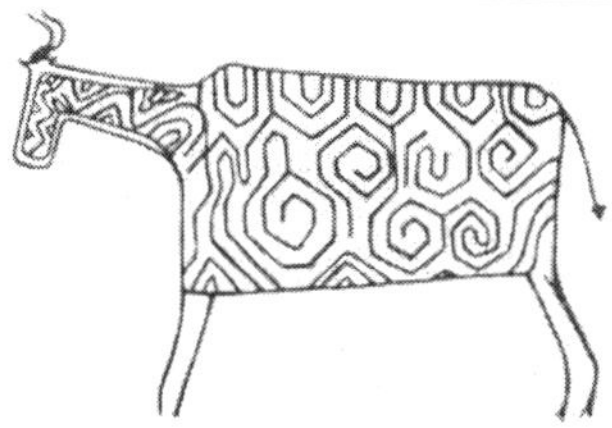
Firangi	Gupha Masir
	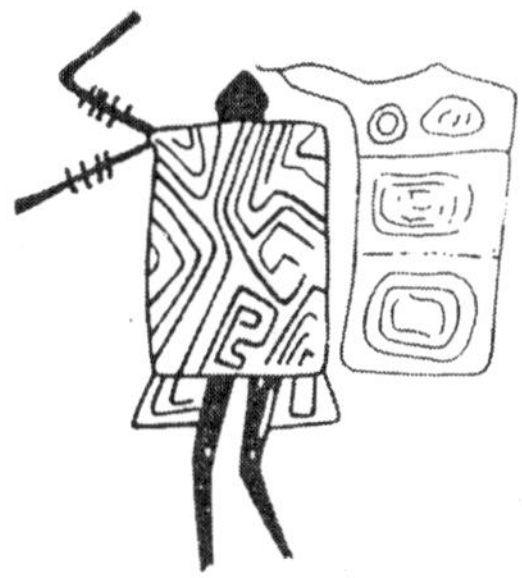
Benakal Forest	Kathotia

The types of motifs executed on various rock paintings and the Chandravati core do denote some connotations in the art of the hunting-gathering prehistoric communities, thereby also indicating a specific artistic tradition, shared by all, having a comparable style of living.

A strikingly similar intricate design, parallel to the above, is also noticed in the Upper Paleolithic Art of Mezin (Ukraine), on Mammoth Ivory Figurines of women and also on an ivory bracelet of 'The Upper Paleolithic of the Central Russian Plain'.

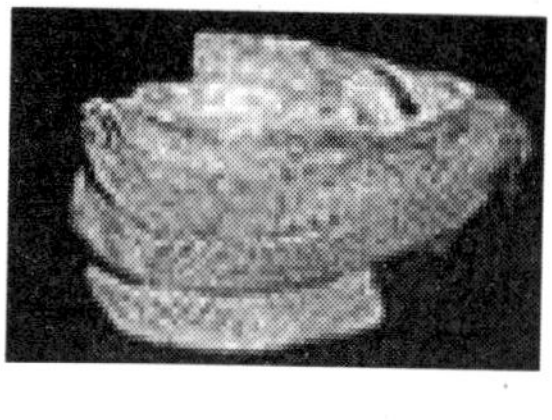 

Bracelet carved out of mammoth ivory from Mezin. Such jewellery was used by the Stone Age hunters of Europe and Asia by 30,000 B.C. It was carved from a single piece of mammoth ivory and it has a magnificent design which can be found to this day in the embroidery of Ukrainian costumes and clothes. This bracelet dates from about 30,000 B.C. and the design is reminiscent of, but predates, the famous Greek meander or the 'maze'.

	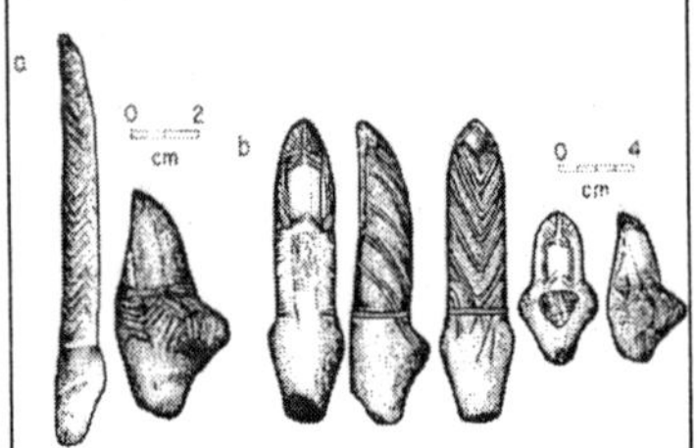	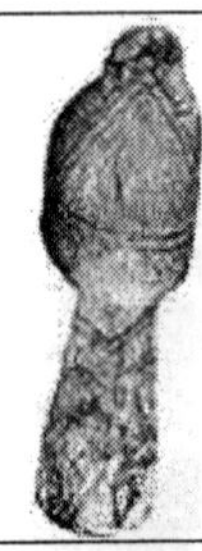
Mammoth ivory needle with eye, engraved with chevrons, from Mezin.	Mammoth ivory 'phallic figurines' and birds from Mezin.	Female statuette carved with engraved chevrons, from Mezin.

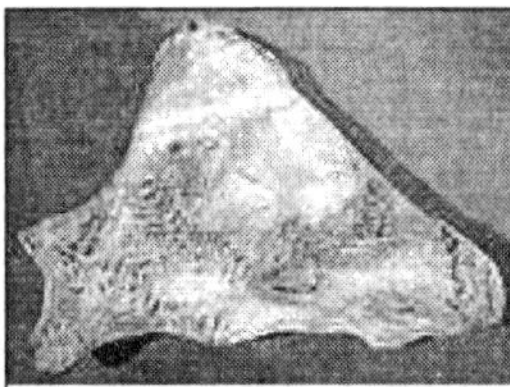	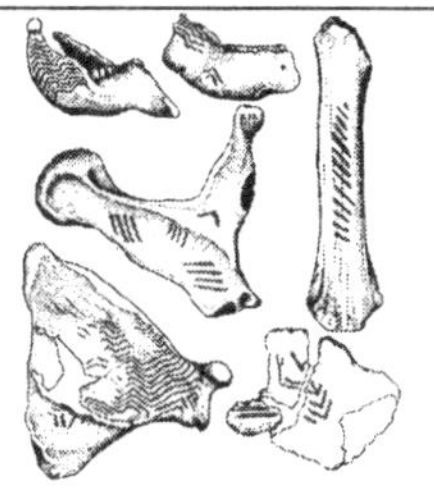
Bones painted with red ochre, from Mezin.	Scapula of painted mammoth used in the construction of one of the huts at Mezin.

Along with the above designs and engravings it is also worth considering another object of religious connotation. They are triangular natural sandstone fragments with concentric

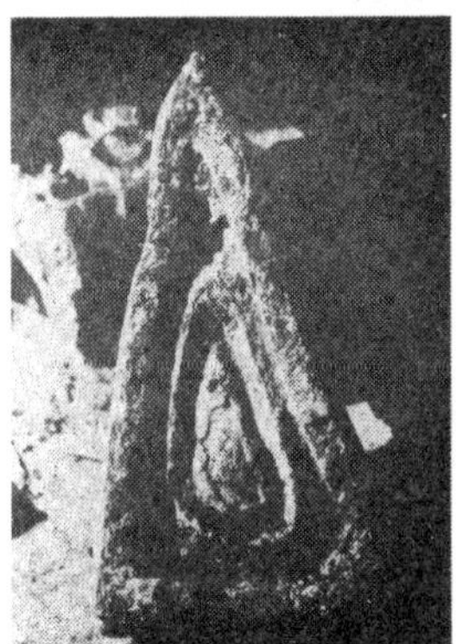

laminations in the form of triangles, found at Bahgor-I (Son Valley, Madhya Pradesh, India) on a partially raised circular rubble platform (Kenoyer, J.M. et. al. 1983, An Upper Paleolithic Shrine in India? Antiquity 57: 88-94). It is interesting to note that even this day the members of the local **Koli** and **Bhagia** tribes worship similar type of colourful natural stones as a symbol of **Mai**, The Mother Goddess or The Goddess of Fertility.

Equally interesting and conspicuous is the fact that rock paintings depicting 'deified animals' are most often linked with mythological tales, prevalent amongst the local tribes, thereby reflecting the then human civilisation and cultures, which their authors observed, experienced, believed, practised and lived as manifestations of the nature and the society.

While the drawings and carvings can significantly be related to either symbols of fertility, mother and temple or a shrine, bearing ethnographic parallels, also a whole row of figurines, found at various places of the world, and as much in the Indian and Russian Subcontinents, bear testimony to the fact that worship or reverence of The Mother Goddess or The Goddess of Fertility must have been a universal phenomenon. This assumption is supported by a close look at such female figurines reported as the "Palaeolithic Venus".

Venus figurines from Russia and The Ukraine

23,000-21,000 BC Limestone, Kostenky settlement

This figurine represents the Palaeolithic 'Venus', with overlarge breasts and belly. The faceless head bends towards the chest while the arms are pressed to the body with hands on the belly. Covering the surface of the head are rows of incisions indicating a hair style or cap. Relief work in the form of a tight plait conveys a breast ornament tied up at the back. There are bracelets on the arms.

This figurine may possibly personify the goddess of fertility, mother-ancestor or the guardian of the home as noted by scholars. Between 1883 and 1895, Louis Alexandre Jullien discovered fifteen figurines at the *Balzi Rossi* area. This is the largest series ever found in one place in Western Europe, and the pieces can be traced back to the Gravettian chronology and culture. Seven of the figurines were displayed in an exhibition at the Canadian Museum of Civilization in 1995.

With the exception of *The Mask*, all of these carvings can be seen as variations on the Paleolithic Venus, a model that we now recognize as fundamental to the artistic repertoire of the Eurasian Upper Paleolithic. Research shows that this model occurs, with regional variations, in many places in Western Europe, Central Europe (the Czech Republic and Slovakia), Eastern Europe (Ukraine and the Russian plain) and even in the Lake Baykal region of Siberia.

It was not until the time of the Aurignacians' successors - the Gravettians of about 28,000 to 22,000 years ago - that the unique form of artistic representation known as the Palaeolithic Venus flourished in many regions of Europe. This occurred in conjunction with a certain standardization of tools, and the coincidence of technological and artistic expansion has been interpreted by some researchers as a first great unifying trend across Europe.

Female Figurines and the Cult of the Goddess of Fertility

Goddess of Fertility, Mother Goddess etc. is a designation that has been ascribed to engraved and painted prehistoric images of women. Although any interpretation is a conjecture based upon a particular reading of the material and culture, the most readily given label (and the one most readily contested) is that of 'goddess' or fertility image, as evidenced by the frequent naming of these statues as a Venus. Identifying and locating the true purpose of these figurines has since nearly become a study unto itself, with scholars and researchers from various disciplines proposing and negating hypotheses and theories. However, if these symbols are to be correctly understood then they must be examined in the context in which they once operated and not at a general level. The essential problem with this type of analysis is the simple fact that their culture is still not fully understood. In light of this dilemma, to say that there was once a universal cult of a Great Goddess is not quite prudent, but nor is it altogether untrue.

It is found that the most obvious place to seek the origin of the Great Goddess would be at the dawn of agriculture, but how then are we to explain the proliferation of female figurines that date to the Paleolithic? One possible answer may lie in the sheer volume of figures and traits they share common and similar physical features. Although problematic, it can be generalized that the figurines from the Paleolithic era meant something more than mere statuettes, as these images appear in various styles and positions for over thirty thousand years.

Many Paleolithic artefacts are reported from the Caucasus, Crimea, Russian steppes, Siberia and Altai. Varied artistic objects from the Stone Age were found in the Malta (Siberia), Maininsk (Siberia) and Kostenky I (River Don) Settlements.

Female figurines from the Malta dwellings are worthy of particular attention; amongst them are exceptionally rare Paleolithic figurines wearing some form of garments. Plates made from a mammoth tusk with depiction of a mammoth and snakes, and figurines of flying birds were also discovered in this settlement.

Artistic objects made during the Paleolithic era occupy an important place in the collection, since this is the only source from which we can reconstruct and study the then culture of the people, whose civilisation is responsible for the creation of such work of art. For instance there are small figurines from Kostenky I and an anthropomorphic figurine from a Mainisk dwelling. The meaning and purpose of such objects from the Paleolithic era are usually identified with ancient cults.

Many objects are decorated with ornamental patterns: from Malta these tend to be depressions and notches forming spiral compositions while from Kostenky more geometrical patterns.

<table>
<tr><td>
1. Anthropomorphic Figurine
20,000-18,000 BC
Maininsk settlement</td><td>
2. Female Figurine 2
22,000-21,000 BC
Malta settlement</td></tr>
</table>

3. Bird Figurine 22,000-21,000 BC Malta settlement	**4. Female Figurine 3** 22,000-21,000 BC Malta settlement

The same tradition is reported to have been continued in the subsequent Periods.

5. Seated Female Figurine Second half of the 4th millennium BC	**6. Figurines of Standing Women** 3rd millennium BC	**7. Female Figurine 4** 4th millennium BC	**8. Cylindrical Vessel** First half of the 3rd millennium BC

Conclusion

In the above context it is possible to infer that there has been a common stylistic pattern amongst the hunting and gathering communities of the Upper Palaeolithic Period. The symbolic representations of Chandravati, Bhagor-I and Mezin mark a striking semblance, which, as speculated, is a derivation of archetypical natural or phosphane motifs, and that they are of the original variants of the kind. Scholars, while talking about 'ritual artefacts of the prehistoric hunter-gatherers in the South Asia", suggested that the Chandravati core was prepared for definite socio-cultural ritual activities and that similar engravings found on the Mezin ivory bracelet represent the earliest examples of non-verbal symbolic communication. They also note that such remarkable engravings to be the roots of civilisation (Gorelick, I. et. al, 1981, The Origin and Development of the Ancient Near Eastern Cylindrical Seal, Expedition, 23/4, pp 17-30). These symbolic expressions have remained in the symbolic repertoire of cultures under study, and they have played an important role in the beliefs and expressions of subsequent cultures that evolved in the same surroundings.

It is, therefore, opined that all motivation of visual impressions found in the Bhagor-I natural stone concentric triangles, the engraved Chandravati core and Mezin ivory bracelet and intricate geometric patterns on rock shelters & cave walls and such identical designs, used by womenfolk both of Ukraine and India, are those abstract forms which embody that energy, fertility (or Shakti), known and worshipped even this day as the **Divine Mother** or **Mother Goddess** and **The Goddess of Fertility**. This evidence is further strengthened in their subsequent manifestations in the various forms of **Tantric Yantras**.

The authors appreciate and acknowledge their students (Meenakshi Chakravarty, Rajesh Kanojia, Julie Thomas and Shabnam Lohani) for their enthusiastic assistance in collecting data for this paper and presentation.

13

Women's Liberation Liberalized

Ritoo M. Jerath

How many times in the recent past has it happened that you are surfing the channels on your TV and you come across a woman dancing in your face with almost no clothes on? When was the last time you picked up the city section of your newspaper and saw articles on women and the clothes they are wearing or not wearing and on the make up they are using and on their sexual habits and desires? Have you been listening to the lyrics of one of the latest Hindi movie songs – the one where the woman says "I want to show my body and move the night away? These and many more are all scenes from urban India in the new millennium. Have you sat back and wondered to yourself what is happening to our society? Have you wondered what exactly it is that you find objectionable in these images? Or have you thought to yourself – I must be getting old? The point is that these images are seen today by some as being 'young and hip and cool and with it'.

Over the last decade these images have become more intense and underlying all of this is the attitude that if you find something objectionable in all this then you are being old fashioned and conservative. It is felt that these are the images of the new bold professional urban Indian woman. Mallika Sherawat, a well known Hindi movie actress who shot to fame because of the bold scenes she has done in her movies when asked to comment on her body exposure has remarked in an interview 'Where are we living today? You see it all the time on the streets, girls wearing short dresses. What's wrong in it? I guess that's the privilege of being a girl and that's how we have an edge over men.'[1] In another interview she said

---

1. http://movies.indiainfo.com/interview/mallika_sherwat.html

'I don't feel scared or daunted by any criticism about exposure. Those people who are criticizing exposure, I think they don't belong to this world. I don't see anything wrong in wearing skimpy tops. I admire those girls who wear small tops and carry themselves comfortably in the society. We must appreciate and encourage this changing attitude. And when she was asked about whether exposure can lead to provocative attitudes in society her answer was "A beautiful body is a gift of God. If I am beautiful, I have full right to take pride in it. I don't think there is anything wrong in keeping myself so glamorous and sexy. In fact, men find me irresistible!"[2]

Mallika Sherawat's attitude is not simply an individualistic one. Many young people think along the same lines. Every other day you read a statement similar to Mallika's made by some one else. Recently there was an article on Delhi school children today and the kind of parties they have, in one of the leading newspapers which reprinted an invitation card for a party sent out by a fourteen year old boy from one of Delhi's best known public schools - the dress code for the party was "the lesser the better [even for my boyfriends and girls please put on the best undies]".[3] In the same article it was reported that some school children from another reputed school had a birthday party where the girls were asked to do a mujra. When questioned about it, the boy said "It's very groovy. You should also try it.... In our last party, we made the girls do Kajra re, the typical Ash way."[4] This attitude is not restricted to the younger generation. The father of the boy also reacted similarly. His take on it was "Once in a while it is okay to do such things. It was not as if the children were having drugs. They were only having fun... the girls had no problems being kothewalis."[5]

Not too long ago, there was another article in the newspaper about the pay packages for women/girls working at the international trade fair. It seems that the pay was decided according to the formula the shorter the hemline, the better the pay pack.[6] This was done

---

2. http://www.hindustantimes.com/news/7242_1577134,00180013.htm
3. Debashree Mohanty, "Class Of 2005", Foray, Sunday Pioneer 23 October 2005.
4. ibid.
5. ibid.
6. Kanu Sarda, "Hemline drives bottom line: Less for more", Hindustan Times 18 November 2005.

because of the belief that nothing works as a bit of leg show in attracting prospective buyers to the stalls. According to a company executive "this is just a business strategy to attract the maximum customers. Honestly speaking, this is what sells".[7]

Interesting that the company executive chose to put it in these words. It is true that today many decisions are made on the basis of what sells. This is perhaps the fall out of the sudden liberalization of our economy and our attempt to be a part of the process of globalization. And as usual the attitude towards women forms a part of this process of liberalization. And as I have said earlier, anyone who finds anything objectionable in all this is seen to be conservative or old-fashioned and anti-liberalization. And those that support or are indulging in it are seen to be modern, with the times and even as fighting for the right of women to do what they want, to exercise their choice.

Apparently the situation in Russia is not very different. Nadezhda Azhgikhina, a journalist working for the magazine Ogonyok, in a report submitted to the Division for the Advancement of Women, Department for Policy Coordination and Sustainable Development talks of how soon after the collapse of the Soviet Union, a truly free press emerged, and almost overnight there was a mushrooming of magazines and newspapers. According to her, as the market economy emerged, so did images of women, proving to be a very profitable commodity. Suddenly, newspapers featuring models and beauty contests sold more than other newspapers. I quote from her report "Beauties in bikinis, their interviews and press coverage of beauty contests started to appear not only in "lightweight" publications, but also in "respectable" ones. The apotheosis of this change, I believe, was the publication in the Communist newspaper Pravda, famous for its Puritanism, of an article about Julia Kourochkina, the winner of the Miss Universe contest. She was enthusiastically described as a true Russian patriot. The photographs matched the tone of the text. Today, TV programs and publications aimed at young people provide a good deal of space and time to advice as to how to become a photo-model, rather than how to enter a university. Faces of beautiful women fill the pages of magazines and the TV screen, famous TV anchor-women and announcers emulate the new stereotypes at the

---

7. ibid.

expense of their own personalities, and this drastically affects the tone of programs."[8] Azhgikina in the same report goes on to talk about the sudden appearance of a lot of pornography with even TV showing semi erotic films. Although according to her the situation has somewhat stabilized now. Azhgikina is not the only commentator on the present day image of women in Russia. Other scholars like Donna Hughes, Sue Bridger and Rebecca Kay have done extensive research in this area. They feel that this change in the image has been brought about by the importation of Western glamour with its emphasis on women's appearance, cosmetics and fashion and that very quickly glamour turned to pornography. Donna Hughes attributes some of this change to the impact of the US TV soap Santa Barbara on Russian Women, where suddenly Russian women were bombarded with Western images of glamour and wealth.[9] Coincidentally, Santa Barbara was also one of the first imported soaps shown on Indian cable TV soon after the process of liberalization had begun in India.

One of the greatest and most progressive revolutions of the 20th century was perhaps the change in the social and legal status of women. At the beginning of the 20th century women did not even have the right to vote. The 20th century is marked with struggles by women to 'get a fair share' in a world dominated by men. The Soviet Union was one of the first countries to have a state policy for the equality of women. In the West women started gaining equality at different times throughout the 20th century. One of the most important landmarks for the women's struggle is the Women's Liberation movement, which began in 1969 in the West, which is often referred to as the second wave[10] of Feminism. It achieved many goals through direct action and pressure group lobbying and had its impact mainly on the English-speaking world and Europe. It is said to have emerged from women's participation in the civil rights movements of the 1960s and the growth of the New Left, which stressed liberation from oppression[11]. The main issues of this

8. http://www.un.org/documents/ecosoc/cn6/1996/media/rmediaen.htm
9. Donna M. Hughes, Supplying Women for the Sex Industry: Trafficking from the Russian Federation, <http://www.uri.edu/artsci/wms/hughes/supplying_women.pdf>
10. Kerryn Williams, Women's liberation — the struggle is alive!, <http://www.greenleft.org.au/>
11. http://www.channel4.com/history/microsites/H/history

movement included not only equal pay and equal legal rights, but also campaigns against rape and violence against women, pornography, and other cultural attitudes – for example, sexist language – that exploit women. One of the documents from the women's liberation movement talked about the women's right to abortion because the woman has the right to "limit the number of [her] children,... for the issue at stake is the right of every woman to the control of her own body" [12]. It also talked about how women are channeled into traditional roles of wife and mother and what also plays an important role in the channelisation of women into traditional roles is the expectations of others and the images of women as empty sex objects.[13]

The women's liberation movement of the West in short stressed: 1) that a woman has a right to control her own body and 2) the need to fight against the depiction of women as sex objects. Similar positions can be found in the women's movement in Russia as well as in India.

The women's movement in Russia[14] is very complex. When the revolution took place in 1917 for the first time the complete economic, political and sexual equality of women was put on the historic agenda. A woman was no longer obliged to live with her husband or to accompany him if a change of job meant a change of house. Property relationships changed to give women equal rights to hold land, be head of a household and to receive equal pay. Attention was paid to women's childbearing role and special maternity laws were introduced forbidding long hours and night work, and establishing paid leave at childbirth, family allowances and childcare centres. Abortion was legalised in 1920, divorce was simplified and

---

12. Female Liberation: A Joint Statement by Six Female Liberation Groups in Chapel Hill and Duham, N.C.,
    Female Liberation - Documents from the Women's Liberation Movement, <http://scriptorium.lib.duke.edu/wlm>
13. ibid.
14. The historical facts about the policies of the Socialist government are taken from Elisabetta Rossi, The Emancipation of Women in Russia before and after the Russian Revolution Part Two, <http://www.marxist.com/womenandmarxism.asp> and Jen Pickard, Women in the Soviet Union <http://www.newyouth.com/womenand marxism.asp>

civil registration of marriage was introduced. Things changed under Stalin. He began to remove some of the laws that had initially been introduced by the Bolsheviks to allow both males and females the full expression of their potential. There are arguments as to whether Soviet women under Socialism truly achieved equality. In fact, there was a whole underground movement of feminists that sprung up around the 70's trying to fight for better conditions for women etc. The aim of this paper is not to argue about the success or failure of the Socialist system vis-à-vis women. The point is that the Soviet Union did at least in its constitution guarantee equality for women and did fight for women to be allowed to make choices and did fight against the degradation of women. And if underground movements did spring up it was only to further the rights of women to control their own lives and their bodies.

In India, women have been historically repressed and exploited. Although the struggle for equality began much earlier, it took active female inclusion in the political world by Gandhi's independence movement to give their voices strength and to eventually have them heard.[15] There was avid political activity on the part of women and female organizations leading up to the 1947 split. The effectiveness of this work foreshadowed the influence women could have on politics when working together, and paved the way for the modern women's movement that began in the 1970's. Since the seventies many women's organizations have come up in India and have been involved in very serious issues regarding women – fighting against violence against women, for laws for equality, against female infanticide, against the exploitation and commodification of women, for the woman's right over her own body etc.

As we can see then that most of the women's' struggles all over the world have raised similar issues with of course some variation depending on the specificity of the social conditions of a particular country.

However, given the present scenario today, the question that arises is where has this struggle for the progress and empowerment of women led to? In India, newspapers, television and films, which today are the most powerful sources of influence and information are selling us an ideal of the 'new age woman'. And this new age woman

---

15. Women In India http://www.freeessays.cc/index.shtml

according to them is "signified by a sultry cleavage."[16] And these 'new age women' are referred to as 'chocolate bombshell', 'item hottie' and 'buxom beauty'[17], whose formula for success is "if you have it, flaunt it".[18] And as pointed out by Azhgikhina the media in Russia is selling a similar image of the 'new age' Russian woman. It is as though the mainstream society of both our countries today has taken the ideals of the years of struggle of the women's liberation movement towards a particular direction and has twisted them to fit in with the needs of a liberalized economy. We seem to have come back almost a full circle where the woman's body has once again become a commodity and an object of the male gaze – the difference being that now the women themselves are 'exercisizing this choice' over their own bodies. And the choice seems to be to commodify and sell their bodies as objects of desire and to meet the needs of the market. And in this 359 degrees turn, women's liberation itself has become liberalized.

---

16. Sex bombs' assets on display, http:// www.hindustantimes.com
17. ibid.
18. ibid.

14

The Russian Economy in the Post-Soviet Period

Meeta Narain

"We are living in an epoch changing time. The end of the millennium, the end of the century, the end of an ideological era. It is all global border-lines, challenging us to give global answers, having large-scale reflections. However, within the smaller cycle of the Russian social life the obvious *volte-face* is taking place. It is going to be quite comparable with perestroika and "democratization" in its significance and consequences. In the ideological sense, perestroika was the transitional period from late Soviet, nominally socialist society, to the liberal and democratic model. The term "post-perestroika" has been applied to the description of that political, ideological and cultural model, which appeared after the radical break with the Soviet past and the establishment of the 'western' capitalist market system in Russia"[1]. This has been rightly framed by A. Dougine in his write-up titled 'Post-Liberal Era' translated by Vladislav Ivanov for Arcotogaia and these changes are visible till date. The following paper has tried to analyse these changes taking place in the Russian economy in the post-Soviet period.

The Russian economy witnessed a number of changes and so did the world from 1991 onwards, that is during the 'post-perestroika' period. The Russian economy had become a subject of heated scientific and political debates all over the world. It was facing crises in all fields. Towards the end of 90s, it started taking concrete steps towards liberalization in all aspects of life. The following paper focuses on the period from 1991-98, which is the epoch of the post-Soviet liberal and democratic period of modern Russian history. The important fact to bring into prominence is that the "post-perestroika" period is drifting towards an end. This means that the 21st century

Russian economy is projecting a reality, which is quite different from the years of the Soviet era.

The paper further distinctly analyses the Russian economy in the post-liberal era on the basis of certain specific questions – Are the events in the Russian economy taking a positive turn in the post-liberal era? By what factors are the developments in the era determined? What impact do the liberal policies have on the development of productive forces? Is liberalization being able to prepare models for productive growth factors and many other related questions?

The economic, political, foreign, cultural, and defence strategy of the Russian Federation was based on the fact that there were differences which existed with the west, which thereby resulted in different social, economic and ideological models. This resulted in the appearance of geopolitical factors, as rightly stated by Vladislav Ivanov, in the translation of Dougine's text in Vtorzhenie #1 "everyone realized that the cold war was not just a display of an ideological duel, but the display of a historical constant, not dependent on social or political factors. It was just one of the stages in the great war of continents"[2]. The geopolitical factors further made the Russian political elite and intellectuals sober down because they started realizing the danger of taking-over of their powers by the aggressive dominating blocs of the West.

With the passage of time, the press too changed its role. In the earlier years of Perestroika, it glorified liberalism of the West, but now it started playing an important role in making the people realize the importance of geopolitical factors. The patriotic opposition also performed a similar function, helping the authorities realize the obvious geopolitical axioms.

This changing phenomenon of the Russian economy has been described by many scholars from different social, economic and political fields. One of the noted scholar, Dr. Vladimir Mau, who is the Director of the Academy of the National Economy under the Government of the Russian Federation and member of the Editorial Board of *Russia in Global Affairs* has very rightly described this in the following manner- "The Soviet economic policy was subjected to cyclical fluctuations since the days of its infancy. Scientists have termed this phenomenon the 'investment cycle in socialist economies' which had the following phases: implementation of an investment program; economic growth slowdown; liberalization measures; acceleration of the rate of growth; increased macroeconomic imbalances; rejection of liberal reforms and enactment of a new investment programme. As opposed to previous periods, however, they did not entail a toughening of the economic regime. Instead, liberalization began to deepen and expand".[3]

The subsequent collapse of the Communist system was primarily due to the fact that there was crisis in the field of industrialization, which called for a transformation. This transformation, thereby took the form of a complete revolution, which could be compared with the great revolutions of the past. The system however, was unable to adjust to this transformation and this took the form of a total chaotic situation in the society. The result was that while the West used the crisis to adapt itself to the new challenges, the Soviet Union showed small but steady growth rates, while at the same time falling into a severe systemic crisis. The heavy industries and the defence production, although dominated the society but the main problem, however, was that in the 1980s the gap between Western and Soviet economic development became apparent to everyone.

To overcome the crisis, the authorities had to adopt the course of liberalization of all aspects of life. As the article, *'Perestroika Through the Prism of History'* by V. Mau says, "The development of productive forces and the relevant models of successful modernization rely on liberal policies (in the developed Western countries), or policies which mark a tendency toward liberalization (in the fast-growing countries of Southeast Asia, for example). It also explains why the Soviet and Russian governments followed a more or less consistent course of liberalization, regardless of their partisan attitudes".[4]

The country's social and economic structure is changed by the revolutions which are a systematic transformation which takes place under the conditions of weak state power. A weak state power, subsequently results in the spontaneous transformation of economic and social system. Several different economic, social and political forces effect the development of a country and hence take the country in different directions. All revolutions go through several stages, where they start from a united structure and go on to radical changes, which result in the break-up of the old system. This then leads to the foundation of a new state order which has to bring stability and the end of the turmoil period.

The transformation of the Russian society which was, as stated earlier, was no less than a revolution, needs to be analyzed in this perspective. The process clearly indicates that Perestroika, in its earlier stages, was giving a positive indication in all fields. However, the total dislike of the old regime and of the legacy of the past did not prove to be a beneficial tool for the society. As stated by many scholars and intellectuals, a combination of the past and the present will only have some long-term consequences for the country.

This is based on the fact that a sudden transformation always leads to hasty decisions, especially in the economic field, which may or may not be in the interest of the country. The social, political, cultural and other reforms too, find it difficult to formulate a stable programme. This is so because, all these fields have a strong ideological and political bondage with the old system, and their sudden changed implementation brings about a large gap between the past and the present. Such programmes cannot be implemented hastily but, since the public notices in them a big change, they start getting the public support. Therefore, they receive the attention of the authorities too. Subsequently, the popularity which the government receives makes it unable to take drastic but necessary decisions when required.

Although, the above factors and analysis help us to understand the pre and post Perestroika period, but they should not be considered as the final cause of the collapse of the soviet system. This is so because, all transformations undergo similar stages and one cannot ignore the instability it brings about in the society. The most prominent sectors namely, the defence and the economic show distinct changes in case of Russia it came into clear prominence that the economic decisions of the late 1980s brought in heavy financial crisis that Russia had to overcome during the entire next decade. However, history of revolutionary age shows that the Russian transformation and the crisis in all the important sectors is very similar to those which took place during the French Revolution, the history of English Land Ownership and others. Instability, financial crisis, property re-distribution are common features of all revolutions.

Hence, the Russian society has to be judged on a comparative basis. The present realities have to be considered and alternatives have to be suggested. The political developments will certainly result in a gradual re-birth and bring about stability to the economy of the nation. This will lead Russia to a new, unique, cultural, geopolitical, social and economic direction. There will be a change in the patriotic policies of the country too. The Russian intelligentsia is heading towards a more liberal, creative, original and constructive thinking. What belonged to the soviet era is being re-examined and re-interpreted to match the realities of the modern historical and geopolitical situations in the world. It is quite clear that presenting something afresh is not easy but is possible through the implementation of new and advanced technologies and policies. Vladislav Ivanov, in the translation of Dugin's text in Vtorzhenie #1 has outlined this fact in a very poetic manner. "The post-liberal era is at a threshold. What will it be? What has not yet been? Much of this issue depends on us, our imagination, our will, our intellect, our honesty and readiness to start everything from the beginning again".[5]

NOTES

1. A. Dougine, Post Liberal Era, translated by Vladislav Ivanov, Arctogaia, Aug. 1998, website http://www.my.arcto.ru/public/eng/eng-lib.htm
2. A. Dougine, Post Liberal Era, translated by Vladislav Ivanov, Arctogaia, Aug. 1998, website http://www.my.arcto.ru/public/eng/eng-lib.htm
3. Vladimir Mau, in his article Perestroika Through the Prism of History published in 'Russia in Global Affairs' vol. 3 • no. 2 • April – June • 2005, website: http://www.isn.ethz.ch/pubs/ph/details.cfm?lng=en&v33=60189&id=13908
4. Vladimir Mau, in his article Perestroika Through the Prism of History published in 'Russia in Global Affairs' vol. 3 • no. 2 • April – June • 2005, website: http://www.isn.ethz.ch/pubs/ph/details. cfm?lng=en&v33=60189& id=13908
5. A. Dougine, Post Liberal Era, translated by Vladislav Ivanov, Arctogaia, Aug. 1998, website http://www.my.arcto.ru/public/eng/eng-lib.htm

REFERENCES

Origins of the Crisis in the USSR, Hillel Ticktin, 1992, USA.

Крысин, Л. П. Социолингвистические аспекты изучения русского языка. 1989, Наука, М.

Филологические Науки, No. 3, 2003

Vladimir Mau, Russia in Global Affairs vol. 3, no. 2, April–June, 2005, website: http://www.isn.ethz.ch/pubs/ph/details.cfm?lng=en&v33=60189&id=13908

A. Dougine, Post Liberal Era, translated by Vladislav Ivanov, Arctogaia, Aug. 1998, website http://www.my.arcto.ru/public/eng/eng-lib.htm

15

Indo-Russian Bilateral Relations in 21st Century

A Brief Report

A. Rajeshwar Raju

One of the distinctive features of the modern world is the rapid expansion of economic, scientific, technological and cultural ties among nations. All the independent nations are now trying to form trade relations with other countries in the world in order to accelerate the development of their economies. Russia's interest in India and Indian people goes back a long way. In the 15th and 16th centuries, the focus shifted from legends about the mysterious wonderland on to insights into India's socio-economic, political and cultural reality. In this connection, before going through the relations with Russia, it would be better to know a little about the pioneers of the above historical movement.

Afanasy Nikitin

While traveling through India, Afanasy Nikitin made a close study of its population, public and state system, economy, religion, people's daily life and nature. His travel notes "The 1466-1472 Voyage Over Three Seas" were translated into many languages. He accomplished his voyage 25 years before Vasco da Gama's expedition had discovered its way to India. Nikitin was a merchant from the city of Tver at the times of the tsar Ivan III (1440-1505) and his voyage was the first recorded contact between India and Russia, which saw India as "a land of priceless diamonds and in mountain caves and pearls of the southern seas" as sung by a famous Indian poet.

Nikolai Roerich (1874-1947)

N.K. Roerich was a Russian painter, archeologist, traveler and writer who lived his life closely connected to India. N.K. Roerich was a member of the St. Petersburg's Academy of Sciences, a member of the association "World of Art" and the initiator of the movement for protecting the cultural monuments and also the founder of the Himalayan Roerich Institute "Urusvat" in Naggar, India. To protect cultural values the International Roerich pact had been concluded in 1954. It was a historic event in the annals of Roerich Centre, Naggar when former Hon'ble Prime Minister of India, Sri Atal Bihari Vajpai paid his visit on 27th May, 2001 to the Centre, the home of famous Nikolas Roerich from 1928 to 1947. The Hon'ble Prime Minister's visit was an acknowledgment of the contribution of the Roerich family in the fields of art, science, culture and their initiatives towards world peace. Though born in Russia, Nicholas Roerich chose Naggar in the Kullu district of Himachal Pradesh as his home and did most of his creative work there.

Evincing keen interest in its accelerated development as a centre of international repute, the Hon'ble Prime Minister announced a grant of rupees one Crore for the development of the Centre.

The former Soviet Union established diplomatic relations with India in 1947, four months before the country officially proclaimed its independence. This fact alone attests to the powerful mutual gravitation that has always existed between the people of the two countries. Nikolas Roerich wrote decades ago that "the Indian magnet attracts Russian hearts".

Rabindranath Tagore

Literary Genius and Humanist: One of India's greatest poets and writers, recipient of the Nobel Prize for literature Rabindranath Tagore (1861-1941) was born in Calcutta on May 7 into a distinguished Bengali family. He first visited Russia in September 1930. Letters written during this visit were later published in the form of a book titled "Letters from Russia". These letters are a running commentary on men and affairs, vividly topical and full of descriptive editions of the Soviet scene. However, this book could not be published in English earlier due to restriction from the British colonizers.

The first impressions cast by the Soviet Republic charmed Tagore. He wrote, "I am now in Russia; had I not come, my life's pilgrimage would have remained incomplete.... But what has astonished me most is the tremendous task that is being carried out here..."

In his letters there was hardly any aspect of life in Russia on which Tagore did not express his opinion. The letters written during his sojourn in Russia presented his reaction to one of the greatest experiments in human civilization. Warmly sympathetic and therefore critical, these rapid transcripts of the poet's reflections are not only a record of an exciting phase of world history but are also of perennial significance because they link up with urgent problems of national reconstruction in India and in the East and this provides a standard of comparative evaluation, as well as a perspective for the future.

In one of his letters written from Moscow on 20th September he opined, "In Russia at last! Whichever way I look I am filled with wonder. It is unlike any other country. It is radically different from the top to the bottom; they are rousing everybody up without distinction..."

Rabindranath Tagore was well known in the Soviet Union and very much loved there. Russian people value the great contribution that Tagore has made towards the national Independence. While he was in Russia, he had extremely interesting conversations with peasants, young people, artists, students which reflected his interest in everything connected with education. He became the real harbinger of the cultural exchange between the Russian and Indian people. Prof. Fyodor Petrov, Chairman of the All-Union Society for cultural Relations with Foreign Countries recalls his meeting with Tagore, "On our first meeting with Tagore we had a three hour talk. We discussed many things. Though he was especially interested in matters connected with education, he also questioned me about the condition of workers and peasants, about the national policy of the Soviet state, about agriculture, about success in industrialization..." Many of his novels, collections of short stories, poems and plays were published in separate volumes in the Soviet Union, while plays and ballets based on his works were staged.

The author's birth centenary celebration became a festival of friendship between the people of both the countries. On this occasion memorial meetings, literary conferences, exhibition of Tagore's books and pictorial exclusion of his visit were organized in the country. Russian people appreciate Tagore's contribution to mankind's culture and his urge for peace and friendship among the people of the world. Reading Tagore's novels, verse, songs, dramas and plays, Russian people understood the spirit of India and its rich culture. They honor Tagore for his humanism, love and belief in man.

A. Indo-Soviet Relations after India's Independence

The first agreement between India and the USSR was concluded on February 2, 1955 for the construction of the Bhilai Steel Plant, which is an outstanding symbol of economic co-operation between the USSR and India. Since then the economic cooperation between the two countries has grown from strength to greater strength. After India's independence, the Indo-Soviet relationship attained appreciable heights in scientific and cultural fields

Once the former Prime Minister of India Late Jawaharlal Nehru said during the period of the struggle for freedom, it would be in India's interest to develop close and friendly relations with the Soviet Union. When the Interim Government was formed in September, 1946 and he was made the Vice President of the Government, he expressed his desire to establish diplomatic relations with the USSR, to which the Soviet Leaders responded favorably. On 13th April, 1947, even before the independence, an announcement was made that the two countries had decided to establish diplomatic relations. The result was the appointment of Mrs. Vijaya Laxmi Pandit as India's first ambassador to the USSR. The friendly ties and mutual understanding which had been established between the people of the two countries in the past was consolidated into a fruitful Indo-Soviet co-operation after the Indian independence.

I. *Nature of Relations between India and Russia*

The relations that have been developing for the past 59 years cannot be described as purely "diplomatic". It is a rare phenomenon in a country of conventional diplomacy and is something more than merely a relationship. It is a deep rooted and time-tested friendship. In the course of these decades, they have been gaining strength, embracing all fields of human activities.

For a human being, the age of 59 years is one of maturity and respectability. The same fully applies to the relations between the two countries. The signing of the historic Treaty of Peace, Friendship and

Cooperation on August 9, 1971 during the Soviet period was symbolic of this relationship which has steadily grown through the decades.

Only few people remember today that India's first autobiotic plant was built in Rishikesh with the Soviet Union's active participation. It was also with Soviet assistance that India built metallurgical plants in Bhilai and Bokaro and launched its first satellites.

II. *Relations between the two countries after the Soviet Unions breakup*

Special significance is being attached to developing and diversifying bilateral trade & economic ties today. Great potential in these crucial spheres of international activities is yet to be tapped. After major democratic transformation of their economies, bilateral relations reached a new level, which was dictated by changes in the international arena. The new stage in Russian-Indian relations was sealed in the Declaration of Strategic Partnership, signed by the two countries during Russian President Vladimir Putin's Visit to India in October 2000.

Indo-Russian relations have been developing for over five decades and are marked by extensive cooperation in political, economic, scientific, technical and cultural spheres. Today this friendship is of great importance in the life of our two people and its role will continue to increase.

This development of bilateral relations is the outcome of the stupendous progress made by Russia and India and for the part played by the Great October Revolution in the world historical process. Indo-Russian relations have passed through various stages in the process of their growth. The most important among the landmarks have been the Treaty of Peace Friendship and Cooperation and the historic visits of Ex- Presidents of former Soviet Union; His Excellencies Mr. Leonid Breznev, Mikhail Gorbachev, Boris Yeltsin and President of Russian Republic Mr. Vladimir Putin.

Our friendship is the result of the tremendous efforts put in by millions of people in both the countries, which forms the material basis of our cooperation. The fruits of this cooperation are there for all to see. The contacts between our countries are embracing newer and newer fields, such as, science, education, culture, public health and sports, and they are all designed to further strengthen the deep and sincere friendship between our countries and people.

B. *List of some very important which events took place in India*

1. *Defexpo India 2004*

Nineteen countries participated in the Defexpo India 2004 – 3rd International Land and Naval Systems Exhibition in New Delhi. Russia presented one of the largest expositions featuring 34 enterprises. They displayed over 370 samples of military equipment and 70 samples of double-purpose and civil products.

2. *Integrated Long-Term Program of Cooperation*

His Excellency Mr. Mikhail Gorbachev and His Excellency late Mr. Rajiv Gandhi signed the agreement on ILTP on July 3, 1987. The 1972 Indo-Soviet S&T agreement was replaced by a new Agreement on Science & Technology between India and Russia signed in 1994 in Moscow. It has been renewed on October 3, 2000. The ILTP is coordinated by the Department of Science & Technology on the Indian side and by the Russian Academy of Sciences on the Russian side. Today there are 88 ongoing ILTP projects and 50 new ones were included into the program.

There are plans to establish Indo-Russian Centers for Bio-Medical Technology (Thiruvananthapuram and New Delhi). Russia and India are committed to the optimal use of existing Institutes and Laboratories to carry out over 135 projects. Most of them are being implemented or identified under the aegis of the ILTP.

Following the decisions of 10th Session of Inter-Government Russian-Indian commission on Trade, Economic, Scientific, Technological and Cultural Cooperation (IGC) in the year of 2005, the working groups for science and technology and working group for information technology were transformed into a working Group for Technologies in order to boost Indo-Russian cooperation in the field of IT, Telecom, developing of advanced computers and technology parks. The first meeting of the reformatted group took place in Moscow in September, 2005.

4. Working Group for Science & Technology.

This Group has been in operation since 1993. It is coordinated form the Indian side by the Department of Science and Technology, Government of India and from the Russian side by the Ministry of Education and Science. Sub-Working Groups are functioning in the following areas:

i. Agriculture – Indian Council for agricultural Research & Russian Academy of Agricultural Sciences
ii. Standardization, Metrology and Certification – Bureau of Indian Standards & GOSSTANDARD
iii. Building Materials – National Council for Cement and Building Materials & Industrial Realization of High Technology Department of the Ministry of Industry, Science & Technology
iv. Meteorology – India Meteorology Department & ROSHYDROMET
v. Biotechnology – Department of Biotechnology & Shemyakin Institute of Bioorganic Chemistry
vi. Medical Sciences – Indian council for Medical Research & Russian Academy of Medical Sciences
vii. Oceanology – Department of Ocean Development and Institute of Oceanology (Russian Academy of Sciences)
viii. Industrial Realization of High Technology – Department of Science & Technology
ix. Seismology – Department of Science & Technology & Institute of Physics of the Earth (Russian Academy of Science)

The Prime Minister, Manmohan Singh who recently visited Moscow said India and Russia must develop long-term energy partnership and expressed India's keenness to join Russia in exploration and production of oil and gas in third countries specially those in Central Asia and also added that talks between Indian and Russian oil companies would soon yield concrete results.

"India-Russia relations are such that although this visit is a landmark one, it is only one in a long journey that the two countries will make together and which shall be of value and benefit to both", Dr. Singh told reporters on his way back from Moscow. On the occasion of the visit of the Indian Prime Minister the two countries signed three agreements; on intellectual property rights, for joint defense work and on cooperation in the field of solar physics.

"Our strategic relationship is based on political consensus in both countries. Despite the historic transformations underway in both countries, the essence of our partnership has not been diluted", Dr. Singh said in his speech at the banquet hosted in his honor by

Russian President Vladimir Putin. He also added that there was no significant sector of our national endeavor in which we have not benefited from Russia. Today, as before, Russia is a valued strategic partner. Our relationship has adapted very successfully and productively to current requirements. "But what we will do together in partnership draws on the legacy of cooperating for mutual benefit", Singh said. Recalling that India's first Prime Minister Jawaharlal Nehru had laid the foundation of an 'abiding friendship' based on mutual trust and confidence years ago, he said "it is fitting to recall the crucial assistance we received from Russia in India's emergence as a country with a fully developed industrial base".

Dr. Manmohan Singh asserted that he was convinced that the two countries would find greater convergence in their efforts as they move forward and that without a doubt, the communication between the two countries were clear and lively.

In a joint statement issued at the end of the four-day visit the two countries said, "As partners standing against WMD proliferation, India and Russia intend to continue their efforts to achieve this objective". Both countries stressed on intensifying efforts for development and diversification of cooperation in trade and economic relations and making it a strong pillar of their strategic partnership. The four-page statement said, "The energy sector is a high priority area in which both countries are fully capable in all respects to forge long-term and large-scale joint collaborations to mutual respect". Both sides expressed satisfaction at the progress in the implementation of major joint projects – Sakhalin I oil and gas project, exploration and production of hydrocarbons in the Bay of Bengal off-shore areas.

India - Russia cooperation is not limited to defense. Identifying India as a major strategic partner in the military-technical, political and economic spheres, Defence Minister of Russian Republic on the above occasion said that India and Russia have similar views on a new world order based on multilateral relations and on key issues of security. He added that the military-technical cooperation between Russia and India dates back to 1960. Since then the overall volume of contacts in the sphere reached 33 billion dollars. Apart from these military projects, there is a much more important influence in terms of real cooperation, that of culture.

It is from this thick and multilevel fabric that our strategic partnership is woven. Defense is only an individual thread of this partnership. It is often believed that our ties are founded on military-technical cooperation. On the contrary, it is our multilateral strategic ties and limitless trust for each other that make deep military-technical cooperation possible. It is worth noting that India and Russia share a common approach towards global terrorism and the principles of inadmissibility of double standards. The two nations also shared their position on the settlement in Afghanistan and the joint efforts of our defense ministries and special services in this sphere prove that the two countries hold similar positions on the settlement of regional conflicts, including those linked to anti-terror operations.

C. Trade Infrastructure in Ties with Russia

Development of trade & infrastructure is expected to become the top priority in the Indo-Russian cooperation. Developing the infrastructure would help increase bilateral investment in mutually interesting areas, such as hydrocarbon surveying, extraction and piping, pharmaceutics and biotechnology, maritime transportation, and harbor construction.

Russian Institutes have unique technologies, and they can be forwarded to India as a basis for joint ventures and joint work. For example, a special working group is now formed within the confederation to collect information about high technologies developed in research institutes, which might arouse interest in India. There is a long-term governmental program of economic co-operation between India and Russia in science and technologies. We are working in this context, attracting the private sector as well.

As paradoxical as it might seem, the fewer number of experts on India in Russia after 1991 and drastic cuts in spending on science has only had a slight effect on the quality and quantity of India-centric studies published over the past decade. The remarkable publications over the past ten years can be divided into three main areas; specific features of Indian culture and civilization; India's historical path, and India's modern development.

D. Indian Studies in Russia

In the first group of studies, we can single out the book *The Tree of Hinduism* (ed. I.P. Glushkova, 1999). The book analyses the sources of Hinduism, its major concepts, diverse cults and traditions from the nationwide to regional levels, and concrete manifestations of religion.

Students and Russians keen on Indian culture have also benefited from a wonderful encyclopedic dictionary *India*, compiled by O.G. Ultsiferov and published in 2003. Recently, I edited and prepared for publication (in collaboration with V.G. Khoros) a collective work entitled *Indian Civilization*. The book singles out the major values and institutions of Indian civilization; Indian civilization's historical dynamics; and Indian civilization in the modern world of globalization. In addition, the book contains a brief anthology of the main works of Indian civilization.

Among fundamental works on the history of ancient India we can single out two monographs by Professor Grigory Bongard-Levin, *Ancient Indian Civilization. History. Religion. Philosophy. Epos. Literature. Science. Dialogue. Among Cultures* (2000) and *Ancient India: History and Culture* (2001).

Among Works on medieval history Ye. Vanina's books *Ideas and Society in India in the 16th-18th Centuries* and *Medieval Urban Arts and Crafts of India. 13th-18th Centuries* are of special interest. They present a broad spectrum of the life of this huge Asian country in the given periods, and dwell on various problems of the country's religious, social and socio-economic development.

In examining modern processes, Russian scholars have focused on India's foreign policy. E. Komarov's book *In Russia and India*, and F. Yurlov's *Russia and India in the Changing World*, both published in 1998, compare Russia and India in the political and economic spheres. Works by V. Belokrenitsky, V. Moskalenko and T. Shaumyan – *South Asia: Conflicts and Geopolitics* (1999) and *South Asia in World Politics* (2003) – examine stages in the formation of the regional system and analyze its prospects. V. Sotnikov's *The Nuclear Problem in Indian-Pakistani Relations* (2003), is devoted to the problems of genesis of nuclear weapons in the region.

It is worrying that Russian scholars are giving less attention to India's internal development. A Volodin's monograph *India: Local Elections and the Development of the Polycentric-Type System* (1994) is the most obvious scholarly work that describes Indian internal political processes. B. Klyuvev's brilliant *Religion and conflict in India* covers confessional relations over thc past 50 years, coupled with an analysis of political processes. *India: The Country and Its Religions* (ed. Ye. Vanina, 2000) is devoted to specific regional problems.

On the whole, it can be said that the Russian readers' interest in India, its history, culture and present-day development has been met to some extent, not only by popular publications – a great many of which have appeared here of late – but also by fundamental scholarly studies.

Conclusion

Relations between India and Russia are a great and a precious asset of our multimillion people. Our task is to strengthen and fill it with new content. While developing relations of friendship between India and Russia today, we are doing a very good thing and not only for the present generation of our people, but also for the coming generations and for mankind's peaceful future.

There are numerous opportunities to expand our economic co-operation, above all in science and technologies, industry and strategic areas. We are in turn ready to establish stable business ties with Russian partners, in particular, pharmaceutics, bio-technologies, and healthcare. We need a more intensive exchange in each of these domains. We should regularly exchange visits and participate in exhibitions. Now we want to arrange a large-scale exhibition of Indian produce in Russia. We also intend to help Russian companies organize displays of their products and services at exhibitions held in India. We need to create a system of interaction between companies.

It has been proved that the prospects are bright of a spectacular breakthrough in economic ties in the field of trade in high-tech machinery and in establishment of joint ventures.

Russia deserves a place in the modern world, which would correspond to its rich history, people's creative potential and its prodigious size. Russia in a short period of time has established working democratic institutions in the country and has put an end to the old ideological and political identity of opinions, and has therefore taken the first steps towards a different life, towards new civilized norms.

For the first time in many decades, may be even centuries, they are not in conflict either with the whole world or with separate countries: they should learn to defend their positions and to win in tough competition, which reigns in the world and most of all on world markets.

The history of mutual visits of Indian and former Soviet Union leaders dates 50 years back. It began with the first visit by India's Prime Minister late Pandit Jawaharlal Nehru to the USSR in the summer of 1955 and USSR's Ex-President H.E. Leonid Breznev in 1961.

India and the Russian Federation have traditionally shared a close and friendly relationship that has today been elevated to a strategic partnership. In 2002 we have celebrated the 55th anniversary of the establishment a diplomatic relations between our two countries. It is significant that over the years, the multifaceted cooperation between India and the Russian Federation has deepened and diversified to mutual benefit. We look forward to the Russian state visit to India later during this year, which I and convinced will help the further diversification of our time-tested ties.

It is a matter of great satisfaction that mutual trust, confidence and understanding have been enduring characteristics of the India-Russia relationship. Particularly in recent years, we have made remarkable progress in expanding the scope and content of bilateral cooperation. The visit will give a strong impetus to the progress of our diverse bilateral initiatives and provide the opportunity to launch new projects. The tradition of an annual summit dialogue reflects the strength and vitality of our strategic partnership.

Our best wishes for continuing good health of Russian people, success in their high responsibility and for the progress and prosperity of the people of the Russian Federation. India and Russia are ready to implement ambitious projects. The Practice of personal meetings, telephone conversations, and exchange of messages has also taken a shape and altogether create a good infrastructure for the development of bilateral relations.

Our relations are free form ad hoc fluctuations; they have a character of strategic partnership. This does not imply that Moscow and Delhi must have no nuances or differences in their stances on this or that problem. That is an expected phenomenon, for the problems are complicated, multifaceted and call for negotiations. The differences in the approaches should not affect the Indo-Russian strategic relationship. Delhi and Moscow proceed from the fact that the strategic partnership between India and Russia in the international arena meets the interests of International stability.

i Special attention should be paid to tap cooperation of the sides in combating terrorism, religious extremism and separatism. This problem exists both in India and Russia, and in this case the assistance of the international community is necessary.

ii. Discussions on prospects for mutually beneficial strategic partnership and pointing out a present-day level of commerce below both countries potential.
iii. Regular talks between cultural, education and defense ministers of India and Russia. The talks should make it possible to make a substantial contribution not only to military technological cooperation, but also to coordination of actions in maintaining peace in all regions, particularly those close to our borders.
iv. Exhibition on the culture and life of Russia's nations from the 18th century till the present day will add to Indian's impressions of Russian culture.
v. Intensive programs of art festivals with its best samples of classic and modern art will bring happiness and produce bright and forgettable impressions of both countries' people.
vi. Identify mutually beneficial investment projects and negotiating financial logistics for these.
vii. Identify the crucial problems in baking cooperation for expansion of trade.
viii. Find out new ways of expanding bilateral trade and to chart new promising aspects of economic partnership, too
ix. Our trade protocols should be envisaged to expand the trade and should have cooperation in new areas, including diamond and computers, and strengthen banking arrangements and the nuclear energy tie-up.

We are tied together by mutual interest in literature and theatre, philosophy and, music, customs and traditions of both countries. The relations between India and Russia in the past and at present continue to reflect positive developments and close cooperation in political, trade, social and scientific spheres corresponds to the high degree of mutual respect and understanding of the two countries towards each other. Now even the field of numismatics adds a little to the positive trend in the bilateral Indian-Russian relations

REFERENCES

New Theme on Russian – Indian Affairs Vol. VII No.4, Oct.2005 & Vol. IV No:2, April-June 2001 published by Oleg Bondarr on behalf of the Information Dept. of Embassy of the Russian Federation in India, 2 Bhagawandas Road, New Delhi-110001. P.14-15

N. Srinivasan: "India discontent with Indo-Russian Economic Relations" Director General of the Confederation of Indian Industry (CII) New Theme on Russian Indian Relations

Sergei Lunev : "India Studies Flourishing in Russia" Researcher at the Russian Academy of Sciences Institute of the World Economy and International Relations, and professor at Moscow State University and the Moscow State Institute (University) of International Relations of the Foreign Ministry of the Russian Federation. Article published in New Theme on Russian-Indian Relations a quarterly journal Vol. VII No: 2, April-June, 2004 published

Dr. S.C. Sharma (1992): "Indo-Soviet Trade since Independence" published by Raadha Publications, New Delhi-110002.

Herald of Friendship – To mark the XX Anniversary of Comrade L.I. Breznev's First State visit to the Republic of India & 75th Birth Anniversary of comrade L.I. Breznev. Russian Language Students Association. Published by Soviet Cultural Centre, Madras.

16

The Dilemma of Ethnicity and Territoriality in Present Day Russia

Ranjana Banerjee

The year 1985 marked the beginning of a new era in Russian history. The two lexis perestroika and glasnost changed the whole scenario of Russia and the other C.I.S countries.Glasnost, the ideological liberation exposed the formerly barred expressions of grievances of all kinds in the Soviet press, including ethnic grievances. The mask of unity was thrown overnight and diversity took the plunge. In place of 'we the soviets,' rang the words 'we the Russians', 'we the Chechens', 'we the Armenians' and so on. Unity,equality,brotherhood were concepts bygone. The Russian researcher V.K. Malkova has shown how the concept of the ethnically understood "us" changed during perestroika. The "we" was associated with the national history; with its language, culture and economy--and with the territory of the group.[1] This marked the beginning of ethnic conflict in U.S.S.R.. Ethnic identity as mentioned below, is in a way "the means of legitimation and delegitimation of political power in transit societies, because it legitimates the national elites action and create necessary conditions for ethno-political mobilisation".[2] The politization of ethnicity,which began roughly in 1988, inflated with time and gradually took the shape of territorial conflict.

Today ethno-territorial conflict, a specific feature of Russia and other C.I.S countries, has become a cause of anxiety. By December 8, 1991 (the date of the official dissolution of the USSR), the number of registered ethno-territorial claims amounted to 168.[3]

However by turning over the pages of the Russian history we see that from the very beginning Russia has been a multiethnic society. Throughout the ages it has experienced the pressure of ethnic assimilation. Russia was the abode of numerous ethnic groups in the pre Soviet era, as well as during the Soviet rule. Thus, the question which arises in one's mind is - what is the cause of the emergence of these conflicts in recent times?

'There is a consensus amongst the experts, that many of the factors that contribute to conflict are derived from the legacies of the Soviet period in general - the legacy of institutionalized ethnicity, the nexus between ethnicity and territoriality, and the ethno-political hierarchy of inequalities in particular. A major role was played by the articulated ethno-hierarchical structure of the USSR "federation," i.e. the "matrioshka" type federalism. One of the fundamental innovations of federal state formation under Soviet rule was the Stalinist linkage of ethnicity, territory, and political administration. Ethnicity was institutionalized on the group level by the creation of a federation of ethno-territorial units, governed by local political elites and organized into an administrative hierarchy. The degree of economic, cultural, political, and many other rights and the opportunities to satisfy the interests of many people depended on the status that was ascribed to an ethnic group within the rigid structures of the USSR federation. "Only fifty-three of the more than one hundred Soviet nations were officially identified with a particular territory and so afforded rights by virtue of their national-territorial status--the so-called "titular" nationalities. The nature of these rights varied widely. Fifteen national groups were given the highest status of Soviet Socialist Republics (SSRs) or "Union Republics," which together included the entire nation. Directly accountable to and within the territories of the Union Republics, in order of descending status, were twenty Autonomous Soviet Socialist Republics (ASSRs), eight Autonomous regions (*oblasti*), and ten Autonomous districts (*okruga*). The rights of each of these formations were listed in the Soviet Constitution, including areas of dependence, guaranteed institutions, and rights of autonomy and – in the case of the Union Republics – secession. Finally, there were also "people without territory," i.e., without ethno-territorial formations of their own, which, under Soviet conditions, meant deprivation of any collective rights of the ethnic group".[4]

Establishing a separate autonomy for the relatively smaller ethnic groups was not feasible, in spite of the fact that they were confined to a specific territory; on the other hand some larger groups had to make do without a homeland of their own: these were the diasporas of different nationalities. There seem to have been two reasons for this exclusion. In most cases these diaspora groups did not live on a compact territory, but were widely dispersed and these groups belonged to nations that had their own separate nation - states elsewhere. But the relocation and assimilation of these ethnic groups could not eradicate them from their roots, their culture.

The other legacies of the past, which became a cause for such conflicts, are the "Russification" policy conducted in the USSR in the pre-*perestroika* period, on the integration type of development, and on relations between the dominant and subordinate groups, the socioeconomic inequity of different ethnic groups.

Consequently the collapse of authoritarian rule post *perestroika* removed the "totalitarian lid" which kept aflame ethnic tensions in control. The democratization of Soviet society resulted in the fact that in many regions of the USSR the dominant-subordinate relations between ethnic groups led to overt conflict. Confrontation between ethnic groups struggling for power, equal rights, and affirmation of their sociopolitical and cultural identities became a regular feature of this soil.

The other cause for this conflict is the legacy of "imposed ethnicity" by the Soviets. As states Dragunsky (1993): "The Russian empire was reborn and reconstituted in the structures of the Soviet Union, which functioned on the principles of ethnocratic hierarchy"[5] i.e. the "imposition of ethnicity", the introduction of obligatory inclusion of each individual's ethnic identity in his official documents (passports). This "imposed ethnicity" later became the major cause of political mobilization and activity of different social groups.

Soviet Union and post-Soviet Russia have experienced ethnic conflict with deep historical roots as well. Recent Russian literature analyzes the historical contexts and events that account for the deep-rooted conflicts in the North Caucasus. Hostility and territorial disputes between Russians and Chechens, as well as some other people of the North Caucasus, date back to the nineteenth century (more than the forty-year-long Caucasian War 1817-64). Khoperskaya and Chernous (1993) review the major landmarks in the political history of Russian-Northern Caucasian relations since the eighteenth century, focusing on the historical roots of the present-day ethnic conflicts in the region. According to these scholars "there have been two main trends in Russia's policies towards North Caucasian people since as early as the nineteenth century: the policies of force and the policies of liberal colonialism (colonial illuminism). The competition between these policies can be observed even today, particularly as suggested by recent dramatic developments in Chechnya".[6]

Repression of and discriminatory policy towards religion under the Soviet regime constitute another legacy that explains some of the causes of post-Soviet ethnic conflicts. The religious factor is evident in the relations between Russia and Tatarstan, Armenia and Azerbaijan, Georgia and Abkhazia, and North Ossetia and Ingushetia.

An important cause and factor influencing the dynamics of ethnic conflict in today's Russia is the rise of new central and local elites: the transformation of the "old guard" into new controller of power; which is apparent in the intensified struggles for power of regional elites in Bashkortostan, in Tatarstan, and in Siberian republics and other regions. National interests are usually interpreted by these titular elites as resurrection of the national language; national culture and religion.

The following categorization of ethno-territorial conflict in the present day Russia and the other C.I.S countries noticeably reflects on the multidimensional characteristics and the intensity of these ongoing conflict : (1) territorial conflict associated with the issue of reunification of separated ethnic groups (Nagorno-Karabakh and, partially, South Ossetia); (2) conflict stemming from the desire of an ethnic minority to exercise the right to self-determination by creating an independent state (Abkhazia); (3) restoration of territorial rights to those who had been subjected to forced deportation (the conflict between the Ossetians and the Ingush over the Prigorodnyi district); (4) territorial claims of a post-Soviet state to a neighboring successor state (claims of Estonia and Latvia to some areas of Russia's Pskov region); (5) conflicts that emerged as a result of arbitrary territorial changes made in the Soviet era (the Crimea and, potentially, boundary issues in Central Asia); (6) conflicts associated with the material interests of the ruling elites (Grozny or Kazan, on the one hand, and Moscow, on the other hand); (7) conflicts associated with factors of a historical nature, preconditioned by the traditions of a long-standing struggle for national liberation against the parent state (the confrontation of the Confederation of Mountain People of the Caucasus and the Russian administration); (8) conflicts caused by the presence of "deported people" on the territory of other republics history of Stalinist repressions and forced population transfers, particularly as these affected Kabardino-Balkaria, North Ossetia, Kalmykia, Dagestan, and other repressed (the Meskheti Turks in Uzbekistan, the Chechens in Kazakstan); (9) conflicts associated with discrimination against the ethnic Russian population in post-Soviet states; and (10) linguistic disputes disguising ethnopolitical grievances and status claims of ethnic groups (Gagauzia and the Trans-Dniester area within Moldova). [7]

The disparity in interethnic relations poses a serious threat to Russia and the other C.I.S countries. "Under the conditions of flourishing ethnic nationalism the multiple cultural identities represent a new reality that is menacing to the accustomed nomenclature of ethnic entitites".[8] To prevent the disruptive conflicts, to revive unity in diversity, it is desirable to introduce a new perception of nationalism that drifts away from ethnic nationalism towards civic nationalism, for one must not fail to remember, that unity, equality and brotherhood is not the catchphrase of the socialists, but the spirit of all caste, creed and religion.

REFERENCES

1. Pal Kolsto, University of Oslo, 'Territorializing Diasporas: The case of the Russians in the former Soviet Republics' printed in Millennium--Journal of International Studies, 1999. Vol. 28, No. 3, pp. 607-631.
2. Journal of Sociology and Social Anthropology, 1999, Vol. 2, Issue 1. available at: http://www.soc.pu.ru/publications/jssa/1999/1/abstracts.html-
3. Liina Areng, 'The Caucasus and Central Asia: Needs and Options for Stabilization', NATO Defense College, Edited by Dieter Ose and Laure Borgomano-Loup available at: www.ndc.nato.int/download/publications/monograph_16.pdf
4. Airat Aklaev, 'Causes and Prevention of Ethnic Conflict: An Overview of Post-Soviet Russian-Language Literature', Institute of Ethnology and Anthropology, Russian Academy of Sciences
   available at: wwics.si.edu/subsites/ccpdc/pubs/aklaev/1.htm
5. Ibid.
6. Ibid.
7. Ibid.
8. Valery Tishkov, 'Against the Rhetoric of Compaints: The Anthropology of Russian Transformations', Institute of Ethnology and Anthropology, New Market of Ethnic Identities
   available at: http://demography.narod.ru/opinions/tishkov.html

17

Transformation of the Silk Road Concept

With Reference toKyrgyzstan-India Relations

Indira Musaeva

Nowadays, the idea of the Silk Road is getting more and more popular and discussed although; today it has a nominal meaning compared to the original context. Silk Road's role then included being a cultural synergy between the East and the West. Buddhism also spread out from India along with trade of silk moving from East to West.

The Silk Road was the oldest ancient trade route that linked East and West. This transcontinental route linked the Roman Empire in the West with the imperial court of China. The Silk Road was the major highway for transporting material goods and knowledge between Europe, the Near East, India, and China — the four major centers of civilization at the time from the first millennium B.C. through the middle of the second millennium A.D. Over this period of almost 2000 years, exotic and commercial goods, skills, knowledge, and religion — as well as silk — crisscrossed the Eurasian continent, and shaped the course of European and Asian history and culture. China's vast western region was accessible to travelers along the classic Silk Road. The trade route was never called such until the term "Silk Road" was first used by the German scholar Baron Ferdinand von Richthofen in 1877 A.D. in his work "China".

Before the discovery of the sea route to India, the Silk Road was the most important connection between the East and West. It experienced its last great era during the time of the Mongol Empire. The best known segment of the Silk Road began in the old capitals of Luoyang and Xian (then called Chang'an, China), extending into Gansu Province reaching the Yellow River at Lanzhou, Tianshui, Zhangye, Jiuquan along the Hexi Corridor reaching Jiayuguan – the giant barrier of the Great Wall and the first key point of the route – Dunhuang in the west end of the Hexi Corridor of Gansu Province, which is one of the well-known Chinese historical and cultural cities, diverging into northern and southern routes that skirted the Central Asian Taklamakan Desert, converging to cross the Iranian plateau, and ending on the eastern shores of the Mediterranean in cities like Antioch and Tyre.

The Silk Road was first traveled by a court official Zhang Qian when he was sent by Han Wudi in the Han dynasty (206 BC-AD 220) on a diplomatic mission in order to seek allies against Xiongnu, who repeatedly invaded the Western Regions. However, on the way to the Western Regions, Zhang was captured by Huns and detained for ten years. After this, Zhang Qian escaped from Xiongnu's detention and continued his journey towards Central Asia. At that time, the local rulers were satisfied with their status and refused to ally with Han Empire. On the return journey, Zhang Qian and his delegation were again captured, and it was not until 125 B.C. that they arrived back in Changan.

In ancient times Kyrgyz people were one of the most powerful nomadic tribes that repeatedly violated the Chinese border and stimulated the Chinese to start building the Great Chinese Wall. Some of the Kyrgyz tribes set themselves free from the Hun domination and moved to the Enisei (Ene-sai-mother River, and Baikal Bai-Kol Lake) regions. There they formed their first state known as the Kyrgyz Kaganat, which existed from 6 to 13 AD. This was also the time when the Kyrgyz culture and the first written Kyrgyz language started to form, confirmed by the unique inscriptions on stone monuments. The Kyrgyz Kaganat collapsed as the result of a foreign invasion and the Kyrgyz people consequently lost their written language. One may infer that ancient Kyrgyz people had their civilization, since written script is a major indication of the existence of a civilization.

The first written evidence of the Kyrgyz people as a nation was found in Chinese chronicles dated from 2nd to 1st century B.C. According to Chinese sources, the Western Region including Djungaria, Ili district and Issyk-Kul Lake were known as the places of nomads. In this region powerful hordes were established. For 2200 years B.C. Yuechji people were there who occupied that place and forced out the Usuni people from north western borders of China, along with the Long Wall. The Chinese history left us some information about this country from Emperor Wudi's time, which was known as Hun's city – Chi-gu (at present a lost city in the territory of Kyrgyzstan). According to Iakinf, Chi-gu (which in Chinese means "Red Valley") was located in Ili Valley to the north-east of Issyk-Kul Lake (Issyk-Kul, in Chinese "Zhe-Hay", means "Hot Lake" in Kyrgyz).

According to Ch. Valihanov, Chi-gu was situated 610 lye north-west of Aksu and to the north-east of Issyk-Kul Lake. We have few sources about Chi-gu from Chinese travelers (Zhang Qian) and from others like Iakinf, Ch. Valihanov, N.M. Prjevalsky, V.M. Ploskih and also one Russian novel by Evgeny Kolesnikov.

The emperor was much interested in what they found. More expeditions were sent out towards the West over the following years. After a few failures, a large expedition managed to obtain some of the so-called `heavenly horses', which helped transform the Han cavalry. These horses have been immortalized in the art of the period, one of the best examples being the small bronze `flying horse' found at Wuwei in the Gansu Corridor, now used as the emblem of the China International Travel Service. Spurred on by their discoveries, the Han missions pushed further westwards, and got as far as Persia. They brought back many objects from these regions, in particular some of the religious artwork from the Gandharan culture, and other objects of beauty for the emperor.

By this process, the route from east to the west was opened up from Hun Dynasty. Zhang Qian is still seen by many to be the father of the Silk Road. Although the mission failed in its original purpose, the information Zhang Qian conveyed to China about Central Asia, and vice versa, made people in each area desire goods produced in the other. Thus, Zhang Qian introduced Central Asia, particularly the Huns in the territory of Kyrgyzstan and inaugurated the trade along the Silk Road.

On a historical-cultural plane, the territory of contemporary Kyrgyzstan formed in ancient times a common territory with Eastern Turkistan where Buddhism took deep root as far back as centuries II B.C. – IV AD and continued to retain influence in several regions for a long time. It is known from numerous sources that the earliest bearers of Buddhism along the route to the East were a large group of natives of Central Asia - Sogdians, Parthians, Khanguis. Of great historical and cultural significance was the activity of the Ak Shigao, a Parthian from Marghilan and crown prince of his country (who rejected the throne like Shakyamuni). He settled in Loyan in 148 AD and till 170 AD he worked on translation of Buddhist works into Chinese. He was undoubtedly the first historical apostle of Central Asian Buddhism. After him there followed a whole galaxy of interpreters of Indian holy texts and authors of new literary and historical works on Buddhist themes, who were known through works of Sanskrit, Khotai - Saka, Tibetan, Chinese, Sogdian and Tokhar literature.

Buddhism prevailed and the most outstanding monuments that were created were considerably distinctive and different from their Indian prototypes. Existence of famous icon painters of Buddhist paintings with Sogdian names and surnames indicating their Central Asian origin speaks in favor of this assumption.

Different researchers draw attention to the leading role of representatives of ancient Central Asian ethnos, who were the first to transfer Indian culture to the East. This is also true of Kyrgyzstan as well, where Buddhist monuments were discovered by A.N. Bernshtam during archaeological exploration of the whole territory of the Republic in 1933-1954. In the western gallery of the shrine (Ak Beshim) a sculpture of Sleeping Buddha was excavated in 1961 and in the southern gallery fragments of paintings were found on the wall.

After the 8th century, Buddhism in Kyrgyzstan did not revive as it did in Tibet, Eastern Turkistan and Far Eastern countries where this religion, beginning from X-XI centuries AD, entered a new phase in its development, undergoing local transformations. Ancient Yenisei Kyrgyz did not stand aside from the influence of Indian Buddhist culture in folklore, geographical names, and moral ethical code and of everyday life and ritual.

In India, before the coming of the Aryans, there, existed the Harappan Civilization. The civilization is also at first called the Indus Valley Civilization. The Harappan Civilization spread over a large area from Baluchistan to Gujarat. Some historians like Prof. B.B. Lal estimated that it covered the eastern valley of the river Indus, spreading over an area measuring 1,600 kilometres east to west and 1,100 Km. north to south. In other words, area covered by the Indus Civilization was much greater than its contemporary civilizations in Egypt and Sumeria.

During the reign of the Kushans, who dominated the areas of Hindu Kush into Kabul, Gandhara, northern Pakistan and north-western India, trade between India, China, Parthia and the Roman Empire became extensive. This provided an ideal medium for the further spread of Buddhism. From the 2nd century BC to the 2nd century AD, Buddhism gradually developed in north western India and the great Kushan ruler, Kanishka, who reigned from 144-172 A.D., was converted. Under his influence, Gandhara, a Buddhist settlement, flourished and created a distinctive Graeco-Buddhist art form, which affected the arts in Central Asia and eastward in the first four centuries of our era.

Kyrgyzstan's ancient Silk Road connections with India have been established on the basis of archaeological sites existent in Naviket, Sujab, Ak Beshim, Balasaghun etc. in Kyrgyzstan, by Voropoeva and Goryacheva. Few Buddhist images (VII - VIII century A.D.) found in Naviket town 35 km., away from Bishkek, are preserved and displayed in the Archaeological museum of Kyrgyz Slav's University and historical museum in Bishkek.

The fact that the Naviket finds resemble the finds in Adjna Tepe, Fayaz Tepe, Kara Tepe and Merv in other Central Asian Republics, offers the conclusive evidence of close historic-cultural links between India and Central Asia. The Great Silk route was not only a means of transferring goods but also the exchange of ideas between cultures and civilizations.

Apart from being a major trading route, the Great Silk Road was of immeasurable significance for the establishment and maintenance of diplomatic relations. Today, while talking about the revival of the Silk Road as a historico-cultural and socio-economic complex, one can not help mentioning the growing process of globalization and increasing interdependence that makes it more vital. The dynamic development of political, trade and economic relations needs to get strengthened if mutually beneficial partnerships are to be developed between all the States on the Silk Road. From this point of view there is a need for focusing on the development perspectives of Kyrgyzstan and India relations.

The Silk Road, after a long period of hibernation, has acquired importance again recently. The trade route itself is also being reopened. The sluggish trade between the peoples of Xinjiang and those of the former Soviet Union has been developing. The circle envelops the five former Soviet Central Asian republics (Uzbekistan, Turkmenistan, Kazakhstan, Kyrgyzstan and Tajikistan), Armenia, Azerbaijan and part of Georgia, Afghanistan, Pakistan, northwest India, Tibet and Xinjiang in China, and southern Russia. To the north, the circle passes to the north of the Trans-Siberian in Omsk. To the northwest, it crosses the Urals and descends parallel to the Volga until it crosses Georgia to the west and descends through the Turkish border towards Iraq. To the southwest, the circle crosses the Persian Gulf and traverses the Indian Ocean towards the south. To the east, it crosses Tibet and Chinese Xinjiang until it gets to Russia's extreme south.

The railway connecting Lanzhou to Urumchi has been extended to the border with Kazakhstan, where on 12th September 1990 it was finally joined to the former Soviet railway system, providing an important route to the new republics and beyond. This Eurasian Continental Bridge, built to rival the Trans-Siberian Railway, has been constructed from Lian Yun Gang city in Jiangsu province (on the East China coast) to Rotterdam; the first phase of this development has already been completed, and the official opening of the railway was held on 1st December 1992. It already promises to be at least 20% cheaper than the route by sea and at 11,000 kilometers is significantly shorter. From China the route passes through Kazakhstan, Russia, Belarus and Poland, before reaching Germany and the Netherlands. The double-tracking of the railway from Lanzhou to the border of the C.I.S. has now been put high on the Chinese development priority list.

On the other sides, there are certain projects being worked out to revive the Silk Road. The Silk Road Foundation is an on-going project to compile an annotated list of all the important travelers on the Silk Road. The travels are arranged in chronological order. Each entry will include a brief description, highlighting where possible issues such as where the person went, and why the journey was undertaken and so on.

Silk Road Seattle is a public education project using the "Silk Road" theme to explore cultural interaction across Eurasia from the beginning of the Christian Era to the Seventeenth Century. The principal goal is to provide, via the Internet, materials for learning and teaching about the Silk Road.

China and the four Central Asian countries located on the Silk Road are seeking to strengthen their co-operation to revitalize the famous ancient trading route. The Silk Road Regional Program (SRRP), a joint initiative between United Nations Development Program (UNDP) and the governments of China, Kazakhstan, Kyrgyzstan, Tajikistan and Uzbekistan, will be carried out in three areas – trade, investment and tourism – with an aim to revive traditional economic cooperation. The project will encourage public private partnership in selected fields such as infrastructure, tourism and hotel development through a Silk Road Investment Forum, an annual or biannual event to attract international and Chinese investment. Througl the project, the UNDP and WTO will identify eight to ten cities along the route to award the title of "UN Silk Road City" to encourage their commitment and long-term planning for the protection of cultural assets.

Being located at the same larger geographical region, which directly corresponds to the close neighborhoods, the two countries share common approaches on many international problems such as struggle against terrorism and extremism of all forms and manifestation, organized crime, illegal drug and arms trafficking. Especially, after the "Tulip revolution" in Kyrgyzstan on 24th March 2005, and after the SCO summit held on 25th July, 2005, in Alma-Ata, there is a trend to strengthen the trade and security cooperation. According to political observers, India and Pakistan might be the members of SCO in the future, in which case SCO's power will significantly increase.

The idea of reviving of the ancient Silk Road is not new either for India, or for Kyrgyzstan. In the era of economic globalization and ambition to expand trade, Kyrgyzstan is looking for expanding economic relations with neighboring countries, in Southeast Asia and South Asia.

The Doctrine of the President of the Kyrgyz Republic, "The Silk Road Diplomacy", declared on 16th September 1998, is the most articulated foreign policy concept for revival of the Silk Road on a new basis and level. Diversification of transport and communication is reflected in the Doctrine as the core issue in establishing and continuing of the economic, cultural and transport links between Asian and European countries. Successful implementation of the Doctrine could promote an unprecedented expansion of trade relations of both sides, as the member countries of the WTO, as well as provide exclusively wide access to the new markets and strengthen the economies of Kyrgyzstan and India. India's experience in the development of tourism, agriculture, industries, trade, education and science and, that of information technologies in particular, can be developed in Kyrgyzstan and promote the irreversibility of mutual relationships between the two countries.

To strengthen and support the bilateral trade and economic relations, the Indo-Kyrgyz Joint Commission on Trade and Economic and Science and Technical cooperation and the Joint Business Council have been formed. During several meetings it was decided to cooperate in various fields of trade and economy, including machinery building, information technology, food processing. The last meeting of the Joint Business Council took place on May 2002. In the sphere of trade-economic relations some progress is noticeable. In 2000-2001, the volume of bilateral trade turnover was 22.25 million US dollars compare to 3.9 million US dollars in 1996-1997 and 11.77 million US dollars in 1998-1999.

Along with political and economic relations there is an evident interest in enhancing relations in the cultural sphere. The Indian epic *Mahabharata* was translated into Kyrgyz by A. Kemelbaev and Kyrgyz epic *Manas* into Hindi by Prof. Varyam Singh (1997). The books *Post-Soviet Condition. Chingiz Aitmatov in 90s* by Prof. Rashmi Doraiswami and *The Epos "Manas": Across the Millenium* by J. Sindhu published recently, are significantly conducive to this relationship. Moreover, as mentioned earlier, India also has its historical links that go beyond the Indo-Soviet Treaty of Friendship of 1971 to the Mughal period and Silk Road.

Reviving the Silk Road directly depends on contemporary requirements of cultural and economic integration as well as globalization. Today Central Asia, which is in the heart of the Silk Road, is facing diverse economic, political and ideological bulks and pressures. Ancient Silk Road had a unique role in foreign trade and political relations, stretching far beyond the bounds of Asia itself. It has left its mark on the development of civilizations on both sides of the continent. There are several potential areas for Kyrgyz-Indian joint cooperation like food processing, information technology, tourism, pharmaceuticals, chemicals, cosmetics, engineering goods, electronics, banking service, and mining. But the existing cooperation needs to enhance in a strategic and long-term cooperation framework within a view to increase investment in energy resources and develop cost-effective transport corridors in near future.

However, the main efforts of politicians and policy makers should be to maintain stability and peace in this geopolitical space. Ancient territories that comprised the Silk route had a rich history and can revive a link between the East and the West with the benefit of modern transport, communication, culture and trade developments. With the latest developments and the changes in political and economic systems, Central Asia and the neighboring region might see international trade flourishing once again.

REFERENCES

1. Abramzon S.M. Kyrgyz and their etnogenetic and historic-cultural relationships. Nauka, Leningrad. 1971.
2. Valihanov Ch. "Zapiski o Kirgizah". Sobranie Socinenyin 5 toms. Tom 2, Gl. Redaktcia of Kazakh Sovetskaya encyclopedia, Alma-Ata, 1985.
3. Shefer E. The golden peach of Samarkand. Book on foreign miracles of Han Empire, Glav. Redakcia Vsemirnoy Litaratury, Moscow, 1981.

18

The Kyrgyz Revolution
Before and After

Konuralp Ercilasun

After the collapse of the Soviet Union in 1991, new independent states have emerged in Central Asia. These Central Asian states, which are consisting from Kazakstan, Kyrgyz Republic, Tajikistan, Turkmenistan and Uzbekistan, have encountered some serious problems. These problems were originated from the Soviet legacy and from being a new modern state. Because of these problems and the fear of unstableness in the region, the leaders of these countries have adopted a strict rule. This way of rule gradually resulted in the emerging of the authoritarian regimes in the region.

Kyrgyz Republic is one of the small and relatively poor countries in the region. Just after the independence, the Kyrgyz Republic and the Akayev regime appeared to be the most open and democratic regime in the region. It was seen as a relatively democratic island surrounded by authoritarian regimes from all directions. In 1995 I talked to a Kyrgyz intellectual. During the conversation, he has criticized Akayev for not being democratic. I argued that Kyrgyz administration is the most democratic one in Central Asia and it would take time to reach a full democracy for a new independent state. He answered that on the contrary Akayev would learn and imitate the neighbouring authoritarian regimes if there were not a strong opposition. After the years passed it seems that this Kyrgyz intellectual's words came true.

I will try to analyze the political turmoil before the revolution, the occurrence of revolution and the developments after the revolution. In the internet site of the Radio Liberty, there is a well-organized and detailed chronology of the political developments in the Kyrgyz Republic since 1990.[1] I will try to make a short summary of these developments after the Batken incident and will analyze the political turmoil and Akayev's path to authoritarianism. This chronology and summary is necessary for understanding the developments in the Kyrgyz Republic. The parts that explain the occurrence of the revolution and the afterwards depend on my observations, observations of a foreigner who was in Bishkek during the revolution and who has a similar cultural mentality with Central Asian people.

Before: Path to Authoritarianism

There is an important turning point in the path from relative democracy to authoritarianism. This turning point is the Batken incident in 1999. At the beginning of the August of that year, an armed group of 20 to 30 men had some clashes with the Kyrgyz border guards. They took some hostages although they have been forced to withdraw. Towards the end of the month, 1,000 armed militants crossed back into the southern regions of the Kyrgyz Republic and they took dozens hostage including four Japanese geologists. A ransom was paid and the Japanese geologists were released.[2] These clashes were a defeat of the Kyrgyz army against an armed group. This incident showed the weakness of the security forces and of the country. Thus, the administrative elite have begun to move towards the authoritarian regime gradually.

Batken incident not only caused a change in the thought of the administrative elite, but also marked a beginning for continuous opposition rallies in the country. After this year plenty of demonstrations and rallies against the government have taken place with different motives in different regions. However the common point of these demonstrations is to back any political figure against the government.

In March 2000, there were demonstrations in the favour of Feliks Kulov. Feliks Kulov had run for parliamentary elections and lost according to the results of the Central Election Committee. Demonstrations continued until April when police broke up them. In August Kulov announced his intention to run for the presidency. Separately from these political events, clashes in Southern Kyrgyzstan took place again in that summer. The Central Election Committee refused to register Feliks Kulov as candidate for the presidency in September. When Kulov planned to attend a seminar in the United States, it was ruled that he could not leave the country.[3] So, the events in 2000 show that Kulov has already taken his part as a well-known opposition leader. He was subjected to trial and was sentenced to seven years in jail. In December another political figure, Kurmanbek Bakiev, also appeared when he was appointed as Prime Minister.

In March 2001 Topchubek Turgunaliev, another political figure was sentenced to six years in jail for plotting to kill President Akayev. Akayev pardoned him after a few months. In the summer of that year again clashes took place in the southern part of the country.[4]

In the global sense, 2001 was the year of the terrorist attacks in the United States. This incident also affected Kyrgyzstan. The Kyrgyz Republic took a quick move and opened a base to US troops for operations in Afghanistan.

The beginning of 2002 marked by charges against Azimbek Beknazarov and this time, demonstrations took place in support of him. In March there are mass protests in Aksy district which made Kurmanbek Bakiev, the then Prime Minister, to fly to Jalal-Abad and investigate.[5] This Aksy incident has left a serious trace in the relations between the government and the opposition.

In May there was another incident took place. When Akayev government had made an agreement with China and ceded a part of land to this country, Deputy Azimbek Beknazarov protested it. Then many supporters of Beknazarov made mass protests and blocked roads. The protests and may be the difference of opinion with Akayev forced Kurmanbek Bakiev to resign and Nikolai Tanaev has become the new prime minister. Protests have continued in the different places of the country. This time the figure that was supported is Azimbek Beknazarov. This year also marked the public announcement of Akayev saying that he would not run for presidency again. Another figure during the end of the year was Usen Sadykov whose application for running for an empty seat in the parliament has been rejected.[6]

In the beginning of 2003, it is announced that a referendum would take place for the amendments of the constitution. This has become a new issue between the opposition and the government. Opposition argued that the time is too short for the referendum and protest the decision. During the end of the January the US has also expressed concerns over the referendum advocating that the draft constitution contained a number of provisions that fall short of international standards, would further concentrate power in the presidency and weaken the role of civil society. OSCE also expressed his opinion on referendum which was nearer to the opposition's ideas.[7]

In the second half of 2003 Akayev who was unsure about the secret intentions of the US came closer to Russia. The sides signed an agreement for Russian command of Kant base and the Russian troops arrived just after two weeks. It was announced that the US-base was temporary while the Russian base was permanent. So, we can see that the restlessness in the country and the opposition backing statements from the US, forced Akayev to choose his side. He quickly tried to balance the US influence by the presence of the Russian troops.

2004 passed with the preparations for the parliamentary elections which would take place in the following year.

When we sum up the 5 years before the revolution, we can easily notice that there was a real political instability in the country. We can summarize the main points of this instability as follows:

1. Mass protests have periodically taken place in the first half of almost every year since 1999, and 2002 was a year of continuous protests.
2. Clashes with some armed groups have taken place periodically for three summers after 1999.
3. The administrative elite gradually moved to centralization of power against these events. However, the more centralization of power brought more protest against the government and in turn it brought more steps to the path of authoritarianism. This process made the front against Akayev grow bigger and wider.
4. The other move of Akayev was to find an outside ally which would guarantee the stability and the unity of the country. This ally was the US first, but after suspected from this country he came close to Russia.

A Sudden Revolution

When we come to 2005 the entire world was watching the Kyrgyz Republic. After the public movements in Georgia, Ukraine and Lebanon in a short period, the question was; which country would be next? The first election in the region in that year was the parliamentary election of Kyrgyzstan and in the autumn there would be a presidential election.

While approaching the parliamentary election in February, there were complaints from the opposition arguing that the election would be unfair as the candidacy of many opposition figures had been rejected. These complaints could not be heard from the KTR, the official Kyrgyz broadcasting channel. Only, they could be known from the opposition newspapers which could hardly be found. Meanwhile, many government figures were excluded and joined to the opposition. The Akayev government became a very little clique which was represented by the Akayev family.

After the first round of the parliamentary election in February, there were some protests in the beginning of the March. According to the election results there was a little success for the opposition; so, the opposition has protested the government for being unfair in the elections. They were demanding the repetition of the election.

On the 16th of March the ambassador of the US made a press conference with interesting remarks. Firstly he repeated his mission-statement which he had also expressed a few months ago. He said:

> As I have said before, my mission as U.S. Ambassador here has been to support the efforts of the people and government of Kyrgyzstan to promote a stable, prosperous and democratic society.
> Frankly, I was surprised last fall when some commentators questioned this statement, as if it somehow was inappropriate for a foreign diplomat to speak in this manner. For I consider these to be shared goals with both the people and government of Kyrgyzstan, and I am very proud of the work that the dedicated men and women in my Embassy perform toward this end.[8]

On a question related with the presidential election that was supposed to be took place in the autumn, he said:

> President Akayev has said he will not run [for the presidency], and we respect that. The constitution says that he cannot run, and we respect that. President Akayev has

> said he will not change the constitution, and we respect that pledge, for to our thinking, constitutions should be changed rarely and with great care. It seems to me, given these facts, that it would be highly contradictory if President Akayev permitted his supporters to launch a campaign to change the constitutional ruling on term limits. President Akayev has done a great deal to develop a modern Kyrgyzstan in the last 14 years, so he will leave a legacy that he should be proud of. I also think his decision to step down this fall would mark a major advance in the development of Kyrgyzstan's democracy, and serve as a powerful example to other states in the region.[9]

So it is clearly seen that in the global sense, the US was pushing a change in the presidency in 2005.

At the 18th of March, the government lost the control of the Osh and Jalal-Abad provinces, but still there were no incidents took place in Bishkek. The tensions went up after the 20th of March. There were some rumours that clashes had taken place and there were deaths from the opposition and from the police.

In the morning of the 22nd of March I went to buy bread from a bakery. Interestingly, the bakery which I had always gone was closed. So I went the nearby one. When I had entered inside, I noticed that the baker was listening to the Radio Liberty which was openly backing the opposition. The exited announcer in the radio was speaking on the events that had taken place in Osh. She was saying "there haven't been a single gun-shut in Osh, there haven't been a single death in Osh; do not believe the news reporting some deaths and clashes". It was a surprise for me to see the baker's intention in Bishkek, in such a de-politicized place.

World televisions broadcasted the turmoil in Osh and Jalal-Abad in which could be seen the throwing of some Molotov cocktails at the same day. Thus, KTR felt obliged to broadcast the same images. However, the presentation of the events was totally different from the world televisions.

In the public square of Bishkek there was another demonstration backing the government and Akayev. This demonstration was not so lively. Akayev made a speech and said that the demonstrations in Osh and Jalal-Abad should dissolve, the requests of the demonstrators were illegal, and could not be accepted. He added that he did not use any force to suppress the demonstrations and would not use in the future.

There were rumours saying that the police and the military forces had joined to the opposition in the 23rd of March. There was a small demonstration at the central part of Bishkek which was suppressed by the police. Akayev appointed a new Minister of Internal Affairs who immediately made a pres conference, aggressively accused the opposition and announced that he would use force to suppress all the demonstrations. The response came immediately from the opposition. Opposition leaders announced that the government ignored and disregarded their demands totally, so they would march to Bishkek in the following day.

And the revolution... The opposition gathered at the two entrance of the Bishkek city. The dealers of the Osh Bazaar -the biggest marketplace inside the city- gave up their business and joined to the demonstrators. Demonstrators began to march to the centre of Bishkek where the Presidential Office placed. There are some rumours that groups of young people plunged into these groups and activated them for marching to the centre. Meanwhile, another demonstration was taking place at the public square backing Akayev. All the police force was ordered to defend the Presidential Office and went there.

Marching groups grew bigger with the joining of the Bishkek people. They came in front of the Presidential Office without any obstacle. This situation indicates that a considerable amount of military forces have already given up and have begun to back opposition. Opposition groups have seized the Presidential Office after a short tumult. Another target of the opposition was the KTR and after capturing the television they began to express themselves from the live broadcast. It was announced that the director of KTR had already sided with the opposition as early as two days before the revolution.

After the seizure of the Presidential Office it was understood that Akayev had fled away. So, the opposition has come to the power. The success of revolution was sudden and unexpected, even for the oppositionists themselves. After the revolution Roza Otunbaeva, one of the leaders of the opposition, has expressed that their aim was not the seizure of the power. They had only wanted to force Akayev for renewing the Parliamentary Elections. However, she said, they decided to march to Bishkek when the government had announced that they were an illegal movement.

One of the characteristics of the Kyrgyz revolution which make it different from the Georgia and the Ukraine cases was the leadership of the opposition. The revolution was so sudden that the opposition did not have the time for producing a single, powerful leader. So, in the first 24 hours of the revolution there was an uncertainty on the leadership of the opposition. This uncertainty was partly solved when Kurmanbek Bakiev was appointed as acting President.

The uncertainty in the leadership has caused confusion among the revolutionaries and has influenced the first decisions in the power. Plenty of political developments happened during the broadcast of KTR. Deputies of the previous parliament were called to hold a session and to decide a date for the new parliamentary elections at the evening of the revolution day. After sometime passed another announcement was made via KTR. The revolutionaries called Akayev to send his resignation. They argued that these steps were required in order to elect a legal parliament and a legal president. However, after sometime passed these steps were forgotten and the revolution made its own laws. An acting president, acting prime minister and an acting government were appointed. So, we can say that there were some unique aspects of Kyrgyz Revolution:

1. There was not a single, strong leader of the movement. Feliks Kulov who has the most support in the public was in prison and could not determine the path of the movement. Instead there was a group of middle-powered leaders who have not a complete control of the public.
2. The motives, the ideas and the demands between these leaders were not in unity.
3. In the beginning of the protests, opposionists clearly asked for the cancellation of the parliamentary election. The goal was to have a considerable number of seats in parliament as this parliament was supposed to elect the president. There was no intention to force Akayev to resign. In Georgia and Ukraine the protests in all over the country and in the capitals have taken several months. However, that was not the case in Kyrgyzstan. The protesters come across almost

no resistance by the police in Bishkek. They easily came to the Presidential Office. They entered inside with some small clashes, and it came out that Akayev had fled away. This was an unexpected event by protesters. The revolutionaries freed Kulov. After a few days of confusion it has appeared that the parliament was not dissolved, it preserved its position.

4. The revolutionaries made announcement for Akayev to sign his resignation and send to them. This was also a different move in the concept of revolution. Revolutions have their own laws. Generally, they don't need the official resignation of the previous government.
5. The main motives of the Kyrgyz revolution were the dissatisfaction of the opposition with the government, the exclusion of some previous important political figures and the poverty among the people.

After the Revolution

The political uncertainty has continued the following few months. The main concern was whether there would be a compromise between Kurmanbek Bakiev and Feliks Kulov, two outstanding figures of the opposition movement. They reached a compromise before the Presidential election in the summer. They have agreed upon the presidency of Bakiev and the premiership of Kulov. So, the election in the summer 2005 was an easy victory for Bakiev who got 89% of the votes.

After the presidential election it can be noticed that political instability continues, but it is not like the situation before the revolution. The former government had lost public support, so it could not stand up against the protests. Now, there is a high support for this new government, so protests do not make so much danger for the administrative elite. However, there were no radical changes in some aspects of administrative elite. After the independence, Akayev had not been able to change radically the Soviet-way of thinking, bureaucracy and mentality. This situation is the same with the new government as this transition requires more time and gradual changes.

In the social aspect, there have been some changes in the attitudes of the people in Bishkek after the revolution. The de-politicized Bishkek has faded away, politics has become the main topic of interest in every place, but it has only lasted for a few months and then it has returned to the former situation.

In the economic aspect, it seems that there is some revival in economy as there are more and more market places opened. Importation of the consuming goods has become more. So, as a consuming economy there can be noticed some improvements.

Another change after the revolution was a small increase in the salaries of all civil servants such as doctors, teachers, etc. This was a move to gain support among the public as the revolution had gotten a significant support from the poor people.

In the January of this year (2006) government released a decree calling universities and institutions to evaluate the revolution. At the end of the January, many discussion panels and conferences on the revolution were organized. Many achievements and shortcomings of the revolution have been stated in these discussions.

As an example, one of these discussions was the *Conference on the Sovereign Kyrgyzstan and Its Future* which took place in the Manas University at January, 31. Many aspects of the Kyrgyz revolution and the afterwards were discussed in this conference, such as the discussions on the constitution, the economic situation after the revolution and the place of the youth in the revolution.

During these discussions on the revolution Kusein Isaev, a sociologist, stated that the corruption and the tribalism, the main problems of the Kyrgyz society, have not been disappeared yet. They were not reduced either.[10] A political scientist Kubanychbek Idinov stated another shortcoming. He said that the Kyrgyz economy shrank 0.6% in 2005, and he added that this is normal as if there is a revolution in a country, the economy will go down in the short-term.[11]

As a result, the Batken incident in 1999 was an important turning point which affects politics of Kyrgyzstan. Mass protests and clashes with some armed groups have periodically taken place almost every year since 1999, and 2002 was a year of continuous protests. The administrative elite gradually moved to centralization of power against these events. However, the more centralization of power brought more protest against the government and in turn it brought more steps to the path of authoritarianism. This process made the front against Akayev grow bigger and wider.

The opposition grew stronger before the parliamentary elections in 2005. After the first round of the elections the opposition has started to organize mass protests and demanded to renew the elections. When the government ignored this demand and accused the opposition of acting illegally, protesters marched to the capital and the revolution has taken place. The motives of the Kyrgyz revolution were the dissatisfaction of the opposition with the government, the exclusion of some previous important political figures and the poverty among the people. There was not a single, strong leader of the movement. Instead there was a group of middle-powered leaders who have not a complete control of the public. The motives, the ideas and the demands between these leaders were not in unity.

After the revolution political uncertainty has continued the following few months. However, now there is a confidence to the government in the public. The shortcomings of the government can be expressed freely, not behind the doors. Although the macroeconomic figures are either went back or made no progress during this time, it can easily be seen that there is a revival of some aspects of the economy. For example, the variation of the consuming goods or the beginning of many new constructions such as buildings or bigger markets can be noticed. On the other hand, the corruption and the tribalism are still seen as the main obstacles to the success for the Kyrgyz government.

REFERENCES

1. Radio Liberty Report (www.rferl.org/specials/kyrgyzelections/timeline. asp)
2. Radio Liberty Report (www.rferl.org/specials/kyrgyzelections/timeline 1999.asp)
3. Radio Liberty Report (www.rferl.org/specials/kyrgyzelections/timeline 2000.asp)
4. Radio Liberty Report (www.rferl.org/specials/kyrgyzelections/timeline 2001.asp)
5. Radio Liberty Report (www.rferl.org/specials/kyrgyzelections/timeline 2002.asp)
6. *Ibid.*
7. Radio Liberty Report (www.rferl.org/specials/kyrgyzelections/timeline 2003.asp)
8. Ambassador Stephen M. Young's Pres Conference at AKI Pres Agency, 16 March 2006.
9. *Ibid.*

10. Kusein Isaev, "Азыркы Кыргызстан элдик ыңкылаптан кийин" (Contemporary Kyrgyzstan: After the Revolution), paper presented in *Эгемендүү Кыргызстан жана анын келечеги Илимий-практикалык конференция* (*Conference on the Sovereign Kyrgyzstan and Its Future*), 31 January 2006, Bishkek.
11. Kubanychbek Idinov, "Элдик ыңкылаптан кийинки Кыргызстандын экономикасынын абалы жана анын келечектеги өнүгүш жолдору жөнүндө" (Economy of Kyrgyzstan: The Contemporary Situation and the Future Developments after the Revolution), paper presented in *Эгемендүү Кыргызстан жана анын келечеги Илимий-практикалык конференция* (*Conference on the Sovereign Kyrgyzstan and Its Future*), 31 January 2006, Bishkek.

19

Cultural Revivalism in Present Uzbekistan

Tashmirza Khalmirzaev

After gaining its independence in 1991, Uzbekistan faced multi dimensional tasks. One such challenge was in the sphere of culture. It was realized that the need of the hour was to look at Uzbekistan's history, because "there is no future, without knowing the past", in order to do justice to the rich cultural, religious and moral values, which, during the Soviet time, in many cases, were ignored or misinterpreted. For example, ideas and works of our ancestors like *Imam Bukhari, Naqshbandi, Khwaja Ahmad Yassavi* – whose contribution to Islamic teachings and mankind's civilization was undisputable – were projected, as they *preached religious fatalism, mysticism and distracted people from the class struggle.*

In the beginning of the 20th century, some progressive minded local intellectuals like Behbudi, Munavvar Qori, Avloniy, Abdur-Rauf Fitrat started the *Enlightenment Movement* in Uzbekistan, which is mostly known as *Jadidlar Harakati* in Uzbek. The founders of the movement wanted to awaken the Uzbek society, bring about a cultural and national rebirth and to inculcate into the people a sense of self identity. These enlighteners strongly believed that fundamental changes in society would be possible only by the spread of mass education. They started opening schools, publishing text books, introducing modern European subjects in their curriculums, opening different centers, theaters and societies like *Milliy Istiqlol* (National Independence) *or Milliy Ittihod* (National Unity).

Behbudi's plan was called the "Cultural Independence of Turkistan". The importance of the press was realized as a vital resource for spreading information and education in society, and therefore newspapers in Uzbek language were also printed. But the noble endeavors of the *Jadids* were brutally disrupted by officials, as *propagating hostile ideology* and leaders of the movement - genuine patriots of the nation, were subjected to tortures, exiled from Uzbekistan and almost all of them were killed. (Here, in connection with *Jadids'* movement in Uzbekistan one may recall activities of Ram Mohan Roy in India, who had the same goal - to educate people and enlighten the Indian society. Fortunately, unlike the Uzbek *Jadids*, Roy was not executed).

In the 1920s-30s there was also a widespread armed unrest in Uzbekistan, called *Basmachi Movement*, which was declared to be *reactionary* and *anti-national*. During 1937-1940, thousands of Uzbek intellectuals, the cream of the nation, writers and even ordinary people, became the victims of the regime for their *nationalistic ideas* or *glorifying the feudal past*.

The sacrifices made by the Uzbek people on the road to Independence of the country were not in vain. In present-day Uzbekistan, the victims of the Soviet system have been declared the true champions of the nation, who devotedly struggled for the Independence of the country. This was made official in May 1999, when the President's Decree "On immortalizing the memory of those, who sacrificed their lives for the liberation of the country and people" was promulgated. Accordingly, all those who were unlawfully subjected to repressions during the Soviet time have now been acquitted and rehabilitated.

The year 1991, along with political independence, brought cultural and religious freedom to the Uzbek people and liberated them from the Soviet past. Fundamental changes in society made a great impact on hearts and minds of people and gave a powerful impetus to rebirth of moral, ethic and cultural values of the nation. In order to fully comprehend a national self identity, one has to restore the broken links between generations by applying to the past and the history of the soil. In this respect the importance of literature comes to the forefront.

Literature

During Soviet times, themes of freedom, struggling for it or depicting of heroes of the past, were like *persona non grata* for Uzbek literature. For example, the famous Uzbek prose writer Pirimqul Qadirov was attacked and severely criticized "for his mistakes made in the book" in official circles as well as the mass-media for his marvelous novel on Zahiruddin Babar.

Now in Uzbek literature one can witness real cultural renaissance. Themes of freedom, patriotism, approach to the past, destiny of an ordinary man, moral-ethic values have become main topics of the literature.

After gaining independence, and specifically within the first 10-12 years, quite a number of merit literary works had been produced on these subjects in prose. To start with, one can mention the *Short Stories* of popular Uzbek writer Asqad Mukhtar, works of Shukur Kholmirzaev, writings of well known Odil Yaqubov or Sayid Ahmad, which are considered *a new phenomenon* in Uzbek literature by the public and the critics alike. The lives and deeds of above mentioned great representatives of Uzbek people became the main theme for Uzbek writers to produce new novels and novelettes on.

Some ten years ago, a new type of literature under the heading *The Heroes of Sovereignty* was brought into publication. Prominent personalities of the past, champions for national freedom, representatives of *Jadidism* and *Basmachi* movements, victims of repressions carried out on a big scale during the 1930-40s became main characters for the new Uzbek fiction. Among prominent writings produced on great historical persons, a few literary works may be mentioned here - Khayriddin Sultan's *Baburi Noma,* Abdulla Aripov's *Sahib Qiron,* Sadulla Siyoyev's on *Khwaja Ahmad Yassaviy* or a novel of Naim Karimov, dedicated to the first Uzbek novelist *Abdulla Qodiriy*, who was also killed during those tragic years. The above-mentioned *Basmachi Movement,* mass repressions got real projection in works of Shukur Khalmirzaev and others. Close to it were novels and stories, giving a true picture of *Jadidism.* Till now, over 30 books have been published on the subject, which became very popular amongst the Uzbek readers.

In poetry, particular attention is now being given to the idea of freedom – freedom of the motherland as well as personal freedom. This is not a new phenomenon in poetry; previously expression was more or less in between the lines. This idea was expressed openly and fearlessly, perhaps for the first time, during the Soviet time in Erkin Vahidov's masterpiece *Ozbegim* (My Uzbek). It was treated at that time as an outburst in Uzbek literature. The poet used bright colors to portray the history of Uzbek people, spread over centuries. The central idea that was conveyed was that the Uzbek people should be proud of their history and should discover their self identity. This theme, along with other such eternal subjects like "love and passion", "time and man", "poet and poetry" get further developed in essence as well as in discovering new forms of expression. At present, apart from the above-mentioned themes, an entirely *new direction* has evolved which may be called *religious-ethic* or *philosophical approach*. The ideas of Islam, Hadiths, Islamic ethics and values are attracting more and more Uzbek poets. Some poetical works of this kind became very popular and have won recognition of readers. Abdulla Aripov's *Haj Note Book* and Asghar Mahkam's *Ishq, Tavajjoh, Naqshbandiya* or verses of Omon Matchon, Sirajuddin Sayid, Tahir Qahhar and others may be illustrative of this. In such poetry, not only are the Islamic ideas depicted, but through them poets try to express a man's inner spiritual world and their own attempts to purify themselves and society.

Islamic Values and Traditions

The Soviet system treated Islam as a big threat to its stability in Central Asia. Therefore from time to time, Muslim majority Republics were subjected to repressions. In Uzbekistan, these actions used to be harsher and carried out on a larger scale, because Islam and its traditions here were stronger and deeper rooted in comparison to neighboring countries (Kazakhstan, Turkmeniya or Kyrgizstan). Efforts were made to pressurize or to arrest Muslim clerics. Many mosques were closed and even destroyed, Islamic teachings distorted. Publications on Islam, Muslim philosophy, Sufism were very limited and carried out under strict government control. Even works of great Alisher Navoi, the founder of the Literary Uzbek language were censored. His unique writing *Munajaat,* where the poet addresses Allah and asks for his mercy, help and encouragement was excluded from the poet's "*Collection of complete works*", published in fifteen volumes during the Soviet time.

Religious freedom also came with Independence. Many Islamic monuments, mosques, had been restored. The large complex of *Imam Bukhari* near Samarkand was completely built up anew. Islamic festivals like *Eid-ul-Fitr* and *Eid-ul-Zuha* as well as *Navroz - Eastern New Year,* which had nothing in common with Islam, had been not only rehabilitated, but declared as gazetted National Holidays.

During the Soviet time, many faithful Uzbeks could not freely go to mosques to offer prayers or to participate in *janaza*, out of fear of being punished by some special government agencies.

Restoration of Islamic values may also be viewed in the following manner – before independence, only fifteen medium sized mosques operated in Tashkent city. Now their number has greatly increased and it is well over one hundred and twenty. The total number of Juma mosques in Uzbekistan has now exceeded five thousand. It is relevant to mention that Muslims in Uzbekistan have traditionally practiced moderate forms of Islam over centuries, and other trends like Wahabizm and so on are completely alien to them. During the Soviet time, the number of Muslims performing *Haj* from the entire USSR annually was about fifteen or twenty. This year the number of *Hajis* from Uzbekistan exceeded five thousand. Few years back in Tashkent, the Islamic University was opened, the only one in Central Asia.

Status of Uzbek Language

A vital component of every nation's culture, more comprehensively expressing its identity and soul, is the *language they speak.* Therefore language policy of the State might be very decisive for the fate of the language.

During the first ten-fifteen years of Soviet power, language policy towards non-Russian Republics of the State was (even on paper) more or less sound and pragmatic. The Center at that time proclaimed, that National Republics have the right to carry out all their educational, judicial and administrative systems, as well as to keep some other documentations on native language. But later on, during the period between 1935 and 1938, this policy was drastically changed. Spreading and cultivating of Russian language in National Republics became the main direction of the national and language policy of the Center. Thus, implicitly, the slow process of *Russification* of other Republics had been started.

In Uzbekistan, where the Uzbek language was a mother tongue of an overwhelming majority of its population, this policy led to confining the social functions of the Uzbek language. In government offices, statistical centers, in education (specially higher education), medical sphere, sports, judicial, science and technology, proceedings of official meetings, different functions and so on had been conducted in Russian. Students, whose medium of instructions in their Institute or University was the Uzbek language, had to learn Russian as a subject, while for Russian medium groups, studying of Uzbek language was not compulsory. The language policy had been planned in such a way, that a good command over Russian would open better job opportunities for the younger generations or could give them a more lucrative position in the society. Therefore, students who had graduated with Uzbek medium of instructions found themselves in a disadvantageous position. Thus, the high social prestige of the Russian language in the Republic, eventually led to a situation where it came to enjoy an undeclared status of the Official Language of Uzbekistan and the status the of native language was decreased to the position of a second or additional one. Its functions were mostly confined to lower administrative and judicial levels, the spheres of literature, culture and public life.

Uzbekistan was perhaps the first Republic in the former USSR where the local language was declared as the official language of the State. On 21st October 1989, about two years before the Independence, the Uzbek language had been announced as the State Language of the Republic of Uzbekistan by the President's Decree. This day is today celebrated as the *Language Day*.

The first clause of the Decree states that the State shall by all means develop and promote the Uzbek language, guarantee its broad use in political, social, economic and cultural life. This proclamation was the first bold step towards Uzbekistan's independence and was an important act which determined the future fate Uzbek language.

Later, in 1995 some Amendments were made to *The Law of State Language of Uzbekistan*. Accordingly all legislative documents, international agreements, work and proceedings of State institutions, judiciary etc. would be carried out in this language. The State was responsible for securing its enrichment and development. For the Uzbek language, instead of Cyrillic, the Roman alphabet was adopted. In coming years all educational institutions, mass-media, official and non-official establishments in their activities shall completely switch over to the new script.

After the adoption of the Uzbek language as an official language, a new Language Policy was worked out. Its implementation is now being carried out in different directions and on big scales. At present, much attention is being paid to the development of the Uzbek language and enrichment of its vocabulary. Many committees are engaged in defining and compiling terminology in such fields, like science, informatics, technology, politics etc. About 120 terminology dictionaries have been published in the period between 1991 and 2004, which is equivalent to the number of publications during the previous 70 years. By the year 2007, publications of the Uzbek National Encyclopedia in twelve volumes and the Dictionary of Uzbek Language in five volumes shall also be completed.

Significant changes are taking place in the vocabulary of the language. Many Russian words have been replaced by old native ones, which during the Soviet power had become out of use. This tendency had become clear during the first few years of independence. Now in coining new words or terminology, along with potentialities of the Uzbek language, resources of other languages are also made of use. Today, the Uzbek language is steadily gaining its rightful position in all spheres of life of Uzbekistan.

20

Functional Specificity of Oriental International Lexicon (OIL) in the Languages of Central Asia and India

Azad N. Shamatov and Sirajuddin S. Nurmatov

Nowadays it is very important to determine different ways and modes of estimation relating to a proper nature of cultural relations between new-born independent states of Central Asia and those of South Asia which have acquired a substantial experience in stable economic development within a framework of market system. This primarily pertains to India demonstrating an illustrious and encouraging example in the realm of high technologies and computer sciences as well. In particular, this phenomenon seems more attractive as a whole given the background where other states of the area like Pakistan and Bangladesh compete with it in growth of population and therefore it deserves to be studied very seriously.

Likewise, similar trends are to be observed in language development spheres of South Asia as well, with widespread of various kinds of speeches such as Hindi, Bengali, Urdu, Punjabi, Telugu and Tamil, which are now listed as amongst the first twenty languages claiming their significance to the world. In this regard a special status belongs truly to Hindi along with Urdu, both of which have beaten all records as the most popular vehicles of the cinema industry production reaching even the remote angles and corners of the world today. Even in a typically western state by means of mentality and culture as Germany, every week on Friday television channels regularly show Indian films dubbed into German according to essential rules of artistic performance.

Thus globalization today does not only cover economic fields, but is more and more rapidly invading the cultural life of many people. Just from this point of view one can consider a factor of mutual intelligibility among representatives of diverse speeches and cultures. The factor indeed does enable a spiritual and moral rapprochement between many people and particularly concerns those who have been engaged in interactions over many centuries for a specific nature of their historical development in the past, impacting each other by bringing over a natural enrichment and versatility in mutual human necessities and endeavors. One can recollect remarkable events which happened in Ancient and Medieval times while the newcomers from Central Asia managed to frequently reach faraway shores of Sri Lanka and Indo-China pursuing various missions like either trade and pilgrimage or spreading a new religion, though many examples of military raids are available through long distances where they used to leave behind certain names of their own tribes and clans.[1]

As for extremely distant points like Sri Lanka, for this Arabs and other Muslim maritime travelers used a melodious name *Sarandib*, apparently derived from Sanskritic *Sinhala Dviipa.* Hence, that is why in the lexicon of local Sinhalese speech one can find, along with numerous borrowings of European origin, a sizable bulk of loan-words of Arabic and Persian roots because of which the Sinhalese might be compared with some Central Asian languages too.[2]

From this point of view it should be underlined that at present in scholarly world there is principally a new branch of linguistics which has formed out to be called 'Interlinguistics', an appearance of which was caused by an acute necessity of establishing general fundamentals in the Plan of Content and the Plan of Expression and elaborating the most optimal means of International communication. As a vivid example of that, one can mention the formation of Esperanto as a special auxiliary code having gained extremely enormous popularity in the middle of past century.

On the occasion many scholars do point out the significance of the international context while searching for solutions of problems in language planning as well as for orientation firstly towards the world languages. This in particular is qualified as a substantial on the wake of emerging and developing a special International Lexicon Systems in various languages, which are interpreted as «objectively existing interlingual synchronic entity, arising in whatever groupings of interacting speeches.[3]

The phenomenon from the point of Language Policy is largely connected with a problem of «acknowledgment of International Lexicon within a process of Speech Communication. This kind of Lexicon as it is well known comes to exist and plays an important part particularly in Bilingual and Multilingual Situations while one is capable more or less actively to switch on from one phonological system to another. Just then a certain mechanisms do enable identification of more or less regularly respective features in common element of Lexicon. As such a «key» perhaps, for example, there might serve a registration of syllables specificity in foreign speech's Lexicon as well as Phonemic correspondences. Thus, a European individual even under limited practical acquaintance with Japanese or Indonesian could find substantial groups of European International Lexicon in these».[4] The same appears relating directly to other languages including Hindi, Tajik and Uzbek as well.

It should be pointed out that at the present stage of World Community Development, while on the wake of collapse of the Soviet Regime there came a serious softening of international tension which practically led to a certain sizable relaxation in ideological, political and military confrontation prevailing during the Cold War period, while there had been involved a lot of powerful states throughout the World. In its own turn it resulted in world wide arms race's cessation and respective abolition of material resources with natural breakthrough in the sphere of international relations. The process is vividly evidenced by the example of our state, Uzbekistan. In Uzbek speech one can easily come across familiar notions and expressions such as *«investment»*, *«fax»*, *«body-building»*, *«show»*, *«hot dog»*, *«digest»* etc. In other words, one can consider here a phenomenon of extensive Internationalization and Globalization in the frame-work of every day events in our life which finds its reflection in Language Development as well.

As mentioned before, an accord between interacting speeches, apart from immense differences in their Phonetics and Grammar, there is gradually forming a special Lexicon Group called the «International one». Just applying it to Uzbek as well as to any other world language, it does not seem to be difficult to distinguish words like *«internet»*, *«international»*, *«interactive»* and so on, which have proved to be the most circulated words in the cultural life of the society. Such elements of Language System do enhance an accord among people, making Communication Process more flexible and thus benefiting the World Progress in general.

Both by nature and usage the units of the International Lexicon can be divided into Distinct and Hidden (or Concealed) ones. The former ones are directly borrowed from certain languages, e.g. English, as is the case with examples given above. As for the latter ones, these are the result of reproduction of newly borrowed notions by own means of the speech. For example, an Uzbek expression *«osmono'par»* or Russian *nevoskroyob* derived from English compound word *«skyscraper»,* consisting of two parts Combining two nations – *«sky»* + *«kissing».* So the Russian word seems to be just a replica of the English pattern.

It is interesting to trace the origin of the Uzbek hidden term *«muzqaymoq»* which literally translates to *«ice + cream»* or *«ice cream»,* formed after the English pattern indeed, but not after the Russian word *«morojennoye»* which is literally understood as *«frozen».* Besides these, there are many such compound word calques like Hindi *antarraashtriiya* or Urdu *bainulaqwaamii* and their Uzbek synonyms *«xalqaro, bainalmilal»* with common meaning *«international».*

It is well known that amongst other reasons, the spread of these words in written speech is also motivated by the translation of some Asian and African Languages into Roman alphabet as a whole. In this respect the adoption of the Roman character by the Uzbek might be considered as an important step towards Internationalization of Uzbek culture and economy, which seems quite natural and it is hoped that the process would lead to further integration of Uzbekistan into the World Community.

Deliberating on the potential sources of the International Lexicon many linguists indicate that along with Language Contacts there is a great part that could also be played by «independent creative activities of languages explained by commonness in psychology, natural conditions, social environment and cultural life»[5]. Hence among the International Lexicon(IL) there might clearly be distinguished two different varieties - the Western (WIL) and The Oriental, including a lot of phraseology idioms as well e.g. a Russian phrase - *«to be in despair» рвать на себе волосы* does coincide with English *«to tear one's hair»,* French – *s'arracher lex cheveux and* German - *sich die Haare ausrafen.*[6]

Similarly, there is an evident coincidence between Tajik-Persian – *na six sozad na kabob* and Uzbek *«six ham kabob ham kuymasin»* likewise with Hindi and Urdu *«na sikh jale na kabaab»*, where in concealed form one can find such a phrase as «sheep are safe and wolves are sate», which in the Oriental languages referred to above is reproduced by Persian claque «just not let burn neither beef, steak nor wooden stick».

Proceeding from the facts mentioned above it may be stated that today a majority of scholars are inclined towards considering that in Modern times a scope of synchronic closings between various languages does not depend on their genetic contiguity but rather on millennia old cultural, political and economic links having been prevailed throughout their historical development.

While a general approach to the data is concerned it seems appropriate to qualify «International Lexicon» notion according to Russian scholar Y.A. Belhchikov as a following. «The words which do coincide formally with respect to regular correspondences between sounds and graphical units, possessing either completely or partially common meanings and denoting international concepts from scientific, technical, political, cultural, artistic spheres of communication and being used mainly in not less than three non-cognate languages».[7]

This phenomenon in modern Linguistic Studies is usually distinguished by the means of three special methods.

The first one of these is Area Approach proper which enables one to define onomasiological isoglosses as well as certain regions showing a spread of the Lexicon on a Linguistic map of the world.

The second one is a Synchronic-Comparative or Contrastive analysis which in its general features reflects various cases of similarity and differences between lots of International lexemes perceived in different pairs or groups of languages under comparison.

Meanwhile, the third one represents many specimens of individual speech investigation in the framework of Bilingualism and Polylingualism. In particular while comparing languages in the Process of Translation one can check up a real ability of International Lexicon to be regularly identified and to serve as a benefiting vehicle for transmission of Information in the conditions of various contacts between diverse languages.

In this regard our paper is dedicated to a problem of mutual intelligibility between various peoples of the many areas irrespective of their origin and typology as well while analyzing a functional correlation between the words of Western and Oriental genesis.

Such Extralinguistic phenomena such as Indian films and Punjabi songs might be regarded as a bold evidence of such an efficiency enabling scores of people to have a broad cultural access to Hindustani and Punjabi which resemble the most mixed varieties of Modern speeches of India and South Asia as whole. These give us a brilliant example of penetration and absorption of Arabic, Persian and Turkic Lexicon in foreign environment.

Functionally these are destined actually to play the same significant role which was usually attributed to Western or European International Lexicon (WIL) of Greek and Latin origin, serving mostly to the needs of industrial and scientific as well as cultural purposes.

Concerning recent political and social changes in present C.I.S. with a special reference to OIL one can notice a visible growth of such a common intelligible words between certain Central Asian and Indian languages. This phenomenon to our mind owes to a socio-political and cultural process of upgrading a social status of Central Asian languages up to an official standard level. Moreover it also is due to development of direct political, social, cultural, commercial, economic and personal contacts between the peoples of both areas too.

Thus in Uzbekistan as a result of that, alongside with cultural resurrection of population on the wake of Independence, there is an unprecedented breakthrough in Uzbek people's mind towards a better understanding of multifaceted culture of India, including languages, literature, philosophy, religions and art which could be observed on many popular examples of borrowing a lot of typical Indian concepts, proper names and phenomena of music and arts.

As a brilliant example of borrowing some typical Indian perceptions one can mention the Ahimsa Theory of Mahatma Gandhi, which attained a high estimation by our respected President Islam Karimov as well as a propagation of spiritual and moral education for young generation, oriented towards a reverence of genuine cultural traditions along with national values as a whole. To our mind, these phenomena might be attributed to the influence of TV serials *«Mahabharata»* and *«Ramayana»* on Uzbek audience. And this trend is considered to be very peculiar for Modern India against a destructive Western Pop culture, spreading on and glorifying violence, sexual instincts and immorality as well.

As for many Indian proper names borrowed in Central Asian Languages apart from *Indira, Raj* and *Jawaharlal* one can also come across many cases of nick names like *Shahrukh Khan, Shahzad, Amar, Ramesh* and *Mukesh* which are now very popular and being easily assumed in Uzbek families for newborn children. The same thing is with names like *Madhuri, Kajol, Aishwarya* and at last *Amitabh.*

Meanwhile, as far as borrowings perceived in Musical art are concerned there are many modern Uzbek variety songs which are usually and frequently tuned on melodious Indian film songs' patterns. These in particular one can treat as a distinct feature of the Uzbek artistic performance by yesterday's widely popular singer *Muhriddin Khaliqov* and nowadays by our superstar singer *Yulduz Usmanova.*

Now let us proceed to concrete details to be seen in usage of OIL and WIL to be seen in the Languages of Central Asia and India. Thus just with special reference to Hindi, Uzbek and Tajik one could observe clearly how a correlation between both varieties of International Lexicon is changing over and resulting in favor of the former under pressing influence of Uzbek and to some extent Tajik's upgrading as official languages of the respective states. For example, we found it as very purposeful to undertake a statistical analysis of certain specimens belonging to the different styles of Modern Hindi Prose targeting an objective to discern and to define a distribution of OIL and WIL in Hindi Vocabulary Lexemes.

Therefore there one does keep in mind that these three languages - Hindi, Uzbek and Tajik are actually non-cognate indeed. As a trustworthy database for our analysis we took three sources.

The first one is a Literary Criticism article by Pankaj Kumar entitled *«Kaise hamaare biic ek insaan rah gayaa»* dedicated to the 93rd anniversary of the famous Indian writer Vishnu Prabhakar, which was published in ICCR's *«Gagananchal»* № 3 dated 2005 (pp. 25-27). In total there are 1180 words of which over 120 are treated as OIL units i.e. above 10%, whereas WIL units embrace only 35 words i.e. around 3%.

In case one refers to the most frequently used words of 0IL, there are sub-ordinative conjunction *ki* «that», Arabic noun *umr* «an age» along with an adjective *jawaan* «young» and noun *yaad* «a memory», which are both of Iranian origin, representing here a pronominal part of the Predicate in a lot of sentences. Besides in a number of frequently used words one can also notice certain conjunctions *lekin* «but» and *agar* «if, in case», a noun of Arabic origin *sawaal* «a question», Iranian noun *zamaanaa* «a period» and Arabic one *insaan* «a man». These words actually do play a significant role in the cultural communication process between the bearers of the Languages under comparison.

As far as a relatively very small group of WIL is concerned, among these one can discern a special denominations of months like *Juun* «June» an adjective *ektiv* «active», as well as a various scholarly degrees denominations abstract nouns like *pwaaint* «a main principle»; «point», *akaadmii* «Academy», *ti.vi.* «T.V.», film and radio etc. In this regard it is extremely important to underline that during the initial Post-Independence years of C.I.S. there were substantial trends perceived towards the purification of Word-Building Policy in many Languages of former USSR, including rejection of many WIL units and formations. Among them there were also thoroughly assimilated words available like *universitet* «university», *gazeta* «a newspaper», *jurnal* «a magazine», *aeroport* «airport» by replacing them with brand new words formed out either of local indigenous words or by activating a corresponding OIL units. But a lot of these new words have not so far acquired proper usage especially in Colloquial Speech due to the tough competition caused by the old European Loans, which proved to be more stable and acceptable for recipient language systems as a whole. We may also refer to some adjectives in Tajik and Uzbek like *aaktiv* «active», *claassic* «classical» and so on.

Therefore, some specimens of Modern Hindi written in specific Journalist Style are characterized by preservation and sometimes by evident preference of the OIL stock i.e. 10 % compared to 3 %. A main nucleus of these words is represented by Abstract Nouns and frequently used Conjunctions and Particles of Arabic and Iranian origin playing an active role in the process of cultural communication.

Now let us proceed to the second source for our investigation which in fact is a typical example of widely spread Literary-Artistic

Style of Modern Hindi today. A short story *«Meghnaa»* by Satyendra Pratap Sinh published in the same number of the *«Gagananchal»* magazine pp. 49-54 might be considered as a regular case of Colloquial Vernacular Speech's intrusion mainly shared by middle class urban people of Hindi speaking area in India who can boast of English education and are to be treated as Bilinguals.

While undertaking a statistical estimation of the text, one has the following results: total number of word-usages is equal to 1650 entries among which 181 word-usages fall on OIL i.e. above 10 %, meanwhile 121 word-usages pertain to the share of WIL indeed.

Moreover in comparison with the Journalist style, as one can conclude there is a specific gravity of OIL; neither does it show any substantial change quantitatively nor qualitatively so far. In particular a major part of that belongs to Abstract Nouns as well as to Conjunctions and Particles of Arabic and Iranian Origin. But as a distinct difference from Journalist style here we have an impressive growth of WIL words which are represented by the most current concepts peculiar to modern life of self-sustained, prosperous strata of Indian population cf. English words as *flight, airport, business, news, waiter, taxi, card, sorry, promise, behavior, company, matured.* These are frequently accompanied by such a typical daily used expressions like phraseology blends – *«I wish you good luck», «Sense of humor», «I love you»* etc.

As a result of that one can perceive something like orientation transfer over of Hindi from the East to the West badly impacting intelligibility between inhabitants of Central Asia and Hindi forcing thus the formers to resort to English too.

The third source as a specimen of text, chosen for a more complete representation of a whole picture reflecting 'International Lexicon' presence in Modern Literary Hindi is taken from the same magazine (see pp. 79-82). So it is a small pamphlet compiled by Shashiprabha Tiwari *«Thumri Utsav» («Thumri Festival»).* To our mind it is designed to show a possibilities of traditionally Indian Style which traces back to Ancient Sanskritic Literary style abundant of typical Old Indian terms belonging to the realm of Classical Musical Mastership.

But despite pressure from the traditional Genre and Thematic limitations laid upon word-usage, one can even notice a trend to preserve connections with colloquial speech in Hindi and simultaneous combination of pure Indian Nomenclature with new tradition winnowed by the Muslim Influence, deriving from the period of Akbar reign while it was a main tendency to promote and encourage synthesis of the best achievements, pertaining to the two polarly opposed performances in Arts as a whole.

Hence one can perceive quite a sizeable striving to utilize the words of Iranian and Arabic origin which many centuries ago became an integral part of Indian Speech Culture. So, in particular, among a total number of the text including 771 word-usages there is a 7 percent of that i.e. 54 word usages are gained by OIL units. For instance, cf. a following words of Iranian origin like *daayraa* «a circle, a cycle», *andaaz* «a style», *xuubsuuratii* «a beauty, an elegance», *sadii* «a century», *bandish* «a composition, creature», *peshkash* «a presentation, performance», *aavaaz* «a voice», *vaahvaahii* «sounds Bis! Very good! Bravo! », *shaagird* «a disciple, student» as well as hybrid words formed out of an Iranian words like *pesh karnaa* «to perform, to present». Rather few, there are Arabic words used like *xaasiyat* «a feature, peculiarity», *shaamil* «present, available», *shuruaat* «a beginning», meanwhile there is a lot of mixed Arab-Turkic proper names of Muslim maestros like *Abdul Karim Xaan, Barkat Aliixaan, Begam Axtar* intermingling with those of Arabic-Indian origin like *Rasuulan Baaii* all of these are usually accompanied by a title *ustaad* «a master, maestro», for instance, *Ustaad Abdul Ghaniixaan.* OIL units can be recognized also within a structure of Raagas or Songs couplets, for example, *main to phulvaa chunan gaii raajaa kii bagiyaa* «I went to the garden of Raja to collect flowers», where bagiyaa is a derivative of Ir. *baagh* «a garden». Another example: *guzar gaii ratiyaaN piyaa nahiiN aaye* «a night has passed over, but (my) beloved didn't turn up». Here a form *guzar gaii* «passed over» is composed of Ir. Present Tense stem *guzar* – «to pass». And the last example: *aayii saavan kii bahaar* «a spring of Shravan month has come over», where *bahaar* is derived from Iranian word for «a spring».

As far as WIL is concerned in this text its units are limited both by number as well as by quality, embracing only 1 percent i.e. 7 word-usages, representing names of months and academic degrees like March and doctor. Besides there is a sole name of musical instrument – *harmonium* from a Greek *harmonia* «a combination, connection».

Thus as a result of the analysis of three different style texts written in Modern Hindi one can draw out the following conclusions:

1) Despite a diversity in genre and stylistic as well as thematic parameters between the most typical specimens of Modern Hindi Prose under present comparative investigation there is an apparently common integrating feature connecting them, which might be identified as a regular availability of OIL units embodied mainly in lexemes of Abstract character constituting a major stock of communicative Syntactical means of speech. One covers approximately 7 to 10 percent of total word-usages, consisting of kernel conjunctions like *agar* «if, in case», *lekin* «but», borrowed nouns used as a part of pronominal predicate along with the words denoting daily popular notions within a cultural communication like *«a man», «a question», «an epoch»* etc. Therefore these should be identified as a constant part in textual structure of Modern Hindi. Thanks to them one can successfully carry on the process of teaching Hindi to Uzbek and in particular Tajik-speaking individuals, where the OIL units mentioned above are perceived in «easily recognizable shape» to be slightly different from Hindi.

2) At the same time it should be stressed upon that as another non-less important peculiarity pertaining to the texts under discussion, a certain presence of WIL also comes to be a very distinct oscillation which differs here from 1 to 3 percent. It is clearly caused mainly by extralinguistic reasons and in particular by an increase of either Anglo-Hindi or Hindi-English Bilingualism among urban strata of India. Here one can find the most special cases of expressing the names of months and the very daily notions, belonging to modern academic activities and culture, encroached into Indian life under direct impact of the British Education System and Western habits and traditions. For example, first of all it is especially visible in the names of academic degrees, like Dr., B.A. and M.A. as well as in the notions of such a popular phenomena like *«film», «T.V.», «radio», «an airport», «a flight».*

On the other hand, there are many cases of blending of pure English words and expressions. These are more freely accepted in comparison with their local correspondences which are usually translated by rather archaic and more or less confessional lexemes. Cf. Eng. «to promise» which stands for Hindi *«vachan denaa»* or Urdu *«vaadaa karnaa»*. Besides, one can confront a stereo typed expression borrowed from English, «a sense of humour» with its equivalents in Hindi *«haasya-ras kaa anubhav»* and Urdu *«zaraafat kaa ehsaas»*.

At the same time judging on the WIL units as a whole and proceeding from their linguapragmatics, peculiarities are rather typical to Colloquial Speech than to the Bookish Written Style and therefore do have an occasional, non-permanent nature of application. That's why these seem as more fitting to be qualified as «a Fluid» or «Changeable» Part in the Modern Hindi Texts distinguished from OIL units, which were already have been treated above as «a Permanent, Constant» element of that.

Nevertheless an extensive and regular functioning of Uzbek and Tajik in such popular walks of everyday life as scientific activities, High Education, State Management and Mass Communication which earlier were completely dominated by Russian as a State Language of USSR, now is contributing immensely to the strengthening and widening of OIL positions within a framework of Vocabulary. Moreover it generated an extremely rapid growth of their Word-Building potentialities in particular concerning such Arabic and Persian affixes like *=iy, = viy, no=, =kor, =gor, =baror* standing for Hindi-Urdu *=ii, naa=, =kaar, =gaar, =giir,* reflecting diverse changes becoming current in socio-economic, political and cultural spheres. In its own turn these trends hade made a very positive impact cherishing a level of intelligibility between Uzbek people and inhabitants of Northern and Central India especially the speakers of Hindi, Urdu and Punjabi.

Thus as a general conclusion it may be stated that the Transition Period in C.I.S. judging from the example of Uzbekistan is nowadays mainly characterized by a cardinal progressive measures in Language Policy enabling a respective upgrading of communication level regarding their interactions with certain ethnical groups of Modern India and South Asia as a whole.

This process is greatly favored by a speedy development of mutual relations between both states in various spheres of present life and first of all in economic, socio-political, scientific, commercial and cultural spheres.

To our mind from the pragmatically point of view these phenomena and tendencies should serve as an effective factor stimulating a development and mastering both the Teaching Methodology and Research Works to be done over our official languages. In particular it is highly appropriate to Uzbek, which is already accepted as a special subject of instruction in one of the leading universities of India – Jamia Milia.

In this respect our Indologists could share their long experience spanning over decades in this direction, for instance, regarding Research Studies in Hindi and Urdu Grammar and Vocabulary as well as compiling text-books, teaching appliances, manuals and dictionaries and not to speak of regularly acting as visiting lecturers in Uzbek Language and Literature to be invited from Uzbekistan.

REFERENCES

1. Cf. Particular names of some cities in Bangladesh like Boghra and Maimansingh.
2. In particular one can refer to a certain of our papers dealing with the problem of Area Linguistics, for example see A.N.Shamatov, Central and South Asia as Medieval Linguistic Areas – 36th Internationale Congress of Asian and North African Studies. Book of Abstracts, from August 27 to September 2, 2000, Palais des Congres, Montreal, Canada, p. 156.
3. A.N.Shamatov, K voprosu o tipologii arealhnyh svyazey yazykov Centralhnoi I Yujnoi Azii – «Voprosy Filologii», No 2, Moskwa, 2003, pp. 23-29.
4. See Internacionalhnye elementy v leksike i terminologii, pod redakciey V.V.Akulenko, Harhkov, «Visha Shkola», 1980, p.208.
5. Akulenko V.V. Voprosy izucheniya leksicheskih intenacionalizmov i processov ih obrazovaniya – «Voprosy socialhnoq lingvistiki», «Nauka», Leningrad, 1969, pp. 79-80.
6. Akulenko V.V. Leksicheskiye internacionalizmy I metody ih izucheniya, - «Voprosy Yazykoznaniya», 1976, No. 6, p. 61.
7. Ibid., p.61.
8. See – International Lexicon , Lingvistiicheskiy Enciklopedicheskiy slovarh, Moscow, 2002, p. 197.

21

On the Reflection of Some New Scientific and Cultural Notions in Indian Life by Means of Modern Hindi

Mahira Nasirova

Language is a social phenomenon as it has a close interconnection with all the processes in the life of a society. It changes and acquires a shape according to the society where it is spoken. The status of a certain language could be stated in accordance with the richness of its vocabulary with new lexicon or new words. It can be said that a language is reflective of all social, political and cultural aspects of the society where it is used.

In our present report, we attempted to analyze some neologisms – new words in Modern Hindi borrowed from English. It has been prepared on basis of our Research work "Some neologism models in Modern Hindi".

It is a world known fact that the tremendous development of science, information technology and the processes of globalization and modernization work towards bringing a huge lexicon into almost all the languages in the world. English, which became the most powerful medium of communication, has a deep influence in most languages. This is seen specially in the fields of science and information technology, where English terms are easily borrowed and widely used in many languages including literary Hindi. Words like *network*, *email*, *internet*, *mobile phone* and *sim card* could be shown as examples.

Though Hindi is considered to be a language with its own indigenous means of word formation, in many cases it is inclined towards being influenced by English in this regard as well. There is a process of involving several English words which are loaned to Hindi vocabulary and usage as well. Moreover, such loans start to compete with the *tatsama* and *tadbhava* words of Hindi.

Our observations mainly deal with a functional style of Hindi current in many periodicals, which in this respect combine different styles like scientific, colloquial and artistic ones. For example, an English loan *bilDar* (from English *builder* - a constructor, a person who is engaged in building) is used side by side with its Hindi synonyms like *ima:rateN bana:newa:la:* and *ra:jgi:r.*[1]

According to our observations some technical terms, which are considered to be English loans, are used more freely than their Hindi synonyms, for example, *vairas* (from English *virus*), though there is a word *vish'a:n'u* in Hindi, and *heykars* (from English *hackers*) - no Hindi synonym was not found for this word. It is relevant to mention here, that these words are mostly used in the field of computer technology. The same situation is observed with a term *netwark* (from English *network*), though there are Hindi words like *ja:li:* and *tantra:*. One could state that there is one more word *sancha:r* – but there were no examples for this word in the meaning of network.

The next word is *Hausing sosa:yti:* (from English *Housing society* - which means the organization which is in charge of providing buildings). We found a word *a:va:s* for *"hausing"*, and *sama:j* and *sanstha:* for the word *sosayti*. But we did not find the words *a:va:s sanstha:* or *a:va:s sama:j* used in this meaning in any source.

The next one is *scri:n sisTam cha:lu* - the process of showing something on the screen. Word by word it can be translated into Hindi like *parde par pradarshit pran'a:li:* or *parde ke dva:ra pradarshan karne ka: kram*. The same situation was observed with usage of this word.

We have gathered more than two hundred new words from many resources like newspapers '*Jansatta:*', '*Navbharat Times*'; magazines like '*Prava:si: Sansa:r*', '*Chintan Sri:jan*' and some Indian TV programs. We would like to give a short list of these words so that it will be clear what and on which fields the English loans are more active in usage. Although the list consists of over two hundred words, we have given just a few of the most active words below:

---

1. The Oxford Hindi - English Dictionary, Mcgregor R.S., 1997, Oxford University.

alyuminiyam prinTed shi:T –aluminium printed sheet
buk ba:inDing mashi:n- book binding machine
brek Ta:im – break time
boks aofis- box office
ilekTra:nik vya:pa:r mela: -Fair of electronic trade
ilekTra:nik udyog – electronic industry
i: - meyl – e-mail
sim ca:rD – sim card
vebsa:iT – website
DaunloaD - (to) download
Dilarship - dealership
peking – packing
pek hona: - packing
posTmorTam (kiya: ja:na:) – postmortem
pla:nT – plant
ma:rkeT velyu: - market value
moba:yl phon – mobile phone
su:par hiT film- super hit film
sheyar ba:za:r – share market
TesT se guzarna: - to be tested
Teknikal bha:sha: - the language of the technique
vayrles neTvark – wireless network
varchual pra:iveT neTwark seva: - virtual privet network service

Here we can mention that there are some words like '*shaoping mol*' (shopping mall) or '*metro*' (metro) which are also borrowed from English, which do not have their Hindi synonyms yet, and can be considered as neologisms in Modern Hindi.

As a conclusion one should state that the impact of English as a highly prestigious word wide language of Modern Science and Technology does affect Hindi with some cases of enlarging its vocabulary and to certain extent of replacing the Hindi Synonyms. It inevitably leads to mixing of two different kinds of speech creating creolized forms of expression. This phenomenon is evident in other languages like Russian and Uzbek as well.

REFERENCES

1. The Oxford Hindi - English Dictionary, Mcgregor R.S., 1997, Oxford University
2. Hindi – Russkiy Slovar, tom I-II, Beskrovniy V.S., M.,1972
3. Samekit Prasha:san Shabda:wali: Parts I-II (Hindi: -Angrezi; Angrezi:- Hindi:), Vegya:ni:k Tatha: Takni:ki: Shabda:vali: A:yog, Kendriya Hindi: Nidesha:lay, Tamil Nadu, 1978
4. Supreme Concise Dictionary (English-English – Hindi) , Compiled and Edited by Sharan and M.A.C. trans, Ph.D, LLB, Delhi, 2000
5. Newspapers 'Jansatta:', 'Navbharat times'; magazines 'Prava:si: sansa:r', 'Chintan sri:jan' (1999-2005)

22

Resurgence of Hindi in the Wake of Globalization

Gajendra S. Chauhan

Modern India is a multilingual nation. Hindi has come a long way since its adoption as an official language by Indian constitution in 1951.It is recognized as a national language in India and it knits the different mother tongue speakers together. In fact, Hindi doesn't have much success stories in the past. Its adoption as an official language sent a ripple of resentment through the southern part of the country. The topsy-turvy journey of Hindi as a national language has come to an end and it has fitted in with the requirement of today's generation and market. It is only after 1990 that revival of Hindi started taking place with globalization and media revolution in India. In today's highly competitive scenario, globalization is less a choice and more a compulsion. The term 'globalization' is not merely confined to economics; it has also extended to our inner self i.e., our culture and society. Consequently, the winds of globalization are bringing about a sea of changes in society and economy. Language and society go hand in hand. While societies undergo transition, so does language, both in its popular and in its purest form. The touch of marketization has not left the linguistic scenario of India untouched.

The paper illustrates how Hindi has come out of its shell and carved its place as a market friendly and popular language. The positive impact is that, due to the expansion of media network in the past decade, pan-Indian Hindi is developing mainly through the audio-visual media. During this period, Hindi is able to make greater impact on non-Hindi speaking states. Non-Hindi speakers in India are like passive smokers of Hindi. Impact of media like television, radio and films is enormous (Mallikarjun.B: 2004)

Say Hello to Hindi

The rebirth of Hindi as the new power language and the Hindification of India has left the brown sahibs baffled. For decades, they were brought up to believe that *firangi* education, *angrezi* accent and western *nakhras* were the passport to social acceptance. Suddenly, it is the other way round. The language has become desirable as it sells. From the morning cup of tea (*chai hoto aisi*) to hoardings (*Mujhme hai woh baat*), from SMS messages (*aati kya*?) to TV commercials (*Thanda Matlab Coca-Cola*) from Hindi Archies cards to children's cartoons and full pages ads in English publications that have slogans in Roman Hindi, from Hindi classes in finishing schools to Hindi folk songs blaring in the discos, there is an entire Hindustan thriving out there. (Shafalee V: 2004) Even USA's George Bush loves it and that's why recently Hindi became one of the languages to be taught in American schools.

Indian Television

It was TV that made Hindi a *raapchik* phenomenon. Today, the Indian TV cable covers over 50 millions homes and provides most of these with almost 100 television channels, both pay and free to air. Welcome to the changing world of News channels. With more than two dozen news channels in languages as varied as multi-cultural India-Indian television industry is set for a sonic boom. When Hindi news channels went 24 hours, MTV turned desi and Hindi serials *Kyuki*… and *Kahani*…became a pre-sleep ritual in every bedroom, no one realized that language of *behenjis* and *babus* are here to stay for a long. The Hindi news channel Aaj Tak is amongst the most popular news channel in the country today and we feel that there is little doubt in the channel's claim that it has changed the way news is delivered to Indian audiences. Aaj Tak has proved that instead of speaking like a pandit, if an anchor uses simple language, he can reach all the sections of society. The importance of Hindi is known from the fact that STAR TV, once an-all-English channel, is now rich in Hindi Programming. Star Plus has not only redefined Hindi television entertainment but also promoted Hindi extensively by snatching the No.1 position as the most popular and watch able Hindi channel. When Star Plus launched '*Kaun Banega Crorepati*?' (KBC) the Indian version of 'Who Wants to Be a Millionaire?' the show quickly became the biggest hit on the Indian Television. Hosted by the megastar of Hindi cinema Amitabh Bachchan, most of its catch phrases such as '*lock kiya jaye*', '*computerji*', '*pucca*' and '*fifty-fifty*' became the part of common Hindi in India. Vividh Bharti is no longer a sole Hindi Radio station. Radio Mirchi and Red FM are gaining momentum as they speak the language of the heart that young generation loves most. It is not strange that Hindi enjoyed unprecedented popularity, even in South, thanks to blockbuster Hindi movies and the universal appeal of Hindi TV programmes like KBC, Indian Idol, Saregama, and Aantkashsree. The Hindi speaking market is the biggest and no foreign channel can afford to ignore it. That's why Walt Disney Television International is ready to cater the larger audiences, especially, kids. Now *Mickey Mouse* & *Donald Duck* are aspiring to learn Hindi language as Disney Toon is available in Hindi besides Tamil, Telugu and English. Even BBC is reportedly toying with idea of airing Hindi programmes.

Hindi Print Media

Those who predicted the fading away of the print media will have to wait slightly longer. Hindi print media is alive kicking, and expanding. Hindi continues to be the only language with the largest number of newspapers, journals and periodicals in India. According to 2005, National Readership Survey, among the top ten dailies, there is only one English daily at No.10 (Times of India). *Dainik Jagran* snatched the No.1 position from *Dainik Bhaskar*, is now India's most read newspaper. Despite the noisiest my-circulation-is-longer-than-yours campaigns being waged by English dailies, it is the only one, which finds itself in the top ten bracket. The rest in the elite ten are all language dailies with as many as five of them being published in Hindi. In magazine section too, *India Today* (Hindi) overtakes *Saras Salil* as the most read magazine (urban plus rural) in the country. Here again all the regional magazines dominate the scene with *India Today* (English) as the only magazine in the top ten.

Hindi Advertising

Gone are the days, when advertisers would think that this particular brand is only for English newspapers. Today, Hindi and other regional newspapers hold an equal importance in the media plan for any brand. The entire Hindi newspaper business has grown in terms of readership and advertising revenue. Today, even brands like Mercedes Benz are advertised on Hindi newspapers. Apart from these, there are lots of other high-end products like expensive watches, luxurious cars and other life-style products that are marketed in Hindi language. The image of Hindi speaking person too is breaking boundaries. It is no longer associated with those who wear *Saris* and *Dhotis*. Now even the social elite accept that Hindi is the '*lift Kara de*' language. It is boom time for Hindi copywriters and advertising professionals. With this Hindi high trend, all the global brands want local flavour and local language. This is recognition of the fact that to stay in Indian Markets, the multinationals need to use a language that overcomes linguistic barriers and cultural differences. Priti Nair Chakravarthy, executive creative director, Lowe, is quite upfront in saying that she favours Hindi. She says, "Hindi rocks because it has the capacity to touch the pulse of the nation. When one uses Hindi or any other local lingo, one can add a lot more insight that is intrinsically Indian." She cites an interesting example; *'Enjoy Coca-Cola'* is insipid when compared to *'Thanda Matlab Coca-Cola'*. Prasoon Joshi, the leading ad man, explains why he supports Hindi vis-à-vis English. He says, "Attitudes are best expressed in Hindi as people understand and immediately connect with the language. Hindi is our street language and it delivers the punch that is required when communicating with the masses. In comparison, English, for most of us, is still a formal language. It is not a street language, like it is in New York". (Anand T 2005).

Bollywood

It is not an exaggeration that if you think of Hindi you think of Bollyhood. Today, there are two kinds of Hindi prevailing in India. The first is the 'official language' that is literary and complex and the second is common Hindi. Thanks to Bollywood for promoting and patronizing common Hindi in the entire world. Hindi films are quite popular throughout India. Indian audiences expect full value for their money with a good entertainer referred to as *'Paisa Vasool'* (literally money's worth). Hindi movies don't have language boundaries. Other language films have very limited market; they hardly find spectators outside their language boundaries. The popularity of Hindi movies is not restricted to Indian subcontinent only. From Bhangra music in Bangkok bars to weepy soap operas in London living room and Bollywood star power on European TV-Hindi entertainment is rocking the world. Once again, it is Bollywood that made *Bhailog Ki Bhasha* hit and hot. Even people don't hesitate to speak slang at hip parties in urban societies. "We don't watch Hindi movies," is no longer the urban snob's punch line. The credit goes to some imaginative filmmakers like Yash Chopra, Karan Johar, Sanjay Leela Bhansali and Ashustosh Gowarikar who altered the downmarket appeal of Bollywood and offered the sugar coated Hindi to the world. The jadoo has worked and Hindi is hip. It spells glamour, cheer and success.

New Language of Mobiles and Computers

Although the Hindi is not technical savvy language but the globalization makes it possible to some extent. Targeting the 43 percent of Indian population that understands Hindi, Nokia recently showcased three handsets with predictive text input to enable users to send and receive messages (SMS) in Hindi besides announcing a Hindi mobile portal. With this initiative on localization, now SMS becomes *Saral Mobile Sandesh* with text in Hindi. Now Hindi is the new language of mobile phones. Many more companies are planning to extent the benefit of mobile revolution to a larger consumer base of Hindi heartland. Hindi is also becoming computer friendly. Microsoft Corporation India Ltd has launched 'Office Hindi' its first offering developed specifically, for the Indian market, which combines computing experiences with familiarity of Hindi language. The package includes a Hindi language interface and support nine Indian languages, empowering Indian users to create documents and communicate with others in the language of their choice. It also makes computer function easy by producing menus and toolbars in Hindi.

Hindi Across India

The new avatar of Hindi is not limited to Hindi belt. A vernacular highbrow attitude is sweeping across India. In extreme northeast, people love to enjoy watching and singing Hindi movies and Hindi songs. Instead of repeated militants' threats and calls for ban on screening of Hindi movies, the cinegoers don't budge on visiting cinema halls. In the entire seven states of northeast, Hindi functions as a link language and commands unparalleled public support. The southern part of the country is not left untouched. In sharp contrast to anti-Hindi move of 1960s, the linguistic divide between north and south is shrinking. Chennai today is one of the cities, besides Bangalore and Hyderabad, where Hindi films are doing better than ever. South has its own Hindi ambassadors, who did great job to promote Hindi and synthesize north flavour and taste into south Indian films. South Indian film makers Mani Ratnam, musician A R Rahman, playback singer, Yasudas, Balasubramaniam, Shankar Mahadevan and Kavita Krishnmurti are saleable artists of Hindi entertainment industry. Our MPs from south, once elected to national parliament, need to speak in new Hindi to be accepted by the main stream, thus reducing the tension between Hindi and non-Hindi speakers. (Shankar S 2005) At Bangalore's high fashionable nightclub Zero G, the weekly Bollywood night when non-stop Hindi Film hits are played, pulls in maximum crowd. The Gujratis and Mumbai Bhais too find it as a trendy option.

New Bhasha - Hinglish

In all this time, the importance of English has never diminished. The advent of the Internet and the globalization only strengthened English. But it has changed the chemistry of relationship between English and Hindi. I think, it is 'BUY *ONE, GET ONE FREE'* syndrome that these two languages enjoy in India. Hindi no longer considers English as its archrival. Globalisation has changed the equation. English and Hindi have come closer and they deliver just perfect, when they work in tandem. Now, it is a winning blend. This blend becomes a new mantra in social acceptance, prestige, and success. Right from the Dabar Chawanprash slogan, '*Banaye Ander Se Strong*' to Coke's '*Life Ho To Aisi*'. The main part is predominantly in Hindi. It is true that this blend of Hindi and English has also flowered on the Internet. Hindi lost it tag of being down market and unfashionable. When I do my yoga lesson with morning Astha channel, Baba Ramdev used to instruct in this new bhasha: '*Pranayama se Hypertension Cure Hota Hai*'. And the rural folk will say "*Life Main Aaj Kal Bahut Tension Hai*". (There is a lot of tension in life these days).

Hindi Goes to Oxford

So what if Prince Charles has added Bollywood to his lingo? The 11th edition of Oxford Concise Dictionary has come out with 900 words of Indian origin. Needless to say, a lot is happening in Hindi, Hindustani, Hinglish, and Pinglish which is making the world sit back and take stock. But more importantly, there are greater dramatic twists and turns in desi lingo itself. Urban India doesn't believe in expressing itself in one form of English anymore. There is a separate bhasha for College, Corporate, Geeky, Tapori and Yuppie India. The uniqueness of this lingo is that it seems Latin and Greek for anybody who does not belong to that particular group. (Nikhat Kazmi 2004) "A surge in the use of Hindi in communication is a reflection of the confidence of New India". Says Piyush Pandey, executive Chairman and national creative director, Ogilvy and Mather Ltd, which has came out with a slang dictionary in which maximum words are in Hindi. *Bole Toh*, it's the staple diet of Hindi movies or we can say *Bhailog Ka Bhasha*. In this slang dictionary, a Tapori is known as '*street smart guy*'. When something goes wrong – '*Life Hai Mamoo*'. A happy-go-lucky guy is known as '*Bindaas*'. Something went terribly wrong – '*Bamboo Lag Gaya*'. A major happening- '*Raapchick*'. A very thin guy is called '*Agarbatti*' and a cool girl is '*Chhamiya*'. Maximum means '*Fulltoo*' and General Knowledge means '*Global Gyan*'. So the list is too long and it is increasingly becoming a part of the Queen's language.

Conclusion

Pushing this trend are three M's: media, marketing and money. The stylish new Bollywood, FM Radio and Satellite Television have not just made Hindi hot but have also redefined the cosmetic DNA of the global Indian. As a reflection, the entire vernacular has become dandy- kurta pyajama, lehanga choli, dhaabe ka khana, the Gujrati dandiya, religious tattoos or the remixed version of Om Jai Jagdish Hare. (Shafalee V: 2004) Hindi is accommodated everywhere. So a language that has survived through the centuries by marrying with different dialects and masters, is bouncing back again in India. But I fear a doubt that the way Hindi is being used today may not be the same in the next 50 years or so. The structure of Hindi is likely to change as it happened with English. Only time can speak how Hindi would hold a balance between the need of the market and the expectation of the purists. May God save the language and its speakers! Amen!

REFERENCES

1. Aanad, Tuhina. "Indian advertising speaks to the heart in Hindi" *<http://www.agencyfaqs.com/news/stories/2005/10/13/12949.html>*
2. Kazmi, Nikhat "Concise Desi Dix". *Times of India* July13, 2004. NE Edition
3. Mallikarjun, B. "Fifty Years of Language Planning for Modern Hindi: The Official Language of India." Language in India, www.languageinindia.com Vol. 4 November11, 2004 *LANGUAGE IN INDIA*.
4. National Readership Survey2005 *<http://newswatch.in>*
5. Shankar, Sadhana. "Meanwhile: A Mix of Hindi, English and 350 Million Speakers." *International Herald Tribune.* January11, 2005. <http://www.iht.com/articles>
6. Vasudev, Shefalee. "The Hindi High." *India Today*. June7, 2004:70-74.

23

Problems of Single Mother

Two Different Approaches

J.P. Dimri
A. Charumati Ramdas

In the 10th issue of Druzhba Narodov* for the year 2005, there appear two stories- one long and one short – about single mothers. The first one, "*A Tashkent Novel*", is written by Suhbat Aflatuni and the second, "*A Rattle*", by Galina Dzugashvily.

Suhbat Aflatuni is a young prosaist from Tashkent. He writes by two names: while writing poetry he uses the name Abdullaev Evgenyi Viktorovich and when he writes prose his name becomes Suhbat Aflatuni. Aflatuni was born in 1971 in Tashkent.

No information is given about Galina Dzugashvily in the journal. Galina is a young female writer from Georgia; she has only a couple of works to her credit. There is another Galina Dzugashvily, Stalin's granddaughter, who has become famous because of her memoirs about her grandfather. This Galina should not be mistaken for the granddaughter of Stalin.

The two stories under consideration deal with the problems the single mothers face while bringing up their child.

Aflatuni's "*A Tashkent Novel*" is the story of Lagi, an emancipated woman of the east, who lives in Uzbekistan in the 1980's and loses her husband as well as her passport before giving birth to her son. She is left in the company of her mother in law who supports her and shows the way to live her life.

"*A Rattle*" is a moving story about a nearly deaf and dumb child and his mother who believes in miracles and does witness them.

Seemingly very simple theme and the subsequent plots are

* The quotes are taken from Druzhba Narodov, No. 10, 2005.

treated differently by both the writers. We shall see in detail how Aflatuni and Dzugashvily narrate the ordeals of their protagonists.

Suhbat Aflatuni's "*A Tashkent Novel*" is not easy to read. Aflatuni does various experiments with the form of the story which remind us of the great masters of the Golden and the Silver ages of Russian literature. The plot expands to around sixty pages. While Dzugashvily's narration is linear in terms of chronology of time and events and is limited to just twelve pages.

"*A Tashkent Novel*" consists of five chapters. The chapters are named Lagi, Rafael, Yusuf, Arthurik and Martha.

As in M Yu Lermontov's "*A Hero of Our Time*", here also, each chapter describes the events of life of that particular person during that period. The connecting link between them being Lagi, like Pechorin in Lermontov's novel.

In addition to these there are a few supporting characters who serve as the backdrop for the development (if we could see such development) of the plot.

The first chapter "Lagi" describes Lagi's life which is depicted in the colors of melancholy and gloom. Lagi is about to give birth to a child. She rushes into the house with unbearable pain. The dark and humid flat on the ground floor seem to be her savior.

By this time Lagi had lost almost everything except her mother in law. Her almost legal husband disappeared in the western Kazakhstan. Then vanishes her job. Then came her father just to curse her, and after that he left her forever and then she found that even her passport was missing.

The clue to Lagi's name takes the reader to her past. In the passport Lagi's name was written as Luisa. Nobody except her father addressed her by this name. While applying for the new passport Lagi decides to bury this name. She is always curious to know why she was named "Luisa" and this search takes her to the years of the Second World War. But that does not happen soon. Aflatuni applies the devices of "Retardation" and "Making Strange" to solve this mystery.

The child, Sultan, filled all the empty corners of her life. Even the mother in law is happy.

When Sultan is one month old, a young mystic healer, Majus, who lived in the opposite building, meets her. Majus is a strange person. Whenever he talks to someone he falls terribly sick. Majus sends his younger brother Malik to take Lagi into the underground cellar. Lagi is lashed just once on her arrival in the cellar because that is the ritual. There, in front of three candles, Lagi comes to know of her true self. She comes face to face with her sharp, transparent thoughts, with her formulae which constituted Lagi.

Lagi is described by the author much in the same way as Lermontov describes Pechorin.

Again a flash back! But these flash backs are also not continuous; they are intercepted by present day events.

When Lagi's stepmother dies suddenly of heart attack while cutting onion in the kitchen, Lagi who consisted of only memories, finds that her memory has branched out into two similar parts like the stream of a river when it meets an obstacle on the way. Since then she never had sound sleep and most of the time, during night, "saw only memories".

She as well forgot to cry!

This tearless Lagi had made a house of books for herself. Though she did not understand much of what she read, the books gave her a feeling of security. In this house of books she invites Yusuf. She gets intimate with him and informs father about him only when she is expecting the child.

The marriage did not take place in the Registrar's office. A Mulla performed the ritual. Even before the son was born Yusuf leaves her and goes away.

Aflatuni has an absurd way of describing his characters.

Lagi's mother in law's life is built on "Science and Life". Each of the characters (like probably every human being) has an Angel of Sleep. Mother in Law's Angel listens to the concert on Radio. Beethoven's "To Alice" is being aired everywhere. This is heard by Lagi's father in a hospital. Lagi's father loved this composition. This reminded him of the woman he fell in love with in Germany during the World War. The vision of snow clad city, the curfew, the firing during that hour always accompany Lagi's father.

Aflatuni gives the life story of each character bit-by-bit in almost all chapters. The plot moves very slowly. The backward and forward swing of time makes the plot not easily comprehensible.

The time goes backward and forward not only by a few years, but it goes to ancient times, when some Buddhist monks are also introduced in the fabric of the plot. The presentation looks like a collage of bits and pieces of life of characters.

Aflatuni's style reminds the reader of the style of symbolists, oberiutians, and faktoviks. It also reminds of the modern "Zhyostkaya Proza".

Let us go back to Lagi.

Lagi receives a telegram that her father is in a hospital in Tashkent. She has to visit him. At the same time Yusuf sends her a letter informing why he was leaving her. His so called "Midnight Sickness" was getting severe day by day. He leaves Lagi and joins a group of archeologists.

If Yusuf is not unfaithful to her, why don't they unite again?

Using the device of "Retardation" Aflatuni shows why Yusuf's letters do not reach Lagi, why Lagi goes into the kitchen precisely at the same moment when Yusuf is being shown on the television along with other archeologists. Finally Lagi meets Yusuf only when she is supposedly in love with another person. He divorces Lagi in a restaurant by uttering "Talaq!" thrice.

Majus had told her, "You will have lots of worries and even men--worries, definitely more,-and men-exactly two. One of them will be a helper and the other -a charmer."

Lagi meets this helper, an elderly man, in the aeroplane when she is going to Tashkent to visit her father. His name is Rafael. He proposes to her, she refuses and he goes to Israel.

Lagi goes to her father who is on the deathbed. He forgives her.

Lagi inherits from her father his old ancestral house and a big box of books. While going through the old papers left by her father, Lagi comes to know about the mystery behind her name. But Aflatuni does not take us there so soon. The reader has to pass through absurd and abstract memories of Lagi's father and his friend. The way to reach them is through the dial of a cuckoo clock. As an hour strikes on the clock a Turkish soldier comes out of the window on the dial and the whole drama, which took place during the war, unfolds...

Lagi's father, Nasreddin Umarovich Khojaev was born in the year 1918. Aflatuni emphasizes that the year of conception was 1917. He had fought the Second World War. He remembers his life....again and again.

Once Lagi is in Tashkent she decides to reconstruct her life. She is scared to stay alone in the old house of her father but she also knows that "Cowardice is inability!" And "Fear is a disease!" (How much like Bulgakov and Chekhov!!).

One very interesting thing in the novel is that answers to many problems are suggested in dreams. (Readymade recipe!)

The backward and forward swing of time is not depicted in terms of real life incidents. Instead, there are symbols everywhere, there is darkness, drowsiness... and on top of it is Lagi's imagination. Her understanding of "Men's world" is depicted in very harsh, not at all aesthetic way. Here is an example:

"The world of Man, attraction towards which Lagi resisted, was hanging above her like a ship of strangers. This world is full of jungle-laws, bloody football matches and obscene photo sessions where special dolls (Lagi initially did not guess that these were living girls) showed themselves up silently. This world was shameless-victory, like the smell from the school toilet "M"...."

Lagi has a constant friend-semi transparent dream. This friend accompanies her when she is awake. Lagi gets clarifications about various problems from him.

Now, from chapter 2, the dream asks her to repeat the verb "Budh" (meaning of this Sanskrit verb is to wake up, to learn, to know). While doing so she enters the world of her dream....but the interesting thing is that this dream is shared by one and all. From here begins the theme of Buddhist monks, which occupies a prominent place in the novel.

Lagi in her semi transparent dream holds Sultan, who was playing a flute, in her hands. Suddenly the space transforms into underground monasteries. There is an unnoticeable swing from real to the unreal and we see the sleepy Buddhaghosha Vinayaka, who took the sound of flute as arrival of winter and he got scared. "Lotus is frozen", but there was no need to get frightened as here, in the country of northern monks, where he was a guest and was going through books, there was no lotus.

Carrying the books with him Vinayaka had come to this place where the monks were living in the hand-made, underground caves.

The theme of monks seems to have a sub-structural significance, with which we shall deal a little later.

Coming back to Lagi: She decides to continue her studies in the University at the Eastern faculty.

In chapter 3 the author tells us about Yusuf. Yusuf had also been a victim of the underground cellar. He sees his dead father in the cellar... the uneasiness; this so called "Midnight Sickness" grows so severe that he has to run away from his house and from his wife. He sends letters to Lagi explaining the whole thing and about his present work but the mother in law does not show these letters to Lagi. Once Yusuf was even shown on the television along with other German excavators with whom he was working, but Aflatuni sends Lagi into the kitchen precisely at the same moment when Yusuf was shown on the screen.

Finally, when Yusuf comes face-to-face with Lagi he utters "Talaq!" thrice and goes to Moscow for further studies.

The younger brother of Majus, the mysterious healer, Malik is also interested in Lagi. But no special chapter is dedicated to him in the novel.

There is Arthurik in the team of excavators. Arthurik is a German. He is given a letter by Rafael for translation. The letter is written in German by Lagi's father. Through this letter Lagi comes to know that her father fell in love with a woman called Luisa in Austria. She was killed by some other soldier during the curfew. Lagi's father loved her so much that back home he named his daughter as Luisa.

Lagi becomes intimate with Arthurik. She spends the New Year eve with him. Later Arthurik also goes away.

With all these things going on Sultan does not seem to be getting any attention from Lagi. One year passed by and again there is a forward swing of time by twenty five years.

The last chapter "Martha" sums up everything that had happened with each character.

Sultan is twenty five years old. They all assemble at a festival, where even the dead are present.

Lagi's father tells Sultan who has done his master's in Vienna, "All that you came to know about me in Vienna took away a lot of your time. And that which requires a lot of time is not 'real'...You should frequently converse with your memory. It has every thing that a man needs". Then he advises Sultan to go to the young people ("Don't dig into the past, go ahead with the river of time").

Even Sultan's grand mother who was present there tells him, "I am not dead. The old guard does not hang its nose."

Sultan says that he was looking for the epigraph for his novel "*A Tashkent Novel*".

This was the marriage of Hasan's daughter. Hasan was the

younger brother of Yusuf. Grand mother also asks Sultan not to forget the blood relations. It is unpardonable.

Majus is still healing... he is famous and rich.

In the end Lagi is seen going with her husband... Yusuf or Malik... could not be seen clearly.

Beneath this story which seems full of absurdities, lies a serious theme, that of the country of the author. The sentence "Uzbekistan is a country of great future" makes one believe that this is not a simple story of the single mother. Single mother is just a metaphor. In reality it is the story of Uzbekistan through ages, since the time immemorial.

A look at the biography of Lagi's father tells that he was born in 1918. Aflatuni also stresses that he was conceived in 1917. (The year of the Great October Revolution). So this phase begins with the Revolution. And it ends with the death of Lagi's father, in the beginning of 80's, when one after the other the Republics were declaring their independence. What follows in the next twenty five years is the uneasiness and uncertainty in the life of the country.

Does the assertion that "the old guard does not hang its nose" point towards a possible return of the pre-80's regime? Also the young generation, Sultan, who is declared as the king of the future is advised not to break relations with the past, it is unpardonable. The ancient past is described through the theme of the monks. The author leaves a note of uncertainty at the end. Lagi is seen going with her husband – who was he? Yusuf, who had left Uzbekistan and gone to Moscow for further progress or Malik who remained in the country? This seems to again start a debate about whether the country should look westwards or look into its tradition for the progress.

Aflatuni's story does not at all throw light on the difficulties Lagi faced while bringing up Sultan. As if the things happened automatically and twenty years pass by just like that. But Galina Dzugashvily's story is the story of real struggle of a single mother, Asya.

When Asya was expecting her child, Galina Dzugashvily says that like every expectant mother she did not want to have a daughter ("I don't need any girl... I myself am a girl.. If she takes birth, I shall not take her, just leave her there itself and that's all...")

And then, to her delight, a boy is born.

The child had some defect. His mouth was a little distorted...the doctors assured her that massage and physiotherapy would set things right in future. Asya did not look at the defect seriously. For her it was more important that the child was a boy, not a girl, and for a boy the defects do not matter.

Even at three years the child could hardly speak 'mama', he seemed even deaf. His eyesight too seemed a little abnormal.

Asya started teaching him with the help of toys... the progress was very slow. He was sent to a special school, but this too did not help much.

Asya's husband remained indifferent to the child. Though initially he would buy things necessary for the education of the child, slowly he started disappearing from the house. Then he opted for a job at a far away place and detached himself from Asya and *her* child. He would come to see Asya just once a year.

The child was growing--only physically, the mental progress is very slow.

Then Asya approaches a healer about whom she came to know from a television program.

Asya and the child watch a television program, in which people from another planet healed a boy from Georgia. After watching the program Asya's child asks her, "Why don't they heal me?"

Since then he started waiting for a miracle to happen, he started waiting for the arrival of a healer from the other planet.

He visualizes his arrival.

Once he feels that someone has entered his room and he is confident that it is the "Other planet man." The belief that someone had visited him makes him feel better.

But when for many days, there was no further miracle taking place, the boy started getting restless. Asya felt that he *had* to feel the presence of an unseen stranger in order to get normal. Then she recorded an unknown whispering voice in the cassette recorder and started playing it for a fraction of a second. The child would feel that someone is talking to him, someone is healing him! And slowly he became almost normal. He even finished the arts faculty in the university, he draws landscapes, is working in a departmental store.

He is now 28!

The struggle and determination of Asya made the child normal.

The miracle was performed by none other but by Asya herself.

"*A Rattle*" is a very realistic story devoid of any absurdity. The narration is simple, chronologically straight.

Thus we see that though the theme of both the stories is the same but the authors have made them look entirely different.

Perhaps that is the difference between the style and approach of a male and a female author towards the problem of a single mother.

24

Contemporary Russian Plays

A New Experience

Nasar Shakeel Roomi

Plays are written to be staged. The plays written should be of such intense emotional temper that the reader having read the play waits impatiently for the text to come alive on the stage. Some plays are such that ,even while reading we feel as if we are actually watching it being enacted and as a spectator the reader thinks that he is actually one of the characters. He starts associating himself with the characters and says it aloud: This is all about me! Just like any literary work of other genre, a play also surpasses all geographical boundaries. Many of us might not have actually seen the contemporary Russian plays on stage but nevertheless while reading many of the plays we actually find ourselves amongst the spectators sitting far away in Moscow, St. Petersburg or Yekaterinburg.

Russia has always been addicted to theatre. Classical Russian plays mesmerized their audience with talented directors and actors making every play a success. Then the plays written were absorbing to the extent that even today we read and reread them with the same interest and passion. However, reading Russian plays of contemporary times is a very different experience. Along with the changing socio-economic order the stage of Russian drama too, naturally, has gone through a sea change. Some plays are extraordinarily interesting, intriguing and captivating. They have taken both Russia and the West by storm. Undoubtedly, the talent has surfaced in a very different atmosphere. This talent is young and diverse.

Today's Russian play has its lexicon derived from today's Russian language with all its specificities. The language of the plays also includes words and expressions which were a taboo and forbidden before. Like in one of the plays of N. Kolyada "The lady of my dreams" the hero uses all possible foul words and remarks that the dictionary of Dal' and Ozhegov have taught me to use foul language. Let me not take it out of context. About this play, I will speak later in the paper. These plays differ from the plays we usually associate the Russian theatre with. The entire structure of the plays has changed. Many of the plays, which do not go unnoticed, are monodramas, where one character speaks about him and in doing so, he speaks about many of us. He is directly in conversation with the reader or the spectator.

There is a huge variety of plays both theme wise and technique wise. There are plays with multiple characters and there are monodramas.

The tradition of monodrama is as old as the theatre itself. This tradition was actually started with bards and storytellers. These were the only central characters and centre of attraction. Before them was only the audience. This form of drama dealt deeply inside the inner world of the hero. As M. Anderson has aptly put it, "the story must be a conflict and specially a conflict between the forces of good and evil within a single person".

One of the playwrights who have many interesting plays to his credit is N. Kolyada. He is the author of more than 70 plays, that is, as one critic remarked, even more than the number of plays that Shakespeare had written. He is not only a talented playwright but also a great actor- director. Besides this, he has been instrumental in nurturing the talents of young playwrights. Many of his students are today world famous playwrights. Oleg Bogaev, Tatyana Garbar, Natalya Malashenko, Tatyana Filatova, Igor Beloglazov, Alexander Naidakov to name a few have attracted the attention of many theatres. Nikolai Kolyada is undoubtedly an institution by himself.

N. Kolyada's "Lady of My Dreams" is one of his best plays. Who is this Lady of dreams? This is actually the name of a film, which was confiscated by the Soviet army after the victory in Germany. Marica Reok is the heroine of this film. The German actor worked for the KGB during the third Reich along with another actor Olga Chekhova and the Swedish actor Zara Leander. This film ran in almost all the theatres in the Soviet Union after the Victory and Marica came to Moscow during the premier. Her name is mentioned many a times during Kolyada's play. It was the dream of the two characters of this play in their prime to be like Marica, maybe not as a spy but certainly as beautiful as Marica.

Kolyada's "The Lady of My Dreams" has all the elements of an absorbing play. It is a serious play with the tones of humor and suspense. At times the reader is even confused as to what is happening and how is it going to end.

The playwright mentions in the very beginning that it is a monologue in one act. The characters in the play are SHE, Voice, VOICES.

The play starts with the scene where a woman is sitting alone in her one room flat and in the adjoining room, loud music is playing. This irritates her. Suddenly the phone rings. She picks it up. She starts to speak to somebody who she thinks is her friend and next room neighbor Ella Nikolaevna. In the beginning, we understand that call is definitely a distance call as repeatedly SHE repeats the word "ne slishna", cannot hear. "Maybe I will call you back". In a dramatic way, which only such plays can offer, we find out that the person she is speaking to is dead long back. In the play we realize that it is not the first time that whenever she gets a phone call by someone who by mistake had dialed her number, she takes that her friend Ella is calling her from the heaven.

The whole haze gets clearer as we approach the end of the play. The monologues take us to the entire gambit of the inner world of the character.

It is not a case of psychological insanity but a case of psychological isolation. Sometimes her monologue seems dull, ordinary. However, if we read with more attention we find that in her monologue She raises many interesting and relevant issues.

Take for example while speaking to Ella, she asks, whether Ella has seen God and spoken to him. However, later after putting down the phone she suddenly realizes that fifty years back she had been a member of the communist party and she herself was a party to the demolition of the St. John's church in 1933 as a representative of the Komsomol atheistic movement and hence there cannot be any god.

These monologues carry many contemporary social issues and changed human attitude. In her monologue conversation, she divides the countrywomen into three kinds: One who goes out in fur coats and suddenly one fine morning they become filthy rich thanks to their husband's speculator friends. Moreover, because they are scared that they might become beggars again as fast as they became rich because as the pitcher goes often to the well, but is broken at last, they show their false kindness is seen clearly.

The second kind is straight from a bourgeois film. They stink of perfume, chew chewing gums and look straight through you if you happen to meet them on the way.

Moreover, the third are those communist "bitches" who even today think that they are living in communist times as if the promises given to them during the communist rule have been fulfilled. These communists always have their hair done such that they never sleep because if you sleep you spoil your hairstyle. Not that they are awake day and night but they use foreign made lacquer and secondly they go to foreign countries and buy special nets made of almost invisibly thin but horribly strong metal in which they even sleep and thus their hair style remains intact.

Her sarcasm and her desperation on not being amongst the privileged are very evident here.

Imagine the condition of the person on the other side of the telephone who unfortunately for himself dialed her number. He shouts in Russian that he is calling from Australia and desperately wants her to receive the fax. He repeats the word fax in Russian факс! факс! факс! Moreover, uses the rhyming word in English (which cannot be repeated in this auditorium). She laughs and says, "O! From Australia! He is shouting as if it is in the other world. From Australia and he is speaking in Russian. Amazing! Our men are all over the place. Everyone has left the land they were born in and forgotten the place they used to play in the snow".

After the man disconnects in desperation she pleads: "Ella do not go! Ok, you were Marika, not me, but do not go".

We have heard of the stream of consciousness and this is what is very much evident in this play.

Maybe Grishkovets, another very talented and famous not only in Russia but even abroad, took the same kind of desperation and confusion but in his own unique way in his classic "The City". He was born in 1967 and is a winner of "Antibooker", Triumph,

I had mentioned earlier, the very style of presenting such plays have changed. This play was staged in conventional theatre but outside the theatre without the prior knowledge of the spectators. The spectators did not even notice when the play started. So the play City was staged right in the city. The mere fact that the spectators did not notice the beginning of the play goes to prove that the aim of the writer, who happens to be the main actor in the play, was to make the spectators see themselves in the actors playing in the play. Because contemporary plays speak the language of the common person, they are about their feelings and the problems they face. In these plays, the number of characters and the duration of plays have decreased. The reasons can be many. What I understand is it is easy to identify oneself with the feelings of the character when one actor is actually speaking to you. The shortening of the duration keeps your attention alive and alert. There is a tendency in many of these plays is to portray the loneliness of the person. Hence, many plays are actually monodramas.

The hero of "The City" argues with the taxi driver for the sake of it. May be for relieving the tension he is going through. He is mixed up with the words but the reader is always in a position to understand him. The hero might be going through the same thoughts as many of his contemporaries. There is utter confusion in his mind. He at times accepts that in this city everything thing he has is good. The house is good. There is nothing wrong in the place he works in. He has a loving wife. However, nothing is good in this good! He is unable to accept this city and wants to leave it without knowing why and where.

The hero finds himself in a place where he feels that nobody understands him. Hence, he switches off the phone. If somebody comes to his house, that too his friend and asks for money as he has to pay for the repair work, our hero cannot even refuse properly. The friend thinks he is angry and has humiliated him though he did not intend to do so. He goes to his father to explain as to why he is leaving the city but just could not because of the internal contradictions that make him more difficult to understand.

This continues fight with himself and his contradictions are probably contradictions within the system he is living. His own actions and his way of speaking go against him. He gets into arguments without any reason and without even realizing. He wants to hurl all his irritation on to anybody he gets to speak be his wife, or father or his friend. Moreover, in spite of the fact that they do understand Sergei's absurd pretensions start reacting, which make things even worse.

He finally leaves the city without knowing where and without enough money. In the taxi from the station, he gets into a meaningless argument with the cabman. Somehow, Grishkovets hero gives the impression of egocentricity. His other plays which became famous worldwide are "How I Ate the Dog" and "The Shirt" and others.

25

Россия на рубеже XX-XXI веков: изменения в культуре, языке, коммуникации

Т.В. Ларина

Изменения, происходящие в политической, социально-экономической областях, затрагивают все сферы человеческой деятельности. Ярким примером этому является современная Россия, где за последние два десятилетия реформ, характеризующихся открытой ориентацией на Запад, мы наблюдаем значительные изменения в идеологии, мировоззрении, ценностях, типе взаимоотношений. Существенные изменения произошли также в языке, речи, коммуникативном поведении.

В статье планируется рассмотреть некоторые характеристики двух типов культур (индивидуалистической в сравнении с коллективистской) и определить, какие из ценностных ориентиров в большей степени характерны для современной России, также обозначить ряд изменений в языке, речи, коммуникативном поведении. Поскольку данный процесс чрезвычайно сложный и многоаспектный, цель данной статьи – лишь обозначить некоторые тенденции, каждая из которых является объектом серьезного и глубокого изучения.

Ключевые слова: тип культуры, коллективизм, индивидуализм, культурные ценности, инокультурное влияние, иноязычные заимствования, демократизация языка, демократизация речи.

1. ПЕРЕОРИЕНТАЦИЯ КУЛЬТУРНЫХ ЦЕННОСТЕЙ

Традиционно, как известно, Россия относится к коллективистскому типу культуры, в центре ценностной иерархии которой находятся *коллективизм, соборность, общение, человеческие отношения, духовность.* Ценности индивидуалистической западной культуры, особенно протестантской, такие как *независимость личности, ее индивидуальность, прагматизм, приоритет материального над духовным*, как правило, осуждались. Однако за последние два десятилетия выросло поколение людей, сформировавшихся в других социально-политических условиях, в сознании которых наблюдается некоторая ценностная переориентация, отход от традиционных коллективистских ценностей.

Наблюдается процесс распада межличностных связей, люди стали меньше общаться, отношения все чаще строятся не на основе личных симпатий и привязанностей, а на прагматически ориентированных правилах. Духовные ценности утрачивают свое место в иерархии ценностных приоритетов. Для молодого поколения россиян на первое место выходят ценности материальные, что влечет за собой переориентацию качеств личности. Помимо качеств общинной личности, важнейшими из которых являются *доброта, сострадание, сочувствие, человеколюбие, бескорыстие, искренность, ориентированность на интересы коллектива* (а иногда и в ущерб им), большую ценность начинают играть качества индивидуалистической личности – *независимость, инициативность, деловитость, амбициозность, предприимчивость, ориентированность на личный успех,* которые ранее ценностями не являлись. Данные ценности пропагандируются средствами массовой информации и кино. Их значимость в новых экономических условиях доказывает и сама жизнь.

Нельзя утверждать, что Россия в результате инокультурного влияния, а также социально-политического и экономического реформирования становится или непременно станет культурой индивидуалистического типа, однако если сравнить характеристики данных типов культур, предложенные Г. Хофштеде [Hofstede 1991] для разных ситуаций (в семье, в школе, на работе, в политике, идеологии и др.), то наблюдается весьма интересная тенденция. Отвечая на вопрос, какие из отмеченных характеристик в большей степени типичны для русской культуры, информанты в возрасте 30-35 лет называют те, что относятся к коллективистскому типу культуры, признавая при этом, что в настоящее время наблюдается некоторая тенденция смещения в сторону индивидуалистических характеристик. Информанты, чей возраст 20-25 лет, выбирают индивидуалистические черты и модели поведения. Так, например, они отмечают, что в России интересы личности важнее интересов группы (семьи, трудового коллектива); приоритет отдается выполнению поставленной задачи, а не поддержанию межличностных отношений; устройство на работу, а также дальнейшее продвижение по служебной лестнице зависит от личных способностей и достижений индивида, а не отношений и связей; в семье родители обращаются с детьми как с равными, а не учат их послушанию и подчинению и т.п.

Данный анализ позволяет предположить, что в процессе адаптации к западному миру, в стремлении интегрировать в него, а также в результате проводимых реформ, Россия, оставаясь культурой коллективистского типа, приобретает некоторые черты, свойственные индивидуалистическим культурам, что находит отражение в сознании людей, проявляется в межличностных отношениях, в моделях поведения и т.д. Вряд ли можно оценивать этот процесс однозначно, приветствовать его или осуждать, как и серьезно повлиять на него. По-видимому, это объективный процесс, являющийся ярким подтверждением того, что культура - способ адаптации к окружающей действительности, и она неизбежно изменяется по мере изменения этой действительности. Положительные моменты существуют в обоих типах культур. Симбиоз наиболее рациональных черт может, безусловно, обогатить русскую культуру и положительно сказаться на поступательном движении страны. Главное здесь не перейти к крайностям, не отказаться от своего в пользу чужого, не увлечься слепым копированием и подражанием.

2. ИНОЯЗЫЧНОЕ ВЛИЯНИЕ НА ЯЗЫК

Широкое проникновение в русский язык иноязычной лексики и ее активное употребление в самых разных сферах является одним из наиболее значимых языковых процессов последних десятилетий. При этом, как отмечают исследователи, следует говорить именно об активизации употребления этих слов, а не только о новых заимствованиях, поскольку наряду с появлением заимствований-неологизмов наблюдается расширение сфер использования специальной иноязычной терминологии, относящейся к экономике, финансам, коммерческой деятельности и некоторым другим областям [Крысин 2004: 184]. Стимулом для этого послужили отмеченные выше политические, экономические, социальные изменения, расширение международных контактов на всех уровнях, интегративные тенденции. Подавляющее большинство иноязычных слов заимствуется сейчас из английского языка, что вполне закономерно, поскольку английский язык приобрел статус глобального языка (Global language) и сфера его распространения и влияния в наши дни огромна.

Изменения в политической системе привели к активному употреблению таких слов, как парламент, президент, премьер-министр, вице-премьер спикер, мэр, префект, префектура, муниципалитет, импичмент, электорат, инаугурация, лоббист и др.

Экономические изменения, ориентация на западно-экономическую и финансовую системы вызвали необходимость приобщения к интернациональной терминологии. В результате в русский язык вошло большое количество экономических и финансовых терминов: аудит, консалтинг, брокер, дилер, маркетолог, инвестор, дистрибьютор, фьючерс, лизинг, логистика, аутсорсинг, рекрутинг и др.

Одним из источников появления новых слов являются компьютерные технологии, откуда пришли такие слова, как дисплей, файл, сайт, вэб-сайт, интернет, хакер, винчестер, принтер, сканер, байт, и др.

Активное освоение иноязычной лексики характерно для развлекательной индустрии: шоу-бизнес, ток-шоу, шоу-мен, дискотека, диск-жокей, ди-джей, римейк, хит-парад, казино, крупье, джекпот, кар-центр, фитнес-центр, триллер, сиквел, пейнтбол и т.д.

Большое количество заимствований наблюдается в области спорта, что связано как с появлением новых видов спорта (виндсерфинг, бобслей, скейтборд, армреслинг, фристайл, кикбоксинг, кайтинг, керлинг), так и с явным предпочтением, отдаваемым английской терминологии, которая вытесняет русскую: вратарь - голкипер, добавочное время – овертайм, судья – рефери, плэй-оф - решающая стадия турнира, хафбек – полузащитник.

Развитие ресторанного бизнеса ввело в обиход слова макдональдс, пиццерия, стейк-хаус, гриль-бар, кофе-хаус, паб и др.

Еще одним проявлением иноязычного влияния на русский язык является калькирование. Как и у заимствований, главный источник калек - английский язык, основными сферами остаются политика, дипломатия, мода, спорт и др. Если ранее преобладали кальки словообразовательные (небоскреб – skyscraper), то в наши дни преобладают кальки семантические (продвинутый – калька с англ. advanced) и сочетаемостные (горячая линия – hot line, утечка мозгов – < brain drain, отмывать деньги - < to launder money) [см. Крысин 2004: 221-226].

Встречается калькирование целых речевых формул. Так, например, в современных средствах массовой информации все чаще можно услышать речевые клише, являющиеся кальками с английского языка: Оставайтесь с нами (Stay with us) / Берегите себя (Take care). В последнем случае, очевидно, можно говорить о функциональном калькировании. Речевая формула Береги-те себя существовала в русском языке и раньше, однако и сфера ее употребления, и семантика были иными. Традиционно она употреблялась при прощании близких людей (перед долгой разлукой, дальней поездкой) и имела буквальное значение. Берегите себя, сказанное диктором телевидения после окончания передачи, на наш взгляд, является калькой английской формулы Take care, которая в английской коммуникации является знаком прощания и не более того и может употребляться в адрес незнакомых людей.

3. ДЕМОКРАТИЗАЦИЯ ЯЗЫКА И РЕЧИ

Демократия, давшая свободу слова, привела к свободе речи. Резко возросла употребительность разговорных элементов, просторечий, жаргонизмов и даже обсценной лексики, что послужило причиной огрубления речи в разных сферах. Исследователи характеризуют этот процесс как «перемещение лексических элементов периферийных сфер языка в центр системы» [Земская 2004: 515] и объясняют его тем, что расширились рамки публичной речи (телевидение, радио, митинги, собрания), к которой приобщились новые слои населения. Политики, общественные деятели свободно допускают в своих выступления и высказываниях не только сниженную, но и обсценную лексику. Разговорные и просторечные элементы, даже жаргонизмы широко употребляются в языке газет как вызов универсальному бюрократическому языку советской прессы, изобилующему штампами и канцеляризмами. Процесс включения сниженных элементов в литературный текст лингвисты называют термином *демократизация языка* [Земская 2004:516].

Сниженная лексика, включая сквернословие, стала все чаще встречаться в речи образованных людей. Отмечается ее распространенность в актерской, писательской, журналистской среде [Крысин 2004: 263]. При этом если раньше она чаще использовалась мужчинами, то теперь роль гендерного фактора снижается и подобная лексика употребляется как мужчинами, так и женщинами. Пока еще сохраняются ограничения, связанные с типом адресата: обсценная лексика употребляется более свободно в среде однородной по полу и возрасту, чем в гетерогенной. Однако, думается, что если этот процесс будет продолжаться, пол коммуникантов перестанет иметь значение, как это произошло, например, в Ирландии, где мужчины свободно используют сквернословие в присутствии женщин или даже обращаясь к ним. При этом важно подчеркнуть, что как в англоязычной коммуникации, так и в русской, в дружеском общении сквернословие выполняет не функцию инвективы, а используется в качестве средства экспрессивности и как знак принадлежности к группе [подробнее см. Ларина 2004].

Следует отметить, что в сфере обслуживания наблюдается противоположный процесс - возрастание вежливости, что является заимствованием модели западного коммуникативного поведения и соответствует новым экономическим условиям. Особенно это ощутимо в сфере торговли, где продавцам магазинов, кассирам предписано улыбаться покупателям и клиентам, здороваться с ними, благодарить за покупку: *Добрый день / Могу я вам чем-нибудь помочь? / Благодарю за покупку / Спасибо за покупку / Заходите к нам еще.* Вместо однословных резких надписей *Не курить! / Ремонт / Учет / Закрыто* можно встретить более мягкие по тональности надписи, ориентированные не только на передачу информации, но и на отношение к адресату: *У нас не курят / Извините. Закрыто на учет / Идет ремонт. Приносим извинения за доставленные неудобства / Мы переехали.*

Изменения социальных отношений и переориентация культурных ценностей незамедлительно отразились на формах обращения. Ушли в прошлое советские и партийные обращения *гражданин, гражданка, товарищ*, являвшиеся маркерами всеобщего равенства и единства, на смену им пришли *господин, госпожа, дамы и господа,* в которых подчеркивается не только высокий статус адресата, но и уважение его личности.

В то же время в асимметричных отношениях, то есть при наличии вертикальной дистанции (возрастной и/или статусной), наблюдается противоположная тенденция - понижение статуса вышестоящего. Примером этому является сужение сферы употребления традиционной русской формы обращения по имени-отчеству и переход на обращение к старшим по имени. В средствах массовой информации, даже говоря о высших должностных лицах, не употребляют отчество *(президент Владимир Путин / премьер Михаил Фрадков).* Во многих компаниях, в первую очередь с западным стилем управления, коллеги обращаются друг к другу по имени, невзирая на разницу в возрасте и должности, это распространяется также на ситуацию *начальник-подчиненный.* Подобные явления наблюдаются во многих странах Запада, в частности, в английской коммуникации, где по имени обращаются не только подчиненные к начальнику, но и студенты к преподавателю. Перенос данной коммуникативной традиции на русскую почву происходит в некоторой степени насильственно. Многие русские информанты жалуются на то, что им очень трудно и неудобно называть своего начальника по имени, в то время как он настаивает на этом.

Еще одной современной тенденцией, наблюдаемой в сфере обращений, является сокращение употреблений в качестве формул обращения терминов родства (*дедушка / бабушка / дядя / тетя*). В результате все чаще встречаются случаи, когда дети обращаются к своим старшим по возрасту родственникам, соседям, друзьям родителей по имени. Молодожены начинают обращаться по имени к родителям мужа/жены (вместо обращения по имени-отчеству). Данное явление, характерное для английского коммуникативного поведения, в русской культуре до недавнего времени считалось недопустимой фамильярностью.

Приведенные факты свидетельствуют об изменениях в русском коммуникативном поведении, в выборе стратегий. Вместо подчеркивания более высокого статуса выбирается стратегия, направленная на демонстрацию равенства, что свидетельствует о демократизации речи. Как и в английском контексте, обращение к старшим по имени в данном случае фамильярностью не является. Напротив, здесь имеет место реализация стратегий вежливости - позитивной вежливости (positive politeness) в терминах Brown & Levinson [Brown & Levinson 1987], или вежливости сближения [Ларина 2003]), нацеленной на устранение статусных различий, что находится в полном соответствии с английской системой вежливости и индивидуалистическим типом культуры, но является новой тенденцией в русской коммуникативной культуре.

Как отмечает Г.Хофштеде, если для коллективистских культур характерна уважительная манера обращения студентов к преподавателю (Students treat teachers with respect), то в индивидуалистических студенты обращаются с преподавателями как с равными (Students treat teachers as equals) [Hofstede 1991:37]. То же наблюдается и в ситуации *начальник - подчиненный*: в индивидуалистических культурах лица, обладающие властью, стараются не демонстрировать эту власть (Powerful people try to look less powerful than they are), в то время как в коллективистских наоборот (Powerful people try to look as impressive as possible) [Hofstede 1991: 43]. Таким образом, демократизация речи также является результатом смещения в сторону индивидуалистических ценностей и моделей поведения.

Заключение

Приведенные факты свидетельствуют о том, что ориентация России в сторону Запада в разных областях жизни привела к серьезным изменениям в культуре. Наблюдается переориентация культурных ценностей и сдвиг в сторону индивидуалистического мировоззрения. Заметны изменения в языке, речи, коммуникативном поведении.

Иноязычное влияние на русский язык в последние десятилетия более интенсивно, чем в предшествующее время, что проявляется в широком заимствовании иноязычной лексики и активизации ее употребления. Изменения в языковом функционировании идут в двух противоположных направлениях: огрубление языка в обиходно-бытовой и публичной сферах и рост вежливости в сфере обслуживания.

Сдвиг в сторону индивидуалистической идеологии с характерной для нее ценностью равенства проявился в формулах обращений, которые стали менее формальными, что позволяет говорить о демократизации речи, об изменениях в коммуникативном поведении.

ЛИТЕРАТУРА:

1. Земская Е.А. *Язык как деятельность: Морфема. Слово. Речь.* - М.: Языки славянской культуры, 2004.
2. Крысин Л.П. *Русское слово, свое и чужое: Исследования по современному русскому языку и социолингвистике.* – М.: Языки славянской культуры, 2004.
3. Ларина Т.В. *Категория вежливости в английской и русской коммуникативных культурах:* Монография. – М.: Изд-во РУДН, 2003.
4. Ларина Т.В. Неформальность как одна из доминантных черт английской коммуникативной культуры // *Язык. Речь. Речевая деятельность.* Вып.6: Межвузовский сборник научных трудов. -

Нижний Новгород: Нижегородский государственный лингвистический университет им. Н.А.Добролюбова, 2004. – С. 65-76.

5. Brown Penelope and Stephen D. Levinson. *Politeness: Some universals in language usage.* - Cambridge: Cambridge University Press, 1987.
6. Hofstede, Geert H. Cultures and Organizations: Software of the mind. London. 1991.

26

Центральная Азия: встреча культурных традиций Востока и Запада

М. Л. Ахмедова

Центральная Азия географически и исторически является связующим звеном между странами Востока и Запада. В далёкой древности здесь находился главный отрезок Великого шёлкового пути, пролегающего из Рима в Китай. Через эту трансазиатскую магистраль край был связан на Востоке с Китаем, на Юге с Индией, на Западе морским путём через Египет и по суше через Иран со странами средиземноморского бассейна. Через Центральную Азию шли также пути с Юга на Север, по которым осуществлялись с древних времен связи Индии и Ирана с народами верховий Волги, Сибири и Дальнего Востока. В силу своего срединного геополитического положения государственные образования данной территории оказывались в составе или зоне влиянии «мировых держан», великих империи, таких как Ахеменидское царство (VI-IV вв. до и.), империя Александра Македонского (IV в. до н.э.), государство Селевкидов (III-I вв. до н.э.), Греко-Бактрийское царство (III-II. В до н.э.), Кушанская империя (1-V вв. н.э.), Тюркский Каганат (VI-V1I вв. н.э.), Арабский Халифат (VII-XIII вв. н.э.) и, наконец, в составе Российской и Советской империй (с середины XIX в. до конца XX в.). А в XV веке при А мире Тимуре Центральная Азия сама стала основой мощного центрально-азиатского государства со столицей в городе Самарканде, включавшего и себя Хорасан (территория современного Афганистана), Иран, Азербайджан, Армению, Грузию, Индию и часть Малой Азии и Сирии. Всё это существенным образом сказывалось на судьбах центрально-азиатских народов, на их культурных традициях, таких их особенностях, как терпимость и религиозная толерантность, восприимчивость и генерирование разнородных идей, синкретизм, или. например, билингвизм (даже порой полилингвизм) интеллектуальной элиты.

На территории Центральной Азии к концу II и середине 1-го тысячелетия до н.э. возник один из древних очагов цивилизации. В середине I тысячелетия до н.э. здесь возникли первые государственные образования - Согд, Бактрия, Маргиана, Хорезм.

Осевое время, понятие которого по К.Ясперсу означает то время в истории человечества, когда человек начинает осознавать себя не только как неотделимую часть рода и племени, но и как нечто самоценное, как неповторимую индивидуальность, перед котором возникает вопрос о смысле жизни и его посмертной участи. В Центральной Азии было представлено такими религиозно-философскими учениями поздней древности, как учение Заратуштры - зороастризм, Мони - монизм, Маздака— маздакизм и др.

Идеи зороастризма о добре и зле, победе добра над злом, о рае и аде, о посмертном воздаянии и наказании, о будущем воскрешении, о пришествии спасителей, о Последнем суде над всеми и о вечной жизни вновь соединяющихся души и тела оказали большое влияние на последующие религиозно-философские искания человечества. Они нашли своё место в мировых религиях - иудаизме, христианстве и исламе, что является одним из ярких проявлении взаимосвязей восточных и западных культурных и философских традиций.

(I в. До н. э). в Центральную Азию проник из Индии буддизм. Именно через Центральную Азию пролетал путь дальнейшего распространения буддизма в Китай и Монголию и далее на Дальний Восток - Корею. Японию, а также в страны Индокитая. Подтверждениям сказанному служат археологические данные, письменные источники, образцы научного и художественного творчества, а также этнографические данные тех времен [1]. В результате археологических раскопок, интенсивно проводящихся в Центральной Азии начиная с первой половины XX в., в том числе «Японской экспедицией по изучению буддизма», обнаружено большое число исторических памятников — остатки больших и малых ступ-хранилищ буддийских реликвий, буддийских молелен, надземных и пещерных монастырей, монет с изображением буддийских ступ. Особенно много обнаружено скульптурных памятников с фигурами Будды, а также многочисленных бодхисаттв, деватов и монахов.

Письменные источники, хранящиеся в рукописных фондах Парижа, Берлина, Пекина, Урумчи, Санкт-Петербурга др., говорят о том, что в Центральной Азии имели распространение как буддизм Хинаяны, так и Махаяны. Усилиями сначала индийских, затем китайских и центрально-азиатских миссионеров осуществлялись переводы буддийских сутр на местные языки, создавались их версии и комментарии к ним. Сохранялись также мемуары центрально-азиатских монахов об их путешествиях в Индокитай. Создавались также религиозно-философские произведения. Возникла буддийская терминология и понятия.

Александр Македонский с 329 по 327 гг. до н.э. провёл кампанию по покорению Средней Азии. В походе его сопровождали учёные, историки и естествоиспытатели, которые не только освещали его походы, но и отражали в своих произведениях культуру и ценности покоряемых народов, и донесли их до греков и в целом до Запада, расширив их представления о мире. Тысячи греческих торговцев и ремесленников, вовлечённых в поход,

---

1. См. Г.А. Пугаченков, Л.И. Ремпель. Очерки искусства Средней Азии. М., 1982; К.П. Содиков «Кадимги туркларда буддизм» («Буддизм у древних тюрков»)//«К;адимги туркий халкдарнинг диний-фалсафий карашлари» («Религиозно-философские взгляды древних тюрков»), Т., 2004, с.49-70; О.Н.Шаматов. «Буддизм маданиятининг Марказий Осиёда таркалиш тарихидан»// «Из истории распостранения буддизма в Центральную Азию»//«Жанубий Осиё тилларига кириш» («Введение в южно-азиатское языкознание»), Т., 2003, с.85-97.

передавали свой богатый опыт и создавали новые отрасли торгово-промышленной деятельности, способствовали расширению торговли и обмену с Грецией. Было построено значительное число новых юродов, вошедших в единую с античными полисами. политическую и экономическую систему. Проникновение греческого языка, образованности и искусства в Центральную Азию и другие страны Востока создали основу для формирования культуры эллинизма - новой синкретической цивилизации, представляющей сплав античных и древневосточных элементов. В эпоху эллинизма культурные традиции, заложенные при империи Александра Македонского, нашли дальнейшее развитие во времена «эллинистических государств» - державы Селевкидов и Греко-Бактрийского государства, в которые входили значительные территории Центральной Азии.

Особенно ярко взаимовлияние культурных традиций Запада и Востока проявились в эпоху Восточного ренессанса. В науке традиционно о Ренессансе (фр. Renaissans, возрождение) шла речь применительно к эпохе расцвета науки и культуры в Европе в XIV-XVI веках, с характерным для них обращением к культурному наследию античности, как бы их “ во рождением». В наше время Ренессанс стал рассматриваться шире - как мировое явление, представляющее собой проявление общей закономерности исторического процесса, обязательно наступающего в определённый момент развития народов с древней, непрерывно развивающейся и в наши дни, культурой . Такие учёные как швейцарский востоковед А. Мец", немецкий философ Г. Лей . известный российский учёный-академик Н.И Конрад . ряд современных узбекистанских авторов, используют применительно к эпохе расцвета науки и культуры в Центральной Азии, Ближнем и Среднем Востоке в VIII-XIII веках понятие *«Восточный ренессанс».* Наряду с ним также используются такие его синонимы, как «Мусульманский ренессанс» и «Арабский ренессанс», поскольку речь идёт о странах, находившихся в составе Арабского Халифата и господствующей роли в нём мусульманской рели ги и Ислама.

В эту эпоху возникли такие обретшие мировую славу центры науки и культуры, как «Байт-ул Хикма», первая восточная Академия, созданная при правлении аббасидского халифа Маъмуна ибн Маъмуна (813-833 гг.), которой руководил выходец из Центральной Азии великий математик Мусо ал-Хорезми, от имени которого происходят понятия «алгебра», «алгоритм»; [2] где творил выдающийся астроном ал-Фергани, в европейской транскрипции - Альфрагамус, о котором говорил Данте в своей бессмертной «Божественной комедии», и многие другие. В Саманидском государстве, при правлении Хорезмшаха Абдулаббаса Маъмуна (999-1016) в Хорезме возникла ещё одна Академия, которую возглавляли выходцы из Центральной Азии аль-Бируни, великий учёный-естествоиспытатель и историк, а также Ибн Сино, в европейской транскрипции Авиценна, выдающийся философ и медик, оставивший огромное научное наследство, нашедшее своё место в развитии мировой культуры. Позднее, в эпоху империи Сельджукидов, в XI веке возник другой научный центр Низамия , по имени визиря Низам аль-Мулька, в котором активно работал всемирно известный богослов, теоретик суфизма ал-Газзали.

Общепризнанно, что культура Восточного ренессанса оказала большое влияние на средневековую европейскую культуру. Как пишет Г. Лей, «Расцвет арабской цивилизации способствовал культурному развитию Запада. Западной Европе потребовалось несколько столетий, чтобы переработать результаты технических, естественно-научных и философских исследований, полученных между VIII-XIII веками на огромном пространстве от Аральского моря и Ирана до северо-западной Африки и Пиренеев»[3].

Взаимовлияние и взаимообогащение восточной и западной культур особенно ярко проявилось в области философии. Формирование арабо-язычной философии в IX-XIII веках происходило под непосредственным влиянием

---

2. I м Л li- b.ipic.n.c 11релислоние. Мусульманский ренессанс. М., 1966 г., с. 3-1 I.
   1'м. А. Меи. М\с\льманскип ренессанс. М.. 1966 г. ' См. Г. Лей. Очерк истории средневекового материализма. М., 1962. [4] См. Н.И. Конрад. Запад и Восток. М., 1972 г.
3. leii Очерки истории средневекового материализма». М.. 1962, с. 22.

античной и эллинистической философии, прежде всего Платона. Аристотеля и неоплатоников. Она была представлена такими философами как Аль-Кинди, Аль-Фараби, Ибн Сино, Ибн Туфейль, Ибн Рушд и др., которые не только переводили груды античных философов, не только создавали комментарии к ним, но и развивали дальше их идеи, и получила название *арабский* или *восточный аристотелизм* (перипатетизм). В свою очередь, арабский аристотелизм оказал обратное влияние на развитие западной средневековой философии, что привело к возникновению в Европе «латинского аверроизма» (от латинской транскрипции имени Ибн Рушда - Аверроэс), оппозиционного официальному католицизму и средневековой схоластике философского течения. В XIII веке в Западной Европе это течение представлял профессор Парижского университета Сигер Брабантский и его последователи. С XIV века до Нового времени латинский аверроизм получил широкое распространение во Франции, Италии и др. старанах.

Арабоязычная философия сыграла уникальную роль в возвращении греческого философского и естественно-научного наследия на европейскую почву. «Аввероизм, - писал Н.И. Конрад. Был первым очагом. в котором затеплился огонёк рационалистической мысли, той самой, которая привела к Декарту. Спинозе, Лейбницу – великим умам, открывшим новую структуру мышления, соединившуюся с тем комплексом новых явлений в экономике, социальном строе, политической сфере, который мы называем Новым временем»[4].

Традиции восточного аристотелизма продолжались и в эпоху Темура и темуридов, особенно в художественной литературе, в творчестве таких великий поэтов как Джами, Низами, Алишер Навои, в воспеваемых ими идеях гуманизма и дружбы народов. В их произведениях фигурировали великие имена античности - Искандер-Александр Македонский, Эвклид, Птолемей, Аристотель,

4. Конрад чС релнеиоеючпое возрождение и Алишер Навои»// Запад и Восток. М., 1972, с.276.

Сократ, Фалес, Анаксимен и др., а героями их произведений выступали грек-Искандер, китаец-Фархад, перс-Шапур, араб-Кайс и т.д.

В новое время с середины XIX кока и и XX веке Центральная Азия оказалась в зоне интересов возникшей на евроазиатском пространстве и стремительно набирающей мощь Российском империи, а затем и Советской империи. Ещё царская власть насильственно включила часть Кокандского ханства в состав России. Позднее остальная часть Кокандского ханства, Хивинское и Бухарское ханства силой были присоединены к Советскому государству. В результате так называемого «национального размежевания» (1924 г.) в Центральной Азии возникли Узбекская, Таджикская, Киргизская, Туркменская и Казахская советские социалистические республики. Объявленный суверенитет этих республик в условиях фактически унитарного государства практически превратился в фикцию. Они были искусственно оторваны от соседних и близлежащих восточных стран, были вынуждены осуществлять внешние сношения через посредство центральных органов СССР. В духовной жизни традиционные восточные ценности, исламская культура столкнулись со ставшей господствующей марксисткой идеологией и государственным атеизмом.

Вместе с тем объективно происходил процесс взаимовлияния и взаимообогащения культур народов Центральной Азии с оказавшимися в едином политическом и экономическом пространстве славянскими народами - русскими, украинцами и белорусами, народами Кавказа и Закавказья, Прибалтики. Здесь стали внедряться европейские стандарты образования, возникли республиканские Академии наук, творческие союзы, появились новые направления музыкального и изобразительного искусства. Традиционные ценности продолжали сохраняться в толще народного сознания и пробивались наружу, преодолевая возникшие сложности и преграды.

Распад Советского Союза стал завершающим звеном характерного для XX века процесса ликвидации мировых империй - австро-венгерской после I мировой войны, колониальных империи после II мировой войны. На этом фоне в мире происходит так называемый «этнический ренессанс», и именно национальные государства становятся основными субъектами международных отношений. Таковыми стали и суверенные государства, образовавшиеся на территории бывшего СССР, в том числе и на территории Центральной Азии - Узбекистан, Казахстан, Киргизия, Таджикистан и Туркмения. Независимый Узбекистан, решая сложные и противоречивые проблемы переходного к новому строю периода, выстраивает свою внешнюю политику со всеми странами, исходя из собственных интересов и исторической целесообразности. На фоне происходящих в мире процессов глобализации, в области культурных отношений Узбекистана восстанавливаются традиционные связи со странами Востока, особенно в гуманитарной сфере, и интенсифицируются связи со странами Запада в таких областях, как опыт демократического строительства, техники и технологии, подготовки кадров.

27

Музыкальная культура Индии в контексте глобализации

Е. М. Гороховик

Известно, что западный мир, и в первую очередь – Европа, давно обратили свой взор к достижениям индийской цивилизации. Индия – один из наиболее стойких мифов европейского сознания, вот уже более пяти столетий будоражащий воображение и умы миллионов представителей Старого и Нового Света. Известно также, сколь многое в европейской, и шире – в западной культуре развилось благодаря изучению Вед, Упанишад, Пуран, древнеиндийского эпоса, образцов санскритской драматургии, шедевров литературы и поэзии на индийских языках, индийской архитектуры, музыки. Индия столь давно и прочно инкорпорирована в европейское сознание, не говоря уже о культурных достижениях самой европейской цивилизации, что, казалось бы, на сегодня для просвещенного европейца нет такой страницы индийской истории и культуры, которая не подверглась бы тщательному научному осмыслению.

Означает ли это, что, исчерпав многовековой интерес западного человека к экзотике, индийская культура уходит сегодня на периферию мирового культурного процесса? Ответ на этот вопрос очевидно повернут к геокультурной ситуации сегодняшнего дня, в которой своего рода «мода на индийское» переживает, несомненно, очередной период ренессанса. Сама Индия – цивилизация с более чем четырехтысячелетней историей, – прочно заняла в современном мире позиции государства влиятельного в политическом отношении, с динамично развивающейся экономической, промышленной и научной инфраструктурой. Представители южноазиатского субконтинента живут сегодня практически во всех странах и регионах планеты, внося значительный вклад в развитие мировой экономики, науки и культуры. Таким образом, существовавшая исторически «Большая Индия», простиравшая когда-то свое духовное и культурное влияние от границ Афганистана до островов Юго-Восточной Азии и Дальнего Востока, от Цейлона до гималайских и тибетских предгорий, в большой степени сохранила, а во многом и значительно приумножила колоссальный объем своего воздействия на мировые процессы культурного взаимообмена. В регионы с неизменно сильным влиянием индийской культуры в наши дни включены, помимо упомянутых выше, также и Европа, Северная Америка, другие континенты, где индийская культура традиционно ли, либо уже придя в наше время, прочно укоренена. Интенсивность процессов «индианизации», происходящих на разных уровнях современного глобализирующегося социума, на пороге нового тысячелетия не только не затухает, но имеет тенденцию ко все большей и большей интенсификации. В свою очередь, не сокращается западное паломничество в Индию, до наших дней сохранившей свое уникальное культурное наследие, припасть к которому как к живительному источнику, до сих пор питающему духовные и художественные идеи человечества, мечтают многие жители нашей планеты.

Вместе с тем, очевидно и то, что воздействие Индии на современный ход мировых процессов не исчерпывается только внешними проявлениями, лежащими в области экономики, политики, промышленного производства, науки и культуры, но уходит корнями вглубь, в духовные завоевания южноазиатской цивилизации, центром которой всегда была историческая Индия. Всем известно, какое огромное духовное влияние оказывала на протяжении многих веков и продолжает оказывать на современные умы индийская мудрость. Пожалуй, не будет преувеличением сказать, что в современном мире в основании многих влиятельных философских, политических, мировоззренческих, художественных концепций лежат завоевания индийской мысли, на протяжении многих столетий и тысячелетий напряженно пульсировавшей в стремлении охватить целостность и единство Вселенной во всем многообразии ее элементов, проникнуть в суть процессов мирового развития и осознать место в них человека. Индия, никогда на протяжении всей истории цивилизации не осуществлявшая территориальной экспансии, всегда охватывала своим духовным влиянием территории, намного превосходящие ее саму. Несомненно то, что не только обозначенные выше политические, экономические, научные, культурные, но также духовные составляющие, берущие начало в сокровищнице индийского духа, во многом определяют сегодня облик современного мира с его поисками гармоничных и созидательных путей развития человеческого сообщества. И вряд ли и в этом смысле влияние Индии когда-либо ослабеет.

В последнее время одной из актуальных тем, характеризующих специфику развития мировой музыкальной культуры на рубеже тысячелетий, стала глобализация. Проблеме глобализации и определяющего влияния ее процессов на развитие современной культуры и искусства посвящаются многочисленные дискуссии, научные форумы, труды исследователей. Обостренно воспринимаемая сегодня антитеза глобализма-антиглобализма, активно вторгающаяся во все сферы нашей жизни и деятельности, заставляет совершенно по-новому осознать смысл, формы и характер тех феноменов культуры и искусства, которые еще вчера представлялись непоколебимыми, монолитными в своих основополагающих смысловых параметрах. По существу, на пороге нового тысячелетия каждая из музыкальных культур оказалась в объективной ситуации, когда в ее содержательно-семантическую структуру включены и имеют равную ценностную и эстетическую значимость достижения музыкального искусства различных социокультурных пластов, географических регионов и исторических эпох.

В свою очередь, смена мировоззренческих позиций, неизбежно диктуемая глубинными изменениями всего современного жизненного контекста, влечет за собой необходимость в системном переосмыслении и пересмотре позиций, в том числе и в области музыкальной культуры (и вслед за ней ее составляющих в виде музыкального искусства и музыкального образования), опирающемся на изменении аксиологических представлений о сущности и характере современной культурной ситуации. На смену старым, уходящим в прошлое директивно-единообразным оценочным категориям приходят и занимают все большее место в общественном сознании представления о плюралистичности, многообразии ценностных систем.

Эпоха европейского культурного монополизма, монополярности и центризма в истории развития мировых культур сегодня динамично сменяется временем, когда на первый план выдвигаются идеи многообразия и культурного релятивизма – тенденций, напрямую влияющих на характер музыкального искусства разных регионов мира, преобразуя его не только внешние, но и глубинные, внутренние аспекты. В современном мире, многополярно организованном и многовекторно ориентированном в отношении культурных приоритетов, по-новому выстраиваются также взаимоотношения между культурами, позиционированными ранее как далекие, мало связанные друг с другом. В наши дни, фактически, каждая из национальных культур осмысливает свое место в современном мире, не только общаясь со своими традиционными соседями, но вступая также в диалог с культурами отдаленных стран и регионов мира. Как известно, в переломные эпохи, подобные той, которую мы переживаем сейчас, каждая национальная культура поставлена в ситуацию переосмысления своего места в мире, своей национальной идентичности, исторического прошлого и будущего. Культурная самоидентификация – сложнейший исторический процесс, в который объективно вступает каждая национальная культура в изменяющихся исторических условиях. Сегодня он выходит на новый виток своего развития, становясь результатом глобального культурно-коммуникативного полилога, поскольку потребность познать себя и глубже заглянуть в свои истоки (то, что можно определить сегодня как актуальную задачу поиска культурой своей аутентичности) всегда объективно связана с необходимостью той или иной культурной системы взглянуть на себя со стороны, со стремлением ее к нахождению своего уникального идентификационного «кода».

Индийская «тема» является устойчивой константой европейского музыкального искусства, на протяжении многих веков, питая творческое воображение композиторов, представлявших разные национальные школы и стили – от Ж.-

Ф. Рамо с его условно-ориентальными «Галантными Индиями» до балетов Л. Делиба, оперных произведений Н. А. Римского-Корсакова в 19 веке, фортепианной музыки М. Равеля, симфонических сочинений и теоретических изысканий О. Мессиана, творческого мышления американских композиторов-минималистов в прошедшем столетии. Европейская публика уже более века тому назад познакомилась с достижениями индийской музыкальной и танцевальной культуры. Музыкальная индология, являющаяся одной из наиболее исторически развитых областей современной музыкальной науки, научная отрасль, сформированная на стыке музыковедения, этномузыкологии, истории, этнографии, литературоведения и ряда других направлений гуманитарного знания, плодотворно развиваясь на протяжении, по крайней мере, последних полутораста лет, заглянула практически во все потаенные уголки этой древнейшей музыкальной культуры, изучив досконально различные ее аспекты. В разных странах Европы и США функционируют факультеты, курсы, центры, которые готовят исполнителей индийской классической музыки из числа европейских и американских музыкантов. Имена ведущих индийских классических исполнителей, таких, в частности, как Рави Шанкар, Али Акбар Хан, Рам Нараян, Шивкумар Шарма, Харипрасад Чаурасия, Парвин Султана и ряд других, приобрели поистине всемирную известность; их концерты проходят в лучших концертных залах разных стран мира, огромное количество аудио и видеозаписей, сделанных с их участием, также во многом способствует популяризации этой древнейшей музыкальной культуры за рубежом. Сегодня западный слушатель знает многое о том, что составляет важнейшие смыслы этой древней культуры, каковы ее основные элементы и составляющие. Такие термины, как «рага», «тала», «шрути», так же, как и имена многих выдающихся индийских музыкантов, сегодня на слуху не только у специалистов, но также у людей, не имеющих профессионального отношения к индологии, но отличающихся широкими духовными и культурными запросами. Сами индийские классические музыканты (Харипрасад Чаурасия, Закир Хусейн, Шанкар и ряд других) активно участвуют в различных творческих проектах за рубежом – традиция, начатая еще выдающимся скрипачом Иегуди

Менухиным, игравшим с известными индийскими музыкантами. Особую область, в которой контакты индийской музыки с западным миром осуществляются в наши дни особенно активно, является сфера киномузыкальной и шоу-индустрии. Думается, не будет преувеличением сказать, что по количеству поклонников Болливуд ничуть не уступает, а вполне вероятно – и превосходит свой американский прототип. Распространяясь практически по всем странам и континентам, музыка индийского кино несет зрителям и слушателям первые незабываемые впечатления от соприкосновения с этой великой культурой. Индийская музыкальная шоу-индустрия, также далеко переступив границы южноазиатского субконтинента, покоряет слушателей и зрителей стран Европы, Азии, Америки. Один из ярких примеров тому – недавняя постановка, сначала в Лондоне, затем – на Бродвее, знаменитого мюзикла "Bombay Dreams", ставшего плодом совместного творчества всемирно известных Э. Ллойд Уэббера и А. Р. Рехмана. Таким образом, имидж индийской культуры, творимый в современном мире, в большой мере создается не только деятельностью представителей бизнеса, высоких технологий, моды и других отраслей деятельности, но также совокупными усилиями индийских музыкантов, аудитория которых растет с каждым годом.

Оборотная сторона этого процесса – влияние западной культуры на индийское музыкальное мышление. Они, в силу ряда причин, проявляют себя не так очевидно и активно, как в случае с такими культурами, как, например, японская, китайская, корейская. Вестернизация как магистральное направление развития музыкального искусства пока еще не коснулась Индии напрямую. Наиболее очевидной причиной тому является, на наш взгляд, все еще мощно развитое, не претерпевающее деградации ощущение аутентичности, испытываемое носителями индийских музыкальных традиций. Музыкальное наследие все еще продолжает оставаться в этом регионе живой, актуальной, не превратившейся в музейный раритет частью индийского искусства, оно успешно заполняет все ниши музыкальной культуры, полнокровно охватывая такие сферы, как собственно музыка, вокальная и инструментальная, танец, музыкальный театр и музыкальная наука. Именно поэтому, в частности, такие формы и жанры западной музыки, как инструментальная (фортепиано, скрипка и др.), симфоническая, театральная (опера и балет), получившие столь широкое развитие и распространение в других азиатских странах как в сфере музыкального искусства, так и образования, в Индии пока еще находятся на периферии музыкально-культурных явлений. Вместе с тем, процесс обогащения индийского музыкального мышления элементами западного музыкального искусства, начавшийся еще в конце 18 столетия, уже очевидно дает свои результаты. Так, в частности, в индийский классический инструментарий (как в традиции хиндустани, так и в карнатской музыке) прочно вошли такие европейские инструменты, как гармониум, скрипка, гитара, кларнет, саксофон. Индийские музыканты, активно общаясь со своими европейскими и американскими коллегами, несомненно в той или иной степени воспринимают опыт западного музыкального мышления, перенося его в свое творчество. Один из интересных примеров тому – исполнительская, композиторская, научная деятельность выдающегося музыканта Рагхавы Рао Менона, творческие усилия которого немало способствовали сближению индийской и западной музыки. Несомненно и то, что современная интерпретация таких базовых концепций индийской классической музыки, как рага и тала, во многом обогащены сегодня за счет взаимодействия индийского музыкального мышления и новых тенденций в мировой музыке.

Таким образом, можно сделать вывод о том, что в современном контексте индийская музыкальная культура – одна из древнейших на нашей планете – переживает период нового подъема, обогащаясь за счет взаимодействия культур и обогащая, в свою очередь, планетарное музыкальное искусство своими выдающимися достижениями.

28

Современное Изобразительное Искусство в Зеркале Мифа: Контуры Новой Эстетики

Н.В. Слухай

Постмодерн вездесущ, и, хотя в течение двух последних десятилетий фиксируется упадок инвентаря его возможностей, он оказывает широкое влияние на этико-эстетический континуум современности. Постмодерная эстетика, которая акцентирует фрагментарную, нестабильную, неопределенную, прерывистую, миграционную и гиперреальную природу существования и соответствует семантике обозначающего ее этимологически противоречивого термина (пост – после и модо – именно сейчас). Онтологические черты постмодерна часто описываются на фоне глобализации, капиталистической универсализации и конца истории и проецируются на соответствующие философско-социологические конструкты, фиксирующие плюрализм, разнообразие, случайность и амбивалентность, и соответствующие лингвистические конструкты, отмечающие нереференциональность, ир- или антирационализм, особенности экспрессивности, интенции, рецепции, репрезентации произведений постмодерной эстетики [1, 327 – 332].

Характерная для постмодерна специфическая континуальность, которая выражается в отсутствии центра, а также периферийного или постоянного значения, и логика бриколажа изначально сближали его с мифом. И, поскольку ни одно направление не может претендовать на статус панхронотопического в художественно-эстетическом континууме социума, неудивительно, что сквозь мировоззренческие концепты постмодернизма уже просматриваются контуры нового направления, мифологическая природа которого определяется совершенно отчетливо. Назовем его пост-постмодернизм. Концептуальное поле пост-постмодернизма принципиально мифологично, соответственно, его основными чертами, помимо характерных для постмодерна, можно назвать космический универсализм, анимо-аниматичность мира деантропной природы, панконтинуальность при акцентированной дискретности, устойчивость временного вектора («вечно длящийся день»), терроцентричность, позитивная аксиологичность, альтернативная реальность (нежесткая референциальность, референциальная воронка). Современное изобразительное искусство отличается разнообразием форм художественно - эстетического отражения мира и обнаруживает в русском и украинском культурном пространстве немало общих черт в силу близости процессов этногенеза и проницаемости культурных границ восточных славян. Тенденции его развития, демонстрируя связь с этническим мифом, обнаруживают ростки новой эстетики, особенно заметной в современном прикладном искусстве, отличием которого служит максимальное соответствие запросам массового потребителя и способность отражать идеи, которые «витают в воздухе», но еще не осмыслены или не полностью осмыслены фундаментальными направлениями живописи.

Так, интуитивизм (например, современное творчество харьковского художника С.А.Малыша), декларирующий абстрагирование от общепринятых форм восприятия мира и «сопричастность пульсу мирового бытия», позиционируется как модерное фундаментальное направление живописного творчества. Интуитивизм обнаруживает тенденции к привлечению классических мифологическим форм «переигрывания мира» (элементов архаичной эстетики, как изоморфы мирового древа - дерево, яйцо, круг; совмещением гиперболизированной антропной с космологичными моделями, особой цветовой гаммой, что отчетливо проявляется на фоне христианской естетики, явленной его полотнами «Зачарованный ангел», «Ангел», «Ангел старого дома», «Город Ангелов», «Затворник Иоанн Святогорский», иконописной версией «Милосердие, 2000»), одновременно демонстрирует комплекс черт постмодерной эстетики (фрагментарность, хаотичность, гиперреальность, нереференциональность, иррациональность, деструктивность, пейоративную аксиологию и так далее).

Произведения прикладного искусства (представленные, к примеру, Happy Art С.Герасименко), декларирующие калейдоскопичность симфонии бытия, счастья от осознания себя сущим в мире живого и одухотворенного космоса, демонстрируют черты новой эстетики. Художественное пространство Сергея Герасименко в аспекте предметно-образного моделирования действительности устроено несложно. Среди моделей по нисходящей частотности представлены **антропная** (число женских образов приблизительно в три раза превышает число мужских), **анимальная** (высокой частотностью обладают образы кота, собаки, птицы, слона, лисы / волка, ослика / коня, быка, рыбы, реже встречается образ улитки), **фитомодель** (образы деревьев, цветов и трав), **архитектурная** модель (образ дома и его метонимических субститутов: вазы, чайника, чашки, а также машины), **артефактуальная** (кентавры и кентаврессы), **астрально-космологическая** (образы солнца, месяца, неба, облаков, звезд-цветов, а также образ корабля, который плывет по небу-морю). Несмотря на формально невысокую частотность, астрально-космологическая модель занимает в художественном пространстве произведений Сергея Герасименко центральное место: в основе иных моделей либо образы-субституты мирового древа (человек, дерево, цветы, дом), либо солярные образы (птица, бык, конь), либо панхронические (улитка, корабль, пирамида, кентавр); особое место среди них занимают образы дерева (цветка) и человека (дома). Симптоматично, что и произведения Сергея Герасименко обретают преимущественно форму названных животных: это либо вазы в виде кота, быка, рыбы, пирамиды, кентавра, либо произведения декоративно-прикладного искусства в форме барельефа летящего мальчика, декоративной рыбы, двух собеседников/собеседниц на лавке. Безусловная доминанта в предметно-изобразительном ряду антропных образов косвенно подтверждается и автором: в качестве произведений самой высокой художественной ценности он указывает объективации антропной модели. Довольно часто встречаются образы, не имеющие четкой референтной отнесенности: один и тот же образ равно читаем как лиса и лошадь, лиса и волк, индюк и петух, собака и ослик. Типичным является предицирование сходных черт образам, представляющим антропную и деантропные модели (например, у рыбы появляются чувственные женские губы, аналогичное симметричное изображение губ у рыбы способствует сближению антропной и ихтиомодели, осознанию проницаемости и единства Вселенной, как и изображение улыбчивых животных).

Особенности художественно-образного моделирования действительности Герасименко обнаруживаются на уровне времени, пространства и признакового континуума его произведений: люди, животные и птицы его мифомира молчат и улыбаются, смотрят широко распахнутыми большими глазами, сидят, стоят, бегут, летят по небу, но главное – выражают приятие реалий земного мира, ощущение радости и самодостаточности бытия и доброжелательного отношения ко всему, что их окружает. Последняя идея калейдоскопичной симфонии бытия, счастья от осознания себя живущим в мире живого и одухотворенного космоса выражается многообразно: босые земные, нехрупкого сложения женщины, тихо летящие против ветра со свободно вытянутыми вперед руками и бесстрашно одетые в красные брюки собеседницы с толстыми икрами ног; принцессы с диспропорциональными добрыми лицами и просто милые носатые дамы; вальяжные коты, приязненно выгибающие хвост, улыбающиеся собаки и задумчивые ослики/кони в яблоках; разноцветные деревья, толстыми стволами опирающиеся о землю; сексуальные рыбы и толстые птицы, бороздящие свои просторы; готические дома, тесно прилепленные друг к другу; крупные яркие цветы, увиденные детским взглядом; быки, усеянные цветами-звездами, с месяцем вместо рогов; полные до краев вазы и чашки. **Доминантным является комплекс признаков «толстый»/ «полный» («наполненный до краев»)** – носителями этого признака являются плотного сложения женщины и мужчины, деревья с толстыми стволами, крупные птицы и почти круглые рыбы, полные губы персонажей и до краев наполненные вазы и чашки; плотно прилепленные друг к другу готические домики; **«добрый»/ «улыбчивый»** - этот признак демонстрирует любой образ антропной и анимальной моделей – выражением задумчивых глаз и улыбкой; **«босой»/ «открытый»** (этот признак характерен для изображения босых летящих женщин, всех персонажей, большие глаза которых почти всегда (за исключением единственного изображения улыбающейся женщины с закрытыми глазами) широко распахнуты, а лица открыты); **«живой и одушевленный» («анимо-аниматичный»)** – относительно всех образов деантропной модели, **«земной»/ «большой, крупный»** («лишенный черт «правильной красоты», асимметричный, с крупными, часто грубыми чертами лица и четко прорисованными линиями глаз, носа и губ»); **«принадлежащий космическому универсуму»** (герои Герасименко легко парят, не зная законов земного тяготения – не только в изображениях, но и явленные барельефами образов; меняют привычную среду обитания – в воздушном пространстве равно представлены птицы и рыбы; игнорируют законы онтологии земного бытия – по небу легко скользят маленькие кораблики, а фигуры летящих по небу женщин расположением рук и видом развевающихся прядей демонстрируют одновременное присутствие встречного и попутного ветра). Произведения Герасименко демонстрируют безусловную матриархичность мифомира автора, причем ненавязчивая доминанта изображений «зрелых матрон» оживляет внутреннюю форму самого термина «матриархичность».

Устойчивость временного вектора «прекрасного мгновения» («вечно длящегося дня») мира образов Герасименко обеспечивается а) доминантой персонажей в возрастном периоде расцвета: это юные девы и зрелые дамы, мальчишки-подростки и респектабельные мужчины в строгих костюмах, испещренных рисунками и разрисованных цветами, но не малые дети и не глубокие старики; б) образом солнца в зените или высокого месяца (примечательна одна из фотографий Герасименко, где голову автора обрамляет венец солнечных лучей, выполненных из майолики); в) символикой вечного яркого дня, высвечивающего многоцветную палитру бытия в мифомире произведений автора (интересно, что на просьбу изобразить полную луну на темном звездном небе художник откликнулся изображением тонкого серпа месяца (возможно – рефлексия интерференции значений русского «месяца» и украинского «місяця”) на фоне глубокого голубого неба, сплошь усеянного корабликами, которые вполне могут быть идентифицированы как мифопоэтические субституты звезд; г) соприсутствием солнца и месяца в обозримом пространстве единого произведения.

Цветовая палитра мифомира произведений Герасименко отличается разнообразием и насыщенностью цветов («У меня нет нелюбимых красок», - утверждает автор), среди которых доминируют основные цвета солнечного спектра во всевозможных сочетаниях оттенков, но без переходов, размытых красок, отсветов и бликов. Насколько можно судить по произведениям 2004 года, некоторое предпочтение автор отдает красно-бордовому, желто-оранжевому, фиолетово-голубому и зеленому цветам. Цвета лишены профанной мотивации (лица белые, смуглые, коричневые, желтые, зеленые и фиолетовые; деревья причудливых цветов, голубые лисы, зеленые быки и желтые в яблоках слоны, собаки и кони), однако с мифопоэтической точки зрения цвета обладают глубокой символической значимостью, которая обеспечивается и совокупностью символических значений отдельных цветов, и символикой общего для всех цветов признака «яркий, насыщенный», что может служить символом радости и счастья, и доминантой теплых, стимулирующих цветов, «связанных с процессами ассимиляции, активности и напряжения» [2, 549].

Пространственные характеристики художественного мира Герасименко сводятся к панконтинуальности, которая выражается в непрерывности и абсолютной заполненности дискурса его произведений при условии его сегментированности. Поверхность произведений Сергея Герасименко любого жанра и формы покрыта множеством сюжетных изображений, каждое из которых имеет свою геометрическую нишу (чаще квадрат – символ устойчивости и порядка), без рельефной окантовки и даже четкого контура (что символизирует проницаемость малых миров), статичных и динамичных, симметричных и асимметричных, равно читаемых во всех направлениях, нормативно расположенных и перевернутых. Образы Герасименко игнорируют геометрическую устойчивость профанного мира и геометрическую канонизированность мифологического мирового древа, однако благодаря панконтинуальности впечатление деструктивности дискурса его произведений не возникает. Числовая символика также деканонизируется: 1, 2, 3, 4, 5, 6, 8, 9 – наиболее активные числа на изображениях.

Творчество Сергея Герасименко представляет собой целостный поток разнообразных форм объективации художественного сознания творца; отдельные тексты освещаются общей концептуальной установкой его творчества, и каждое из них представляет концепт своеобразием авторского воплощения идеи посредством сильных позиций и категорий текста. В рамках лингвистики текста под сильными позициями, как известно, подразумевают специфическую организацию текста, которая обеспечивает выдвижение на первый план важнейших смыслов текста, установление иерархии смыслов, фокусирование внимания на важнейшем, усиление эмоциональности и эстетического эффекта текста [3, 23–24]. Типичными сильными позициями словесных произведений являются заголовок, начало, концовка, ключевые слова, пролог, эпилог, эпиграф, посвящение и так далее.

Сильными позициями знаковой системы прикладного искусства есть основания считать форму и цвет произведения: именно они являются регуляторами направления и интенсивности ассоциативного потока реципиента. Форма произведения играет в этом процессе основную роль: сравним малоинформативную форму вогнутого четырехугольника или косой трапеции с формой кентавра или мальчика с простертыми в полете руками, или кота (рыбы, быка), или пирамиды с сорванным верхом (значимые объективации пирамиды такой формы находим в последнее время и в произведениях словесного искусства – например, „Пирамиды" Т.Пратчетта). Это обусловлено высокой степенью символичности составных компонентов (подобных названным образам) ведущих моделей мифопоэтического мира, в то время как символика искривленных геометрических фигур прочитывается с трудом. Сравним: кентавр – символ физической силы и доминанты разума над инстинктом и в то же время – символ человека, который пребывает в плену собственных первобытных инстинктов [4, 142–143]; пирамида, или возвышенность света, изоморфный образ мирового древа, -

символ бессмертия и креативной силы солнца [4, 279–280], бык – символ силы, власти, божественности, величия [4, 31–32] и так далее. Таким образом, формы произведений Сергея Герасименко тяготеют к **структурам с высокой степенью символичности**. Сильная позиция цвета обеспечивает ореол эмоционально-экспересcивного восприятия произведения, прежде всего в пределах оппозиции хроматические – ахроматические, светлые – темные, холодные – теплые, яркие – приглушенные цвета. Многоцветная палитра каждого из произведений автора навевает соответствующее эмоциональное состояние радости и приподнятого настроения и символизирует жизнь, солнце, день/утро, весну/солнце, юность/полную сил зрелость фактом объективации цвета (отсутствие цвета – часто – примета хтонического мира) и семантикой светлых, теплых, ярких цветов.

Дискурс каждого произведения С.Герасименко разворачивается через систему текстообразующих категорий, которые обычно определяются как абстрактные семантико-функциональные значения, соотнесенные с отношениями явлений объективной действительности, выраженные теми или иными языковыми средствами [5, 11] или, добавим, ресурсами иных семиотических систем. Основное внимание среди категорий анализируемых текстов привлекают категория пресуппозиции (благодаря комплементарной парадигме мифа), семантической связности и интеграции, реестр которых совпадает с аналогичным, который разворачивается словесным произведением [6, 43–87]. Однако характер реализации текстообразующих категорий в данном случае существенно отличается от особенностей их развертывания в вербальном тексте. Например, при условной автономности восприятия двух-четырех проекций плоскости изображения (пирамид, треугольной или плоской вазы) семантическая связность компонентов рисунка обеспечивается полилогом символически резонансных носителей цвета (желтого цвета изображений кота, стволов и крон деревьев, людей, слона, солнца, домов или красного цвета изображений солнца, деревьев, волос, крыш) в диапазоне контрарности и комплементарности; повторяемостью комплекса мифопоэтически значимых признаков в широком диапазоне оппозиций открытый/закрытый, одетый (обутый)/обнаженный (босой), прямой/кривой, толстый/худой и других; несовпадением логико-семантических параметров художественного мира сравнительно с реальным (перемещение кораблей на небо, звезд – на спину быка, полеты людей и животных), логикой абсурда или нарочитой хаотизацией мира, которые четко противопоставляют семантически связный континуум художественного произведения миру внешнего бытия; реестром символически резонансных субъектов мифопоэтического мира автора.

Субъекты мифомира произведений Герасименко, до краев испившие чашу красоты земного мира, кружащегося в просторах космического универсума, излучают добро имманентно собственному мироощущению, и яркий хаос этого круговорота обещает рождение нового светлого космоса (что отражает внутренняя форма неканонического названия – Happy Art (искусство счастья), которое присвоил направлению один из ценителей творчества Герасименко). Благодаря этому высокохудожественные творения Сергея Герасименко отличаются позитивной аксиологией и демонстрируют тенденции оформления черты новой эстетики.

Новая эстетика принимает те черты постмодерна, которые изначально сближали его с мифом (специфическую континуальность, логику бриколажа и подобные). Однако концептуальное поле новой эстетики демонстрирует чуждые постмодерну черты: высокую конструктивность мышления, креативность, явленную чертами космического универсализма, анимо-анимитизма мира природы, панконтинуальности при акцентированной дискретности, устойчивости временного вектора («вечный круг времен»), терроцентричности, позитивной аксиологии, созидательном потенциале альтернативной реальности. Произведения новой эстетики служат творческой альтернативой многочисленным патогенным текстам современности, демонстрируя обнадеживающие тенденции развития современного художественного мира.

ПРИМЕЧАНИЯ

1. Барський Р. Постмодерність Енциклопедія постмодернізму / За ред. Ч.Е.Вінквіста, В.Е.Тейлора. – К., 2003.
2. Керлот Х.Э. Словарь символов. – М., 1994.
3. Арнольд И.В. Значение сильной позиции для интерпретации художественного текста // Иностр. яз. в шк. – 1978. – № 4.
4. Тресиддер Дж. Словарь символов. – М., 1999.
5. Чикина Л.К. Лингвистика текста: Учеб. пособие. – Саранск, 1986.
6. Слухай Н.В. Художественный образ в аспекте лингвистики текста. – Симферополь, 2001.

29

Некоторые Особенности Возникновения и Развития Документализма в Кыргызской Литературе

Х. М. Шамбеталиева

Документализм в кыргызской литературе как принцип создания художественного образа берет свое начало в 1930-е годы и присутствует на протяжении всего литературного развития. 1980-1990 годы XX века дали обширный пласт художественной литературы, созданной на фактографическом материале. Причем, и появляются и развиваются различные формы воплощения документализма. Они требуют научного исследования истоков и разнообразных путей трансформации документального материала в художественное повествование, роли и функций документа в ткани художественного произведения.

Определение границ исследования непосредственно зависит от терминологической характеристики понятий «документ», «документализм», «документальная литература». В «Большом энциклопедическом словаре» дается следующее толкование: «Документальная литература – очерки, реже произведения других жанров, содержанием которых являются реальные и характерные явления, события, лица. Документальная литература, как правило, включает публицистическую оценку автора. Многие произведения документальной литературы имеют художественное значение»[1].

В академическом 17-ти томном «Словаре русского языка» слово «документ» раскрывается в следующем значении: «1.Деловая бумага, служащая письменным доказательством чьего-либо права или обязательства… Исторические д о к у м е н

Это же явление отмечает и профессор А. С. Кацев: «Писатели, переводя произведения русской литературы, не только приобщаются через образцы к русской культуре в целом, но и осваивают в своем оригинальном творчестве жанры, не характерные для традиций национального словесного искусства».[8]

Нехватка опыта, мастерства приводит к тому, что многие кыргызские писатели обращаются к опыту русских писателей. Пробел в жанровом развитии заменяется переводами из инонациональной, в частности, русской литературы. Именно этим можно объяснить выбор автобиографических, документальных произведений русской литературы, которые к концу 1930-х годов были переведены на кыргызский язык. Сюда относятся и «Железный поток» А. Серафимовича, «Мятеж», «Чапаев» Д. Фурманова, отрывки из автобиографической повести «Детство», «Мои университеты» М. Горького, повесть Л. Толстого «Хаджи-Мурат»[9], написанные на основе документальных и автобиографических материалов.

По образцу русской литературы в 1930-е годы рождается совершенно новый жанр кыргызской литературы - автобиографическая повесть. Молодые кыргызские писатели, еще не имевшие достаточного опыта, старались в первую очередь воспользоваться автобиографическими материалами.

Известно, что автобиографизм – это первая стадия осмысления окружающей действительности, первое восприятие, трансформированное в художественный текст. Для первых письменных прозаических произведений характерно создание статичных образов, так как авторы, как правило, еще в достаточной мере ориентируются на фольклорные традиции (в кыргызской литературе 1920-30-х годов еще господствует фольклорное мышление писателей), на акынскую поэзию, для которых наиболее характерна именно описательность. Художественные произведения строятся по принципу «что вижу, о том и пою (рассказываю)», в которых еще отсутствует развитие художественного образа, его динамика. Автору важно передать свои ощущения и мысли. В произведениях этих лет ощущается личностный, нередко декларируемый подход, оказывающий воздействие на характер повествования, когда «я» автора является наиболее важным и выдвигается на первый план. Современники могут отрицать, не соглашаться, сомневаться с той или иной трактовкой или изложением материала, а потомки уже будут судить о прошлой эпохе по воспоминаниям, по художественным произведениям тех лет. То есть по истечении определенного промежутка времени эти произведения будут восприниматься как «живой голос эпохи» и приобретают объективный характер повествования.

Если в 1920-30-х годах в автобиографических произведениях основное внимание было акцентировано на событийную основу, то в конце 1980 – начале 90-х годов писатели стремятся осветить глубину душевных переживаний личности. Если в первых автобиографических произведениях судьба народа выступает как часть судьбы автобиографического героя, то теперь все происходит в обратном направлении: личная судьба рассматривается как составляющая часть судьбы народа. Примерами могут служить рассказ С. Алиевой «Запах фиалки» и рассказ М. Байджиева «За три секунды до преступления».

Масштабы исторического события определяет время. Проходят годы, и сама история осмысливается по-новому. Те громогласно одобряемые художественные произведения, которые воздействовали на сознание читателей, в контексте исторических перемен приобретают новое звучание, иногда противоположное тому, которое придает им автор. Иногда наоборот, произведение не только претерпевает смысловые изменения, а с течением времени определяется новое место конкретного произведения в литературном ряду.

В кыргызской литературе, так же как и в русской, 1950-80-е годы характерны широким использованием документальных источников, действительных фактов в художественном повествовании. Литература повествует не только о современности (о чем речь пойдет ниже), но и начинает широко и многогранно воссоздавать региональную историю советской власти.

Трансформация жизненного факта в ткань художественного произведения очень сложный процесс, который имеет некоторые отличительные особенности, так как нельзя забывать о специфике документального образа, о границах художественной интерпретации и обобщения. Не разрушая свои связи с действительностью документальный факт должен стать эстетически значимым. Ведь только тогда документальное произведение живет, когда реальные события, легшие в основу повествования, становятся необходимым звеном в художественном открытии.

Повесть, в которой процитированы документы, еще не может расцениваться как художественно-документальное произведение, так как большое значение играет эстетическая значимость, эстетическая нагрузка, выполняемая документом в этой повести, степень авторской интерпретации, талантливости художника.

Преобразования, начавшиеся во второй половине 1980-х годов, отмена цензуры сказались на литературной жизни не только советской, но и национальных литератур. Так, например, в 3 номере «Литературного Киргизстана» за 1990 год печатается новый вариант повести Ч. Айтматова «Лицом к лицу». Сам автор так охарактеризует это явление:

«… я решил вернуться к ней и восполнить то, от чего мне в свое время пришлось отказаться по цензурным соображениям, – от каких-то глав, каких-то поступков моих героев, которые прежде весьма осложнили судьбу моего произведения».[10] Основной конфликт произведения – конфликт отдельной личности и долга – наиболее явственно раскрывается после второй редакции, когда уже не обойдена тема раскулачивания, что явилось не только фактом классовой борьбы, а что еще важнее, составило основу столкновения, противоречия, в результате чего главный герой Исмаил становится дезертиром.

Выходит в свет не только литература о современности, но и произведения о далеком прошлом кыргызского народа. Так, в начале 1990-х годов появляется повесть «Мать-и-мачеха» Е. Колесникова о первых русских переселенцах. Сам автор напишет в предисловии: «Когда явился мне Егор Саламатин – первый лапотный курский крестьянин, пришедший на киргизскую землю – в документах, в свидетельствах очевидцев, – я почти сразу написал повесть «Черная кость»… Теперь есть «Мать-и-мачеха» – продолжение повести «Черная кость», где в основном действовали курский крестьянин и киргизский джигит…».[11]

В основу повести Е. Колесникова «Мать-и-мачеха» положены реальные события, происходившие в Пржевальском уезде в 1919 году, и больше известные как «Тюпский мятеж».

Интерес читателей к документам, соответствие изображаемого и фактического материала в середине 1980-х и началу 1990-х годов находились на очень высокой отметке. Прежде всего, это объясняется, наверное, тем, что перестройка, гласность, демократизация общества вызвала у читателей желание разобраться в сложных, порой противоречивых мнениях, взглядах. Люди захотели сами доискаться, найти истоки того самого «застойного явления». Характерной особенностью десятилетия становится резко возросшая общественная активность, заинтересованность людей не только в литературе, но и в вопросах экономики, политики, истории.

Вдруг выясняется, что некоторые отрезки времени в истории бывшего Советского Союза литература не освещала, не нашли должного отображения в искусстве художественного слова отдельные драматические моменты развития общества. И писатели решили восполнить эти «пробелы» истории.

Н. Анастасьев справедливо отмечает, что к концу нашего столетия «документальная литература приобрела всемирный размах».[12] Это еще одна особенность всей литературы конца XX века. Исследуя современность, современный мир, литература начинает обращаться, прежде всего, к истории далекого и ближнего прошлого. Читатель недоверчив, чтобы принять придуманную версию истории или, другими словами, «мифологизированную историю». Он жаждет правды и о недалеком прошлом, и о настоящем, сегодняшнем дне. Поэтому такой повышенный, неподдельный интерес к литературе фактов. Ведь общеизвестно, что в документальной прозе оценочная сторона не главенствует. А отсюда появляется возможность самому сделать выводы, самому разобраться в происходящих переменах. Важной особенностью этого времени становится наличие полного спектра различных оценок, мнений, взглядов на те или иные события и возможность самостоятельного, а не навязанного выбора. Читатель самостоятельно ищет «кристалл правды». Права С. Алексиевич, утверждающая, что «в конце XX века, уже неоспоримо, что искусство о многом в человеке не подозревает, не догадывается.

Отсюда такое доверие к факту, удовольствие от подлинности, каким давно заразился современный человек».[13]

И еще одной характерной особенностью, на наш взгляд, отмечена литература этого десятилетия: это некая исповедальность повествования. Писатели хотят высказаться, торопятся рассказать то, что было скрыто где-то в тайниках души. Выплескивается недосказанное. Если раньше «документ часто не открывал, а скрывал правду» (М. Шагинян), то теперь происходит обратный процесс. Документы обнажают определенный срез времени, раскрывают и передают «дыхание эпохи», «атмосферу времени». Исповедальность характеризует искусство художественного слова в это десятилетие, и как результат появляются рассказы-исповеди, автобиографические рассказы об определенном периоде в истории развития общества. Открывается трагедийный герой нашего времени, появляется обобщенный образ-герой, через которого каждый художник старается передать трагедию своего времени, его беду. В этих героях (зачастую автобиографических) отражается и жестокость, и боль, и противоречия всей эпохи.

Бесспорно одно – документализм сыграл большую роль в развитии литературного процесса. И наблюдаемая многофункциональность документа в литературном процессе объясняется ростом профессионализма писателей. Начиная от простого, прямого, «лобового» включения документа в текст произведения, от устоявшейся описательности событий, литература начинает раскрывать новые грани, иные возможности документа в создании художественного произведения.

Литературная практика конца XX века убедительно доказала: документализм в кыргызской литературе существует и приобретает все усложняющиеся формы. Кыргызскую литературу на современном этапе отличает стремление к глубокому художественному осмыслению жизни. Свой вклад в решение этой проблемы внесла и художественно-документальная проза, которая занимает заметное место в современном литературном процессе. Анализ источников показал, что в литературе советского периода помимо межнациональных традиций, воздействия русской литературы на процесс развития новописьменных литератур, существовали глубоко национальные традиции, и кыргызская литература, имеющая богатые древнейшие фольклорные традиции, использовала их в первых письменных произведениях.

СНОСКИ

1. Большой энциклопедический словарь. (Гл.ред. А. М. Прохоров). – М.: Советская энциклопедия, 1991. –Т.1. – С.403.
2. Словарь русского литературного языка. –М.-Л.: АН СССР, Т. 3. – С.352
3. *Явчуновский Я. И.* Документальные жанры. – Саратов, 1974. – С.22
4. *Гушанская Б.* На путях научно-художественного документализма. – В кн.: Художественное и научное творчество. – Л.: 1972. – С.143
5. *Адамович А.* Выступление в дискуссии «Жизненный материал и художественное обобщение»// Вопросы литературы,1966, № 9. – С. 7.
6. Там же, с.23.
7. *Джолдошева Ч. Т.* Роль художественного перевода в формировании и развитии киргизской прозы. В кн.: Закономерности развития новописьменных литератур и проблемы социалистического реализма. – Бишкек, 1980. – С.48.
8. *Кацев А. С.* Русская литература в переводах на кыргызский язык. – В кн.: Русская литература в переводах на кыргызский язык. Диахроническая библиография. Вып.1: 1922-1960 гг. – Бишкек,1999. – С.5.
9. *Толстой Л.Н.* Кажымурат: (Повесттен ъзъндъ) / Котор. М. Элебаев// Кыргыз совет адабияты. – 1936. – № 2. – Б.4-16; № 3. – Б.18-25; № 6-7. – Б.18-22.

   Толстой Л. Н. Хаджи-Мурат: (Повесттен ъзъндъ) /Котор. Ж. Боконбаев //Кыргызстан совет жазуучулар союзунун алманахы, –1936. – Б.37-40.

   Фурманов Д. А. Козголон: (Роман) /Котор. М. Элебаев. – Ф. –Казань: Кыргызмамбас. –1936. –200 б.

   Горький М. Таятамдын ъйъндё; Чиймечиникинде(ъзъндълёр) М. Абдыкеримов жана О. Жакишов. Адабият: орто мектептин V кл. ъчън окуу китеби.I бёлум. – Ф.: Казань,1937. – Б. 5-34.

   Фурманов Д. А. Чапаев (Романдан ъзъндъ) /Котор. М. Элебаев//Кыргыз совет адабияты. –1937. –№5-6. –Б.37-42.

   Горький А.М. Менин университеттерим: (Повесть) /Котор. М. Догдуров. – Ф. –Казань: Кыргызмамбас. –1938. –198 б.

   Фурманов Д. А. Чапаев: (Роман) /Котор. Т. Байджиев. – Ф. –Казань: Кыргызмамбас,1939. – 376 б.
10. *Айтматов Ч.* Лицом к лицу // Литературный Киргизстан,1990, № 3. – С.7 (Подчеркнуто нами. - *Х.Ш.*)
11. *Колесников Е.* Мать-и-мачеха // Литературный Киргизстан, 1991, № 2, № 3.
12. *Анастасьев Н.* Прямая речь // Иностранная литература, 1989, № 11.
13. *Алексиевич С.* В поисках вечного человека //Вопросы литературы, 2000, № 1. – С. 38.

30

К вопросу о решении гендерных проблем в Кыргызстане

Назгул Абалова

Как известно, "*Гендер – социальный пол*...смысл понятия "гендер" заключен, прежде всего, в идее *социального моделирования или конструирования пола*. Социальный пол конструируется социальной практикой. В обществе возникает *система* норм поведения, предписывающая выполнение определенных половых ролей; соответственно возникает жесткий ряд представлений о том, что есть "мужское" и "женское" в данном обществе".[1]

Таким образом, смысл понятия «гендер» заключен, прежде всего, в идее социального моделирования или конструирования пола. Социальный пол конструируется социальной практикой.»[2]

Гендер не только влияет на представление человека о себе, но и учит его поступать определенным образом. Поэтому и возникает понятие «гендерные роли», под которыми понимаются «установки и виды деятельности, которые общество увязывает с тем или иным полом».[3]

Значит, гендер является одним из измерений социальной организации, определяющим наши отношения с окружающими и представлением о себе. И дифференциация понятий «пол» и «гендер» означала выход на новый теоретический уровень осмысления социальных процессов. В конце 80-х годов прошлого тысячелетия феминистские исследовательницы постепенно переходят от критики патриархата и изучения специфического женского опыта к анализу гендерной системы. Женские исследования постепенно перерастают в гендерные исследования, где на первый план выдвигаются подходы, согласно которым все аспекты человеческого общества, культуры и взаимоотношений являются гендерными. В современной науке гендерный подход к анализу социальных и культурных процессов и явлений используется очень широко.

В Кыргызстане понятие «гендер» появилось относительно недавно. Гендерная концепция, гендерные исследования, гендерный анализ законодательных актов в Кыргызской Республике стала разрабатываться и проводится в последнее десятилетие прошлого столетия, когда на мировой арене интенсивнее стали актуализироваться гендерные проблемы. Как известно, на этот период пришло прохождение ряда значимых международных форумов и конференций, которые затронули проблемы гендерной системы, норм, гендерной идентичности, гендерной идеологии: Каирская международная конференция по народонаселению и развитию 1994 года, Пекинская Четвертая Всемирная конференция по положению женщин 1995 года, Копенгагенский Всемирный саммит по социальному развитию 1995 года, Гамбургская Пятая Международная конференция ЮНЕСКО по образованию для взрослых 1997 года.

До 1995 года в Кыргызской Республике не существовало единой концепции в отношении улучшения положения женщин, так как тоталитарный режим социалистического общества, несмотря на светский характер декларируемых принципов, не предлагал новых принципов и стимулов для участия женщин в общественно- политической жизни, за исключением заказных квот. Особая активность в решении гендерных проблем приходится на 1996 год, который был объявлен Годом Женщин в Кыргызстане. Это было началом разработки новых реальных программ по достижению гендерного равенства и баланса в демократическом, суверенном кыргызстанском обществе.

Отрадно отметить, что в этот период в молодой независимой стране было сделано много по институциональной поддержке женщин:

- создана Государственная комиссия по делам женщин, семьи и молодежи (1996);
- проведены парламентские слушания по положению женщин (1996);
- была утверждена и начала реализоваться Национальная программа по улучшению положения женщин «Аялзат» (1996-2000);[4]

А в 1997 году Кыргызстан принял национальную стратегию по устойчивому человеческому развитию и вошел в число 10 пилотных стран, где были взяты на вооружение решения Всемирной конференции ООН по положению женщин (Пекин,1995). В основных документах, которые определяют стратегию развития Кыргызской Республики на среднесрочную и длительную перспективу - Комплексной основе развития до 2010 года и Национальной стратегии сокращения бедности, - повышение внимания к проблемам и перспективам решения гендерных проблем рассматривался как важный элемент демократического строительства, усиления возможностей страны по борьбе с бедностью и по стимулированию социального и экономического развития Кыргызстана. Достижение гендерного паритета в образовании и культуре является одним из стратегических направлений Национального плана действий по достижению гендерного равенства в Кыргызской Республике на 2002-2006 годы[5], утвержденного указом Президента КР от 02.03.2002 г. Закон Кыргызской Республики «Об основах государственных гарантий обеспечения гендерного равенства», принятый Законодательным собранием Жогорку Кенеша Кыргызской Республики от 31 января 2003 года, «регулирует отношения по предоставлению равных прав и возможностей лицам разного пола в социальной, политической, экономической, культурной и иных областях жизнедеятельности человека».[6]

Компонент по гендеру, как составная часть Программы социального управления ПРООН в Кыргызстане, был основан в 2001 году. Основными направлениями деятельности Компонента по гендеру Программы социального управления ПРООН являются:

- предоставление консультаций правительству в области разработки гендерной политики;
- развитие гендерной статистики;
- внедрение гендерных подходов в политику и стратегию министерств и ведомств;
- поддержка гендерного образования в высших учебных заведениях;
- поддержка женского политического лидерства;

- поддержка гендерного бюро Правовой клиники «Адилет».

С 1996 года «Бюро гендер в развитии» ПРООН, в настоящее время Программа социального управления ПРООН, оказывает поддержку Национальному Статистическому комитету Кыргызской Республики в подготовке и публикации сборников гендерной статистики. Ниже приводится гендерная характеристика Кыргызстана, подготовленная Программой социального управления ПРООН:

- В целом образовательный уровень мужчин и женщин не имеет значительных отличий, однако в городах женщины образованнее мужчин: доля женщин с высшим образованием составляет 17,5% по сравнению с 15,6% у мужчин, со средним специальным образованием, соотвественно, 16,9% и 9,9%;
- За 1996-2000 гг. уровень экономической активности среди женщин снизился на 4,9%, среди мужчин – на 1,9%;
- В 2001 году среднемесячная зарплата женщин составила 67,6% от заработной платы мужчин. Различия в размерах заработной платы обусловлены тем, что работа в «женских» отраслях оплачивается ниже, чем в отраслях, где работают мужчины
- Ожидаемая продолжительность жизни мужчин 64,9 лет, женщин – 72,4 года. Разница в 7,5 лет связана с различиями на уровне смертности полов. Основные, определяющие эту разницу потери, связаны с более высокой смертностью мужчин в результате несчастных случаев, отравлений и травм;
- Женщины уделяют ведению домашнего хозяйства в среднем по 4-5 часов ежедневно, затрачивая более 20% суточного фонда времени. У мужчин эти затраты не превышают 5% и составляют немногим более одного часа;
- Средний размер пенсии женщин составляет 86% от среднего размера пенсий мужчин;

- В 2001 году досрочная отмена моратория на куплю-продажу земли фактически дала старт рынку земли.

Земельными долями наделены около 2 млн. 462 тыс.человек, из них 50,8% женщины. В распределении этого стратегического ресурса женщины юридически имеют равные с мужчинами права на владение землей как частной собственностью. Но существующие традиционные стереотипы фактически ограничивают правоспособность женщин в этом вопросе.[7]

В марте 2002 года был подписан договор о сотрудничестве между Программой социального управления ПРООН, Управлением верховного комиссара по делам беженцев ООН, Американской Ассоциацией юристов о поддержке Правовой клиники «Адилет» (Кыргызская Ассоциация молодых юристов). Программа социального управления поддерживает Гендерное бюро, которое является составной частью клиники. Учитывая уровень правовой культуры населения, в особенности женщин, основными видами деятельности Гендерного бюро являются распространение информации и предоставление юридических консультаций по гендерным вопросам населению, в том числе и беженцам, а также проведение обучащих семинаров по вопросам гендерных отношений и насилия. В рамках направления «Поддержка женского лидерства» был осуществлен проект «на 100% больше женщин в парламенте», в результате которой составлена гендерная статистика об участии женщин в сфере политической жизни общества. Это статистика подверждает данные до 2005 года и выглядит следующим образом:

- Женщины, составляя 52% электората, имеют представительство в Законодательном Собрании Жогорку Кенеша Кыргызской Республики пропорциональное 6,7%. Сохраняется тенденция «пирамиды», когда женщины составляют 12 % на уровне областных. 13 % - на районных и городских, и 16% - на уровне сельских кенешей.
- В 2002 году из 12 министров только 2 женщины, 1 женщина, занимающая должность губернатора области, из 455 глав Айыл Окмоту – только 21 женщины.
- По данным 2001 года среди руководителей органов власти и управления женщин на высших

> государственных должностях составили 14,7%; среди руководителей структурных подразделений, департаментов, управлений – 24,4%.

Доминирование мужчин в политических структурах, низкий уровень гендерного сознания, недостаток поддержки со стороны партии и СМИ, отсуствие соотвествующих связей с различными общественными организациями – все это служит серьезной преградой для расширения представительства женщин в политике.

В 2005 году в Кыргызстане прошли очередные выборы в Парламент Жогорку Кенеша, но к сожалению, как отмечает Ж. Бекбаева, «страной ближайшие 5 лет будет править «законодательный мальчишник», так как в новом однопалатном Парламенте женщины не имеют в нем ни одного представителя.»[8]

Почему в новый парламент не прошли женщины-кандидаты? По словам депутата прошлого состава Т. Боромбаевой: «...все дело в отсуствии одинакового старта для мужчин и женщин. Женщины практически не имеют мощного финансового источника для предвыборной компании.»[9]. Она, как лидер партии «Эл Мурас» («Народное наследие») предлагает один из выходов из сложившейся ситуации - это выбор по партийным спискам. Какова же ситуация в данный момент по партиям, которые функционируют в Кыргызстане? В блоке «Манас» женщины занимают 30,8%, в партии «Моя страна» - 20%, в партии Коммунистов 18,8%, а в партии «Ата Мекен» («Родина»), которую возглавляет экс-спикер нынешнего Парламента О.Текебаев, вообще нет женщин. Среди лидеров всех партий есть только 3 кандидатуры. Это Р.Отунбаева – лидер партии «Ата Журт» («Отечество»),.Боромбаева – лидер партии «Эл Мурасы» («Народное наследие»), К.Ажибекова - лидер радикальных коммунистов. Все эти 3 партии отрицают, что их политическое движение имеет четко выраженный гендерный признак. Единственная пратия, созданная по половому признаку и под неофициальным патронажем прошлого правительства «Демократическая партия женщин» еще на выборах 2000 года с треском провалилась.[10]

Выступая 7 марта 2006 года на торжестве, посвященном Международному женскому дню, Президент К. Бакиев подчеркнул, что около 37% руководящего состава всех уровней составляют представители прекрасного пола. Однако, как и повсюду в мире, женщины Кыргызстана почти не оказывают влияния на принятие решений. В политике и политических структурах главенствует опыт, сконструированный мужским видением мира. Наше общество давно нуждается в женщинах-лидерах, которые бы внесли обновляющий фактор и в политику, и в экономику, – продолжил Президент. - Представьте себе, мы имеем только 1 женщину-министра, члена Правительства, а в Жогорку Кенеше нет ни одной женщины – депутата. Мы все надеемся на мудрость наших избирателей на следующих выборах в Парламент».[11]

«Государство, - сказал Президент К. Бакиев, - поддерживая равноправие мужчин и женщин, тем самым обеспечивает гармоничное развитие общества в целом». Сегодня власть стремиться найти новые возможности для улучшения положения женщин, семьи, их социального статуса и условий жизни. Наращивая эти усилия, подчеркнул глава Республики, руководство Кыргызстана старается уйти от традиционных локальных женских проблем и концепции гендерного равенства полов к идее паритетной демократии при главенстве законов «Об основах государственных гарантий в ведении гендерного равенства» и «Мерах социально-правовой защиты от насилия в семье». Сегодня в Счетной Палате, ЦИК, Верховном и Конституционном судах законом предусмотрено наличие лиц одного пола не более 70%. Президент сообщил, что такой же законопроект будет разработан и об испольнительной ветви власти – Правительстве».[12]

Для того, чтобы женщины занимали в Парламенте республики достойное место, необходимо, чтобы, в первую очередь, женщины-избиратели поняли важность и смысл избрания демократичеким путем женщин-парламентариев. Тогда и будет обеспечен успех. И хочется порекомендовать женщинам Кыргызстана: «Вперед! Красиво, бережно, стремительно!», ведь многие кыргызские женщины унаследовали неподражаемые черты своих далеких прабабушек, как мудрая Чиирды, величавая Каныкей, великолепная Кыз

Сайкал, гордая Жаныл Мырза, дальновидная Курманжан Датка, стойкая Уркуя Салиева. В процессе исторического развития кыргызстанского общества на его общественной арене появлялись и появятся новые женские имена, которые своим доблестным трудолюбием и профессиональным талантом завоюют признание и любовь народа.

ПРИМЕЧАНИЯ

1. Основы гендерных исследований.Хрестоматия, 2001, стр. 12.
2. Там же, стр. 12.
3. Масионис Дж., Социология, 9-е изд. 2003., стр. 439.
4. Национальная программа расширения возможностей женщин «Аялзат» (1996 -2000гг), Бишкек, 1996.
5. Национальный план действий по достижению гендерного равенства в КР(2002-2006гг), Бишкек, 2002.
6. Закон Кыргызской Республики «Об основах государственных гарантий обеспечения гендерного равенства», Бишкек, 2003.
7. www.sgp.undp.kg
8. Бекбаева Ж.,.Вся власть мужчинам.//Ц-А. Интернет журнал «ОАЗИС»//www.ca-oasis.info/oasis/.
9. Там же
10. Там же
11. Президент намерен сохранить во власти гендерное равенство: поручено подготовить законопроект о сохранении в испольнительной власти гендерного равенства www.cdf.gov.kg/ru/new/?=29
12. Шепеленко А., Душой их человечество согрето //Слово Кыргызстана, 27.03.06//www.sk.kg/2006.23/1/htm

31

Концепция Пространства и Времени в Мировосприятии Кыргызов

З.Т. Рысалиева

Все известные события обладают двумя предельно общими атрибутами – пространством и временем. Они происходят в некотором пространстве и им свойственна определенная временная динамика. Представление о пространстве и времени так существенны для интегральной картины мира, что их нередко называют «фабрикой Вселенной»(1). Можно с уверенностью утверждать, что всякой картине мира во всех сменяющихся друг друга истории человечества культурах, соответствовало определенное пространственно-временное видение. От начала человеческой истории и до наших дней, с расширением познания и развитием науки, это видение углублялось и совершенствовалось. Но «почти все фундаментальные представления о пространства и времени уже давно были созданы нашими далекими предшественниками. Во всяком случае, трудно найти такие современные концепции или модели пространства и времени, у которых не было бы весьма архаичных прообразов» (2). Это говорит о том, что первые концепции пространства и времени были созданы в мифологии.

В данной статье мы попытаемся дать анализ концепции пространства и времени в мировосприятии кыргызов на основе материальной и духовной культуры народа.

Как отмечал известный историк В.В. Бартольд, кыргызы являются одним из древних народов Центральной Азии. Первые сведения о кыргызах мы встречаем в «Исторических записках» китайского историка Сыма Цзяня, которая датируется 201 годом до н.э. Это свидетельствует о том, что история кыргызов насчитывает более 2000 летний период существования. За этот долгий путь материальная и духовная культура кыргызского народа прошли сложный путь исторического развития. Ее становление неразрывно связано с кочевой цивилизацией, «которая впоследствии была названа номадической, предложившая истории свой способ и метод видения мира: постижение безграничных просторов бытия, не скованных пространственными рамками».(3) В поисках лучших пастбищ и водных источников скотовод вместе с семьёй и своим родом часто переходил из одного места в другое. На каждом этапе развития материальной культуры и традиции происходили существенные изменения. Вся культура, образ жизни, идеологические представления и мировосприятие находились в состоянии постоянного обновления и совершенствования. Не было застывших, замкнутых систем. Наоборот, проявлялось постоянное стремление к новизне, к аккумулированию этнокультурных достижений других племён и народов. Кыргызы не случайно говорят: «Элуу жылда эл жаңырат» т.е. по прошествии 50 лет сам народ и его культура обновляются. В этой пословице выражено народное понятие об историческом отрезке времени.

В традиционном мировосприятии кыргызов пространство превалировало над временем, обуславливая пространственность как характерную черту мышления. Время понималось своеобразно, как циклическое, которое определялось существованием природных циклов развития, имеющих свои особенности на фоне общего движения в истории жизни кочевника-кыргыза.

Как уже было отмечено выше, первые концепции пространства и времени были созданы в мифологии. Мифология представляет собой своеобразную, исторически первую форму мировоззрения. В качестве системы взглядов она прошла длинный эволюционный путь. И на каждом этапе этого пути создавалась своя картина мира, изображающая его зарождение и структуры. «В самом общем виде, пишет М.Д. Ахундов, - динамику мифологического мира можно раскрыть как переход от Хаоса к Космосу».(4) В этом контексте можно отметить, что высшую ценность в мифическом сознании составляет время и место возникновения мира, т.е. центр мироздания, который ассоциируется с понятием "мировое дерево", "дерево жизни".

Мировое дерево - это связующее звено между землей и небом, между верхним и подземным мирами.

В космогонических мифах древних кыргызов мы не можем найти четко и ярко выраженной картины происхождения мира. НО мы можем встретить некоторых мифоэпосах представления о происхождении мира. Например, в эпосе "Манас" встречаются такие строки: «Жер жер болгондо, С'уу суу болгондо, Манас Манас болгондо». Эти сюжеты иллюстрируют традиционное моделирование мира, которое встречается в мифах Шумера, Китая, Индии, т.е. космическое отделяется от хаоса, земля от воды, появляется первочеловек - Манас. Например, в Ригведе, переход от хаоса к космосу описывается следующим образом: «Не было ни сущего, и не сущего. Не было ни воздушного пространства, ни неба над ним... не было ни смерти, ни бессмертия тогда. Не было ни признака дня, (или) ночи..»(5). Точно такую же схему можно найти в Законах Ману: «Этот мир неведомый, неопределимый, недоступный для разума, непознаваемый, как бы совершенно погруженный в сон, был тьмой» (6). Для структуры подобных текстов характерны следующие особенности: 1) построение текстов как ответа на некий вопрос; 2) членение текста, заданное описанием событий (составляющих акт творения), которые отражают последовательность временных отрезков с указанием начала; 3) описание последовательной организации пространства; 4) введение операции порождения для перехода от одного этапа творения к следующему; 5) последовательное нисхождение от космологического и божественного к «историческому» и человеческому.(7)

Вселенная это нерасторжимая связь трех миров: мира нижнего, верхнего и подземного. Каждый из этих миров выстраивался по аналогии либо с телесной, либо с психической, либо с духовной организацией человека. В силу этого, Вселенная оказывалась целостной и по всем параметрам изоморфной человеку: любой человеческой структуре соответствовала изоморфная ей - космическая. Изоморфными такой картине мира оказывались не только человек и Вселенная, но и составляющие их миры - телесный (физический), душевный (метафизический) и духовный (трансцендентный). Таким образом, в мире действует принцип структурного изоморфизма: каждый элемент природного целого имеет единую структуру. Символом структурной упорядоченности является, как уже отмечали выше, мировое дерево (мировая гора, мировой столб). Мировое дерево - характерный для мифопоэтического сознания образ, воплощающий универсальную концепцию мира. Образ мирового дерева реконструируется на основе мифологических, в частности, космологических представлений. При членении мирового дерева по вертикали выделяются нижняя (корни), средняя (ствол) и верхняя (ветви) части. По вертикали обнаруживаются противопоставления: верх-низ, небо-земля и др. С помощью мирового дерева различимы основные зоны вселенной - верхняя (небесное царство), средняя (земля), нижняя (подземное). Мировое дерево - это ось, которая объединяет все сферы мироздания. В эпосе "Манас" главный герой - Манас ассоциируется с мировым деревом, и через этот образ организуется весь пространственно-временный континуум. Другой образ мирового дерева - это мировая гора. Горы всегда ассоциировались с мудростью и величием, поэтому многие народы до сих пор поклоняются горам и эти места считаются священными. Например, в Кыргызстане встречаются такие места как, мазар Дунгуромо на Ыссык-Куле и Кочкор-Ата в Кочкорке. Таким образом, образ мирового дерева, корнями уходящего в землю, а вершиной возносящего в небеса, выражал идею единства небесной, земной и подземной сфер. Несмотря на то, что разные уровни мироздания символизировали различные миры, у них есть и общее объединяющее начало - это земля и жизнь. Земля - феномен, порождающий жизнь, это источник жизни, связанный с рождением, развитием человека. Земля - это и мир людей, символ света и счастья. Такие философские представления отражены в эпосе "Эр-Тоштук". Согласно мифопоэтической модели мира в эпосе показано, что Земля это источник жизни, а подземный Мир - символ мрака, ночи и небытия. Эти представления были связаны с вертикальной структурой мироздания. Пространственные слои могут быть ориентированы также и горизонтально - по сторонам света. В мифах народов мы часто встречаем слова "четыре стороны света", которые символизируют основные ориентиры мира: восток, запад, юг и север. В эпосе "Манас" пространство имеет четыре направления, четыре стороны. Надо отметить, что понятия пространства и времени существовали на эмпирическом уровне. Постепенно эти категории эволюционизировались от сравнительной связи до диалектического единства. Например, в эпосе "Эр-Тоштук", происходящие события слишком фантастичны, время не имеет определенного порядка, а героиня эпоса Кенжеке носит ребенка 7 лет. В эпосе "Кожожаше" время уже конкретизировано, а события происходят в определенной местности. Несмотря на то, что герой эпоса "Кожожаш" гоняетеся за Сур-Эчки в течении года, в эпосе можно обнаружить определенную систематизацию времени и пространства. В эпосе "Манас' время динамично, одни события идут после других, главные герои сменяют друг друга, образуя единую трилогию (Манас - Семетей - Сейтек). Но некоторые герои живут вне времени. Свидетельство этому присутствие главных героев Бакая и Каныкей от начала и до конца эпоса.

В мифическом сознании понятие пространства и времени также связаны с различными уровнями мироздания. Например, шаман обладает способностью путешествовать во времени, то он может отправиться в будущее или прошлое, присутствовать при событиях, которые еще не произошли или уже произошли. Надо отметить, что понятие времени - одна из самых таинственных и трудных для понимания категорий человеческого мышления - и мифологического, и философского, и научного. Уже в самых архаических картинах мира время неоднократно, релятивно, циклично и спиралевидно. Оно течет, то уплотняясь, то разряжаясь (неоднородность), то ускоряя, то замедляя свой бег (релятивность), из прошлого в настоящее и через будущее вновь возвращается в прошлое, повторяясь буквально (цикличность) или в улучшенном варианте (спиралевидность). В традиционном жилище кыргызов – юрте (боз уй), мы можем найти яркую иллюстрацию, как номады представляли пространство и время.

Что означает юрта для кочевника? Можно с уверенностью отметить, что в юрте были заключены в конкретизированном виде древнейшие черты культуры народа. Юрта представляет собой вершину кочевой архитектуры и народно-прикладного искусства. Кроме этого, она была прекрасно приспособлена к кочевому образу жизни: мягкость, простота конструкций, удобность в транспортировке, всесезонность - были её неизменными качествами. Юрта состояла из деревянной конструкции; остов, собираемый из нескольких частей складных решетчатых стенок «кереге», придающих юрте в плане круглую форму. «Кереге» состояли из отдельных звеньев «канат», над которыми на жердях «уук» поднимали купол юрты — «түндүк». Отчет времени суток, месяца и года кочевники обычно вели по солнцу, а именно по углу падения солнечного луча через тундук. По мере того, как лучше солнце скользил по окружности и по кончиком жердей, падающий через свод юрты, кыргызы определял время.

Размер юрты зависел от количества звеньев «канат», при сравнении говорили «алты канат уй», «он канат уй», — «шестиканатная юрта», «десятиканатная юрта» или от количества жердей — «уук», которые загнутым концом «ууктун алаканы» прикрепляются к верху раздвинутых «кереге», «ууктун учу» упираются в отверстия обода «түндүк» — «жүз баштуу», «сексен баштуу», «алтмыш баштуу уй» — баш — голова, верхушка остова юрты — «керегенин башы». В зависимости от качества «кереге», юрту делили на «тор көз», «жел көз», «ара көз». Особо крепкими и качественными были юрты, если решётки «кереге» были маленькими — «тор көз кереге».

В юрте кыргызов заключены в конкретизированном виде древнейшие черты культуры народа, социальных и общественных отношений.

Чрезвычайно интересна организация жилого пространства в юрте. Оно делится на четыре части. «Төр» — место противоположное от входа в юрту, самое почётное. Здесь располагались гости, старшие мужчины семьи. Здесь же на сундуках и других предметах сооружали стопки одеял, войлоки, ковры, меховую и др. верхнюю одежду — «жүк». «Эр жак» — мужская сторона, левая от входа часть юрты. Здесь располагались мужчины средних и молодых лет, на ночь здесь находилась спальня для молодожёнов. «Эпчи жак» — правая от входа часть юрты, принадлежит женщинам, здесь за оградой из циновок находились домашняя утварь, продукты питания. Затем «улага», около порога. Здесь в левой, ближе к входу стороне, находились конские снаряжения — «ээр токум», «ат жабдыктар» и др. принадлежности бытового назначения. В центре юрты находи- лось место, на котором разводился огонь — «коломто». При установлении юрты вход ориентировали по-разному, в зависимости от рельефа местности и направления ветра. Однако, преобладали ориентации на восток, на центр аила. У кыргызов существовал целый ряд обычаев, обрядов, связанных с юртой. Прежде всего, к юрте и её принадлежностям относились бережно. Не принято было плохо отзываться о юрте. Мастера юртовщики «үйчү», «уста», а также мастерицы — «уздар» пользовались среди кыргызов особым уважением. Существовал обычай «үй тою» — нововоселье. Когда семья ставила новую юрту, то обязательно устраивали праздник. В отношении огня — «коломто», существовал целый ряд обычаев. Огонь в представлениях кыргызов имел очищающую силу. В него не плевали, не обрызгивали водой, нельзя было ходить вокруг огня, перепрыгивать. Не давали горящую золу соседям затемно. Если умирал кто-нибудь из членов семьи, то тело покойника, по обычаю, держали в течение трёх дней в юрте. В таком случае из юрты выносилось все убранство, утварь, оставались только войлочные ковры — «кийиз», «шырдак», «килем», на которых сидели плакальщицы. Если покойник был мужского пола, то его располагают в мужской стороне юрты, а если женского, то в женской стороне.

Таким образом, представления древних о пространстве и времени отмечались огромным разнообразием. Каждая культура имела на сей счет свое особое представление. Но если брать мифологию в целом, то в ней оказываются представленными в мифологически-образной форме практически все известные концепции и модели пространства и времени – открытого, закрытого, однородного, неоднородного, линейного и нелинейного, статического и динамичного, субстанционального и релятивного, однослойного и многослойного.

ЛИТЕРАТУРА

1. Ахундов М.Д. Пространство и время: от мифа к науке. // Природа, №8. С.53
2. там же, С.53.
3. Урманбетова Ж.К. Философия культуры- Бишкек, 2000. С.143
4. Ахундов М.Д. Пространство и время: от мифа к науке. С.54
5. Гимн о сотворении мира //Ригведа. Избранные гимны. - М.: Наука, 1972. С.263
6. Законы Ману.- М.: изд-во вост. Литер., 1960. С.21.
7. Топоров В.Н. Первобытные представления о мире. Общий взгляд.//Очерки истории естественнонаучных представлений в древности. – М.:Наука, 1982. С.8.

32

Государство и Культурные Процессы в Современном Казахстане: Новые Парадигмы и Реалии

Sattar Fazylovich Mazhitov

Современные культурные процессы в Казахстане многолики и разнообразны. Под ними понимается широкий спектр изменений, инноваций, коренных преобразований, охватывающих различные отрасли и сферы образования, науки и культуры, включая все развивающиеся в настоящее время виды и жанры искусства. По причине комплекса исторических обстоятельств Казахстан является государством с полиэтническим обществом. Поэтому культурный процесс здесь вбирает в себя явления, связанные с взаимодействием и взаимовлиянием национальных культур. При этом следует отметить, что как ни в какой другой сфере социального развития в Казахстане, в области культуры национальное выступает в наиболее индивидуальном, можно сказать «чистом» виде, впитывая все лучшее из инонационального. В то же время, культурные процессы в казахстанском обществе не ограничиваются национальными культурами географических масштабов страны. В Казахстане, благодаря происходившему на его территории многообразным политическим, историческим, общественно-экономическим изменениям, выработалась благодатная почва, которая способна впитывать все наилучшее из духовного наследия человечества. Примеры этому можно проследить еще со времен функционирования первых магистралей Великого Шелкового пути, которые как известно проходили через территорию как Казахстана, так и Индии.

Складывавшиеся в Казахстане со второй половины 80-х годов –времени распада СССР - культурные процессы, отражали, с одной стороны, кризис советской тоталитарной системы, отход от культивировавшихся в тот период принципов классовости, партийности, социалистического реализма. Культурное развитие страны характеризовалось трудностями и коллизиями становления нового независимого государства. После декабрьских событий 1986 г. в Казахстане свой отпечаток на решение культурных вопросов оказало и обвинение казахского народа в "национализме". С другой стороны, в культуре конца 80-х - 90-х гг. наблюдается отражение первых шагов утверждающего плюрализма, различных форм собственности, общественно- политического обновления и многообразия мнений. Народное образование, наука и культура получили широкое пространство для саморазвития, свободы от идеологических догм и стереотипов.

Государства постсоветского пространства на протяжении относительно короткого исторического периода столкнулись с комплексом проблем сферы духовного и культурного развития. Среди них: уход в прошлое былых приоритетов единого культурного пространства и появление новых парадигм национальной идентификации; девальвация коллективистских взглядов и возрождение на их руинах разных по своей идейной и мировоззренческой направленности ценностей. Последние и определили, в конечном счете судьбы ряда традиционных сообществ и государственных формирований. Эволюция процесса демократизации непосредственным образом определила многообразие и реальный контент общественных структур. В то же время по ряду показателей идеалы плюрализма и мультикультурализма не оправдали себя и даже вызвали обратные процессы. В этих условиях для возрожденного Казахстана ключом к сбережению нации, стабильности общества, национального единства и общественного согласия стал ориентир на богатое историческое и культурное наследие казахского и других этносов. Тем более, что возрастающие темпы глобализации актуализировали задачу выработки универсальной модели сохранения этнической самобытности и неповторимости.

Обращение к культурному наследию приобретает особую актуальность, когда встает задача выявления этнодифференцирующих функций в развитии национальных культур. Исследователь сталкивается здесь с разного рода жанрово-стилевыми предпочтениями и лексико-семантическими ориентациями при прослеживании судьбы фольклорного, профессионального развития отдельных национальных культур, путей совершенствования и взаимообогащения их самобытных творческих школ. Отсюда актуализация вопросов «что» и «как»: что означают культурные ценности для их создателей и породившей их социально-этнической среды, а с другой стороны, как они воспринимаются и оцениваются в инонациональной среде «потребителей». Под последними подразумеваются как читатели, зрители, слушатели, так и художники-творцы, и интерпретаторы, и аналитики искусства, осваивающие культурное наследие сообразно своим профессиональным установкам. «Психологи нашего столетия неоднократно рассуждали об архетипах, трудно определяемых больших идеях, образах или системах идей и образов, выплывающих в сознании людей из сферы бессознательного. Национальная сказка, мифология, древние законы, архитектура, литература, история, культура, музыка и т.д. способствуют тому, что в сознании каждого из людей каким-то таинственным образом формируются образы, способствующие возникновению собственных оценок истории и культуры, а также порождающих деление на «Мы» и «Другие». Без таких архетипов вообще невозможно говорить о национальной памяти, национальном образе мира, национальном духовном и материальном наследии» (Назарбаев Н.А. В потоке истории. – Алматы, 1999. - СС. 147-148).

В настоящее время цивилизационное формированис Казахстана, как равноправного субъекта мирового сообщества, требует глубокого переосмысления места и роли культурного достояния народа, давшего имя республике. Согласно принятой ЮНЕСКО «Конвенции о всемирном культурном и природном наследии», а также «Рекомендации об охране культурного и природного наследия» ответственность за сохранность и прерогатива регулирования нормативной системы в этой сфере ложится на плечи государственных структур.

Однако настала необходимость и на общенациональном уровне, с привлечением широкой общественности, произвести освидетельствование и выявить приоритеты историко-культурного наследия с точки зрения сохранения и развития языка, материальных, интеллектуальных и духовных достижений, на основе которых складывается современный этнический образ казахского народа. Сопоставительный анализ историко-культурного ядра казахстанского общества в контексте общечеловеческих гуманитарных ценностей даст возможность не только обогатить имманентную социокультурную инфраструктуру, но и четко позиционировать Казахстан в современном мире как страну с уникальной историей и культурой.

Достигнутые Казахстаном к началу XXI века темпы экономического роста оказали неминуемое положительное влияние на развитие культурных процессов. Примером плодотворного контакта государства и культуры в современном Казахстане по праву может считаться Государственная программа «Культурное наследие». Первый этап Программы «Культурное наследие» рассчитан на 2004-2006 гг.

Реализация программы основана на выдвинутой Президентом Республики Казахстан Н.А. Назарбаевым двуединой задаче «формирования такой социокультурной общности, которая опиралась бы на богатейший пласт языковой, духовной и материальной культуры казахского народа, а также всех этносов, проживающих в нашей стране. И одновременно – на органическом восприятии многогранного опыта духовно-культурного развития всей мировой цивилизации».

Настоящая Программа определяет основные аспекты, связанные с изучением, охраной, использованием и пропагандой культурного наследия страны, преемственностью развития и возрождения историко-культурных традиций, предусматривает меры по созданию целостной системы изучения культурного наследия, в том числе и современной национальной культуры, фольклора, традиций и обычаев, обобщению многовекового опыта национальной литературы и письменности, по созданию развернутых художественных и научных серий, а также, реставрации, консервации и музеефикации памятников истории и культуры, укреплению и развитию научно-исследовательской, материально-технической составляющей вопросов культурного наследия.

Разработка данной Программы была продиктована необходимостью более активного, конструктивного вмешательства в организационную ситуацию, сложившуюся в сфере культурного наследия, путем планомерного финансирования деятельности по сохранению и рациональному использованию имеющихся культурных ценностей.

Начиная со второй половмны 80-х годов XX века практически было приостановлено издание основополагающих трудов мировой научной мысли в области философии, истории, юриспруденции и т.д., а также художественной литературы для казахскоязычной аудитории. В этой связи, в целях воспитания подрастающего поколения в духе казахстанского патриотизма и восполнения пробелов в полноценном изучении исторического, культурного наследия, а также обобщения многовекового духовного опыта казахского народа, становятся особо актуальными вопросы создания развернутых исторических, художественных, научных серий на государственном языке.

Комплексное решение обозначенных выше проблем в рамках настоящей Программы будет способствовать дальнейшему развитию системы изучения, сохранения и популяризации культурного наследия народа Казахстана.

В целях развития духовной и образовательной сферы, обеспечения сохранности и эффективного использования культурного наследия страны масштабный проект «Культурное наследие» включил в себя разработку теоретических проблем исторической науки и издание лучших образцов национальной литературы и письменности, достижений мировой научной мысли, культуры и литературы на казахском языке.

Кризис современного исторического сознания исследователи связывают в первую очередь с проблемой методологии истории. Наличие большого числа направлений, концепций и позиций по проблеме сущности и направленности общественного развития, о месте в нем отдельных народов и цивилизаций, а также осознание специфической сложности феномена человека и общества ставит перед учеными-историками и общественностью суверенного Казахстана вопрос как о синтезе столь многоплановых данных, так и выборе системообразующего критерия для построения цельного исторического знания.

Современные культурные процессы, и в частности наука, немыслимы без обращения к наследию мировой философско-исторической мысли. Настоятельная потребность выйти за пределы конкретных эмпирических данных и обобщить их на уровне смысла и вызвало необходимость создания сериала книг «Мировая историческая мысль». Немаловажную роль в выборе этого проекта сыграло и то, что в условиях расширяющейся сферы действия и возрастающих функций казахского языка как государственного, казахстанское общество столкнулось с фактом отсутствия переводов на казахском языке огромного массива произведений мировой исторической мысли.

В рамках реализации Указа Президента Республики Казахстан «О Государственной программе «Культурное наследие» на 2004-2006 годы» и Постановления Правительства Казахстана «О Плане мероприятий о реализации Государственной программы «Культурное наследие» на 2004-2006 годы в 2004 году начато создание серии книг «Мировая историческая мысль» в 10-ти томах на казахском языке. Работы по подготовке этой серии к изданию возложены на Институт истории и этнологии им. Ч.Ч. Валиханова. Автор этих строк является руководителем данного проекта.

В серию «Мировая историческая мысль» вошло множество трактатов мыслителей и ученых мира, посвященных проблемам развития человеческих цивилизаций, культур, стран и народов, огромное количество теорий, концепций исторического развития и школ, а также имена представителей целой плеяды талантливых историков мира.

Считаю весьма уместным и отрадным отметить на данном научном форуме тот факт, что в 1 и 7 тома серии «Мировая историческая мысль» включены в виде антологии извлечения из классических произведений Древней Индии: «Артхашастра», «Джатаки», «Законы Ману», а также трудов лидеров индийского освободительного движения - Махатмы Ганди и Джавахарлала Неру. Благодаря реализации в казахстанском общества Государственной программы «Культурное наследие» через многие столетия впервые «заговорили» на казахском языке древнеиндийские трактаты, легенды и сказки, многие положения которых актуальны для современного Казахстана. Трудно переоценить большую значимость произведений М. Ганди Дж. Неру для понимания не только той исторической действительности, в которой они жили и творили, но и для тех обществ, которые ныне переживают подобные же процессы.

Примером сотрудничества государства, общества и культуры в современном Казахстане является деятельность Института истории и этнологии им. Ч.Ч. Валиханова Национальной академии наук. Этот Институт поддерживает культурные контакты и научное сотрудничество с Посольством Республики Индия в Казахстане и Индийским культурным центр при Посольстве Индии (г.Алматы). В 1999-2005 гг. проведены следующие мероприятия совместно с Посольством Индии в Казахстане:

- подготовлены обоснования и открыты в г.Алматы – улица (2002 г.), школа (2003 г.), памятник Махатмы Ганди (2004 г.);
- сотрудниками Института С.Ф. Мажитовым и Э.Ж. Валихановым организован и проведен круглый стол «Джавахарлал Неру и современность» (г.Алматы, 2003 г., 3 июля)

В январе 2005 г. состоялась неофициальная встреча Посла Индии в Казахстане Ашока Кумара и директора Индийского культурного центра в Алматы – доктора Мишры с администрацией, сотрудниками Института и членами Ассоциации историков Казахстана

Институт принимал участие в организации и проведении мероприятий, посвященных 50-летию первого визита Премьер-министра Индии Дж.Неру в Алматы. В частности, директор Института, профессор М.К. Койгелдиев и автор этих строк выступили с докладами на Международном семинаре «Джавахарлал Неру и сотрудничество в Азии» (г.Алматы, 2005 г., 17 июня).

В настоящее время Посольство Республики Индия в Казахстане в сотрудничестве с научными учреждениями Казахстана готовит к изданию книги о деятельности и значении наследия М. Ганди и Дж. Неру в условиях современного

Казахстана. К настоящему моменту мною для этих книг написаны статьи «Mahatma Gandhi - The Great Soul of Mankind», «The Heritage of Jawaharlal Nehru in the Conditions of the Kazakhstan Sovereignty».

На этапе возрождения и становления самостоятельной государственности Казахстана особую значимость приобретает наследие видных исторических деятелей, чьи имена связаны с историей борьбы за свободу и независимость, мир и социальный прогресс, строительством суверенных государств.

Ныне наступили иные времена. И в такие моменты особенно ощущаешь суть слов «суверенитет», «независимость». Казахстанские исследователи имеют возможность не опосредованно изучать историю любого государства нашей планеты. Разве это не достижение независимости? Ныне от нас самих – казахстанцев, зависит то, станут ли достоянием нашей истории Великий Ганди-джи и равные ему другие выдающиеся отцы человечества. Другое дело, что это требует не просто больших материальных и физических затрат, но особого душевного настроя, любви к своему делу.

Современные реалии Республики Казахстан внесли коренные изменения в понимание перспектив параллели «государство и культура». Новые парадигмы в этой плоскости служат идее консолидации казахстанского общества, где наряду с утверждением межнационального согласия очень важным является укрепление внутринационального единства. В нашей республике строится демократическое общество с многоукладной, рыночной экономикой, открывающей человеку возможности для реализации его экономических, социальных, национальных, политических и культурных интересов позволяющей свободно интегрироваться в общемировую цивилизацию. Для внешней политики Казахстана взаимодействие и сотрудничество с быстро развивающейся Индией является весьма актуальным и приоритетным.

ПРЕДЛОЖЕНИЯ ПО СОТРУДНИЧЕСТВУ

1. Организация и проведение совместного научного форума «Казахстанско-индийские отношения и сотрудничество в Центральной Азии».

2. Организация и проведение научной экспедиции в Индию с целью выявления материалов о Казахстане.
3. Подготовка специалистов со знанием языка в области историко-культурных контактов Казахстана и Индии.
4. Обмен докторантами, аспирантами, соискателями.
5. Издание серии книг под названием «Казахстан и Индия в потоке всемирной истории». Цель серии – публикация работ специалистов из Казахстана и Индии, посвященных историко-культурным контактам и сотрудничеству.
6. Выпуск книги «Дж.Неру и Казахстан» (на казахском, английском, русском языках). В нее войдут работы казахстанских специалистов о Дж.Неру и фрагменты из его трудов на трех языках.
7. Организация и проведение совместных научных исследований в области истории, культуры, дипломатии двух стран.

33

Русский Язык в Профессионально-Деловой Сфере

С.А. Хавронина

В последние десятилетия при некотором снижении интереса к изучению русского языка в мире наблюдается сохранение и даже укрепление его позиций в странах Восточной Европы, Дальнего Востока, государствах СНГ в качестве средства профессионально-делового общения. Изменения, произошедшие в экономической и социально-политической жизни не только в России, но и во многих других странах, открыли широкие возможности для взаимовыгодного сотрудничества иностранных компаний с русскими деловыми партнерами.

В последние годы наблюдается стабильное увеличение контингента иностранных граждан, заинтересованных в изучении русского языка профессионально-делового общения. К этой категории учащихся относятся, прежде всего, дипломированные специалисты, профессионально занимающиеся бизнесом, а также сотрудники посольств, фондов и благотворительных организаций, представители правительственных структур зарубежных стран и многие другие. В связи с экономической интеграцией России в зарубежную экономику и созданием транснациональных компаний появились и новые, перспективные группы пользователей русского языка профессионального общения-специалисты и менеджеры среднего и крупного звена, так называемый «элитный персонал» современного крупного бизнеса.

Русским языком профессионального общения стремятся

овладеть также учащиеся различных учебных заведений в России и за рубежом, которые связывают свою будущую карьеру с использованием русского языка в области бизнеса. Преподавание русского языка иностранным студентам в высших учебных заведениях России (ранее Советского Союза) с самого начала ориентировалось на обучение языку как *средству получения высшего образования и специальности.* Изучение иностранными студентами русского языка шло параллельно с изучением специальных предметов. В соответствии с профилем будущей специальности основу обучения составлял научный стиль, точнее определенный подстиль - гуманитарный, естественно-научный, технический и др.

В отличие от студентов, иностранные «деловые люди», как правило, уже сложившиеся специалисты. Они изучают русский язык параллельно с профессиональной деятельностью и для того, чтобы использовать его *в качестве рабочего языка.* Им необходимо овладеть официально-деловым стилем, устной деловой и обиходно-деловой речью.

Интеграция русского языка профессионально-делового общения (сфера бизнеса) в европейскую систему обучения иностранным языкам является составной частью общей интеграции России в международное экономическое и единое образовательное пространство.

Процессы интеграции русского языка в международный контекст диктуют необходимость учитывать рекомендации относительно описания разных языков в целях преподавания, сформулированные в проекте Совета Европы «Языковая политика для многоязычной и многокультурной Европы».[1] Эти рекомендации предполагают

- унификацию целей и содержания обучения языку;
- единую систему описания уровней владения языком;
- использование тестирования в целях объективного контроля и сертификации уровня коммуникативной компетенции учащегося.

С появлением нового контингента изучающих русский язык перед методикой преподавания русского языка как иностранного встала проблема разработки системы обучения русскому языку как средству общения в профессионально-деловой сфере. С начала 90-х годов прошлого века «бизнес-русский» становится предметом изучения и описания в целях преподавания его иноязычным бизнесменам.

Выявлены наиболее актуальные темы и типовые ситуации устного делового общения. Важнейшими представляются несколько макротем, отражающих общие для всех деловых людей фрагменты экономической действительности, такие как «Виды предпринимательства», «Презентация фирмы», «Направление деятельности фирмы», «Место фирмы на российском рынке», «Коммерция», «Реклама», «Финансы», «Выставки, ярмарки», «Биржа» и некоторые другие. Выявлены наиболее частые ситуации делового общения, к числу которых следует отнести разговор по телефону, деловую встречу, деловую беседу, рабочее совещание, переговоры.

Сегодня преподавание русского языка иностранцам является адресным, в максимальной степени учитывающим коммуникативные потребности каждой категории учащихся. Установлено, что коммуникативные потребности зарубежных бизнесменов связаны с необходимостью:

- общаться с деловыми партнерами при непосредственном контакте и по телефону;
- участвовать в деловых беседах, рабочих совещаниях, переговорах;
- выступать на презентациях, пресс-конференциях, выставках;
- понимать содержание документов, деловых писем, рекламных объявлений;
- понимать звучащие по радио и телевидению объявления, рекламу, бизнес-хронику;
- оформлять деловые документы;
- писать деловые письма, заявления, доверенности, служебные записки.

Названные коммуникативные потребности диктуют соответствующие коммуникативные задачи, которые приходится решать иностранным бизнесменам на русском языке. В соответствии с выявленными потребностями были исследованы жанры устной и письменной коммуникации, в том числе документации и деловой переписки. Изучение языковых средств – лексических единиц и синтаксических конструкций, функционирующих в устных и письменных текстах делового общения, позволило определить языковой, речевой и текстовой материал, необходимый для обучения зарубежных бизнесменов общению в профессионально-деловой сфере на русском языке.

С начала 90-х годов выходит в свет целый ряд специальных пособий, в том числе «Бизнес-русский», «10 уроков русского языка для бизнесменов», «Контакты для контрактов» и другие.

В 1997 году был издан учебник **«Русский язык в деловом общении»** Russian language for business communication. Washington. ACTR-ACCRLS Edition, подготовленный авторским коллективом в составе Л.П. Клобуковой, И.В. Михалкиной, С.А. Хаврониной и позднее изданный в национально-ориентированных вариантах – испанском, немецком, польском, болгарском. Учебник содержит материал, целью которого является формирование, развитие и совершенствование коммуникативной компетенции, под которой понимается умение решать жизненно важные, в том числе и профессиональные задачи средствами иностранного, в данном случае русского языка.

Занятия по данному учебнику позволяют учащемуся достичь базового, а затем и основного уровня владения русским языком профессионально-делового общения. В современной теории и практике преподавания иностранных языков можно считать утвердившимся *уровневый подход* к формированию коммуникативной компетенции и способам ее проверки и оценки.

Уровневая система позволяет сопоставлять результаты обученности иностранным языкам, достигнутые в рамках различных национальных образовательных систем. Это является необходимым условием для:

- обеспечения академической мобильности,
- конвертируемости соответствующих документов (дипломов, сертификатов),
- объективного оценивания работодателем уровня владения иностранным языком претендента на определенную должность.

Под уровнем владения иностранным языком понимается определенная степень сформированности коммуникативной компетенции, позволяющая решать на изучаемом языке экстралингвистические, в том числе и профессиональные, задачи общения в соответствии с условиями коммуникации.

Уровень не представляет собой нечто изолированное: он существует только в системе уровней. Эта система применительно к профессионально-деловому общению на русском языке представлена следующим образом:

высокий уровень
продвинутый уровень
основной уровень
базовый уровень

В самом общем виде различия между выделенными уровнями определяются такими объективными критериями, как:

- количество решаемых коммуникативных задач,
- характер ситуаций общения,
- количество и характер обсуждаемых тем.

Базовый уровень владения обеспечивает решение *минимального числа коммуникативных задач* профессионально-делового общения *в стандартных ситуациях* обсуждения *ограниченного круга тем.*

Основной уровень владения языком обеспечивает решение основных коммуникативных задач в изменяющихся ситуациях обсуждения расширенного круга тем.

Продвинутый уровень владения языком обеспечивает решение основных коммуникативных задач в условиях профессионально-делового общения в изменяющихся ситуациях обсуждения широкого круга тем.

Высокий уровень предполагает свободное владение языком и обеспечивает решение неограниченного числа коммуникативных задач в любых ситуациях профессионально-делового общения.

От уровня к уровню происходят качественные и количественные изменения коммуникативной компетенции учащегося: расширяются коммуникативные потребности, тематика и набор ситуаций общения; увеличивается набор жанров и типов текстов, объем языкового материала; совершенствуются коммуникативные умения, что и обусловливает качество коммуникативной компетенции иностранца, соответствующей определенному уровню владения языком.

Данные уровни владения русским языком профессионально-делового общения положены в основу разработки российской системы тестирования и сертификации уровней владения русским языком в профессионально-деловой сфере, созданной под эгидой Министерства образования Российской Федераци.[2] Разработчики российской системы тестирования и сертификации учитывали опыт выделения уровней для языка бизнеса в рамках различных национальных тестовых систем и прежде всего Лондонской торгово-промышленной палаты LCC (London Chamber of Commerce and Industry) и Кембриджского экзаменационного синдиката UCLES (University of Cambridge Local Examination Syndicate) - в разделе BEC (Business English Certificates).

В России и в ряде других стран уже в течение нескольких лет проводится тестирование иностранных граждан, позволяющее им подтвердить владение русским языком профессионально-делового общения на одном из четырех уровней. По результатам тестирования выдается соответствующий сертификат государственного образца.

ЛИТЕРАТУРА

1. The Common European Framework of Reference for Languages Learning and Teaching. – Strasburg. Council of Europe, 1997.
2. Журавлева Л.С., Клобукова Л.П., Михалкина И.В., Трушина Л.Б., Ускова О.А., Хавронина С.А. Концепция единой российской тестовой системы по русскому языку профессионального общения (модуль «Бизнес»)// X Международный конгресс МАПРЯЛ. Русское слово в мировой культуре. – СПБ., 2003.

34

О Некоторых Тенденциях Развития Лексики Русского Языка: Лингвокультурологический Подход к Постановке Вопроса

В.М. Шаклеин

Как известно, в конце XX столетия в российском обществе произошли значительные изменения: поменялись социальные приоритеты, изменилась структура общественных отношений, появились новые профессиональные группы, возникли новые поведенческие нормы. В структуре источников информации все меньшее место стали занимать лучшие образцы русской словесности. Предпочтение отдается, как правило, произведениям, изначально направленным на сюжетно-линейное восприятие текста, в котором собственно языковая форма, социальный, философский и нравственный подтексты уже не имеют, как раньше, первостепенного значения. Отрицательное влияние на русский язык нередко оказывает телевидение с некачественными отечественными и зарубежными фильмами с присущим последним специфическим переводом, примитивизм и схематизм которого бросается в глаза даже не искушенным в области филологии зрителям. В связи с этим представляется актуальным рассмотрение вопросов, связанных с изменениями в словарном составе русского языка, влиянием языковых процессов на личность, т.е. проблем, требующих комплексного лингвокультурологического подхода.

Это констатация в целом известных фактов. Куда более актуально попытаться рассмотреть то, по какой причине в современном русском языке наблюдаются интенсивные изменения в лексическом, семантическом составе, происходящие за счет проникновения в общеупотребительный язык слов из жаргонов ранее весьма ограниченных социальных слоев. Также интересно проанализировать способы образования неологизмов в современном русском языке. Все это может служить в качестве обозначения задач статьи. Однако разговор о новом в русском языке не будет более менее объективным, если не сказать о влиянии происходящих языковых процессов на личность человека-носителя русского языка, который переживает происходящие изменения в значительной мере с помощью форм этого языка.

Иными словами, перед нами возникают проблемы более широкого плана, чем собственно языковые, культурные или социально-психологические. Обозначенные вопросы имеют скорее комплексное содержание, выходя к лингвокультурологическим способам обозначения и решения.

Еще не так давно разобщение гуманитарных наук не способствовало решению таких серьезных вопросов. Так, в конце XX века Н.К. Михайловский писал: «В науке, в тех редких случаях, когда действительно говорится новое слово, одна из задач авторов нового слова состоит в том, чтобы примкнуть к одному из существующих течений, найти себе опору и оправдание в целом ряде предшествовавших работ, наблюдений, выводов. При этом о новом слове собственно даже не думают, оно является само собой. В публицистической критике и т.п. отраслях словесности, имеющих дело непосредственно с массой читателя, такого неукоснительного контрольного аппарата нет»[1].

Разумеется, строго определенного механизма или, своего рода, «контрольного аппарата», позволяющего осуществлять четкий нормативный анализ языка ещё окончательно не выработано. Вместе с тем нельзя сказать, что процесс засорения языка неоправданными неологизмами, фразеологизмами и жаргонизмами неуправляем, что регресс в языке столь же необратимое явление, как и различные унификационные тенденции. Последние, а под ними имеется в виду прежде всего американизация восточных и евразийских культур, известных своим особым отношением к миру духовной культуры, явились важнейшими фактором восприятия языковой формы как крайне незначительного феномена по сравнению с конкретными действием и прагматическим результатом этого действия. И дело здесь не в низкосортности массовой американской культуры. И в Америке, и в Европе сегодня создаются истинные шедевры в рамках именно массовой культуры. Например, подбор актеров в историческом английском фильме «Екатерина», повествующем о восшествии на престол Екатерины II, ничуть не уступает лучшим театральным труппам России сегодняшних и прошлых лет. Вероятно, чувства, переживания, внутренние муки своих героев европейские актеры передают очень мастерски, но все-таки чаще всего невербально. С точки же зрения языка, можно наблюдать немногословность и, на первый взгляд, примитивизм. Но это только на первый взгляд. В действительности чем меньше слов, тем больше актер. Многословие же носителя русского языка с его монологами и интеллектуальное кино с его подтекстуальными смыслами не совсем стыкуется с европейским менталитетом. Так, если русский актер в ответ на затронувшие его героя события, отразит в десятиминутном монологе, то актер европейский может промолчать, но в этом молчании будет свой смысл. Поэтому, говоря об унификации культур как объективном процессе, нельзя только указывать на то, что западный примитивизм поглощает русскую традицию. Это скорее, это иная культура слова. Возможно, не менее великая, чем культура слова в русской литературе, русском театре и русском кино. Все это так. Но, говоря другими словами, русскому языку от этого не становится легче.

Возникает традиционный русский вопрос: Что делать? Смириться? Выстроить вновь «железный занавес»? Ответ очевиден: ни то ни другое современное общество вряд ли примет. Необходимо задуматься прежде всего об управляемости происходящих процессов и явлений, о лингвокультурной экологии общества.

Для понимания внутренней механики учёта принципов лингвокультурной экологии необходимо обозначить во взаимосвязи основные социальные, культурные и языковые процессы, произошедшие в России в 90-е годы прошлого столетия.

Прежде всего следует вспомнить, что нормативная чистота русского языка в советский период истории России во многом поддерживалась политико-административными методами. Так, круг читаемой литературы, просматриваемых кинофильмов, репертуар театров в своей основе имел произведения классической литературы. Знание классики, увлечение ею считалось необходимым и достаточным признаком не только образования, но и общекультурного уровня каждого образованного человека. Кроме того, читать классику было модно. Проникновение в язык просторечной лексики и фразеологии вместе с управленческим звеном рабоче-крестьянсокого происхождения, лингвистических экспериментов писателей и поэтов, мемуары участников Великой Отечественной войны сыграли, конечно, свою роль. Вместе с тем новые литераторы осознанно гласно воспринимали Пушкина, Гоголя, Лермонтова как нечто высокое, к чему следует стремиться и которого вряд ли когда можно достичь. То есть существовал некий официально утвержденный языковой идеал, в конечном итоге «переборовший» советский новояз.

Правда, на этом фоне одновременно существовал и язык лагерей, и следственных изоляторов, язык, которым в СССР владело немало людей. Разумеется, все они сталкивались с «языком зоны». Например, мало кто из старшего поколения жителей современной России не знает одну-две песни о бежавших или об отправленном в тюрьму молодом грабителе. Очевидно, начало было положено известной песней «По диким степям Забайкалья». Иными словами, многие представители бывшего СССР, включая и слои интеллигенции, частично знали язык «фени». Однако вследствие непрестижности, явного указания на социальный низ, тюремный жаргон всё-таки не получил массового выхода в общеупотребительный русский язык. Владея жаргоном, бывшие «зеки» редко употребляли его в беседе с другими гражданами.

Первые признаки проникновения тюремного жаргона в общеупотребительный русский язык в крайне ограниченных пределах стали наблюдаться в конце 70-х годов XX века, когда распространилась практика призыва на действительную военную службу бывших заключенных или лиц с нарушенной психикой. Призывали их, конечно, в непрестижные, нестроевые войска. Тем не менее внутри армейской среды уголовная лексика распространилась довольно быстро, перейдя затем в разговорный язык вместе с миллионами демобилизованных молодых людей. Эта лексика изначально затрагивала прежде всего градацию солдат по сроку службы, имела уголовные корни (например, человек, не принявший присягу, т.е. недавно призванный, назывался «синяк», «сапог», «покойник»; человек, отслуживший менее полугода – «щегол», «зелень», «кирзач»; человек, отслуживший полгода – «молодой», «летун»; человек, отслуживший один год – «черпак», «карась», «усталый»; человек, отслуживший два года – «обиженный», «дембель», «гражданский», «объедающий»). Касалась данная лексика и градации по внутригрупповому влиянию (солдат, пользующийся наибольшим влиянием назывался «король», его ближайшее окружение – «быки»; работающий солдат – «мужик»; солдат, отслуживший весь срок в дисциплинарном батальоне и работающий все это время – «звонарь»; солдат, выполняющий любые поручения старших по внутригрупповой градации – «шнырь», солдат, выполняющий наиболее грязную работу, не следящий за собой – «чмо», «опущенный»; солдат, сделавший попытку покончить жизнь самоубийством, - «самострел», «бритва»).

Вместе с аналогичной лексикой в русский язык стала проникать тюремная фразеология и невербальные средства коммуникации (например, развести руки чуть в стороны обозначало «холодная погода».

Тем не менее нельзя сказать, что армейская среда в конце 70-х – начале 80-х годов стала существенным каналом проникновения тюремного жаргона в русский язык (значительная часть солдат срочной службы, будучи элементарно воспитанными людьми, все-таки предпочитала пользоваться нормативным языком, часть – сознавала, что такие слова совсем не украшают язык), но все же молодежь оказалась под влиянием вышеуказанного процесса.

С начала 90-х годов ситуация стала быстро меняться. Еще в 80-е, когда были организованы первые частные предприятия, структурировались и преступные сообщества, специализировавшиеся на отъеме у них денег. С этого момента лексика бандитских группировок стала входу в среде молодежи, особенно специализировавшиеся на купле-продаже каких-либо товаров. Это была так называемая лексика «барахолок» своего рода «дикого рынка».

Изначально носители данной лексики отличались глубоким цинизмом по отношению к рабочим, крестьянам, то есть к людям, зарабатывавшим себе на жизнь традиционными для СССР способами. В крупных городах России это особенно проявилось в отношении к крестьянскому труду. «Карц», «Вася», «крест», «колхозан» - названия крестьян в среде торговцев. Прилагательное «плуговатый» (от «плуг») означало «недалекий», «глупый». Следует отметить, что эта часть лексики в своем семантическом составе до сих пор не испытала существенных перемен.

Лексемы данного ряда наиболее явно пересекались с уголовной лексикой, где также имелось немало слов, отражающих презрение к честно работающим людям. Вместе с тем лексика языка несвободы характеризовалась большей остротой, семантической напряженностью. Например, и сегодня одно из воровских названий крестьянина, как и любого человека, занимающегося тяжелым физическим трудом, – «парижанин».

Более динамичными оказались те слова «рыночного» жаргона, которые обозначали денежные единицы. Называя «двадцариком» и «полтинником» не 20 и 50 копеек, а 20 и 50 рублей, «рублем» - 10-рублевую, а затем – 100 рублевую купюру, «двушкой», «трешкой» - 200 и 300 рублей, торговцы проявляли своего рода кураж, отделявший их от имущественного положения простых людей. Так, в конце 80-х на любом рынке можно было услышать разговор типа: «Для тебя твоя двухсотрублевая зарплата – кусок хлеба, а для меня кусок – 1000 рублей».

Ограниченность функционирования подобной лексики, как известно, закончилась в связи с начавшейся в 1991 году обвальной инфляцией. Вышеперечисленные слова стали практически общеупотребительными. Кроме того, в язык молодежи вошли такие слова, как «бабки» - «деньги», «башлять» - «платить», «забашлять» - «заплатить», имевшие свои корни в тюремном жаргоне.[1a]

С другой стороны, жаргонные названия денег, возникшие в 50-70-е годы, оказались неустойчивыми («тугрики», «рупии», «монеты», «мани»). В то же время некоторые названия денежных знаков обнаружили, напротив, удивительную устойчивость. Так, фамильярные наменования 100-рублевой купюры «катя», «катька», «катенька», восходящие к царской сторублевке с портретом Екатерины II, пережив «керенки», советские, и российские деньги разных образцов, продолжали оставаться употребительными. Вот, например, запись 1992 г., сделанная автором статьи: «Пятихатку не разобьешь? (то есть – не разменяешь ли 500 рублей?) – только катьками.» По мере роста инфляции общеупотребительным стало слово «лимон», обозначавшее миллион рублей.

Усиление роли жаргонизмов в этот период российской истории было вполне объективным процессом. Так, еще в конце 20-х годов Б.А. Ларин писал: «Всюду, а не только в Союзе, отмечается в последнем полустолетии усилившееся просачивание в разговорную (в художественно-литературную) речь элементов воровского жаргона. Разве только близорукий наблюдатель может удовлетвориться объяснением этого явления как частного, обусловленного, например, революцией. Отчего же тогда это имеет место и во Франции, и в Америке? На самом деле в этом случае мы имеем только более яркий пример общего и постоянного языкового взаимодействия всех слоев языкового коллектива, обычное использование «иной» речи социальных соседей и антиподов, пример непрестанного искания новых экспрессивных средств в ближайших источниках (оно всегда успешно, когда обращаются к богатому «языковому дну» города).[2]

Примерно к 1993 году в России прекратился процесс гиперинфляции, криминальные сообщества накопили значительное количество денежных средств. В связи с этим стал меняться образ криминального авторитета. Если раньше это был человек, откровенно отказывавшийся подчиняться каким-либо официальным законам, сотрудничать с властями, кроме того, большую часть жизни проведший в тюрьме, покрывший все тело знаковыми татуировками, не имевший практически никакой собственности и надеявшийся лишь на воровской «общак», то в 90-е годы образ идеального криминального авторитета приобрел иной вид: это уже стал броско и дорого одетый человек, украшавший себя золотом, разъезжавший на иностранной машине, имевший значительную собственность, банковские счета, ни за что не желавший попасть в тюрьму и поэтому довольно активно сотрудничавший с властями и даже входящий во власть. Организуя собственные предприятия, вкладывая свои криминальные капиталы в коммерческие операции, новые криминальные авторитеты в значительно меньшей степени стали употреблять в своей речи лексику языка несвободы. Данное обстоятельство обуславливалось тем, что многие из таких авторитетов сами никогда не сидели в тюрьме или в свое время отбыли там незначительные сроки. Им также приходилось иметь дело с вполне респектабельными чиновниками и бизнесменами. В целом владея неплохим русским языком, даже довольно образным, они употребляли воровскую лексику в целях удержания тех, на кого непосредственно опирались.

В то же время, вливаясь в среду торговцев, предпринимателей, они определили моду на их язык. Употреблять воровскую лексику, воровские средства невербальной коммуникации стало для последних своеобразным показателем защищенности, связи с криминальной средой, знания этой среды, без чего, собственно, предпринимательство в начале 90-х и не существовало. Однако лексика, пришедшая в язык предпринимателей из тюремного жаргона, прошла определенную адаптацию к языку нормативному, т.к. употреблялась, в конечном итоге, не для выражения смысла, а для участия в разговоре с юмористическим оттенком (например: «Он ментам забашлял, чтобы братва не наседала, а бык пришел и говорит: «Делись!» Ну тот в отказ. Так его через два дня в подъезде замочили. Говорил я ему, с ракетчиками по понятиям жить надо». – Он милиционерам заплатил, чтобы от него бандиты отвязались, а один из бандитов пришел и говорит: «Отдай часть заработанного». Тот отказался. Через два дня его убили в подъезде. Я говорил ему, законы, по которым живет криминальный мир, необходимо соблюдать)».

По всей видимости, криминальная лексика в среде предпринимателей – явление неустойчивое. Так, в среде крупных предпринимателей она уже не используется, но продолжает функционировать в языке предпринимателей мелких, уходя из их языка по мере ослабления влияния явного криминалитета.

Показательно, что распространенные в тюрьмах невербальные средства коммуникации, а это, главным образом, «язык» манипуляции пальцами рук, перешел в среду предпринимателей лишь в своем внешне-поверхностном виде. Еще в середине 90-х годов можно было наблюдать беседу двух предпринимателей или людей, изображающих из себя криминальных авторитетов, с использованием характерных движений пальцами рук, что, по мнению жестикулировавших, было показателем их принадлежности к криминалитету. Вместе с тем подобные движения рук («пальцы веером») с точки зрения невербального «языка» жестов, распространенного в тюрьмах, не имеет никакого смысла[3]. Как правило, движения рук предпринимателей, производившиеся ими во время беседы, на воровском «языке» жестов обозначало настойчивое приглашение собеседника выпить денатурата, причем за его счет.[4]

Если в целом проникновение жаргона языка несвободы в язык предпринимателей можно расценить как явление временное и неустойчивое, то в других сферах жизни российского общества будет наблюдаться иная картина.

Так, специфика распространения наркотиков, напрямую связанная с криминалитетом, определяет и специфику языка наркоманов – быстро растущей социальной группы. Наркомания, имевшая ранее место, главным образом, в криминальной среде, войдя в гражданское общество, «потянула» за собой и весь набор тюремной лексики, связанной с производством, доставкой, хранением и употреблением наркотиков. Например: «дозняк» - доза наркотика; «курок» - тайник для хранения наркотиков; «насморк» - кокаин; «сено» - маковая соломка.

Скорее всего, в среде наркоманов подобная лексика будет крайне устойчивой, поскольку декриминализации сферы наркобизнеса в России в ближайшее время не ожидается. Более того, по некоторым оценкам, количество наркоманов в стране будет расти, особенно если не будет выправлено экономическое положение основной массы населения страны. Следовательно, не исключено, что лексика наркоманов в том или ином виде будет проникать в общеупотребительный язык.

Примерно то же можно сказать и об уже сформировавшейся, структурировавшейся профессиональной сфере деятельности – проституции, организации секс-услуг, торговли женщинами как сексуальными рабынями. Данная сфера деятельности во всем мире (кроме отдельных стран Европы) подконтрольна организованной преступности. Поэтому нельзя ожидать ни от проституток, ни от сутенеров или работорговцев использования в своей профессиональной деятельности нормативного языка. Приведем несколько примеров: «комод» - охранник гостиницы; «баллон» - милиционер, берущий взятку пойманных проституток; «охмуреж» - кокетство перед возможным клиентом; «пойти в отвез» - сбежать от сутенера.

Подобная лексика довольно быстро проникает в общеупотребительный русский язык. Основным каналом ее переноса являются люди, пользующиеся услугами проституток, т.е. люди из самых разных социальных слоев российского общества – от чиновников и политиков высшего ранга до простых рабочих.

Лексика, отражающая новое состояние российского общества, сказывается прежде всего на молодежи. Однако здесь не следует полагать, что молодежный сленг есть абсолютно новое для русского языка явление.

На несоответствие истинных устремлений молодежи тому, что предлагает общество всегда вызывало своего рода языковую реакцию. Так, отношение молодежи 70-х – начала 80-х годов прошлого века к реалиям советской педагогики выражалось в таких лексемах, как «продлюга» - группа продленного дня, в которой школьники оставались под присмотром педагогов в течение всего дня; «шарага» - профтехучилище; «фазан» - учащийся профтехучилища; «классуха» - классная руководительница; «пивонер» - пионер; «шакал» - преподаватель начальной военной поготовки.

В то же время основой молодежного сленга нельзя считать только отрицательную реакцию на окружающий мир. Скорее, такой основой являлось шутливое отношение к миру. Например, «нарисовать рожу» - сделать макияж; «дерибас» - подделка под импортный товар; «пестрить мульку» - имитировать импортное изделие, прилаживая к отечественному изделию импортную этикетку; «ехать пешкарусом» - идти пешком; «отвалить» - оставить в покое; «прощайки» - немодные ботинки; «спокойка» - передача «Спокойной ночи, малыши».

Отличительной чертой молодежного сленга всегда был прием языковой игры[5]. Например, пародийное использование лексики не своей группы: диалектизмов («надоть» - надо, «надысь» - недавно); воровского жаргона («шмонать» - искать); детской речи («би-би» - автомобиль.

Молодежный сленг, подверженный языковой моде в наибольшей мере, чем язык какой-либо другой социальной группы, в 90-е годы отразил все изменения, прошедшие в русской культуре и в русском языке. Современный молодежный сленг – это, в частности, язык дискотек, ночных клубов. Иными словами, в молодежном сленге можно встретить лексику из всех новых сфер жизни российского общества. Эта лексика присутствует в сленге иногда в прямом заимствованном виде, иногда в шутливо переиначенном, например: «штабель» - компания; «клоп» - магазин; «хит» - поп. музыка; «сочняк» - высокая оценка.

Можно заметить, что принципы образования лексики молодежного сленга в 90-е годы не изменились, однако изменилась сама лексика. И если в 50-е – 70-е годы он не имел прямого влияния на общеупотребительный язык, то сегодня такое влияние можно определить как существенное. Это связано с тем, что, во-первых, масса молодых людей – посетителей ночных клубов и дискотек являются менеджерами, профессиональными торговцами, т.е. людьми, обеспечивающими себе жизнь самостоятельно, многие являются представителями низшего звена наркомафии, наркобизнеса, проституции, т.е. люди, задействованные в криминальные структуры; во-вторых, молодежный сленг стал языком наиболее престижных развлекательных программ на телевидении и радио; в-третьих, владение молодежным сленгом вошло в моду.

Таким образом, молодежный сленг, в отличие от жаргона языка несвободы, наркоманов стал одним из каналов проникновения ненормативной лексики в общеупотребительный русский язык.

Следует также отметить, что вместе с новой экономической системой в русский язык пришло большое количество слов англо-американского происхождения, о чем, конечно, уже написано и сказано немало. Такие слова, как «менеджер», «дистрибьютор», «гет», «дилер» во многом засоряют русский язык. вместе с тем, исходя из возможностей лексического состава русского языка, иногда невозможно подобрать точные эквиваленты подобным слова. Следовательно, их дозированное употребление оправдано. В.В. Блажес отмечает: «… самым общим свойством менталитета, выраженном в речи практически всех социальных групп (…) является дистанцирование от власти... Вот небольшой, но выразительный текст, иллюстрирующий слова се́нс – экстрасе́нс и полтерге́йн – полтергейст, мифическое существо, появляющееся в жилище и вредящее жильцам: «Се́нсов развели, полтерге́йнов разных», - негодует пенсионерка на новые порядки».[6]

Однако можно ли говорить об общественном нормировании языка, когда за очень короткий срок – 10 лет его лексический состав поменялся приблизительно на 10%. Произошло это за счет ухода в пассив целых лексических групп и появления новых групп. Иными словами, перед нами возникает картина объективной смены языка. Насколько возможно применить здесь традиционные способы нормирования?

Долгое время понятие нормы рассматривалось в статическом плане, что на сегодняшний день, по крайней мере, дискуссионно. Явное противоречие традиционного понимания нормы с динамической природой языка привело в итоге к осознанию нормы как явления динамического. Это «обусловленный социально-исторический результат речевой деятельности, закрепляющий традиционные реализации системы или творящей новые языковые факты в условиях их связи как с потенциальными возможностями и с реализованными образцами…»[7]

Говоря об экологии языка можно прийти к выводу, что собственно экологичным язык может стать в некоем идеальном обществе, где нет таких негативных социальных явлений. Иными словами, где нет социальных пороков, там нет проблемы экологии языка. Ставить жс вопрос так, что от идеально построенного, составленного, «экологичного» языка изменится общество, а вместе с этим изменением и исчезнет «лексика порока»- вряд ли на сегодняшний день реально.

Сегодня, если в русском языке образуется слово, то первое требование, которое должно ему предъявляться - это соответствие системе и структуре языка. С этой точки зрения вполне нормативно появление таких слов и выражений, как «видеобум», «неформал», «электронная почта», «универсам».

«Они мотивированы прежде всего экстралингвистически, поэтому нормативно оправданы; кроме того, соответствуют синтагматическим связям и отношениям языковых элементов. Тем не менее в свое время многие возражали против неологизма «универсам», считая его уродливым образованием. На Западе универсамы называют супермаркетами. Это название мелькает и в наших газетах. Хорошо ли это? Лучше ли заимствованное слово, чем гораздо более понятное универсам».[8] Это обсуждалось более двадцати лет назад. Сегодня слово «супермаркет» используется не менее активно, чем «универсам».

Для оценки неологизмов необходимо уточнить некоторые наиболее продуктивные способы их образования в современном языке.

Так, в 90-е годы существенно активизировались слова на – ация. Как известно, языковая система предоставляет два способа назвать процесс: через глагол и через существительное, абстрагированно, вне времени и вида. Словообразовательная система способствует наименованиям абстрагированного типа, минующим при своем возникновении глагольную ступень. В русском языке появилась целая группа таких инноваций. Например, «декоммунизация», «департизация», «дегайдаризация», «омонизация», «хуторизация», «эгоизация» (по типу известного ранее «политизация»). Повысилась частотность употребления таких слов, как «либерализация», «социализация», «гуманизация».

В ряду абстрактных процессуальных существительных находится слово «разгосударствление». Данная система весьма популярна вот уже на протяжении более десяти лет. Но так ли необходимо это неудобопроизносимое слово? Данная лексема была образована от слова «государство» для обозначения процесса перехода из государственной собственности в частную и другие виды собственности предприятий, средств транспорта, земель, банков, жилых и общественных зданий. Обычно аналогичные существительные образуются при помощи суффиксов от глаголов «черезступенчато» от имен, префиксально-суффиксальные образования такого типа для русской языковой системы не характерны. В результате получилось слово, режущее слух и напоминающее некий современный новояз.

Популярны в современном русском языке составные слова, где первая часть, как правило, состоит из корня иноязычного происхождения («диско-музыка», «брейк-мода», «фанк-музыка»), где первые части называют те или иные музыкальные или танцевальные стили, пришедшие из западного искусства. «В конце 70-х годов стали появляться слова с первым элементом «гала» (франц. gala). Раньше этим словом, как известно, называли торжественный придворный праздник; в современном языке оно встречается в составе сложных слов: «гала-концерт», «гала-спектакль», «гала-представление», «гала-обозрение» - и обозначает особенно торжественное зрелище. У многих возникает вопрос: зачем образовывать новые сложные слова с иноязычным компонентом - гала, если можно вместо них употребить словосочетание «торжественный спектакль», «торжественное представление» и т.п.». Однако же «гала-концерт» и «праздничный концерт» - это театрализованное представление с большим числом исполнителей, сопровождаемое световыми, звуковыми эффектами и проходящее на больших сценах, аренах, стадионах. Этот дополнительный оттенок значения во многом оправдывает употребление французского слова «гала».[9]

Тем не менее использование слова «гала» - более исключение из правил, нежели само правило. Так, в современном русском языке совершенно неоправданно в качестве неологизмов употребляются иностранные слова, которые имеют традиционные русские аналоги. В качестве примера можно привести популярное ныне слово «бизнесмен», имеющее свой аналог в русском языке – «предприниматель». В этом случае лексему «бизнесмен» можно рассматривать лишь как засоряющую язык.

По аналогичному поводу В.В. Колесов отмечает: «Не имея образа, ясного всем, чужое слово так эластично. Так хочется передавать им всякие мысли, какие приходят в голову(…). Многие слова проникают в общее употребление из специальных сфер. Принимая или отвергая такие вхождения, надо, думается, исходить опять-таки из следующих соображений: нужно ли слово языку, не будет ли оно дублировать уже имеющееся и хорошо несущее свою службу слово? Правильно ли оно образовано? С этих позиций совершенно не выдерживает критики глагол «задействовать». В лингвистической литературе высказывалось мнение о том, что слово проникло на страницы газет, в радио- и телепередачи из речи военных. Этот глагол не термин, «задействовать» значит ввести в действие, пустить в ход; есть и другие слова, которые могут называть то же самое: «запустить», привести в действие», «организовать».[10]

Также в русском языке имеется немало глаголов, которые образованы путем прибавления приставки за- к уже существующему слову («заблокировать», «заспециализировать»). Данный тип глаголов очень продуктивен. Вместе с тем здесь есть проблемы с образованием непереходного глагола. Например, нельзя сказать «задействовать линии электропередачи», можно «ввести их в действие», нельзя «задействовать группу», можно «организовать группу». Однако на такие тонкости уже мало кто обращает внимание, особенно на фоне образования потока неологизмов куда более броских и ярких.

В целом лингвисты негативно относятся к любым инновациям в языке. Или, говоря мягче, новые слова для них не всегда нежелательны даже в том случае, если они образованы в рамках словообразовательных типов. Противодействие инновациям со стороны ученых особенно ощущалось в 50-е – 70-е годы, когда русский язык был относительно постоянен. В этом случае лингвистика даже с теоретической точки зрения оказалась не готова не только обрабатывать материал современных инноваций, но и дать авторитетные рекомендации по регулированию процесса появления новых слов. Рекомендации, к которым бы прислушались дикторы, журналисты и все те, кто имеет дело со словом по характеру своей профессии. Как правило, научные работы по этому поводу сводятся к констатации либо отрицательной оценки новых явлений в языке.

Вместе с тем известно, что одним из основных требований словоупотребления является уместное применение слова в присущем ему значении.

В.Г. Костомаров в свое время отмечал, что принимаемый в мире стиль по большей части задает английский язык – не только в бросающихся всем в глаза формах песен и танцев, комиксов, модной одежды и поведения, «маскультуры» в целом, но и в завидно положительном вкладе в технику и науку, в медицинские и иные открытия всемирного значения, что закрепляется новой терминологией, разносимой по всем языкам мира. Этому служит могучий инструментарий радио, телевидения и компьютерных банков хранения информации. «Биржа», «брокер», «дилер», «бартер», «инвестор», «лизинг», «лот» - эти слова стремительно входят в наш обиход, с каждым днем становясь более привычными. Те перемены, которые происходят в нашей жизни – политической, экономической, - обусловили появление инноваций.[11]

По всей видимости, подобные слова не следует «изгонять» из русского языка, поскольку их употребление профессионалами (банкирами, биржевиками, экономистами) во многом оправдано. Но дело в том, что наиболее широкое их употребление присутствует на страницах средств массовой информации.

Если внимательно отнестись к работе В.Г. Костомарова «Языковой вкус эпохи»[12], то выяснится, что значение неологизмов во многих случаях доступны для их обработки с помощью русского языка:

«бартер» - товарообменная сделка с передачей права собственности на товар без платежа деньгами, натуральный обмен; «лизинг» - сдача во временное пользование имущества с периодической оплатой стоимости.

Конечно, трудно представить англоговорящего экономиста заменить представленные выше лексемы русскими эквивалентами. Однако, до сих пор звучат возражения против употребления, например, слова «бартер». Английское «бартер» равнозначно русскому товарообмен. Тем не менее *бартер* явно предпочитается исконному эквиваленту. Причина этого кроется, видимо, в том, что единая система экономических отношений требует единой системы наименований, поэтому международный стандарт прокладывает себе дорогу.

Скорее всего, именно эта причина способствует закреплению в языке английского слова «рейтинг». Английское rating – оценка, класс, разряд, чин. Вначале это иноязычное слово употреблялось в составе словосочетания «личный рейтинг», известного в шахматной терминологии, а потом и за ее пределами. В настоящее время слово «рейтинг» употребляется самостоятельно, вне какого-либо несвободного сочетания:

«рейтинг директора», «рейтинг станочника», «рейтинг политического деятеля», а также «рейтинг банков», «рейтинг завода», «рейтинг картины».

В данном английском слове, впрочем, есть определенный смысловой оттенок. Слово «оценка» можно толковать следующим образом: действие по назначению глагола «оценить», «оценивать»; мнение, суждение о качестве, достоинстве, значении чего-либо; обозначение степени значений и поведения учащихся.

При определенном творческом подходе слово «меценат» могло бы расширить свое значение и заменить собой английское заимствование. Слово «попечитель» для выполнения новой функции должно было бы пройти метафорический путь в развитии своей семантики. Но по вполне объективным причинам этого не произошло. Исконные слова русского языка, отягощенные многозначностью, ассоциациями с прошлыми эпохами не смогли обозначить новое явление: «спонсор» - лицо, организация, финансирующие с определенной целью какое-либо мероприятие.[13]

Масса заимствованных слов из английского языка не может вызвать каких-либо возражений, поскольку в русском быту и культуре отсутствовали сами предметы и явления, обозначенные этими словами. К такого рода словам можно отнести лексемы «армреслинг», «роллер», «дискрет», «холдинг», «роаминг».

Современный русский язык, несомненно, до крайности засорен ненужными словами, лишними в языке, которые вполне можно было бы заменить словами исконно русскими. Тем не менее, скорее всего данные слова уйдут в сферу специального употребления, поскольку, во-первых, мода на слова иностранного происхождения быстро проходит, а во-вторых, данные заимствования не оправданы коммуникативной потребностью широких слоев населения. Хотя не исключено, что многие из заимствованных ныне слов останутся в языке, во всяком случае в качестве пассивного запаса слов. По мере необходимости они будут реанимированы, как это случилось с лексемами «плюрализм», «альтернатива», «приватизация».

Значительно бóльшую опасность для русской лингвокультуры представляет процесс постепенного обеднения языка. Происходит это по большей части из-за уже вышеназванного процесса смены общественных приоритетов.

Нельзя сказать, что и в этом отношении в современном русском языке происходят одни лишь отрицательные явления. Например, многие исследователи в своих работах обращают внимание на процесс реанимации многих исконно русских слов, отмечая, что активизация данной тенденции во многом обусловлена современными общественно-политическими факторами и, главным образом, изменениями в экономической и политической сферах.

Во многих же случаях тексты донесли до нас «стереотип общественного сознания, в котором понятия «предприниматель» и «преступник» оказались слишком тесно переплетенными».[14] Например: «Российские предприниматели? – с отвращением переспросил один из недавних моих собеседников – Что вы! С ними ни в коем случае нельзя иметь дело! Все они – мафия!» - «Все?» - «Конечно, все! А потом стали возмущаться тем, как предприниматели – мироеды – обирают народ»[15] И там и тут оба директора (они же новоиспеченные капиталисты - предприниматели) пытались в борьбе со своим коллективом прибегнуть к помощи полицейских структур».[16]

Таким образом, слова «предприниматель», «предпринимательство», реанимированные и воспринимающиеся как неологизмы, в одних случаях употребляются в положительном смысле, а в других – в отрицательном. С точки же зрения сугубо лингвистической проникновение в современный русский язык масштабно используемого слова «предприниматель» есть явление положительное, перекрывающее неологизм «бизнесмен».

Тенденцию возрождения вышедших из употребления слов иллюстрирует также слово «господин», которое все еще трудно входит в речевой обиход при обращении к собеседникам или при именовании лица. Очень возможно, что российскому обществу подходило слово «товарищ», однако будучи во многом политизировано, оно по объективным причинам скорее всего выйдет из активного употребления. Наилучшая ему замена – «господин». Вместе с тем это слово крайне неохотно употребляется в широких кругах населения, как, впрочем, и слово «товарищ».

Как положительное явление в экологии современной русской лингвокультуры следует отметить возвращение городам, улицам, переулкам их исторических названий. Это свидетельствует о снятии своего рода напряженности в обществе, связанного с излишней политизированностью жизни. В такой ситуации, несомненно, улучшается не только общее психологическое состояние общества, но и оздоравливается лексический состав языка, связывая жителей городов и поселков с их историческим прошлым, напоминая о том, что история великой России началась отнюдь не в 1917 году.

Хотя в данном случае есть один немаловажный нюанс, связанный с временным дискомфортом для определенной части людей, проведших молодость или часть жизни в городах с названиями советского периода. Привычки и воспоминания юности уносят их не в Городовой переулок, не на Тверскую и Мясницкую, а на улицу Горького, улицу Маркса-Энгельса, Марксистскую. Недаром и по сей день пожилые жители Москвы именуют улицы и места с уже новыми названиями старыми именами. Им привычнее называть метро «Китай-город» «Площадью Ногина».

Вместе с тем обозначенная проблема не является причиной сохранения названий времен социализма, поскольку в итоге не удовлетворяется ни одна из мировоззренческих ментальных потребностей русского народа – ощущение себя в неразрывной связи с прошлым своей страны. Ведь какие «перестройки» и «шоковые терапии» не устраивай, русский народ всегда остается русским народом со всеми свойственными ему этническими чертами.

Также важно в этой связи был пересмотр знаков и символов России, возвращение старого византийского герба с двуглавым орлом, триколора, Андреевского флага, праздника Рождество, возведение православия в ранг национальной религии. В результате русские вспомнили, что живут в России.

Таким образом, лингвокультурная экологическая ситуация в современной России отличается целым рядом особенностей. Это прежде всего проникновение в язык лексики языка несвободы, неоправданных заимствований из английского (американского) языка, непомерное увлечение молодежи сленгом, употребление молодежного сленга на радио и телевидении. Существенное отрицательное значение имеет расширение социальной базы жаргона, последствия которого в настоящий момент российское общество еще не может оценить адекватно, поскольку проблема находится лишь на начальном этапе своего развития.

Наблюдаются также и положительные сдвиги в современной русской лингвокультуре. Это возвращение исторических названий городам и улицам, возвращение старой государственной символики.

Как видно, лингвокультурная ситуация на сегодняшний день может быть охарактеризована, с одной стороны, как не совсем благоприятная, но и не катастрофическая. Ее улучшение напрямую будет зависеть от упорядоченности общественных отношений: экономических, личностных, отношений «человек - природа», человек – «чистота улиц», «человек – удобный город», экология природы – экология человека – экология языка.

ПРИМЕЧАНИЯ

1. Цитируется по кн.: Колесов В.В. Культура речи – культура поведения. – м., 1988.- с.140.
2. Ларин Б.А. О лингвистическом изучении города // История русского языка и общее языкознание. – М., 1997. – С. 176. (Первая публикация статьи – 1928 г.).
3. Алферов Ю.А. Пенитециарная социология. Аудиовизуальная диагностика (татуировки, жаргон, жесты) – ч.II. – Домодедово, 1999. – с. 124-125.
4. Там же. – с.125
5. Блажес В.В. Языковая игра в языковом поведении горожан // Языковой облик уральского города. – Свердлвск, 1990. – С. 113-126
6. Блажес В.В. Языковая игра в речевом поведении горожан. – С. 120
7. Скворцов Л.Н. Теоретические основы культуры речи. – М., 1980. – С. 43
8. Калинин А.В. Культура русского слова. – М., 1984. – С.11.
9. Морской А.В. Современные тенденции развития лексики русского языка// Инновации в современно м русском языке. Научная конференция. Доклады. Новосибирск, 1987. –С.19.
10. Колесов В.В. Культура речи - культура поведения. – Л., 1988. – С.177.
11. Костомаров В.Г. Перестройка и русский язык // Русская речь. – 1987. - №6. – С.11
12. Костомаров В.Г. Языковой вкус эпохи (из наблюдений над речевой практикой масс-медиа). – М., 1994.

13. Большой англо-русский словарь / Под об. рук. И.Р. Гальперина. – М., 1979; The Rocket Oxford Dictionary of current English. – Oxford, 1969, The American College Dictionary. – New York. 1970.
14. Правда. – 10 октября. – 1990.
15. Литературная газета. – 12 февраля. – 1992.
16. Ленинский путь. - №11. – июнь. – 1993.

35

К Вопросу о Новой Стратегии Работы в Области Образования со Странами Бывшего Советского Союза

Степаненко В.А.

Изменение политической ситуации в России в конце восьмидесятых – в начале девяностых годов, распад Советского Союза прямым образом отразились на культурных связях, а также и на сфере образования. Какова культурная ситуация сегодня? 70 лет мы были вместе, конечно же, вся культура стран СНГ была охвачена процессом русификации.

Национальная и русская культура были тесно переплетены. В школах обучение велось в основном на русском языке, средства массовой и культурной информации – на русском языке, русский язык открывал детям мир как в русскую, так и в европейскую культуру. Нельзя забывать, что во многие республики письменность пришла только после революции вместе с кириллицей. Мы долго жили одними писателями, одними культурными событиями, одними литературными героями.

Чингиз Айтматов: тематика произведений этого писателя восточная, киргизская; тем не менее герои, форма выражения, да и сам писатель, пишущий на русском языке, воспринимаются нами как русские. В произведении «Плаха» евангельская тема Понтия Пилата перекликается с этой же темой в произведениях русских писателей (ср. М.А. Булгаков. Мастер и Маргарита). Расул Гамзатов: песню «Журавли» на стихи Гамзатова пела вся Россия. Военная тематика – тема войны – общая для всех людей бывшего СССР. Произведения Василя Быкова написаны на белорусском языке, на русский переводились автором, его герои были актуальны одинаково для белорусов и русских, а также для всех, кого коснулась война. Кинематограф: белорусский режиссёр Пташук, грузинские Иоселиани, Абуладзе, Данелия, тбилисский армянин Параджанов (учился в Москве, работал в Киеве, снимал фильмы по украинским авторам), узбекский Ишмухамедов – были известны и популярны в России, может быть больше, чем у себя на родине.

Слова Л.И. Брежнева, воспринимавшиеся нами тогда иронически, о том, что «возникла новая историческая общность "советский народ"» на самом деле имели под собой основание.

Такая культурная общность была возможна только благодаря общему языку культурной коммуникации, а именно русскому языку.

После распада СССР, проблема национализма обострилась. Русский язык оказался в конкурирующих условиях. «В наследство от СССР нам оставлена достаточно эффективная система образования и подготовки кадров как для самой страны, так и для других стран. Однако сегодня многие ключевые посты в странах, ранее ориентированных на СССР, занимают молодые лидеры, получившие образование не в СССР или России, а в США и Западной Европе, что не укрепляет рыночные и политические позиции России в мире. <...> Резко сузилось образовательное пространство русского языка, усложнился доступ к получению знаний и информации на русском языке не только для жителей Прибалтики, но и для граждан других стран СНГ, включая Украину и Казахстан, традиционно ориентированных на русский язык в качестве второго языка общения»[1]. Однако пятнадцать лет не прошли даром. Политическая ситуация постепенно менялась. Сейчас процессу интеграции уделяется большое внимание, существует Федеральная программа поддержки интеграционных процессов в странах СНГ. 2006 год объявлен годом СНГ. По материалам НОФМО (Научно-образовательного форума по международным отношениям) «Сила воздействия глобализации на новые государства оказалась мощнее, чем усилия по развитию регионального сотрудничества на постсоветском пространстве. Возникшие на постсоветском пространстве региональные группировки имеют скорее формальный, нежели реальный характер»[2]. Вполне очевидно, что до 2010 г. в структурировании постсоветского пространства сохранится преобладание глобализации над регионализацией. В СНГ не стоит на повестке дня вопрос о каком-либо коллективном обособлении от внешнего мира, не говоря о выработке единой позиции по отношению к третьим странам.

В настоящее время интерес к получению образования в России в странах СНГ значительно вырос. Для многих становится очевидным, что путь в Европу, связь с ней лежит через Россию. Российским правительством увеличивается количество бюджетных мест для студентов из СНГ. В 2006 году только для учащихся из Киргизии будет выделено 300 мест. С чем же мы сталкиваемся, с какими проблемами при обучении русскому языку нынешних учащихся из СНГ. Конечно же, они очень различаются по уровню владения языком. Среди них можно по уровню владения языком выделить три основные группы:

– обучавшиеся в своих государствах в школах, где преподавание идёт на русском языке и по программам российского образования; эти студенты отлично владеют русским языком (как письменной, так и устной речью); знание русской литературы достаточно высокое;

– обучавшиеся в национальных школах с преподаванием русского языка: хорошо владеют устной речью, но требуют усиленной работы над развитием письменной речи; изучаемые в средней школе РФ произведения русских писателей знают.

– обучавшиеся в специальных школах, где преподавание идёт на иностранных языках (в основном это турецкие школы); выпускники таких школ имеют весьма слабые знания русского языка в устной речи, письменная речь у этой категории учащихся совершенно отсутствует; в русской литературе и в целом в культуре ориентируются слабо.

Наиболее популярные специальности: юриспруденция, экономика, перевод.

Таким образом, в настоящее время многие учащиеся их стран СНГ нуждаются в достаточно серьёзном курсе не просто русского языка, а русского языка как иностранного, что требует создания новых методик, учебников и учебных пособий. Необходим культурологический курс, восполняющий недостаток фоновых знаний. Мы знакомим их с русской культурой, но не в таком плане, как это делалось в советские времена.

Мы стараемся знакомить их с русской культурой, не превознося её, а раскрывая и показывая её связь с европейской. Так, например, рассматриваются различные архетипы, проводятся параллели между литературными образами: Дон Кихот – князь Мышкин в русской литературе (образ которого перекликается также с образом Христа); Дон Жуан – Печорин, Онегин. Перекликаются не только литературные образы, но и исторические: Игнатий Лойола – Протопоп Аввакум – Николай Островский (прототип литературного персонажа Павки Корчагина). Что между ними общего? Что отличительно-национального? С этой точки зрения показательна анкета казахского автора Хакима (Хакимжана Акишевича Булибекова), размещённая на сайте «Русскоязычная Азия», где напротив графы "Какие произведения (литературы, живописи, музыки, кино и т.д.) и какие авторы оказали на вас влияние?" содержится ответ: *Н.Гумилев, В.Вернадский, В.Шекспир, Евангелие* (см. в конце статьи).

Это тема неисчерпаема, она вызывает интерес как исследователей, так и студентов и требует совместных размышлений, к чему мы вас и призываем.

Анкеты Казахстанских авторов

Фамилия	Булибеков
Имя	Хакимжан
Отчество	Акишевич
Псевдоним	Хаким
Дата и место рождения	23 июня 1953 г. г.Алма – Ата
Образование	высшее
Профессия	поэт, кинодраматург, режиссер.
Место работы	планета Земля, Солнечная система
Основные публикации	“Русскоязычный монолог” и “Альманах любви” - сборники стихов.
Какие произведения (литературы, живописи,	**Н.Гумилев, В.Вернадский, В.Шекспир, Евангелии.**

музыки, кино и т.д.) и какие авторы оказали на вас влияние?	
Определите близкие вашему творческому сознанию темы, жанры, сюжеты, образы.	**Исторические.**
Что значит для вас понятие “художественная литература”?	**Близкая к философской.**
Какой ряд мгновенных ассоциаций вызывает у вас словосочетание “искусство XXI Века”?	**Познание**

ПРИМЕЧАНИЯ

1. По материалам сайта Международного фонда Шодиева http://www.chodiev.ru/publish/index.php?id=2.
2. Available at: http://www.obraforum.ru/archive_2004.htm.

36

Языковая Картина Мира и Преподавание Русского Языка

Ф.И. Панков

Введение.

Содержательное пространство каждого языка в своих структурах (функционально-семантических полях, системах значений и др.) отражает как интернациональные черты категоризации мира, так и определённую специфику национального менталитета, которая закреплена в концептосфере данного языка и в его модусе. Эта сфера непосредственно связана с областью когнитивистики и культурологии. Способность языка отображать экстралингвистическую действительность создает языковую картину мира каждого народа, которую необходимо учитывать в практике преподавания языка.

В национальных языковых картинах мира помимо универсальных черт существуют и принципиальные особенности. Языки различаются между собой как наборами формальных средств, так и системами тех смыслов, которые при помощи данных средств могут быть выражены.

Русская языковая картина мира получила своё отражение и в лексике, и в синтаксических моделях, и в морфологических формах, и в просодике, и в речевом этикете, даже в мимике и жестах. В преподавании русского языка должны быть учтены такие его фундаментальные характеристики, как системность, объективный характер языка и субъективный характер речевых реализаций, материальный характер лексики и идеальный характер грамматики [Всеволодова 2000].

Отсутствие учёта преподавателем специфики национальной языковой картины мира и фундаментальных характеристик каждого языка приводит зачастую к грамматическим, лексическим и коммуникативным ошибкам учащихся – так называемому «отрицательному» языковому материалу [Щерба 2002].

Рассмотрим особенности русской языковой картины мира в области таких универсальных функционально-семантических категорий, как время, пространство и причина, их связь с преподаванием русского языка.

1. Категория времени.

Во взгляде на категорию времени возможны глобальные расхождения в национальных языковых картинах мира. Эти расхождения проявляются, в частности, в ориентации во времени, в делении суток на части, а также в формах приветствия и прощания.

Ориентация во времени: прошлое – будущее. Разные народы имеют разную ориентацию во времени. Так, для русских (и, видимо, вообще для европейцев) прошлое оказывается «позади», а будущее – «впереди». В некоторых же неевропейских языках, например в армянском и китайском, вектор движения времени воспринимается как направленный в другую сторону: прошлое – «впереди», а будущее – «сзади». Это легко объяснимо логически: собственная история известна говорящему и поэтому обозреваема взглядом, будущее же неведомо, оно за спиной. Русский (или вообще европеец) представляет себя во времени движущимся вперёд по жизненному пути. Китаец же или армянин ощущает себя неподвижным, а время проходит сквозь человека, как ветер, дующий сзади. Таким образом, русские ориентированы во времени в будущее, а, например, китайцы и армяне – в прошлое. Отсюда возможны коммуникативные ошибки учащихся при восприятии таких типично русских высказываний, как (1а) и (1б):

(1а) ***Впереди*** *у нас экзамены*;

(1б) *Самое страшное* ***позади***.

В примере (1а) речь идёт о том, что экзамены предстоят в будущем, а в предложении (1б) – о том, что самое страшное осталось в прошлом, а не наоборот. Безусловно, недооценивать в преподавании специфику языковой картины мира недопустимо.

Деление суток на части. Кроме того, разные народы делят сутки на части по разным основаниям. Поэтому русские идут в театр или в гости на вечеринку *вечером (сегодня вечером)*, а англоязычные – *ночью (tonight, at night)*. Для русских с 12 до 16–17 часов – *день*, а для испанцев и португальцев после 12 начинается *вечер (tarde)*. Для русских *первая половина дня, до обеда* – это, как правило, время до 13–14 часов, но для многих европейцев оно ограничено двенадцатью часами, полуднем. Оказывается, в современном русском языке *полдень* и *полночь* – это обозначение не середины дня (ср. англ. *midday*) или ночи (ср. англ. *midnight*), а их начала. Поэтому для русского высказывание (2а) или (2б) обычно означает, что встреча назначена на время после 14.00:

(2а) *Встретимся **во второй половине дня***;

(2б) *Встретимся **после обеда***.

Приветствие – прощание. Специфическое деление суток на части нашло отражение в наличии традиционных русских приветствий: *Доброе утро!, Добрый день!, Добрый вечер!* и в пожелании *Спокойной ночи!* В китайском и корейском языках деление суток на части раньше (примерно до 1970-х – 1980-х годов прошлого века) было связано со временем приёма пищи и соответствующие приветствия звучали как (3а), (3б), (3в) или как более общее (3г) – эквивалент нашего *Здравствуйте! Как поживаете? Как дела?*:

(3а) *Вы уже позавтракали (Вы уже съели утренний рис)?*

(3б) *Вы уже пообедали (Вы уже съели дневной рис)?*

(3в) *Вы уже поужинали (Вы уже съели вечерний рис)?*

(3г) *Ели ли вы?*

Поэтому бывало чрезвычайно странно слышать, когда китайские или корейские учащиеся на русском языке с подобным вопросом обращались к собственному преподавателю.

Причём употребление русских приветствий, начинающихся со слова *добрый,* возможно только при встрече, а пожелание *Спокойной ночи!* – только при прощании. В то же время, например, по-турецки можно сказать (4а) – только как приветствие, а (4б), (4в) и (4г) – как при встрече, так и при расставании:

(4а) *Gün aydın!* (т. е. *Доброе утро!,* буквально – *День светлый!)*;

(4б) *Iyi günler!* (т. е. *Добрый день!)*;

(4в) *Iyi akşamlar!* (т. е. *Добрый вечер!)*;

(4г) *Iyi geceler!* (т. е. *Спокойной ночи!)*

Это приводит к таким ошибкам, когда турецкие учащиеся, прощаясь с преподавателем, говорят ему: *Добрый день!* или *Добрый вечер!*, что законами русского речевого этикета не допускается. Интересно, что в современных теле- и радиопередачах в России, начинающихся ночью, звучит приветствие ***Доброй** ночи!* (не ***Спокойной** ночи!*), которое ещё лет пятнадцать назад невозможно было представить. В Интернете же, когда общающиеся по-русски между собой люди могут находиться в разных часовых поясах, закрепилось обращение *«**Доброе** время суток!»* или *«**Доброго** времени суток!»* (не *Спокойное время суток!* и не *Спокойного времени суток!*). Таким образом, в русском языке использование эпитета *добрый* закрепилось за приветствием, а *спокойный* – за прощанием.

2. Категория пространства.

Расхождения в национальных языковых картинах мира проявляются также во взгляде на категорию пространства и выражаются нередко в грамматических формах, в частности, при выражении значений местонахождения (где) и направления – директива-финиша (куда) и директива-старта (откуда), в употреблении тех или иных пространственных предлогов.

Местонахождение (где) – направление (куда). В некоторых языках, например английском или датском, отсутствует формальное различие между значениями местонахождения и направления, т. е. между *где* (англ. *where*) и *куда* (англ. *where*). Это приводит к ошибкам учащихся типа (5а) или (5б):

(5а) **Вчера мы ходили в* ***театре*** (вместо *Вчера мы ходили в* ***театр***);

(5б) **Летом мы ездили в* ***Москве*** (вместо *Летом мы ездили в* ***Москву***).

Ещё пример. В русском языке (так же как, например, в английском) глагол *писать* имеет валентность *«где»* (указание местонахождения), а в турецком языке глагол *yazmak (писать)* имеет валентность *«куда»* (указание направления – директива-финиша). По-русски нужно сказать (6а), а по-турецки – (6б). В русском языке подобную валентность имеет глагол *записывать* (6в). Ср.:

(6а) *Я пишу (где?)* ***в своей тетради***;

(6б) ***Defterime*** *yazıyorum* (т. е. **Я пишу (куда?)* ***в свою тетрадь***);

(6в) *Я записываю что-либо* ***в свою тетрадь***.

Местонахождение (где) – направление (откуда). Так же как глагол *писать*, русский глагол *покупать* имеет валентность *«где»* (указание местонахождения), т. е. русские покупают что-либо где-либо (7а). В то же время в турецком языке глагол *satınalmak (покупать)* имеет валентность *«откуда»* (указание направления – директива-старта), т. е. турки покупают что-либо откуда-либо (7б). Ср.:

(7а) *Я купил книгу (где?)* ***в магазине***;

(7б) *Kitabı* ***mağazadan*** *satınaldım* (т. е. *Я купил книгу (откуда?)* ***из магазина***).

Точно так же русские берут книгу *в библиотеке,* т. е. *«где»* (8а), а тюркоговорящие или англоговорящие – *из библиотеки,* т. е. *«откуда»* (8б), (8в):

(8а) *Я взял книгу (где?)* ***в библиотеке***;

(8б) *Kitabı* ***kütüphaneden*** *aldım*;

(8в) *I borrowed a book* ***from the library***.

Отсутствие учёта подобной специфики может приводить к грамматическим ошибкам иностранных учащихся.

Предлоги *на – в, из – с.* Законы развития языка, как известно, носят объективный характер, а его конкретные речевые реализации могут быть и субъективными. Проиллюстрируем это на конкретном примере. Так, в последнее время на Украине и в среде некоторых политиков и журналистов в России распространилось употребление русских именных локативных групп *в Украину* вместо традиционной *на Украину, в Украине* вместо *на Украине, из Украины* вместо *с Украины.* Мотивация довольно странная: если теперь Украина стала самостоятельным государством, значит, по-русски нужно говорить не *на*, а *в*, не *с,* а *из*. Но ведь мы говорим и о самостоятельных государствах *на Кубу – на Кубе – с Кубы, на Мадагаскар – на Мадагаскаре – с Мадагаскара, на Кипр – на Кипре – с Кипра.* То есть украинские политики субъективно захотели повлиять на объективные законы русского языка. Однако носителями языка являются не отдельные политики или журналисты, а весь народ, который не может употреблять по заказу те или иные грамматические формы. Люди говорят так, как диктует им традиция. Конечно, язык меняется, развивается, но медленно и по своим собственным, а не по политическим законам.

Системность языка – асистемность отдельных участков. Одной из фундаментальных характеристик русского языка является его системность, однако это не значит, что в нём отсутствуют асистемные участки. Так, асистемно образование названий лиц – жителей той или иной местности: города, страны, региона. Преподаватель русского языка не может дать своим иностранным учащимся алгоритм образования подобных существительных. Он может лишь продемонстрировать различные способы такого словообразования. Покажем их в виде таблицы.

Образование названий лиц – жителей той или иной местности

Названия лиц – жителей городов	Названия лиц – жителей стран	Названия лиц – жителей регионов
Москва – москвич (м.р.), москвичка (ж.р.), москвичи (мн.ч.); **Санкт-Петербург** – петербуржец (м.р.), петербуржка (ж.р.), петербуржцы (мн.ч.); **Минск** – минчанин (м.р.), минчанка (ж.р.), минчане (мн.ч.); **Киев** – киевлянин (м.р.), киевлянка (ж.р.), киевляне (мн.ч.); **Тула** – туляк (м.р.), тулячка (ж.р.), туляки (мн.ч.); **Архангельск** – архангелогородец (м.р.), архангелогородка (ж.р.), архангелогородцы (мн.ч.); **Гусь-Хрустальный** – гусевец (м.р.), гусевка (ж.р.), гусевцы (мн.ч.)	**Россия** – русский (м.р.), русская (ж.р.), русские (мн.ч.); **Индия** – индиец (м.р.), индианка (ж.р.), индийцы (мн.ч.); **Франция** – француз (м.р.), француженка (ж.р.), французы (мн.ч.); **Англия** – англичанин (м.р.), англичанка (ж.р.), англичане (мн.ч.); **Турция** – турок (м.р.), турчанка (ж.р.), турки (мн.ч.); **Чехия** – чех (м.р.), чешка (ж.р.), чехи (мн.ч.); **Германия** – немец (м.р.), немка (ж.р.), немцы (мн.ч.); **Польша** – поляк (м.р.), полька (ж.р.), поляки (мн.ч.)	**Европа** – европеец (м.р.), европейка (ж.р.), европейцы (мн.ч.); **Азия** – азиат (м.р.), азиатка (ж.р.), азиаты (мн.ч.); **Сибирь** – сибиряк (м.р.), сибирячка (ж.р.), сибиряки (мн.ч.); **Камчатка** – камчадал (м.р.), камчадалка (ж.р.), камчадалы (мн.ч.); **Юг** – южанин (м.р.), южанка (ж.р.), южане (мн.ч.); **Север** – северянин (м.р.), северянка (ж.р.), северяне (мн.ч.); **Восток** – житель Востока (м.р.), жительница Востока (ж.р.), жители Востока (мн.ч.)

Примечание к таблице: м.р. – мужской род, ж.р. – женский род, мн.ч. – множественное число.

3. Категория причины.

В русском языке при выражении причины предметные имена существительные или личные местоимения, указывающие на предмет или лицо, способны употребляться в значении пропозитивных имён. Таким образом они выступают во вторичной семантической функции. Так, по-русски можно сказать не только (9а), но и (9б), не только (10а), но и (10б), что недопустимо во многих других языках, в частности в английском. Ср.:

(9а) *Я опоздал на урок* ***из-за поломки автобуса***. –

(9б) *Я опоздал на урок* ***из-за автобуса***.

(10а) *Мы рады* ***видеть вас***. –

(10б) *Мы рады* ***вам***.

Такую особенность русского языка следует учитывать в преподавании как русского языка иностранцам, так и английского языка русским. Тогда можно будет избежать распространённых ошибок, когда вместо типа (11а) русские по-английски говорят (11б):

(11а) *We are glad* ***to see you***. –

(11б) **We are glad* ***to you***.

Выводы.

Таким образом, изучение неродного языка – это в определённой степени постижение языковой картины мира его носителей. Соответственно непонимание, трудности в усвоении грамматики, лексики, просодики могут быть связаны с различиями в языковой картине мира родного и изучаемого языков, что следует учитывать в процессе преподавания языка, введения и закрепления лексического и грамматического материала – как звучащего, так и письменного, как книжного, так и разговорного.

Изучением содержательного аспекта языка и средств выражения смыслов (изучением языка «от смысла к форме» и «от формы к смыслу») занимается функционально-коммуникативная грамматика русского языка и, в частности, идеографическая грамматика – её составная часть.

ЛИТЕРАТУРА

1. Всеволодова М.В. Теория функционально-коммуникативного синтаксиса: Фрагмент прикладной (педагогической) модели языка: Учебник. М., 2000.
2. Всеволодова М.В., Панков Ф.И. Практикум по курсу «Теория функционально-коммуникативной грамматики»: Рабочая тетрадь: Учебное пособие. М., 2005.
3. Мы и мир. Психологическая газета. М., 1998, февраль, № 4.
4. Щерба Л.В. Преподавание языков в школе. Общие вопросы методики: Учеб. пособие. – М., 2002.

37

Проблема Культурного Диалога в Российской Традиции Философского Образования

Ирина Полякова

К диалогу в различных его аспектах прямо или косвенно обращаются многие мыслители XX в., достаточно вспомнить имена М. Бубера, Г.-Г. Гадамера, М. Хайдеггера и др. Проблема диалога культур признается не менее существенной для выживания человечества, чем экологические проблемы.

Теоретическая и методологическая база для понимания философских оснований диалога и его образовательного значения складывалась на протяжении многих лет и в работах отечественных мыслителей: В.С.Соловьева, П.А.Флоренского, С.Н.Трубецкого, С.Л.Франка; позднее – А.Ф.Лосева, М.М. Бахтина, Ю.М. Лотмана, М.К. Мамардашвили, В.С. Библера.

История как «предание» (традиция), по мнению известного русского философа и педагога С.И.Гессена, невозможна там, где нет задания, т.е. тех неисчерпаемых целей, которые в своей совокупности составляют культуру. Прошлое не исчезает бесследно, но сохраняется, передается именно потому, что оно служит этапом на пути к вечной и неисчерпаемой цели [3]. Философия и богословие, философия и поэзия, разум и сердце в философских дискуссиях XIX в. могут рассматриваться в контексте построения диалога как главной культурной задачи. В духовно-академической традиции основанием культурного диалога становится христианский платонизм.

Подчеркивая внутреннюю связь диалектики с онтологическим идеализмом, С.Л.Франк отмечал, что «весь ее смысл состоит в том, что в глубочайшей основе мирового бытия совершается некий мировой «разговор»..., размышление мира о самом себе, и тем самым духовное борение, определяющее путь его развития, строй его жизни» [8, с. 46].

Историческое столкновение ratio и Λόγος'a, которое, по мнению В.Ф. Эрна может произойти лишь в России, также предполагало построение культурного диалога [10, с. 85]. Предпосылкой этой «встречи» русский философ считает тот факт, что оба начала, и ratio, и Λόγος, русская мысль имеет внутри себя, имеет не как внешне усвоенное, а как внутренне ее раздирающее. «Русские мыслители, очень часто разделенные большими промежутками времени и незнанием друг друга, *перекликаются* между собой и, не сговариваясь, в поразительном согласии *подхватывают один другого»* [10, с. 98]. Диалогическая природа свободной традиции философии Λόγος'a, выражающей внутреннее метафизическое единство человечества, способна преодолеть различные формы «культурного непонимания».

Защищая научное понимание философии и вместе с тем, не соглашаясь с теми, кто приравнивает философию к математическому естествознанию, еще один представитель русской философской мысли – Г.Г. Шпет настаивал на том, что одна из самых древних примет философии – ее «существенно диалектический характер» [9, с. 468]. «Диалектика как метод есть метод строгий и точный, — только это не строгость математического доказательства. Но, кроме того, диалектика, по определению Сократа,– совместное мышление, *διαλογοζ* в самом подлинном и полном значении» [9, с. 468]. Отсюда вытекают специфические особенности философии, отличающие ее от других видов знания. Как нельзя свести драматическое действие к монологу, так нельзя требовать от философии, чтобы она была знанием, в точности подобным математическому естествознанию, чтобы ее ценность и ее смысл определялись технической приложимостью. Собственная жизненность и оригинальность философии заключается в диалоге, в жизненном действии.

Особое значение в утверждении места диалогической проблематики в методологии гуманитарных наук, имеют работы М.М. Бахтина. Точные науки – это монологическая форма знания: «интеллект созерцает вещь и высказывается о ней», –

писал Бахтин [1, с. 383]. Для гуманитарных наук необходимы иные принципы: активно-диалогическое понимание (спор-согласие), включение в диалогический контекст, диалектическое соотношение тождества и нетождества. Философия начинается там, где кончается точная научность и начинается инонаучность. Ее можно определить как метаязык всех наук (и всех видов познания и сознания). Подчеркивая ограниченность догматической мысли, Бахтин сравнивает ее с рыбкой в аквариуме, наталкивающейся на дно и на стенки и не могущей плыть дальше и глубже.

М.К. Мамардашвили в своих лекциях по истории философии проводил идею диалога в историко-философской традиции. Требование реконструкции, задача «домыслить», что ответил бы Сократ Аристотелю. Прошлое становится современным через наше диалогичное по своему характеру причастие той особой реальности, которую Мамардашвили называет «умным бытием».

История философии, которую Мамардашвили пытается представить как историю некой единой, хотя и растянувшейся во времени, попытки людей философствовать и посредством философии узнавать о себе и о мире то, чего без философии узнать нельзя, необходимо учит принципам диалогического мышления. Читать тексты и рассуждать о них имеет смысл только тогда, когда ты не наполняешь себя догматической ученостью, а восстанавливаешь живую сторону мысли, из-за которой эти тексты создавались [6]. Лишь в этом случае, при встрече с текстом через две тысячи лет после его создания, он оказывается для нас не элементом книжной учености, а живой реальностью, «проникнув» в которую, мы можем оживить те мысленные состояния, которые находятся за текстом и возникли в людях посредством этого текста. Проблема не в том, чтобы прочитать и потом помнить текст, а в том, чтобы понять и суметь высказать мысль, содержащуюся в нем, как возможность актуального, теперешнего мышления людей.

Диалог не случайно называют «ключевой метафорой» нашего времени, а «диалогизм» – ведущим течением современной мысли, ставящим перед философами цель осмысления феномена отчуждения человека от предметного мира, человека от человека. Диалогическая ситуация сосуществования культур, о которой неоднократно писал М.Ю. Лотман, в центре внимания современных гуманитариев.

В последние десятилетия в России разделяются мировые тенденции поиска новой образовательной парадигмы. Освободившись от идеологического диктата и вновь обретя академический статус, философия решает проблему разработки плюралистической модели философского образования. Именно через образование, прежде всего философское, осуществляется важнейший из способов постижения культуры, усвоения опыта предшествующих поколений. Философия, непосредственно изучая эти ценности, призвана играть парадигмальную роль как в системе образования философского, так и в системе образования в целом (учитывая обязательность курса философии в учебных программах всех российских вузов).

Существенное влияние на процессы, происходящие в сфере философского образования в России, в последние десятилетия оказало развитие философской компаративистики с убеждением в том, что философия может стать важнейшим фактором снижения напряженности в области культуры, пространством взаимопонимания и понимания иных мировоззренческих и культурных традиций.

Сравнение и сопоставление философских традиции, выявление интеркультурных коммуникативных оснований философского диалога, связывание созданных в различных цивилизациях и культурах типов мышления, творчества и восприятия действительности становится не только содержанием академических дискуссий, но и практикой образовательного процесса. Принципы компаративистской методологии в последнее время восприняты в построении учебных философских курсов, воспроизводящие ее тексты используются в качестве первоисточников в учебном процессе, что способствует выявлению коммуникативного характера гуманитарного знания и, тем самым, утверждает диалог как норму современного философского мышления и историко-философского процесса. С этих позиций мы смотрим на историю философии как на историю диалога философских культур, используя историко-философский материал не в его общепринятом хронологическом ракурсе, а проблемно-избирательно.

Предрассудки о непреодолимости различий между цивилизациями и «универсалистские претензии европоцентризма» остались в прошлом. Это позволяет овладевать в образовательном процессе методологией, признающей ценность различных моделей культуры и форм мышления. Отказ от предвзятых стереотипов, установок и претензий на конечную истину, попыток выстроить философские идеи различных эпох и культур в некую жесткую линию позволяет современному мышлению ориентироваться на такую особенность культуры, когда «высшие» достижения человеческого мышления, сознания, бытия вступают в диалогическое общение с предыдущими формами культуры, когда в едином духовном пространстве современности сходятся («стягиваются» – В.С. Библер) многообразные формы культуры, заставляя современное мышление духовно сопрягать их.

Характеризуя современное философское умонастроение в России, академик В.С. Степин пишет: «Мы расстались со старой и малопродуктивной установкой утверждать себя в качестве непререкаемых обладателей истины и конфронтировать со всеми другими, отличными от нас направлениями философской мысли. Более продуктивным оказалось видение себя, как части мирового философского процесса, его особой составляющей, которая нацелена на диалог и дискуссии с другими школами и направлениями в философии» [7]. На передний план в этом диалоге выходят эвристические функции философии, направленные на выработку таких новых идей и категориальных структур, которые могли бы стать основанием культуры будущего человеческого мира.

Одной из важнейших функций философского образования считается формирование культуры мышления. Философское мышление диалогично по своей природе. Принципы Сократической диалектики возрождаются вновь в практике образования, как за рубежом, так и у нас. К сожалению, в условиях существования, с одной стороны, достаточно жестких образовательных стандартов, привычной формы организации учебного процесса с весьма ограниченным количеством часов, выделенных на изучение философии, а с другой, совершенно произвольных подходов к преподаванию философских дисциплин, это еще не стало по-настоящему «практикой», однако в этом направлении ужу сделаны конкретные шаги.

Как подтверждение вышесказанного – в дискуссиях о

модели преподавания философии в России все чаще прослеживается мысль о необходимости дополнить философскую методологию инструментарием герменевтики, в которой диалогичность мышления служит важнейшим из условий понимания. Обращаясь к русским читателям в предисловии к своей книге «Актуальность прекрасного, Г.Г. Гадамер подчеркивал, что герменевтика – это практика, фундаментальная истина человека такова: истину не может познавать и сообщать кто-то один. Всемерно поддерживать диалог, давать сказать свое слово и инакомыслящему, уметь усваивать произносимое им – вот в чем душа герменевтики» [3, с. 8].

Сегодня в России диалог рассматривается как основа рефлексивной модели практики образования. В связи с этим активно обсуждается концепция М. Липмана и других сторонников программы «Философия для детей», в основу которой положена методология сократического диалога и педагогическая максима о том, что самореализация личности достигается через коллективизм.

Коллективный поиск истины, о котором так много говорил Сократ, здесь выступает в качестве важнейшей регулятивы. В процессе диалога необходимо научиться слушать другого и самому адекватно реагировать на сказанное. По определению Липмана, «это включает в себя умение следовать линии рассуждения, возникающей в ходе дискуссии, видеть допущения, лежащие в основе каждого высказывания, делать выводы, проверять логичность, учиться думать независимо, выбирая свой собственный стиль [5, с.116.]

Такой диалог представляет собой форму совместного рационального рассуждения. Его задача – дополнить научное исследование. Рациональное рассуждение помогает нам расширить знание с помощью логического вывода, защитить его с помощью доводов и аргументов, координировать знание средствами критического анализа. Примером практического воплощения принципов диалога в России стала школа «Диалога культур» (В.С. Библер и др.).

Новую педагогическую установку, из которой можно исходить, участники данного проекта связывают с типом мышления современного человека, с происходящим в настоящее время (пусть и медленными темпами) переходом в мышлении от «человека образованного» к «человеку культуры», сопрягающему в своем мышлении и деятельности различные, не сводимые друг к другу культуры, формы деятельности, ценностные, смысловые спектры. Отсюда – проецирование на весь процесс обучения особенностей современного мышления, – мышления «человека культуры». Современное мышление строится по такой культурной схеме, когда «высшие» достижения человеческого мышления, сознания, бытия вступают в диалогическое общение с предыдущими формами культуры (Античности, Средних веков, Нового Времени). В диалоге разных культурных смыслов бытия, – суть современного понятия, современной логики мышления. В.С. Библер говорит о том, что диалог – это не просто эвристический прием усвоения монологического знания и умения, но – определение самой сути и смысла усваиваемых и творчески формируемых понятий (понятие – диалогично по своей логической природе и по своей психологической – для сознания диалогическая ситуация сосуществования культур данности). Тексты культуры в их диалогическом сопряжении должны стать реальным предметом осмысления, спора, индивидуального творчества.

Диалогический подход в процессе приобщения к философии открывает необычайные познавательные и творческие перспективы. В этом действительный образовательный смысл диалога. Логика творческого мышления, по замечанию В.С. Библера, это логика диалога.

Нет ни первого, ни последнего слова и нет границ диалогическому контексту он уходит в безграничное прошлое и в безграничное будущее, писал М.М. Бахтин. Даже прошлые, рожденные в диалоге прошедших веков, смыслы никогда нс могут быть раз и навсегда завершенными, конченными, они всегда будут меняться, обновляясь в процессе последующего развития диалога. В любой момент развития диалога существуют огромные, неограниченные массы забытых смыслов, но в определенные моменты дальнейшего развития диалога, по ходу его они снова вспомнятся и оживут в новом контексте. Нет ничего абсолютно мертвого: у каждого смысла будет свой праздник возрождения.

По общему признанию, к началу XXI в. сложились предпосылки для парадигмального сдвига, формирования нового синтеза науки, философии и других форм духовного опыта. Приоритеты новой формирующейся парадигмы философского образования связаны, прежде всего, с расширением пространства культурного самоопределения, в котором одной из важнейших задач является построение культурного философского диалога, возможности постижения в образовании многообразия культур через усвоение различных, стилей и форм философствования. Альтернативой «монологизму» классического философствования сегодня выступает «диалогическая философия», позволяющая решать задачу создания единого коммуникационного пространства и вместе с тем конструирования новых смыслов сквозь призму собственного «я».

По замечанию В.С. Библера, философия теперь претерпевает такой сдвиг, который она претерпевала в начале философского мышления. Начало XXI века требует не просто продолжения разных философских культур, которое было от античности до нашего времени, но некоторого крупнейшего перелома, крупнейшего изменения философского мышления.

В заключение, обращаясь к мысли М.М. Бахтина, хотелось бы сказать: диалектика родилась из диалога, чтобы снова вернуться к диалогу на высшем уровне диалогу личностей [1, с. 384].

БИБЛИОГРАФИЯ

1. Бахтин М.М. К методологии гуманитарных наук // Бахтин М.М. Эстетика словесного творчества / Сост. С.Г. Бочаров… – 2-е изд. – М.: Искусство, 1986.
2. Гадамер Г.-Г. Актуальность прекрасного. М.: Искусство, 1991.
3. Гессен С.И. Основы педагогики. Введение в прикладную философию. М: «Школа-Пресс», 1995.
4. Диалог и коммуникация – философские проблемы // Вопросы философии. – 1989. – № 7. – С.3-27.
5. Липман М. Становление мыслительных навыков с помощью философии для детей // Философия для детей. М., 1996.
6. Мамардашвили М.К. Лекции по античной философии. Под редакцией Ю.П. Сенокосова. М., 1999.

7. Степин В.С. Эпоха перемен и сценарии будущего. М.: ИФ РАН, 1996.
8. Франк С.Л. Непостижимое (Онтологическое введение в философию религии) // Франк С.Л. Сочинения. М.: Правда, 1990.
9. Шпет Г.Г. Философия и история // Русская философия конца XIX – начала XX вв. – Антология. – СПб., 1993.
10. Эрн В.Ф. Борьба за Логос // Эрн В.Ф. Сочинении. М.: Издательство «Правда», 1991.

38

सामाजिक एवं सांस्कृतिक संक्रमण की प्रक्रिया और साहित्य

हिंदी के नये साहित्य पर कुछ टिप्पणियाँ

देवेंद्र चौबे

[यह संगोष्ठी पत्र हाल के वर्षों में साहित्य में उभरकर आये स्त्री, दलित और आदिवासी साहित्य के संदर्भ में संक्रमणकालीन स्थितियों पर एक विमर्श प्रस्तावित करता हैं। इस पत्र में बंगला और हिंदी की कुछ–एक रचनाओं को केंद्र में रखते हुए इस बात पर विचार किया गया है कि संक्रमण की स्थितियाँ निर्मित करने में स्थान–परिवर्तन (Migration) भूमिका क्या है।]

पिछले डेढ़–दो सौ वर्षों में भारतीय समाज का सामंतवाद और साम्राज्यवाद के खिलाफ जो संघर्ष हुआ है, उससे जनता एक संक्रमण के दौर से गुजरी है तथा उसका गहरा असर भारतीय और हिंदी साहित्य पर भी पड़ा हैं। खासकर हिंदी में कहानी, उपन्यास, आलोचना, खड़ीबोली काव्य आदि जैसी विधाएँ एवं रचनाएँ भारतीय सामंतवाद एवं अंग्रेजी साम्राज्यवाद के खिलाफ संघर्ष करते हुए ही विकसित हुई हैं। इसका अनुमान इसी बात से लगाया जा सकता है कि **बालकृष्ण भट्ट** जैसे लेखक अपने आलोचनात्मक लेखन के कारण ही ब्रिटिश सरकार की दमनकारी नीतियों के शिकार होते हैं और उनके द्वारा प्रकाशित पत्रिका ***हिंदी प्रदीप*** 1908 में एक सरकारी अध्यादेश के बाद बंद हो जाती हैं। **महावीर प्रसाद द्विवेदी** अपने आलोचनात्मक लेखों में कवियों की नायिका भेद (चित्रण) जैसी सामंती प्रवृतियों का विरोध 1903 में ***सरस्वती*** के संपादक बनने के साथ ही शुरू कर देते हैं। **प्रेमचंद** 1918 में प्रकाशित अपने प्रथम उपन्यास ***सेवासदन*** से लेकर 1936 में प्रकाशित ***गोदान*** में क्रमशः एक तरफ जहाँ भारतीय सामंतवादी व्यवस्था का विरोध करते हुए समाज में सुमन जैसी स्त्रियों की दुर्दशा का बयान करते हैं, वहाँ दूसरी तरफ अंग्रेजी साम्राज्यवादी नीतियों की भी। **महादेवी वर्मा** 1942 में प्रकाशित ***श्रृंखला की कड़ियाँ*** में भारतीय

समाज की पितृसत्तात्मक सामाजिक व्यवस्था में महिलाओं की दुर्दशा का बयान करती हैं और स्त्री मुक्ति की बातें करते हुए विकास के लिए उन्हें ज्ञान की परंपरा से जुड़ने की सलाह देती हैं। ध्यान देने की बात है कि यह सब एक खास दौर में यानी कि स्वाधीनता आंदोलन के दौरान होता है। लेकिन क्या कारण है कि अचानक हिंदी में 1965 के बाद, खासकर, 1967 में नक्सलबाड़ी की घटना के बाद एक नये प्रकार का साहित्य आना शुरू हो जाता है। महत्वपूर्ण बात यह है कि यह आंदोलन और उससे उपजा साहित्य भी 1947 में देश की आजादी के बाद पहली बार, सातवें दशक में खेतिहर मजदूरों और किसानों सहित समाज के कमजोर तबके की एक नये प्रकार की गुलामी और सामंती व्यवस्था की चर्चा करने लगता है और 22 अप्रैल 1969 में गठित **भारत की कम्युनिस्ट पार्टी** (मार्क्सवादी–लेनिनवादी) **चारू मजुमदार** के नेतृत्व में उत्पीड़ित समाज की मुक्ति के लिए एक नयी लाकतांत्रिक व्यवस्था की मांगे करने लगता है। **महाश्वेता देवी** इसी दौरान नक्सलवादी आंदोलन से जुड़े युवाओं की पुलिस द्वारा की जा रही नृशंश हत्याओं पर ***हजार चौरासी की माँ*** (1974) जैसा उपन्यास लिखती हैं और हिंदी में, सातवें दशक में **धूमिल, राजकमल चौधरी** जैसे कवि भी यह घोषणा करने लगते है कि यह आजादी झूठी है, तत्कालीन लोकतांत्रिक पद्धतियाँ आदमी को नपुंसक एवं अपाहिज बना रही हैं; इसीलिए अब एक दूसरे प्रजातंत्र यानी कि एक नयी लोकतांत्रिक व्यवस्था की जरूरत है। **कृष्णा सोबती** 1967 में प्रकाशित उपन्यास ***मित्रो मरजानी*** में एक ऐसी स्त्री चरित्र को लेकर आती है जो पितृसत्तात्मक सामाजिक व्यवस्था की सारी हदों को पार करते हुए स्त्री के एक स्वतंत्र वजूद की माँग करती हैं। **जगदीशचंद्र** 1973 में प्रकाशित उपन्यास ***धरती धन न अपना*** में भारतीय सामंती व्यवस्था में जीवन–यापन कर रहे काली जैसे दलित चरित्र की मार्मिक दशा का बयान करते हैं जो बाद में, सही मायने में क्रमशः 1995, 1997, 2002 एवं 2006 में प्रकाशित **मोहनदास नैमिशराय** के ***अपने अपने पिंजरे*** , **ओमप्रकाश वाल्मीकि** के ***जूठन*** , **सूरजपाल चौहान** के ***तिरस्कृत*** (एवं 2006 में ***संतप्त***) और **भयौराज सिंह बेचैन** के ***बेवक्त गुजर गया माली*** (***हंस*** , फरवरी : 2006) में दिखलाई पड़ता है जहाँ अपनी–अपनी जिंदगी की हकीकतों का बयान करते हुए ये दलित आत्मकथाकार भारतीय वर्ण–व्यवस्था की विसंगतियों का विरोध करते हुए गैर दलित समाज के प्रति अपना प्रतिरोध दर्ज करते हैं। रही सही कसर 2004 में आकर **निर्मला पुतुल** जैसी आदिवासी लेखिकाएँ ***अपने घर की तलाश में*** जैसे काव्य–संग्रह में पूरा कर देती हैं, जब भोश पूरे भारतीय समाज से यह सवाल करती हैं कि बिना उनकी (आदिवासी समाज) रजामंदी और जिंदगी की हकीकतों को समझे उनकी जमीनों पर बाँध क्यों

बनाया जा रहा है अथवा सड़कें क्यों और कैसे बन रही हैं : *इसलिए इतना जरूर पूछना चाहूँगी / कि नदी पर बांध क्यों बन रहा है ?/ किसलिए नाप–जोख हो रही है हमारे / गोचर जमीन की ?/ क्या चीज का सर्वे चल रहा है ?/ और यह जो सड़क बन रही है / कितने के बजट की है ?/ इसका ठेकदार कौन है ?/ कहाँ का है ?/जरूर पूछना चाहँगी !* (***अपने घर की तलाश में***, रमणिका फाउंडेशन, दिल्ली, पृष्ठ : 98–99)

यह सवाल इसलिए भी महत्वपूर्ण है कि इस प्रकार के परिवर्तन और विकास का गहरा असर संबंधित समाज पर पड़ता है तथा एक निश्चित अवधि के लिए संबंधित समाज संक्रमण की अवस्था में चला जाता है। **नर्मदा बचाओ आंदोलन** से जुड़ी **मेधा पाटेकर** विस्थापन की अवस्था से गुजर रहे जिस आदिवासी समाज की चिंताओं से पिछले कई दशकों से आंदोलनरत हैं, वह परिवर्तन और विकास की इन्हीं असमान प्रक्रियाओं की देन हैं। ***डूब*** (1991) में **वीरेंद्र जैन** विकास योजनाओं के नाम पर विनाश के लिए अभिशप्त एवं संक्रमण की जिंदगी जी रहे समाज की त्रासदियों का बयान करते हैं। यहाँ तक कि इस प्रकार के परिवर्तन और विकास उस समाज को ऐसी स्थिति में ला पटकते हैं, जहाँ से उन्हें मुक्ति का रास्ता दिखलाई नहीं पड़ता है; शेष समाज को बेहतर विकल्प और विकास के लिए मौका जरूर मिल जाता है जिसकी तरफ **निर्मला पुतुल** की उपर्युक्त पंक्तियाँ संकेत करती हैं। ***'भानीचरी'*** कहानी में **महाश्वेता देवी** ने विकास के लिए जंगल से बाहर मुख्यधारा में गये आदिवासी समाज की स्त्रियों की संक्रमणकालीन स्थितियों एवं दुर्दशा का चित्रण करते हुए लिखा है कि *" ईट बिठाओ, ईट बिठाओं भानीचरी। कहाँ आयी तू, किस देश में –– कुछ समझ में आया ? रहमत का बच्चा पेट में लेकर दूर–दूर तक फैले धान के खेत को उदास आँखों में आँसू लिए देखते रहती हो। ऐसा बँधुआपन ! तुम शायद जानती हो, यह तुम्हारा कैदखाना है। तू जानती नहीं इस देश की भाषा। किस रास्ते से आयी थी, शायद उसका पता भी भूल गयी है। "* (**ईंट के ऊपर ईंट**, बंगला से अनुवाद : प्रमोदकुमार सिन्हा, पृष्ठ : 68)

महाश्वेता देवी की ***भानीचरी*** कहानी की उपर्युक्त पंक्तियाँ बताती हैं कि संक्रमणकाल में एक आदिवासी स्त्री को किन प्रकार की अमानवीय स्थितियों से गुजरना पड़ना पड़ता है। ये स्थितियाँ एक तरफ जहाँ अमानवीयता की सीमाओं को पार करती हैं, वहाँ दूसरी तरफ इस बात का भी संकेत करती हैं कि अपने मूल स्थान से दूर जाने और नयी जगह पर व्यवस्थित होने के बीच आदिवासी या कोई भी समाज अपनी संस्कृति, भाषा और भूगोल से भी दूर होने लगता है। उसकी आदतें बदल जाती हैं। उसके चरित्र में परिवर्तन आने लगता है। यहाँ तक कि अगर कोई आदिवासी

विकास की प्रक्रिया से जुड़ने के लिए अपना मूल स्थान छोड़कर शहर जाता है, कहना न होगा कि यह वही संक्रमणकालीन दौर होता है, जब कोई व्यक्ति अथवा समाज **हाशिया का आदमी** या **हाशिया का समाज** (Marginal Man or Marginal Societies) में तब्दील हो जाता हैं। प्रसिद्ध समाज शास्त्री **राबर्ट इ. पार्क** ने लिखा है कि *" संक्रमण–काल में उनके चरित्र में नैतिक द्वंद्व और संघर्ष की भावना विकसित होने लगती है, जिसके परिणामस्वरूप वे पुरानी आदतें छोड़ने के लिए बाध्य हो जाते हैं। लेकिन नयी आदतें इतनी जल्दी बन नहीं पाती हैं, जिसके कारण अपने आपको वे हाशिये पर खड़ा महसूस करते हैं। "* (Human Migration And The Marginal Man : Robert E. Park, ***The American Journal of Sociology***, May : 1928, Number : 6, page-893.)

दरअसल जिन नयी स्थितियों की तरफ बंगला और हिंदी में रचित यह साहित्य और उनके लेखक संकेत करते हैं, वह अचानक नहीं बनी थी। इसकी एक लंबी और ऐतिहासिक परंपरा तथा प्रकियाएँ रही हैं तथा संबंधित समाज को यहाँ तक पहुँचने में अनेक प्रकार के संक्रमण के दौर से गुजरना पड़ा है। खासकर जवाहरलाल नेहरू के निधन और नक्सलबाड़ी आंदोलन के बाद हिंदी साहित्य में कृषि–संबंधी संघर्ष के साहित्य के समानांतर जो नये प्रकार का साहित्य आता है तथा जिसकी पहचान हम फिलहाल स्त्री, दलित और आदिवासी साहित्य के रूप में कर रहे हैं, वह अनेक मायने में इन्हीं संक्रमणकालीन स्थितियों की देन रहा है। यहाँ इस बात का उल्लेख करना जरूरी है कि इन स्थितियों को बनाने में सामाजिक और राजनीतिक आंदोलनों के साथ ही विकास की विनाशकारी भूमिका और असमान समुदायों एवं समूहों के बीच की घटनात्मक टकराहट, संघर्ष तथा संस्कृतियों के संयोग से उत्पन्न स्थितियों की बड़ी भूमिका रही हैं। इस पूरी प्रक्रिया में **स्थान–परिवर्तन** (Migration) पर विचार करना जरूरी है क्योंकि स्थान–परिवर्तन के कारण ही कोई व्यक्ति अथवा समाज घर की पारंपरिक संस्कृति और आमदनी तथा जीवन–यापन के स्थायी आर्थिक स्रोतों से कटने के लिए बाध्य होता है। इतना ही नहीं घर की संस्कृति से कटने के बाद व्यक्ति या कोई सामाजिक–समूह अपने आपको नये परिवेश अथवा समाज में व्यवस्थित नहीं कर पाता है तथा बीच के संक्रमणकालीन समय में दोहरी मानसिकता में जीने के लिए बाध्य हो जाता है जैसा कि **शेखर जोशी** ***'दाज्यू '*** या **संजीव** ***'दुनिया की सबसे हसीन औरत'*** ,***'घर चलो दुलारी बाई'*** जैसी कहानियों में दिखलाते हैं अथवा दलित लेखकों में **ओमप्रकाश वाल्मीकि** ***'घुसपैठिये', दयानंद बटोही 'सुरंग'***; स्त्री लेखिकाओं में **ममता कालिया** ***'जाँच अभी जारी है',*** **सुधा अरोड़ा** ***'महानगर की मैथिली'*** ,**चित्रा मुद्गल** ***'भूख'*** तथा आदिवासी लेखकों में

रोज केरकट्टा ***'भंवर',*** **पीटर पॉल एक्का** ***'राजकुमारों के देश में',*** **कैलाश वनवासी** ***'सुरक्षित–असुरक्षित'*** में। **स्थान–परिवर्तन** की प्रक्रिया में संक्रमणकालीन जीवन के तीन स्थितियों की चर्चा करते हुए समाज शास्त्री **एवर्ट वी. स्टॉनक्वीस्ट** ने इस बात का उल्लेख किया है कि *'कई बार व्यक्ति अथवा समाज को यह पता ही नहीं चलता है कि वह दो संस्कृतियों में के बीच पल रहा है। वह इस बात से अनभिज्ञ रहता है कि उसका व्यक्तित्व किन समस्याओं से गुजरने वाला हैं।'* दूसरी स्थिति, *' संकट के चक्र की होती है जिसमें व्यक्ति को इस बात का एहसास हो जाता है कि वह दो संस्कृतियों के अंतर्द्वंद्व के बीच जी रहा है। इस अवस्था में व्यक्ति के अंदर कुछ विशेष प्रकार के लक्षण दिखलाई पड़ने लगते हैं। उसकी बेचैनी बढ़ जाती है तथा वह अन्य लोगों से खिंचा–खिंचा रहने लगता है। किसी बड़ी घटना से उसकी आँख खुल जाती है तथा दोनों संस्कृतियों के बीच के खिंचवा को महसूस करते हुए उसकी एक महत्वपूर्ण आदत क्रियाशीलता बन जाती है।'* तीसरी स्थिति संक्रमणकाल की चरमावस्था —– *'प्रतिरोध की होती हैं। इसमें व्यक्ति अथवा समाज अपनी दिशा तय कर लेता हैं।'* (The Problem of Marginal Man : Evertt V. Stonequest, ***The American Journal of Sociology***, vol. XLI, July : 1935, Number : 1, page-1)

इतना ही नहीं, इस अवस्था की चर्चा करते हुए **स्टॉनक्वीस्ट** ने इस बात की तरफ भी संकेत किया हैं कि संक्रमणकाल में रह रहा व्यक्ति अथवा समाज ऐसी स्थिति में कई बार ताकतवर समूह की ओर बढ़कर उसमें भाामिल होने की कोशिश करता है या कई बार उस प्रभावशाली समूह के प्रति विरोध जाहिर कर क्रांतिकारी अथवा उग्र राष्ट्रवादी भी बन जाता है या कई बार इन सारी स्थितियों से अपने आपको विमुख कर लेता हैं जैसे कि कुछ हुआ ही नहीं हो । इस संदर्भ को **भुजंग मेश्राम** द्वारा संपादित एवं गोंडी भाषा में प्रकाशित आदिवासी कविता संग्रह ***'मोहोल'*** में शामिल **प्रमुराजगडकर** की कविता ***महाकाय शहर*** की निम्नलिखित पंक्तियों के माध्यम से समझा जा सकता है, जिसमें अपने मूल स्थान से रोजगार के लिए शहर गये एक आदिवासी की उस त्रासदी का बयान किया गया है, जिसके अंदर क्रांति की आग तो है, पर पेट की आग संक्रमण काल में क्रांतिकारी मानसिकता का गर्भपात करा देती हैं और वह सारी स्थितियों से विमुख हो जाता है:

बोलता येते, क्रांतिचिभाशा / पण येते / भकास सुकून डबक झालेल्या / पोटात काहीचनब्हते / म्हाणूण भाक्ष्या क्रांतीच्या भाशेचाच / गर्भपात झाला।

अथार्त, *बोलना भी आता है, क्रांति की भाशा / भी आती है / वीरान, सूखकर डबरा बने पेट में / कुछ नहीं था / इसलिए मेरी क्रांति की भाशा का ही / गर्भपात हो गया* (पृश्ठ : 49)

जाहिर है, संक्रमण काल एक तरफ जहाँ व्यक्ति, समूह अथवा समाज को प्रतिरोध के लिए तैयार करता है, वहाँ दूसरी तरफ उन्हें तोड़ता भी है।

पर कई बार संक्रमण काल में निर्मित अजनबीयतपन या बेचैनी की स्थितियाँ किसी बड़े विद्रोह को जन्म देती हैं या विद्रोह को ताकत प्रदान कर उसे एक बड़े आंदोलन में तब्दील कर देती हैं। ब्रिटीशकालीन भारत में आदिवासियों द्वारा किये गये विद्रोहों को भी इसी नजरिये से देखा जा सकता हैं। उदाहरण के लिए **बिरसा मुण्डा** द्वारा 1899–1900 में किया गया **बिरसा (मुण्डा) विद्रोह** को हम ले सकते है जिसमें मुण्डा एक तरफ जहाँ जमींदारों के शोषण से उत्पीड़ित थे, वहाँ दूसरी तरफ अपनी जाति और धर्म छोड़कर ईसाई बनने के बाद भी नयी सामाजिक जिंदगी में दोहरा जीवन जीने को बाध्य थे। धोबी के उस गदहे की तरह जो न घर का होता है, न घाट का। कहा जाता है कि यदि धर्म परिवर्तन के बाद नये धर्म में अजनबीयत की जिंदगी जी रहे इन ईसाई मुण्डाओं का साथ, इस विद्रोह को नहीं मिलता तो **बिरसा मुण्डा** के लिए अंग्रेजों के खिलाफ इतना बड़ा आंदोलन चलाना मुश्किल होता। इस विद्रोह की सबसे बड़ी भूमिका यही थी कि इसने आदिवासियों के मन में इस बात को साफ कर दिया कि उनके वास्तविक शत्रु साहब लोग और अंग्रेज सरकार हैं। इसीलिए आज भी जब आदिवासी समाज अपने आपको संकट में पाता हैं, बिरसा मुण्डा को याद सबसे पहले करता हैं :

हमने नहीं देखा तूझे पहले / लेकिन केवल तुम ही / हमारे विद्रोह को / दिशा देते हो
तब तुमने ही तो किया था संघर्ष / गोरो को खदेड़ने की खातिर /... आज न गोरे है / न सपनों की आजादी / आज न घने बीहड़ हैं / ना तूं है / है केवल बीहड़ों में फैलता असंतोष /होठों पर तेरा नन्हा–सा गीत /ऊलगुलान ! ऊलगुलान ! ऊलगुलान ! / जो बन गया है हमारी संस्कृति की लड़ाई /सच बताउं अब हमें जल्दी है / नहीं चाहते अब हम ओढ़ी हुई सभ्यता / धिक्कारते जैसे अंधकार को / जंगल बांटती दुलाली प्रथा को / हम नकारते हैं / गूंजती है घाटियों में पीछा करती आवाज
बिरसा तुम्हें कहीं से भी / आना होगा /.... कहीं से भी आ मेरे बिरसा / खेतो की बयार बनकर / लोग तेरी बाट जोहते ! (आ मेरे

बिरसा : **भुजंग मेश्राम**, *युद्धरत आम आदमी* : सं. **रमणिका गुप्त**, अंक: 55, विशेषांक : 2001, पृष्ठ : 157–158)

जाहिर **भुजंग मेश्राम** की यह कविता एक तरफ जहाँ संक्रमणकाल में जी रहे आदिवासी समाज की त्रासदियों का चिंताजनक चित्र खींचती हैं, वहाँ दूसरी तरफ **बिरसा मुण्डा** को संक्रमण या किसी भी प्रकार की समस्याओं से मुक्ति दिलानेवाले सबसे बड़े नायक के रूप में स्थापित करती हैं। यह एक बड़ी बात हैं। इसीलिए कई बार संक्रमणकलीन स्थितियाँ व्यक्ति अथवा समाज को अपने वास्तविक शत्रुओं की पहचान और उनसे मुक्ति के रास्ते भी बताती है। इसे **शेखर जोशी** की कहानी ***दाज्यू*** और **संजीव** की ***दुनिया की सबसे हसीन औरत*** जैसी कहानियों से समझा जा सकता है। दोनों कहानी के केंद्र में पहाड़ से मुख्यधारा में आये नायक हैं, पर **शेखर जोशी** की ***दाज्यू*** का नायक मदन जहाँ संक्रमणकलीन समय में अपने ही समाज के जगदीश बाबू और हेमंत जैसे शत्रुओं की पहचान कर अपने आपको उनसे यह कहकर विमुख कर लेता है कि *" बॉय कहते हैं शा'ब मुझे! "* (***मेरा पहाड़*** : **शेखर जोशी**, लोकभारती, इलाहाबाद,1989, पृष्ठ : 34), वहाँ ओरॉव जाति की सब्जी बेचकर गुजारा करनेवाली महिला विकास की असमानता और मुख्यधारा की अराजकता का विकार होकर भाग्य को दोष देते हुए अपने आपको संक्रमणकालीन संकटों से मुक्ति के लिए शेष समाज से सहयोग की अपेक्षा करती है : *" रो रहा है हम अपन नसीब पे "* (***दुनिया की सबसे हसीन औरत*** : **संजीव**, यात्री प्रकाशन, दिल्ली, 1990, पृष्ठ : 147)। जबकि यह आदिवासी महिला उसी **ओरॉव (महिला) समाज** की है जिसके पूर्वजों ने कभी बिहार के रोहतास जिला के आसपास के जंगलों में सरहुल के पर्व में नशे में डूबे पुरूषों के नहीं जगने पर स्वंय मर्दाना पोशाक पहनकर मध्यकाल में मुगलों की सेना के तीन–तीन हमलों को नाकाम किया था। **संजीव** ने इस कहानी में बताया है कि बाद में जब लड़ती हुई कुछ बहादुर औरतें पकड़ गयी, तब मुगलों को पता चला कि उनका युद्ध तो ओरॉव महिलाओं से हो रहा था। इस अपमान का बदला लेने के लिए मुगलों ने पकड़ी गयी महिलाओं के चेहरे को तीन बार दागा। बाद में ओरॉव महिलाओं ने इसे अपनी ताकत और प्रतिरोध की क्षमता मान **सिंगार** के रूप में अपना लिया। जाहिर है, रेलगाड़ी में सब्जी लेकर जाती वह ओरॉव महिला जब टी. टी. और कुछ यात्रिओं से अपमानित होती है, तब अपने भाग्य को दोष देती है, जबकि उसका अपमान अपने समाज से निकलकर एक दूसरे समाज में जाने, संवाद करने एवं जगह (Space) पर कब्जा करने की प्रक्रिया में (संक्रमणकालीन स्थितियों) में होता हैं।

कहना न होगा कि समकालीन हिंदी और भारतीय साहित्य में पिछले तीन–चार दशकों में स्त्री, दलित और आदिवासी केंद्रित जो साहित्य आया है, उसकी निर्मिति में संक्रमणकलीन स्थितियों की बड़ी भूमिका रही हैं। और सच यह भी है कि इस संक्रमण में **स्थान–परिवर्तन** (Migration) एक निर्णायक भूमिका निभाता है। पर, इस बात को भी ध्यान में रखना जरूरी है कि स्थान–परिवर्तन मात्र गतिशीलता नहीं है। कारण, स्थान–परिवर्तन में कम–से–कम जन्म–स्थान अथवा मूल–स्थान में परिवर्तन होता है तथा जो पुराने बंधन होते हैं, वे टूटते हैं। अर्थात् व्यक्ति, समूह अथवा समाज का **घर** से नाता टूटता है। उदाहरण के लिए, यदि **प्रभा खेतान** के उपन्यास ***छिन्नमस्ता*** की नायिका विवाह करना नहीं चाहती हैं, या **ओमप्रकाश वाल्मीकि** की कहानी ***प्रमोशन*** का दलित नायक सुरेश साथी मजदूरों की निगाह में दलित से मजदूर न बनकर अस्पृश्य यानी कि दलित ही बना रहता है, अथवा **अरूण प्रकाश** की कहानी ***बेला एक्का लौट रही है*** की बेला गैर आदिवासी समाज में शिक्षिका के बदले एक आदिवासी स्त्री ही बनी रहती है तो कहीं–न–कहीं ये वहीं भयावह स्थितियाँ हैं जो किसी व्यक्ति या सामाजिक समुदाय को जन्म–स्थान से दूर जाने से रोकती है अथवा स्थान–परिवर्तन के बाद की संक्रमणकालीन स्थितियों (जैसे – अस्थायीपन, बेचैनी, संकट, तनाव, अजनबीपन, अशांति, मानसिक एवं शारीरिक क्लेश आदि।) से जूझने के लिए छोड़ देती हैं, जैसा कि सुरेश या बेला एक्का के साथ होता हैं। यहाँ, यह कहना अति योक्तिपूर्ण नहीं होगा कि यह एक ऐसी स्थिति है जिससे आज बहुलांश भारतीय अथवा वैश्विक समाज गुजर रहा है, भले ही हम अपने आपको एक–दूसरे की तुलना में बेहतर स्थिति में क्यों न महसूस करें!

39

हिन्दी कविता में भूमंडलीकरण की झलक

विजयकुमारन. सी.पी.वी.

आधुनिकता का उद्गम हम ज्ञानोदय में देख सकते हैं। यद्यपि इसका नतीजा उन्नीसवी शताब्दी में हासिल हुआ। तथाकथित ज्ञानोदय परियोजना का निरूपण बुद्धिवाद, औद्योगीकरण और ज्ञान तथा उत्पादन के प्रमाणीकरण में हुआ और उसका विश्वास रैखिक विकास एवं विश्वव्यापी परम सत्यों में था। आधुनिकता की परियोजना उसके ज्ञान और विज्ञान, उसके बुद्धिवाद, सर्वमुक्तिवाद और मानवतावाद आदि के विरुद्ध प्रतिक्रिया और नकार को ही उत्तर आधुनिकतावाद माना जाता है। यह मान्यता प्रो. रणधीर सिंह की है जिसे कि उन्होने 'अब' के शताब्दी अंक २०००-२००१ में व्यक्त की है। इस शताब्दी के अन्तिम दशक में वैश्वीकरण, उदारीकरण, निजीकरण और बाजारवाद का शोर सर्वत्र मचा है। आज त्रिलोचन, नागार्जुन और केदार के वर्ग संघर्ष की चर्चा नहीं है। ओम भारती का संकलन 'जोखिम से कम नहीं', मदन कश्यप 'नीम रोशनी में', निलय उपाध्याय का संकलन 'कटौती', बोधिसत्व का 'हम जो नदियों का संगम हैं', प्रेम रंजन अनिमेष का 'मिट्टी का फल' और संजय कुन्दन का 'कागज के प्रदेश में ' जैसे काव्य संग्रहों की कविताओं में आज की कविता का, भूमंडलीकरण का दौर है। वरिष्ठ और युवा कवियों के काव्य-संग्रहों, 'अतिरिक्त नहीं' -विनोद कुमार शुक्ल- 'वर्षा में भीगकर'-इव्वार रब्बी- 'एवजी में शब्द' -विनोद कुमार श्रीवास्तव- 'मगर एक आवाज'-लीलाधर मंडलोई -'और जोखिम से कम नहीं - ओम भारती- आदि को पढते हुए समकालीन कविता के कई चेहरे उजागर होते है। ये कवितायें बाजारवाद, उपभोक्तावाद, सम्प्रदायिक कट्टरता और सांस्कृतिक राष्ट्रवाद के तहत सांस्कृतिक एकरूपता के विरुद्ध प्रतिवाद कर रही हैं।

समाज में व्याप्त उपभोक्तावाद ने हमारी सहज मानवीय संवेदना को कितना अमानवीय और क्षत-विक्षत कर दिया है कि ऐसा लगता है कि हम सभी बाजार के बीच खडे हैं जहाँ हर आदमी को खर्च कर देने के लिए घात लगाए बैठा है । पहले यह काम क्रूर व्यवस्थाएँ किया करती थीं, अब यह काम बहुराष्ट्रीय कम्पनियों और उनके द्वारा फैलाया बाजार कर रहा है। त्रिलोचन के गाँव का सारा नक्शा ही बदल गया । अब शाम होते ही बडे-बूढे, बालक- बच्चे और औरतें अलाव की जगह टी. वी. तापते हैं। आज सबसे अधिक अमीर और क्षमतावान वह है जिसके पास ज्ञान और सूचना प्रौद्योगिकी पर सबसे अधिक कब्जा है। त्रिलोचन का

दूसरा गाँव उत्तर आधुनिकता से प्रभावित है।उत्तर आधुनिकतावाद का मुख्य दबाव आधुनिकता की परियोजना का विघटन या विखंडन है।

पूँजी ने हमारी मानवीय संवेदनाओं को तहस नहस कर रख दिया है। पारिवारिक रिश्ते भी अर्थ के आधार पर मजबूत एवं कमजोर बन रहे हैं। टेरी ईगलटन उत्तराधुनिकता की प्रवृत्ति के रूप में 'उच्च संस्कृति' और 'जनवादी संस्कृति' को मिटाने की प्रवृत्ति को तीसरी दुनिया के भौमीकरण से जोडते हैं-"Post modernity is a style of thought which is suspecious of classical notions of truth, reason, identiy and objectivity... Post Modernism is a style of culture which reflects some thing of this epochal change in a depthless, ungrounded self reflexive, playful, derivative, aclestic, pluralistic art which blurs the boundaries between " high' and "popular' culture, as well as between art and everyday culture." (Terry Eagleton, 1997, vii). अतः यहां उत्तराधुनिकता को संस्कृति की एक शैली मानी।

बहुराष्ट्रीय कम्पनियाँ भारतीय मानसिकता को विदेशी बनाकर हमारी राष्ट्रीय एवं सांस्कृतिक अस्मिता को छिन्न भिन्न कर रही हैं। प्रसिद्ध समीक्षक मनमोहन का तो यहाँ तक मानना है कि "यह नयी दुनिया मायावी है और किसी के हाथ नहीं आने वाली।'

अरुण कमल के एक संकलन 'पुतली में संसार' में एक कविता 'बिछावन' में जो सांस्कृतिक गुलामीपन पर व़्यंग्य है, वह तीसरी दुनिया का नमूना बनता है। हम किस अर्थ में स्वतंत्र हैं ये पंक्तियाँ प्रमाणित करती हैं- 'वाइसराय का बिछावन देखने वह व्यक्ति गया, जो व्यक्ति कभी तुम्हारा गुलाम था...' और कविता का अंत यों होता है- 'अब हम गुलाम नहीं।' इसमें आज़ाद भारत के मंत्री की विलासिता की तुलना करते वइसराय की विलासिता को किंचित आश्चर्यक नहीं माना।

मुकुट सक्सेना की 'बढते नाखून की चुनौती' में अमेरिका का वीटो पवर, परमाणु परीक्षण प्रतिबंध संधि में तीसरी दुनिया को हस्ताक्षर करने पर जोर देना, आर्थिक उदार पर प्रतिबंध लगाना कि उस गरीब देश में परमाणु परीक्षण किया गया हो, आदि की ध्वनि है। वे कहते हैं- 'जब लोग वढा रहे हों / नाखून / सैकडों योजन दूर बैठे व्यक्ति का मांस / नोच खाने के लिए / औह लगा रहे हो प्रतिबंध / कि नहीं करोगे / तुम कोई परीक्षण / अपने नाखून बढाने का / चाहे वह अपनी फांस निकालने के लिए ही क्यों न हो।'

आदमी की पहचान चीज में होती है। वह अपनी आलीशान कोटी से नामी हो, अपने नये नये औजार से, या कार-मोटर गाडी से। इस सत्य को उद्घाटित करनेवाली श्री हिलतेश व्यास की पंक्तियां हैं- ' चीजों सं भर जाएगा घर / घट गया है आदमी।' कवि की इन पंक्तियों में वही व्यापार तंत्र ध्वनित है कि अब जरूरत के मुताबिक चीजों की आपूर्ति का पुराने व्यापार के स्थान पर अपनी शान-शैकत के लिए घर को चीजों से सजाने की, मुक्त बाजारव्यवस्था बनी है।

आदमी खुद चीज बनता है। स्त्रियों का सबलीकरण या मुक्ति का संदेश इससे मुक्ति लाने के लिए होता है। रीता हजेला 'अराधना ' की अद्यतन कविताएं (१)-' सब्ज बाग',

चारदीवारी', आदि में नारी विमर्श का स्वर मुखरित हैं। स्त्री को परंपरागत कैद से मुक्ति दिलानेवाले स्वर में आपने पारिवारिक जीवन की कैद को तोडने की बात भी की है-

> नहीं जीना चाहती वो / खाट पर पडी / वस्तु बनकर, /
> तैयार है बदलते मूल्यों धारणाओं मे, घुलने मिलने के लिए।'

ओमप्रकाश मिश्र की 'एक अधूरी कवित' में वह बेरोजगार बिंबित है जिसको व्यक्ति, समाज और राष्ट्र जैसे शब्दों के लिए कोई संवेदना नहीं, जबकि बहुराष्ट्रवाद के आइने से तीसरी दुनिया के हर बेरोजगार की यही नियति बनती है। उन्हीं की दूसरी कविता' थके हुए लोग' में श्रमिकों और सर्वहारा वर्ग की वर्तमान हादसा बतायी जाती है- 'इस्तेमाल किये जा रहे हैं / परिवार के सदस्यों में / हाशिये पर इनका नाम आता / सूचना प्रौद्योगिकी के इस युग में / समाज के माथे पर बोझ हैं / ये थके हुए लोग।' हाशियेकरण की प्रवृत्ति में घर ही नहीं, अपना समाज, राष्ट्र आदि भी समान दबाव थके हुए लोगों पर डालते हैं। आज राष्ट्र को उन मतलबी शक्सों की जरूरत है, जो ज्ञान-विज्ञान के क्षेत्र में अपने देश को विकसित राष्ट्रों के मुकाबले करा सकें।

आज के भूमंडलीकृत अर्थ-तंत्र से कोई भी वस्तु बच नहीं सकता। बाजार की ग्रसी यह दुनिया छोटी से बडी वस्तु में भी यही अर्थ खोजती है। कुबेर दत्त की कविता (२) -'श्रीमती कनकनयनी की नाक ' भी इसी तंत्र को खोलती है-

'श्रीमती कनकनयनी / दौडती हैं लेजर-गति को / अछाड-पछाड / उनकी नाक / पहले पीतल की हुई, फिर अष्टधातु की / फिर चाँदी की / फिर सोने की / फिर हीरे की / अब तो वहां / नाक की जगह / एक आसमान फोडती मीनार है। 'अब साहित्यकार भी उपभोक्ता ही तो है। वे भी -' श्रीमती कनकनयनी की नाक पर / लंबी-लंबी कविताएँ लिख रहे हैं आधुनिक और उत्तर आधुनिक भाट-चारण... पूंजी की रक्तिम नौटंकी / जिसमें मटक रहे हैं या ही ही पत्रकार / या हू हू टी. वी. कार / उई उई गजलकार / फिदा-फिदा चित्रकार / और / अश-अश गीतकार.... ।'

त्रिलोचन का दूसरा गाँव उत्तर आधुनिकता से प्रभावित है, जिसकी परख १९८० में प्रकाशित 'ताप के ताप हुए दिन' काव्यसंग्रह की कविताओं से की जा सकती है। इसमें चित्रित मजदूर को पैसे के चक्कर में अपनी पत्नी तक की याद नहीं आती। पूँजी ने किस तरह हमारी मानवीय संवेदनाओं को तहस-नहस कर रख दिया है, इस मानवीय पहलू को यों उद्घाटित किया गया-

> 'सचमुच इधर तुम्हारी याद तो नहीं आई,
> झूठ क्या कहूं, पुरे दिन मशीन पर खटना'

'चंपा काले अछर नहीं चीन्हती' में पहले ही आपने कलकत्ता जैसे महानगर की भूमंडलीय स्थिति को एक आदिवासी महिला की लघुमानसिकता के साथ उकेरा है-

> 'कलकत्ता कभी नहीं जाने दूँगी
> कलकत्ता में बजर गिरे' जैसै सत्यापन इसका निदान है।

उत्तर आधुनिकता का बाजारवाद गांव में हिंसा, कूटनीति, ईर्ष्या, द्वेष एवं आपसी फूट के रूप में उभरा है। पारिवारिक रिश्ते भी अर्थ के आधार पर मजबूत एवं कमजोर बन रहे हैं।

उत्तर आधुनिकतावाद का मुख्य दबाव आधुनिकता की परियोजना का विघटन या विखंडन है। आधुनिकता का उद्‌गम हम ज्ञानोदय में देख सकते हैं। यद्यपि इसका नतीजा उन्नीसवीं शताब्दी में हासिल हुआ। तथाकथित ज्ञानोदय परियोजना का निरूपण बुद्धिवाद, औद्योगीकरण और ज्ञान तथा उत्पादन के प्रमाणीकरण में हुआ और उसका विश्वास रैखिक विकास एवं विश्वव्यापी परम सत्यों में था (३)। आधुनिकता की परियोजना उसके ज्ञान और विज्ञान, उसके बुद्धिवाद, सर्वमुक्तिवाद और मानवतावाद आदि के विरुद्ध प्रतिक्रिया और नकार को ही उत्तर आधुनिकतावाद माना जाता है। यह मान्यता प्रो. रणधीर सिंह की है जिसे कि उन्होने 'अब' के शताब्दी अंक २०००-२००१ में व्यक्त की है। आज सबसे अधिक अमीर और क्षमतावान वह है जिसके पास ज्ञान और सूचना प्रौद्योगिकी पर सबसे अधिक कब्जा है। इस शताब्दी के अन्तिम दशक में वैश्वीकरण, उदारीकरण, निजीकरण और बाजारवाद का शोर सर्वत्र मचा है। आज त्रिलोचन, नागार्जुन और केदार के वर्ग संघर्ष की चर्चा नहीं है।

बहुराष्ट्रीय कम्पनियाँ भारतीय मानसिकता को विदेशी बनाकर हमारी राष्ट्रीय एवं सांस्कृतिक आस्मिता को छिन्न भिन्न कर रही हैं। प्रसिद्ध समीक्षक मनमोहन का तो यहाँ तक मानना है कि "यह नयी दुनिया मायावी है और किसी के हाथ नहीं आने वाली। '

जनकवि नागार्जुन अपने काव्य-संकलन, 'अपने खेत में' की पहली कविता में एक किसान के रूप में उपस्थित हैं। जानता है कि "मकबूल फिदा हुसैन की/चौकाउ या बाज़ारु टेकनीक/हमारी खेती को चौपट/ कर देगी/जी, आप/ अपने रुमाल में/ गांठ बांध लो, बिल्कुल।।" नागार्जुन हल, खेत, बीज के साथ ही प्रसिद्ध चित्रकार एम.एफ. हुसैन और बाजारु टेकनीक को काव्य-प्रतीक बना लेते हैं। धार्मिक पहचानवादी का यह प्रमाण कलाकार के द्वारा भी निसृत है, जो सलमान रुशदी ज़ैसे विख्यात साहित्यकार से संभव हुआ है। देश और काल की धार्मिक कट्टरता का लाभ उठाते कई प्रकाशक भी भूमंडलीकृत पाठक को समझा बुझाते हैं कि उन्हें धर्म केवल बिकाऊ माल है। लंदन-अमेरिका जैसे देश भी खुलकर ऐसे प्रकाशकों पर कटाक्ष करते हैं। राजनैतिक शरण का मामला भी इसीसे बनता है।

अमेरिकी लेखक डेनियल बेल ने 'विचारधारा का अंत' शीर्षक पुस्तक लिखी और केवल मार्क्सवाद का ही नहीं, द्वितीय विश्वयुद्ध के बाद समस्त धाराओं को अप्रासंगिक घोषित कर दिया। पूंजीवादी व्यवस्था के अनुकूल होने से पश्चिम में भी इस का स्वागत हुआ।

"मूसलचंद की फंतासी - अर्थात् बीसवी सदी के अन्तिम दशक में एक बार फिर मेघदूतम' शीर्षक कविता प्रदीप सक्सेना ने रची और इसने समाजार्थिक व सांस्कृतिक क्षेत्र में प्रभावी छल के साथ ही मार्क्सवादी नारों के नीचे छिपी तथाकथित वामपंथी कलाबाजी का पर्दाफाश किया-

'आओ हम चलें समाजवादी देशों में नौकरियां करने / दांत दिखलाने या आँख साफ करवाने, लौटे / उधर से दिल्ली में, फ्लेट खरीदते हुए, लादे हुए फ्रिज, / टी.वी.... 'कहीं धर्म का राजनैतिक उद्देश्य के लिए इस्तेमाल का राजनैतिक तंत्र भी दिखाई देता है। अब यह समझ़ाना कठिन नहीं रह गया है कि 'इश्वर-अल्लाह-मसीह' विचार के नहीं, मात्र भावनात्मक-

आवेश के विषय है। इस कटु चेतावनी का व्याख्यात्मक रूप केदारनाथ सिंह की "उत्तर कबीर" कविता में देखा जा सकता है।

चर्चित कवि आशोक वाजपेयी ने एक लम्बी कविता 'शताब्दी के अन्त के कगार पर" सन् १९९८ में रची। इसमे कुम्हार, लुहार, मछुवारा, बढई, कबाडी और कुंजडा अपने-अपने वक्तव्य देते हैं और पूरी बीसवीं सदी के विषय में अपने अनुभवों पर आधारित निष्कर्ष निकालते हैं। नरेश मेहता के जैसे इस कवि के भी कुछ प्रश्न अनुत्तरित रह जाते हैं - 'मैं सोच रहा था कि यह घडे की कौन-सी शताब्दी है? / पीने के पानी का इतिहास क्या है? / अनाज को याद है अपने पहली बार होने का समय?/ और क्य काल इस चक्के के घूमना शुरू करने के पहले से / चक्कर लगा रहा है? 'अंत में कवि ने एक खिडकी खोली एक दूसरे काम के लिए - 'चकाचौंध और चौंक के हाशिये पर / इतिहास के चिकने-चुपडे भवन से बाहर / वे जो कुछ लोग खडे हैं / मुझ कवि के साथ / अपनी-अपनी जगह पर / मैं सिर्फ एक खिडकी खोलता हूं।' दलितों की भूमंडलीय अवस्था का परिचय माइकल चेसुदोव्सकी (४) ने दिया है।

टाइपिस्ट और मज़दूर बाज़ार के मालिक यानी बहुराष्ट्रीय कंपनियों की समृद्धि बरकरार रखने के लिए भरपुर भूमिका निभा रहे हैं। अखिल पूँजी की गिरफ्त में पडकर आदमी उसके इशारे पर खिलौने की भांति खेल रहा है। ओम भारती की पंक्तियाँ इस प्रकार है-' कितनी छोटी दुनिया उसके सामने / तीन डगों से नाप /धरती-समूची / आ गयी वह विदांस हमारी देहरी पर - (जैसे खिलौने हम)

निलय उपाध्याय ने आत्मनिर्भरता का हिमायत करते हुए घोषणा की है -दुनिया में/ विरोध के सारे हथियार चूक जायेंगे। अई.एम.एफ व विश्व बैंक गरीब देशों से यही सलाह देते है कि उन्हे आर्थिक संकट से बचने केलिए इसी उद्योग पर ध्यान केन्द्रित रखना चाहिए । ऐसी हालत में 'सेक्स टूरिसम' को

बढावा देने की सलाह मालिक लोग दे रहे हैं।

औरत की वर्तमान बदियती व बदहालत (५) का एकान्त श्रीवास्तव ने अपनी छोटी कविता 'लडकी और आम' में बहुत ही सहज एवं दिलकश चित्रण किया है-

"लडकी का जन्म हुआ/ तो आम का पौधे रोपा गया/ लडकी बिकी अपने बाजार में /जहाँ चखे जाने का कानून चलता था।"

कात्यायनी की 'रात के संतरी की कविता' भी उल्लेखनीय है जिसमें दुनिया भर की तमाम दलित जाति कैसी दुर्निवार हालत की गिरफ्त में आ गयी है। भूमंडलीकृत अफ्रीका इसका उदाहरण बनता है-

"नेलसण मण्डेला के देश में
विश्व सुन्दरी प्रतियोगिता के लिए मंच सजा रही है।"

मुक्त बाजार को, वरिष्ठ कवि कुंवर नारायण और केदारनाथ सिंह[६] ने अन्य कवियों के समान स्वर में प्रताडना की है-

'बाजार एक ऐसी जगह है/ जहां मैने हमेशा पाया है / एक ऐसा अकेलापन जैसा मुझे / बडे-बडे जंगलों में भी नहीं मिला।' - (कुंवर नारायण)

'सच यही है कि बाजार में नहीं मिलते घोंसले / वहाँ सिर्फ पिंजडे मिलते हैं / इसलिए टूट जाने के बाद उन्हें हर बार / बनाना पडता है नए सिरे से / उतने ही धीरज / और शायद उससे भी ज्यादा जोखिम के साथ।' - (केदारनाथ सिंह)

मार्क्सवाद का खोखलापन प्रकट करते हुए संजय चतुर्वेदी [७] ने व्यंग्य किया-

'क्या मौं सपना देख रहा हूं
कोई मार्क्सवादी ऐसा भी होगा
जिसके सामने मार्क्सवाद छोटा पड चुका हो
कोई क्रांतिकारी बरअक्स जिसके
अब्र क्या चीज है हवा क्या है
और इन्कलाब तो खुदा कसम हुआ क्या है।'

अकविता की कोटि में आनेवाली कविता भी कहीं उत्तराधुनिक माहौल सजाती है। 'कचरे का सिमसिम' ऐसी है जिसमें उपरोक्त कवि ने कविता की अंत्येष्टि की बात की-

'राजनीतिक रूप से सही होने के वीभत्स संस्करण ने
साहित्य की आड में
अधिकांश हिन्दी कविता की यह अंत्येष्टि की।' (वही, १२)

कुछ कवितायें संचार माध्यमों की उपज बनकर विश्वजालों में अपना पैर जमा चुकी है। 'वागर्थ' पत्रिका में सालों पहले वाणी मुरारका के काव्यालाप का जिक्र किया गया। कहा गया कि जब वह कवितापाठ प्रत्यक्ष इलाहाबाद के मंच पर हुआ तो कोई प्रभावशाली अस्तित्व नहीं जमा सकी। लेकिन उसे जब विश्वजाल में दिया तो कवयित्री को विश्व के कई कोने से अच्छी टिप्पणियां तुरंत मिलती रही। इस से वागर्थ ने कविता का क्षणिक अस्तित्व समझाया। हिन्दी का दुनिया का पहला पोर्टल महाराष्ट्र के पूना में बना 'वेबदुनिया डॉट कॉम' है, जो अब तक असंख्य आलोचनायें, कविता, नाटक तथा सर्जनात्मक साहित्य का सामयिक वेबपत्रिका बनकर फिरती है। हिंदी के असंख्य विश्वजाल अब तक बने हैं।

इस प्रकार हम देख सकते हैं कि हिन्दी कविता में भूमंडलीकरण का दौर पहले से ही शूरू हुआ है। वह वर्तमान संदर्भ को आत्मसात करके ही उपभोक्तावाद की नयी जमीन खडा करता है। इसलिए कविता का कलेवर और प्रस्तुति में भी विश्वजाल या पृष्टजाल का अनुरूपन होता है। वेबकविताएं देश और काल की सीमा को तोडकर वैश्विक पाठक की मांग करती है। साहित्य की आम प्रवृत्ति के रूप में भूमंडलीकरण को ली जा सकती है, जिससे हिन्दी कविता भी बच नहीं सकी।

संदर्भ

१. *दस्वावेज, १०८, गोरखपुर, जुलाई-सितंबर २००५, पृ.७२-७५.*
२. *नया ज्ञानोदय, नई दिल्ली, अक्तूबर २००५, पृ. २३.*
३. Adjunct of a free market economy, post modernism concerns itself with mass production and image... as Baudrillard demonstrates, the similacrum

gives a copy which no longer refers to a reality. … Cola is not the real thing in a Baudrillardian world but Coke, the logo, is (Juliane Welfreys, 2002, Literary Theories, Edinburgh University Press, Edinburgh, 360.)

४. Michel Chossudovsky, 1997, The Globalisation of Poverty: Impacts of IMF and World Bank Reforms.

५. Gayatri Spivak Chakravarti, Feminism and Critical Theory in the book David Lodge & Nigel Wood, ed. 2003, Modern Criticism and Theory, Delhi, Peerson Education, P. 483

६. *उद्धृत ज्योतिष जोशी, 'नई धारा', दिसंबर-जनवरी २००५, पृ. २५.*

७. *नया ज्ञानोदय, नई दिल्ली, सितंबर २००५, पृ. १०.*

- Terry Eagleton, 1997, The Illusions of Post Modernism, Oxford, Blackwell, p vii.
- *हिन्दी उपन्यास : समकालीन विमर्श / सत्यदेव त्रिपाठी/अमन प्रकाशन, कानपुर- उद्धृत शशिकला राय, आलोचना, पुस्तक वार्ता, मार्च-अप्रेल २००३, २८.*
- *हंस, मार्च २००१, नई दिल्ली, पृ. २७.*
- *सुधीश पचौरी, २०००, आलोचना से आगे, दिल्ली, राधाकृष्ण प्रकाशन।*
- *१९९६, उत्तर आधुनिक साहित्य विमर्श, नई दिल्ली, वाणी प्रकाशन.*
- *गोपीचंद नारंग, २०००, संरचनावाद उत्तर संरचनावाद एवं प्राच्य सौन्दर्यशास्त्र, दिल्ली, साहित्य अकादमी.*

List of Contributors

Ms. Abalova, Nazgul, Ph.D. Scholar, School of Social Sciences, Jawaharlal Nehru University, New Delhi, India.

Prof. Ahemdova, M.L., Professor, Tashkent State Institute of Oriental Studies, Tashkent, Uzbekistan.

Dr. Banerjee, Ranjana, Department of Slavonic and Finno-Ugrian Studies, University of Delhi, South Campus, New Delhi, India.

Prof. Basu, Sankar, Professor, Centre of Russian Studies, School of Language, Literature and Culture Studies, Jawaharlal Nehru University, New Delhi, India.

Dr. Chauhan, Gajendra S., Languages Group, BITS, Pilani, India.

Dr. Choube, Devendra, Associate Professor, Centre of Indian Languages, School of Language, Literature and Culture Studies, Jawaharlal Nehru University, New Delhi, India.

Prof. Dasgupta, Debal, Professor, Department of Russian, Maharaja Sayajirao University of Baroda, Vadodara, Gujarat, India.

Prof. Dimri, J.P., Professor, Department of Russian Studies, Central Institute of English and Foreign Languages (CIEFL), Hyderabad, India.

Ms. Ercilasun, Güljanat Kurmangaliyeva, Senior Lecturer, Department of History, Kyrgyz-Turkish Manas University, Bishkek, Kyrgyzstan.

Dr. Ercilasun, Konuralp, Assistant Professor, Department of History, Kyrgyz-Turkish Manas University, Bishkek, Kyrgyzstan.

Dr. Gorokhovic, Elena, Reader, Department of Music History, Belarusian State Academy of Music, Minsk, Belarus.

Prof. Hasan, S.A., Professor, Centre of Persian & Central Asian Studies, Jawaharlal Nehru University, New Delhi, India.

Dr. Jerath, Ritoo M., Associate Professor, Centre of Russian Studies, School of Language, Literature and Culture Studies, Jawaharlal Nehru University, New Delhi, India.

Prof. Khalmirzaev, Tashmirza, Institute of Oriental Studies, Tashkent, Uzbekistan.

Prof. Khavronina, S.A., Professor, Department of Russian, People's Friendship University of Russia, Moscow, Russia.

Dr. Larina, Tatiana, Department of Foreign Languages, People's Friendship University of Russia, Moscow, Russia.

Prof. Maurya, Abhai, Professor, Department of Slavonic and Finno-Ugrian Studies, University of Delhi, South Campus, New Delhi, India.

Dr. Mazhitov, Sattar Fazylovich, Scientific Researcher, Department of Historiography and Source Studies, Ch. Ch. Valikhanov Institute of History and Ethnology of Ministry of Education and Sciences of the Republic of Kazakhstan, Kazakhstan.

Ms. Merchant, Mahnaz, Assistant Coordinator, Secretariat for the Promotion of the Discourse on Science, Religion and Development, New Delhi, India.

Dr. Mittal, Manu, Associate Professor, Centre of Russian Studies, School of Language, Literature and Culture Studies, Jawaharlal Nehru University, New Delhi, India.

Dr. Musaeva, Indira, Research Scholar, School of International Studies, Centre for Russian, Central Asian and East European Studies, Jawaharlal Nehru University, New Delhi, India.

Dr. Narain, Meeta, Associate Professor, Centre of Russian Studies, School of Language, Literature and Culture Studies, Jawaharlal Nehru University, New Delhi, India.

Ms. Nasirova, Mahira, PG Scholar, Department of South Asian Languages, Tashkent State Institute of Oriental Studies, Tashkent, Uzbekistan.

Mr. Nurmatov, Sirajuddin S., Teacher, Department of South Asian Languages, Tashkent State Institute of Oriental Studies, Tashkent, Uzbekistan.

Dr. Pankov, Fedor Lecturer in Russian Philology, M.V. Lomonosov Moscow State University, Moscow, Russia.

Dr. Polyakova, Irina, Associate Professor, Department of Philosophy and Culture Studies, Kaliningrad State Technical University, Kaliningrad, Russia.

Dr. Raju, A. Rajeshwar, Lecturer, Department of Russian Language, APS University, Rewa, Madhya Pradesh, India.

Dr. Ramdas, A. Charumati, Reader, Department of Russian Studies, Central Institute of English and Foreign Languages (CIEFL), Hyderabad, India.

Dr. Roomi, Nasar Shakeel, Associate Professor, Centre of Russian Studies, School of Language, Literature and Culture Studies, Jawaharlal Nehru University, New Delhi, India.

Ms. Rysalieva, Zainura, Ph.D. Scholar, School of Social Sciences, Jawaharlal Nehru University, New Delhi, India.

Prof. Shaklein, V.M., Professor, Department of Russian, People's Friendship University of Russia, Moscow, Russia.

Prof. Shamatov, Azad N., Professor & Chairman, Department of South Asian Languages, Tashkent State Institute of Oriental Studies, Tashkent, Uzbekistan.

Dr. Shambetalieva, Hadicha, Lecturer, Department of Russian Language & Literature, Kyrgyz State Pedagogical University, Bishkek, Kyrgyzstan.

Dr. Sharma, N.K., Psychiatrist, Kangra, Himachal Pradesh, India.

Prof. Slukhai, Natalia, Professor, Institute of Philology, Taras Shevchenko Kyiv National University, Kiev, Ukraine.

Prof. Sonawane, Vishwas H., Professor, Department of Archaeology and Ancient History, Maharaja Sayajirao University of Baroda, Vadodara, Gujarat, India.

Prof. Stepanenko, Vera, Deputy Head, Center for International Education, Moscow State University, Moscow, Russia.

Dr. Upadhyay, Neelmani, Retired Principal, District Mandi, Himachal Pradesh, India.

Dr. Usacheva, Veronica V., Visiting Scholar, Centre for Russian, Central Asian and East European Studies, School of International Studies, Jawaharlal Nehru University, New Delhi, India.

Dr. Vijaykumaran, C.P.V., Reader, Department of Hindi, Payyanur College, Kannur University, Kerala, India.

Prof. Yegorova, A.V., Director, Department of International Relations, Yaroslavl State University, Russia.

Ms. Zade, Zarrin Abdukhalik, Student, Department of Philosophy, Tashkent State Institute of Oriental Studies, Tashkent, Uzbekistan.